In Search of God and Self
Renaissance and Reformation Thought

Nearly all the wisdom we possess, that is to say, true and sound wisdom, consists of two parts: the knowledge of God and of ourselves. But, while joined by many bonds, which one precedes and brings forth the other is not easy to discern.

John Calvin
Institutes of the Christian Religion,
Chapter One

1559

In Search of God and Self

Renaissance and Reformation Thought

Donald J. Wilcox

University of New Hampshire

Houghton Mifflin Company · Boston
Atlanta · Dallas · Geneva, Illinois
Hopewell, New Jersey · Palo Alto · London

Copyright © 1975 by Houghton Mifflin Company

Printed in the U.S.A.

Library of Congress Catalog Card Number: 74-10026

ISBN: 0-395-17178-4

Contents

Preface   *xi*

General Introduction   *3*

THE RENAISSANCE   9

Part One   The Background of the Renaissance   11

1   Political Context of the Early Renaissance   *11*
The Traditional Powers: The Papacy   13
The Rise of the Lordships   18
The Republics   23
Naples and Venice   27
Conclusion   28
Bibliography   29

2   Crises of the Fourteenth Century   *31*
Economic Crisis: Depression   31
Population Crisis: Plague   33
Political Crisis: New Politics in Florence   35
Religious Crisis: Change in Popular Preaching   37
Intellectual Crisis: Boccaccio   39
Conclusion   41
Bibliography   42

3   Dante and the Medieval Tradition   *43*
Historical Background of De Monarchia   44

95532

Scholastic Assumption in De Monarchia   48
The Role of Analogy   52
The Renaissance Reaction   54
Bibliography   56

Part Two   The Growth of Humanism in Italy   57

4   Petrarch and the Beginning of the Renaissance   *57*
Early Humanism   57
Petrarch   60
Bibliography   72

5   Humanism   *74*
Bibliography   88

6   Humanist Education and Scholarship   *90*
Education   90
Scholarship   98
Conclusion   104
Bibliography   104

7   Neo-Platonism   *106*
The Birth of the Platonic Academy   107
Philosophy in the Platonic Academy   112
Magic   115
Bibliography   121

8   Science   *123*
Technology   124
Astronomy   125
Medicine and Chemistry   139
Bibliography   140

**Part Three   The High Renaissance: Climax and
Dissolution   143**

9   Political Upheaval   *143*
Internal Problems in the Fifteenth Century   146
Diplomatic Problems in the Fifteenth Century   149
Invasions   151
Bibliography   155

10 Thought and Letters: Machiavelli *157*
      Bibliography *171*

11 Graphic Arts *173*
      Patronage *173*
      Painting *175*
      Architecture and Sculpture *185*
      Bibliography *189*

12 The End of the Renaissance in Italy *191*
      Bibliography *200*

THE REFORMATION 201

Part Four Introduction and Background 203

13 Introduction *203*
      Bibliography *208*

14 The Rise of Territorial States *209*
      Law *211*
      Taxation *214*
      Regionalism *215*
      Bibliography *221*

15 The Church Before Luther *223*
      The Growth of Papal Government *224*
      Opposition to Papal Power *227*
      Bibliography *230*

16 Intellectual Background *232*
      Augustine *232*
      Aristotle *234*
      The Thirteenth-Century Synthesis *235*
      Bibliography *237*

**Part Five The Building of the Reformation
             Vocabulary 239**

17 Mysticism *239*
      Practicing Mystics: Catherine of Siena *240*
      The Theology of Mysticism: Meister Eckart *245*
      Bibliography *251*

18   Nominalism   *253*
     The Philosophy of Nominalism: William of Ockham   254
     The Pastoral Effects of Nominalism: Confession and
        Gabriel Biel   258
     Bibliography   266

19   Northern Humanism   *268*
     Early Humanism in the North   268
     French Humanism   272
     English Humanism   275
     German Humanism   277
     Erasmus   281
     Bibliography   285

Part Six   The Sixteenth-Century Reformation   288

20   Martin Luther   *288*
     Encounter with Erasmus   288
     The Stages of Luther's Youth   290
     Luther's Thought: The Doctrine of Solafidianism   294
     Luther's Thought: Other Elements of the Protestant
        Tradition   303
     Bibliography   306

21   John Calvin   *308*
     Calvin's Life and Career   309
     Calvin's Thought   315
     Bibliography   324

22   The Spread of Protestantism   *326*
     The Lutheran Reformation   327
     The Lutheran Reformation Outside Germany   333
     The Calvinist Reformation   336
     Conclusion   339
     Bibliography   341

23   The Catholic Church in the Sixteenth Century   *342*
     Reform of Abuse   343
     Moral and Spiritual Reform   345
     The New Orders   346
     The Jesuits   348
     The Fight Against Heresy   355

The Council of Trent   356
Conclusion   358
Bibliography   360

24   The Radical Reformation   *361*
Radical Movements in the Catholic Tradition   362
Radical Movements from Lutheranism   364
Radical Movements from the Swiss Reformed Church   367
Bibliography   388

Conclusion: To Live Appropriately   *374*
Bibliography   389

Index   391

Maps
Italy in the Fifteenth Century   142
Europe in 1526   216–217

Preface

This book is intended as an introduction to Renaissance and Reformation history. Its purpose is to stimulate the reader's curiosity to learn more about the period by presenting a unified general picture rather than overwhelming detail. A basic background in the social, economic, and political history of the period is included, but the emphasis is on intellectual and cultural history, for reasons discussed in the Introduction. The intellectual history of the Renaissance and Reformation manifests certain values common to both, particularly a heightened awareness of the personal dimensions of life. These shared concerns make the epoch more coherent to the reader, without, I hope, obscuring its immense diversity.

I have also tried to give the reader a sense of the vitality of the study of history. The product of recent scholarship is incorporated in the book not to demonstrate how much more accurate or sophisticated present-day historians are than their predecessors, but to suggest that our questions about the past change with our contemporary concerns. I have tried never to condescend to the past, but rather to present the Renaissance and Reformation as manifesting a life style different from our own but nevertheless satisfying similar human needs and longings. Our interest in the past is diminished if we perceive it as only a primitive precursor to our own times.

I wish to thank my students, at both the University of New Hampshire and Harvard University, for their help in the conception of this book. Their questions and comments have sharpened my own perceptions of the field. They have made me aware of those aspects of the period most difficult for twentieth-century students to grasp and of what the Renaissance and Reformation have to say to our times. I also wish to thank the patient and long-suffering friends outside the field of history who read the manuscript with care and recommended improvements. Finally, Professor Theodore Rabb of Princeton University and Professor Lewis Spitz of Stanford University read the manuscript and made many useful and important suggestions. I wish to thank them for their time and critical acumen; the book is much better for their help. The faults that remain, of course, are my own.

Donald J. Wilcox   *Durham, New Hampshire*

In Search of God and Self
Renaissance and Reformation Thought

General Introduction

Intellectual and cultural history is a proper focus for a study of the Renaissance and Reformation because these movements, which occur during the period from 1300 to the end of the sixteenth century, were held together by common intellectual concerns. The period had less coherence in the realm of economic, political, or social history. This is not to say that such factors were of little account. The economic background of the period was an essential ingredient of its contributions. The Renaissance, for instance, certainly depended on trade and commerce to provide the wealth supporting the burst of culture that was the movement's glory. Such intense artistic activity is hard to imagine in a wholly agricultural society, but the commercial revolution that fostered this wealth began in the twelfth century, not the fourteenth. Similarly, the political commitments of Renaissance men were related to the independence the Italian city-states enjoyed from imperial or royal control as well as to the vigor of Italian political institutions, but this independence dated, too, from the twelfth century. Indeed by the fourteenth century these institutions had lost much of their original vigor and freedom for experimentation. They were already hardening into stable and legitimate governments whose efficiency and fiscal might were the envy of the rulers of northern Europe. In social terms as well there was little that made the Italian Renaissance unique. Renaissance society was dominated by established families of landed and commercial wealth, but similar social groups had dominated other cultures and would continue to wield a preponderant influence in Europe well into the industrial revolution.

Nor is it easy to tie the Reformation to particular political, social, or economic changes. The growth of territorial monarchies in northern Europe made possible the support Martin Luther received, but these monarchies were no innovation of the sixteenth century. The thirteenth century witnessed a marked growth of territorial power on the Continent, and in England the process can be traced back to the Norman Conquest in 1066. Attempts to locate the rise of modern capitalism in the sixteenth century have met with little success, and no relationship between Protestantism and the new merchant class, if indeed there was such a class, has been clearly established. In short, the three hundred years from 1300 to 1600, in which the Renaissance and Reformation occurred, were not great turning points for any of the political, social, and economic trends that formed modern Europe. The period was distinguished instead by the appearance, development, and maturity of new intellectual vocabularies in both northern and southern Europe.

The Renaissance began in Italy in the early 1300s when men attempted to gain a clearer understanding of the ancient world through a fresh look at the classics. During the same years thinkers in northern Europe were seeking a more personal and immediate formulation of religious experience than the scholasticism of the preceding century. Out of these two beginnings grew the mature Renaissance and Reformation.

Intellectual history is not only the best way to introduce the Renaissance and Reformation; it is a valid and appropriate means of treating any period. Many historians have felt that intellectual history is a secondary field to be studied only after the economic, political, and social "facts" are established, but what men want, or think they want, is as central to human history as what they eat, how they wield power, or how they combine in societies. The fact that all these elements are interrelated has been almost universally accepted in the twentieth century, and few historians would try to isolate either ideas or economic trends from other human activities. Intellectual historians agree that ideas spring from the same matrix that produces political institutions, economic organization, and social forms. They seek only to show that ideas are best studied in intellectual documents. No social data can convey the force of an idea as clearly as a poem or a philosophical treatise. Just as the sonnets of Petrarch tell us little about the wool trade, so the account books of the wool guild provide only the vaguest insights into the sonnets. The historical genesis of an idea is found more surely in the intellectual milieu that preceded it than in the political, economic, or social background.

I have tried to take advantage of the peculiar strengths of intellectual history in choosing the topics in this book. While it is often difficult to expose the student who is new to a field, or who wants only a general introduction, to the detailed primary sources of social and economic history, this is not a great problem in intellectual history. The documents the intellectual historian uses have an availability that account books, political debates, and social memoirs seldom do. I have taken this into consideration by referring to works readily available in inexpensive editions when I analyze the contributions of the thinkers in the period. The student who consults these works can easily find the basis on which particular generalizations are made and at the same time broaden his awareness of the complexity of the field.

What follows is not an encyclopedic survey of the period. I have sought not to cover the Renaissance and Reformation by giving a short summary of each major thinker's contribution, but to introduce the period by analyzing its major concerns and by dealing in depth with particular thinkers who illustrate these concerns. In some cases my choice was obvious; in some, other thinkers could just as easily have been chosen. For example, in Chapter 3, which treats the intellectual tradition against which the Renaissance was reacting, a more "scholarly" discussion would deal with particular scholastic thinkers in Italy in the early fourteenth century and analyze their actual disputes with some of the early humanists. I have chosen instead to discuss the basic scholastic assumptions in terms of a single text, Dante's treatise on world government *(De Monarchia)*, which is easily available to the student who wishes to see for himself how these assumptions were manifested. A short bibliographical section at the end of each chapter offers suggestions for further reading. These suggestions include not only the material covered in the chapter but related topics not directly discussed.

The Renaissance and Reformation are treated here as parallel historical phenomena that are related but distinct. Each appeared in the early fourteenth century in reaction to those aspects of medieval life that seemed to create a closed and coherent system for the perception of experience. Each can be said to end by 1600, when men began again to devise systems for organizing the very insights of the Renaissance and Reformation into different patterns and methods of observation. Until the sixteenth century these movements had little communication with one another, largely because they developed in separate parts of Europe. Nevertheless, from the beginning they had certain common concerns that stemmed from the fact that each was reacting in its own particular way to a common medieval vocabulary of experience.

The book will treat the Renaissance and Reformation separately. In each section, following a brief analysis of the economic, political, and intellectual background, chapters will be devoted to key figures who created the basic intellectual approaches of the age: Petrarch, Salutati, and Bruni for the Renaissance; Meister Eckhart, William of Ockham, and Gabriel Biel for the Reformation. The Renaissance section will continue to discuss the mature development of the Renaissance in Italy, the establishment of educational programs and scholarly techniques, the appearance of Neo-Platonism in the middle of the fifteenth century, and the culmination of Renaissance ideas in the works of Machiavelli and the painters of the High Renaissance. The section will conclude with a short essay on the dissolution of Renaissance sensibilities in Italy following the French and Spanish invasions of the early sixteenth century.

The Reformation section will move from the early thinkers to the great sixteenth-century reformers, Luther and Calvin, and show how their contribution reflected a creative synthesis of the earlier thinkers' ideas. Other aspects of the sixteenth-century Reformation will be treated, including the Roman Catholic reformers and the radicals, who resisted inclusion in any of the major movements. A final section will discuss the great thinkers of the last age of the northern Renaissance, Montaigne and Shakespeare, who must be understood in the context of both Renaissance and Reformation and whose achievements reflected the strengths of both movements.

The single greatest obstacle to understanding the thought of this period is its omnipresent religious language. Not only the leaders of the Reformation but the more secular writers of the Italian Renaissance used terms like "God," "faith," "divine foreknowledge," and "judgment" with a frequency and evident seriousness that seem strange today, when such language is heard only from theologians and clerics. The religious vocabulary of the period has an important significance, but it does not mean that men of the Renaissance and Reformation were necessarily more pious, superstitious, or credulous than men of any other age. An essential step to understanding the Renaissance and Reformation is to see that period as peopled by human beings whose basic physical, spiritual, and intellectual attributes were similar to our own.

If the use of religious language does not connote greater piety, what then does it tell us? It shows that the men of the Renaissance and Reformation were both unwilling and unable to separate moral and spiritual considerations from practical ones. Neither the language nor the science of that day permitted men to make measurements or observations without considering the value and worth of their subject. The scientific world-view presented a stationary earth at the center of the universe surrounded by a sphere containing the sun and stars. Motion occurred because solid objects were attracted to the earth, ethereal ones to the stars. Thus the study of motion required considering questions of direction and goal. Even more important, most of the words that we use to study the Renaissance and Reformation and that enable us to analyze experience apart from values were not available to that period. Words such as "analyze" and "synthesize," "abstract" and "concrete," "deduction" and "induction," were added to the language only in the seventeenth century as part of the scientific revolution that shaped our current approach to the world.

During the scientific revolution, Descartes and others discovered that a more precise picture of experience could be acquired by devising techniques and a vocabulary to observe and record this experience independent of any question about its ultimate worth and goal. Descartes did not consider moral questions to be unimportant or unreal; he simply thought they could be separated from the process of scientific observation. His approach proved immensely fruitful in the development of scientific ideas and methods. Our control over nature is discernibly greater than that enjoyed by Calvin or Machiavelli. Yet our pride in that achievement should not blind us to the advantages of the earlier world-view, which gave explicit and deep consideration to questions of value and ultimate goals as an intrinsic part of its grasp of the universe.

The Renaissance and Reformation, then, boast of no atheists. All thinkers spoke of God with a comfort and familiarity to be found in few twentieth-century intellectual circles. But the acceptance of religious language did not prevent some from being anticlerical or from rejecting the teachings of the church. Their religion did not preclude hypocrisy and worldliness, nor did it even mean that they attended church with regularity or sought seriously to introduce the precepts of religion into their lives. Men of the Renaissance and Reformation were, in short, human beings with the needs and capacities of any other human beings, but they also were men who saw the world in terms of certain assumptions and who expressed their vision in a certain language quite different from our own. The following chapters will try to penetrate those assumptions and decipher that language so that the men of that period can convey their insights in terms more easily understood by our own age.

The Renaissance

Part One
The Background of the Renaissance

1 Political Context of the Early Renaissance

The Renaissance began in Italy shortly after 1300, matured there over the course of the next two centuries, but did not exert a significant influence north of the Alps until the sixteenth century. During much of this period Italian intellectuals who traveled to the North — on diplomatic missions, in search of new manuscripts, or to find employment as resident scholars in some northern court — complained loudly about the barbarity, backwardness, and general lack of culture in the intellectual circles of France, England, and Germany. Poggio Bracciolini, who spent some time in England during the early fifteenth century, sent letters to his Italian colleagues lamenting the complete lack of intellectual companionship he found on the island.

The North was neither devoid of culture nor without outstanding men of intellect, but its schools and thinkers posed different questions from those that occupied the Italians of the Renaissance. Furthermore, Northern thinkers sought to answer these questions in ways the Renaissance found alien and unproductive. The clarity of this division between Northern and Southern intellectuals during the fourteenth and fifteenth centuries suggests strongly that political and economic differences might lie behind the peculiar values and characteristics of the Renaissance in Italy.

The political, economic, and social conditions that differentiated Italy from the rest of Europe seemed clear to historians a generation ago. Three large trends were believed to underlie Italian life in the Renaissance. Legitimate political authority, represented by the pope and Holy Roman emperor, had declined. Powers that lacked a legitimacy rose to fill the vacuum and created political institutions of great strength and effectiveness free from traditional restraints. A merchant class rose to political dominance especially in Tuscany, which was the center of the international trade and banking on which Italian wealth depended. None of these three trends look as clear to historians today as they did twenty years ago. The exercise of power seems less illegitimate and more tied to traditional forms, despite certain important innovations in Italian politics in the early fourteenth century. The commercial activity of Italy was carried on not by a separate merchant class in opposition to the landed aristocracy but by families who held wealth in both land and commerce and who regarded their landed properties as more solid and prestigious holdings. In short, Italy in 1300 was indeed wealthier and more politically sophisticated than the rest of Europe, but these advantages should not conjure up images of a rising middle class overcoming a backward landed and feudal aristocracy to found the modern state.

This chapter will look at examples of the three basic types of power in Italy during the Renaissance. The papacy will serve as an example of a political institution relying heavily on traditional and spiritual means to exercise its power. The Holy Roman Empire, the other traditional power, seldom troubled Italy during this period. Milan, the largest of the cities of the Lombard plain, will serve as a typical lordship, or *signoria,* and Florence will represent the republics. Naples and Venice will be considered briefly at the end of the chapter. While they were important states, they had peculiar problems and intervened only irregularly in the affairs of the other Italian states until the fifteenth century.

The Traditional Powers: The Papacy

Historians formerly accepted the view that there was a sharp, steady decline during the Renaissance of the traditional means by which the papacy exercised power — the spiritual authority based on its claim to apostolic succession. This interpretation appealed strongly to the nineteenth century, which explained much of its own achievements in terms of breaking the spiritual restraints of the medieval church. The old Cambridge Medieval History, for instance, in many ways a culmination of Victorian historical writing, entitled its volume on the thirteenth century *The Decline of the Empire and Papacy.* The influence of the papacy was viewed as reaching a high point during the reign of Innocent III (1198–1216), who used his spiritual authority to depose kings, elect emperors, and bring the temporal governments of Europe to obedience. The decline after his death was caused by the development of strong national states whose leaders did not respect the power of the popes and resulted in the dramatic humiliation of the papacy at Anagni. There in 1303 Philip IV of France took Pope Boniface VIII prisoner and tried to force his resignation.

This interpretation saw the popes' transfer of residence to Avignon in 1305 as a further reduction in prestige, making the popes docile tools of the French kings. The final blow was the Great Schism, which broke out in 1378 when two claimants both asserted they had been elected to the papacy and European Christendom divided into two obediences. The disputes of the opposing claimants irreversibly weakened the spiritual authority of the church and prepared the way for the more profound and lasting split of the Reformation. Thus from its pinnacle of influence under Innocent III the church steadily declined to a nadir at the beginning of the fifteenth century. The Renaissance popes brought a burst of culture to Rome, but their scandalous private lives further diminished the prestige of the papacy until finally it came to be regarded as no more than another Italian power — and not a very strong one at that. This interpretation spoke clearly to nineteenth-century readers, who saw in the struggles the rise of nation-states. We find it not so adequate today, less because we are more sophisticated than our predecessors, than because we ask different questions, more attuned to our own age. Among other things, we are more willing to acknowledge the twofold nature of papal power.

The thirteenth century did not make an absolute division between spiritual and political power. Popes, from their earliest days, when they were simply bishops of Rome, regarded their authority as both spiritual and political. They claimed not only the spiritual authority Christ gave to Peter but also temporal rights over the territories around Rome that came to be called the Papal States. These lands had come to the papacy in various ways. After the conversion of the emperors to Christianity in the fourth century, the early popes inherited much of the land around Rome through pious bequests of individuals. Specific donations of territory in the eighth and eleventh centuries added considerably to these original holdings. It was not until the sixteenth century, however, that all the lands were united into an effective single administration. Before that time the popes consistently claimed suzerainty as temporal lords over their territories, but their control was at best intermittent.

Papal policy was governed by the assumption that each of the two bases of power depended on the other. The popes were firmly convinced that the exercise of effective spiritual authority throughout Christendom demanded a firm base of temporal power in Italy. There is no other way to explain the tenacity with which they defended their rights to the chaotic lands of the Papal States. Financially the states were a liability. They cost five times as much to maintain and administer as they returned in revenues. Without them the papal budget could have been cut in half. The popes attempted to offset the deficit by securing taxes from northern monarchs, but this policy caused bad relations with the rulers and a weakening of papal influence in the North. The Papal States were not even a military asset. The troops they provided were barely enough to suppress internal revolts.

Just as the popes saw temporal power as necessary to spiritual jurisdiction, so without embarrassment they used spiritual weapons for political ends. The interdict, which prevented the sacraments from being administered within a given territory, and the excommunication, which separated specific people from the ministrations of the church, were employed against recalcitrant cities and rulers within the Papal States and throughout Italy. These sanctions did not depend for their effect merely on religious feeling; they had political and economic effects as well. Excommunication provided an accepted pretext for revolt by releasing subjects from the obligation to obey their ruler, and popes seldom excommunicated a lord who was not already in difficulty from restive subjects or foreign invaders. Because the interdict placed a territory outside international law, treaties could be broken, and debts owed to citizens of that territory could be repudiated. Against the Italian cities in particular, with their growing trade and international banking, the interdict was a formidable weapon. Where the political and economic sanctions were not available, the spiritual weapons were usually ignored, and the popes resorted to military force.

The association of political and spiritual power seemed callous and reprehensible to men of the nineteenth century, but to contemporaries of Innocent III or Boniface VIII it was part of the nature of things, and papal policy in Italy was seldom questioned before the Reformation either by popes or by the secular rulers. Nor is it easy to prove that the popes were wrong in assuming the interdependence of these functions. They held the Papal States until 1870 and were driven from them only after it was clear that landed property was giving way to capital investment as a fulcrum of political power. In any case, the popes from 1200 to 1400 pursued a single policy of strengthening the Papal States and preserving the spiritual influence of the church. These were not two goals but one.

As soon as the unity of papal policy is realized, it becomes less clear that papal authority actually declined. In fact the popes exercised a more effective control of the states in 1400 than Innocent III had in 1200. Innocent, upon his coronation in 1198, had great difficulty securing a simple oath of loyalty from his leading subjects, and it was nearly ten years before he felt strong enough to ask their consent to some major reforms at the parliament of Viterbo. These reforms, approved in 1207, merely granted the pope the basic rights of government, including the right to mediate quarrels and prevent wars among the towns, the right to appoint administrators to hear judicial appeals from local courts, and the right to summon a parliament.

In the eighteen years of his reign Innocent governed the Papal States with a firmer hand than any of his predecessors, but his immediate successors were unable to follow his example. Frederick II (1215–1250), who was both king of Sicily and Holy Roman emperor, combined his imperial title with his Italian power base to exert a crushing pressure on the states. The papal cities rebelled. Rome, the most unruly of all, expelled Pope Honorius III five times between 1219 and 1226. Honorius' successor spent only four of the first twelve years of his reign there, and Innocent IV abandoned the city completely to take up residence in Lyon. Frederick's death brought little relief, for the new king of Sicily, Charles of Anjou (1268–1285), proved equally interested in controlling the states, despite the fact that papal support had placed him on the throne. He made himself senator of Rome, insisted on the appointment of large numbers of French cardinals, and stirred up revolt in the cities. As a result the popes found Rome as uninhabitable during his reign as they had when Frederick was alive.

Against this background of unrest, instability, and interference by the Sicilian kings, the humiliation of Boniface VIII in 1303 and the subsequent transfer to Avignon become clear. Boniface responded to growing unrest in Rome and burgeoning French influence in the college of cardinals by a vigorous administration that moved into areas popes had not dared to touch in the preceding century. He secured an unprecedented control over appointments and judicial matters but made many enemies — particularly among the partisans of the French. One of these partisans, Sciarra Colonna, in fact seized Boniface at Anagni. The career of Boniface (1294–1303) should not be seen as a dramatic indication of papal decline. His defeat was one of many temporary reverses in that period, and even in defeat he left the Papal States more firmly under the sway of the popes than he found them.

The increased control over its lands that the papacy had won during the thirteenth century was not lost during its residence at Avignon. From a religious point of view this was the great period of ecclesiastical expansion; the popes pursued a vigorous political policy that resulted in the recovery of their Italian possessions. They had left Rome largely because the unsettled conditions offered them no permanent seat, and they were determined to return to a stable territory. By far the largest expense of the papacy during the period from 1305 to 1377 was the cost of soldiers and administrators in the Papal States.

The policy was hard to put into operation. Because of the distance between Avignon and Italy the first interventions were ill informed and awkward. Clement V, the first Avignonese pope, vacillated in his policy toward powers outside the states. On matters within the states he was frequently so ill informed that he intervened on the side of his enemies or those who had already lost. His successors did better. Clement VI (1342–1352) reasserted control over

Rome by manipulating the strange Roman revolutionary Cola da Rienzi, who dreamed of restoring the city to its rightful place as ruler of the world. Cola was finally overthrown by the mob that had supported him, but the papacy continued to exercise greater authority in the city than it ever had in the past. The capstone of this policy was the mission of Cardinal Albornoz, who was sent to Italy in 1353 and by 1366 had forced all major lords in the Papal States to recognize papal authority. Albornoz is now recognized not as the creator of papal policy but simply as the last and best in a long line of administrators who prepared the way for the pope's final return to Rome in 1377.

The return to Rome was immediately followed by the Great Schism. Though the schism had an undoubted impact on the spiritual authority of the church north of the Alps, its impact on the Papal States is hard to assess, varying as it did with the intelligence and energy of particular popes. The greatest Roman pope during the schism was Boniface IX (1389–1404). With the support of King Ladislaus of Naples he secured a control of the states that no pope before him had ever enjoyed. He appointed all officials within the states, demanded the right of appeal on all judicial matters, and governed in a manner that would have been the envy of Innocent III. His successor, by contrast, lost most of the Papal States, and when the schism was mended the new pope, Martin V, had to win them back anew.

The continued political and spiritual strength of the papacy played a part in the development of the Renaissance. The popes of the fifteenth century contributed in important ways as patrons and writers to the cultural life of Italy. Their role as patrons of art is particularly noteworthy and will be treated in chapter II. These activities required wealth and a measure of political independence, but we have seen that those factors cannot be divorced from spiritual claims. Between 1200 and 1400 the papacy experienced successes and setbacks like any other temporal power, but these vicissitudes cannot be traced to a decline in its spiritual authority. Throughout the period it maintained a policy of developing its spiritual and political sources of strength together. Spiritual weapons were a strong element of policy. They were used both in and outside the Papal States, but in a way that showed the papacy's continuing importance as both a particular political power and a universal source of legitimate authority.

The Rise of the Lordships

Despite the continuing strength of traditional supports for the exercise of power, the period of the Renaissance witnessed important political innovations involving institutions and fiscal practices. These innovations gave the leaders of the Italian states greater control over the inhabitants than that enjoyed by the rulers of northern Europe. The new practices were established slowly and only with difficulty. They never gave the Renaissance states an authority as pervasive as that of the modern state, and the Renaissance state should not be considered as a simple prototype or simplified version of the territorial, national states that matured in the nineteenth century. To do so obscures many of the key features of Renaissance politics.

The two main areas of political experimentation were the Lombard plain and Tuscany. These areas, dominated respectively by Milan and Florence, competed throughout much of the Renaissance for hegemony in Italy. Each had characteristic strengths and weaknesses that must be understood in order to grasp the complex picture of Renaissance political life.

As in the case of papal authority, our understanding of Renaissance politics has undergone a change. The classic synthesis of Renaissance culture is Jacob Burckhardt's *The Civilization of the Renaissance in Italy,* published in 1860. Burckhardt suggested that the Renaissance arose in the vacuum left by the decline of legitimate powers. The intense personalities and individualism that characterized the movement constituted a response to the political chaos and institutional experimentation of the fourteenth century. With no firmly established political forms, men were thrown on their own ingenuity to force their way to power and keep themselves there. Scholars have since questioned this aspect of Burckhardt's thesis. On closer analysis, power seems not nearly so unstable in the fourteenth century as Burckhardt thought it was. The establishment of legitimate governments in the cities of Italy, which Burckhardt found in the fifteenth century, is actually the work of the fourteenth. The Renaissance developed not in an age of experimentation but in an age when forms were becoming increasingly rigid.

Even this trend toward established institutions is not so clear as one might wish. Outside of Tuscany (where republican institutions remained strong) the political form that developed in the fourteenth century was the signoria (*signorie* in the plural). [The holder of a lordship was a *signore* (*signori* in the plural).] Throughout northern Italy by 1400 independent communes had given way first to a locally appointed lord, then to a foreign one — usually the lord of Milan. The signoria did not come to power easily. Even the great signori were faced in the fifteenth century with unsolved problems and obstacles to stable and legitimate government. Recent studies of signorie in the Romagna outside Lombardy have stressed both the continued vitality of communal institutions and the illegitimacy of lordships throughout the fourteenth century.

The problems besetting the signoria can be seen in the development of the most successful one of all: the lordship established by the Visconti family in Milan. Milan was the most populous of the northern communes; its 200,000 people made it the largest city in fourteenth-century Italy. Its population supported a strong manufacturing economy based on wool, general commodities, and most of all arms and metallurgy. It lacked, however, the vigorous international trade that made Florence prosperous, and many of Milan's political problems reflected its dependence on a regional economy. Milan particularly needed to control the Lombard plain in which it is situated. Long before 1300 the city had come to dominate its nearest neighbors and secure markets for its goods. In the fourteenth century Milan began to assert its hegemony over all the cities of the North except Venice and even established itself south of the Apennines among the communes of Tuscany.

The Milanese commune, which the Visconti lords supplanted, was founded in 1057. An Italian commune was nothing like a complete state. Most were established among residents of a city and its surrounding countryside for self-defense and were nothing more than an oath of association for this specific purpose. The commune was one of several institutions within a city. In Milan, criminal justice was usually administered through the guilds or the Motta, an association of minor knights. Great magnates, noble families who generally lived outside the city, administered their own justice and originally used the commune only insofar as it suited them. In fact the three groups who made up the Milanese commune — the magnates, the Motta, and the merchants — more often than not found themselves disagreeing over how their military power should be deployed. The merchants wanted to protect the trade routes, the magnates their landed estates, and the knights their role as fighters. To deal with these disagreements the institutions of the commune had to be expanded. A council of justice was created, and, when this came to be dominated by the magnates, a council of citizens was formed to speak for the merchants. By 1214 a foreigner called a *podestà* was regularly invited in to command the army. The success of this impartial figure was so great that he soon was given judicial and legislative functions as well. The communes did not surrender their independence by the creation of an executive officer. His election, and that of all other major officers, remained in the hands of the councils, who also retained the right to veto any of his acts.

The podestà became a universal figure in Italian politics but was seldom able to convert his power into a permanent lordship. The signoria in Milan grew not from the office of the podestà but from the captaincy of the people. This office was first created in 1225 and was designed to counterbalance the power of the nobles. In 1263 Philip della Torre had himself elected both captain of the people and perpetual lord of the people of Milan. The della Torre family was unable to hold the lordship, and it eventually passed to the Visconti family, who were much more cautious than their predecessors. Holding a firm base of power in the church (Otto Visconti, the first scion of the family, had been made archbishop in 1262), they assumed title gradually. Not until 1349 did they allow the councils to make them hereditary lords.

As lords of Milan, the Visconti pursued three objectives. They sought to establish orderly lines of succession within the family, to institutionalize their rule in Milan, and to extend their control to the other cities in Lombardy. By 1400 a firm institutional structure had been established, but difficulties still remained with inheritance and control of the subject towns. The institutional accomplishments of the family have led historians to overrate the general success of the Visconti signoria. In fact the three objectives depended on one another, and Visconti rule was troubled until the end of the dynasty.

The succession was a constant problem. The Visconti family easily maintained the lordship, but it never established clear rules for succession. Each time a reigning signore died, a crisis developed that usually resulted in a struggle within the family and the division of the lordship. The first major crisis occurred in 1339, when Azzo Visconti died leaving three young cousins and two uncles. The councils elected both uncles, Luchino and Giovanni, joint signori.

This solution worked because Giovanni was already archbishop and was willing to leave state matters to his brother. But when Luchino died, Giovanni had his brother's sons declared illegitimate to avoid the rule of a child and took over full control of the city himself. Thus the first crisis for Visconti control passed solely because of Giovanni's statesmanship and canniness.

A second crisis broke out in 1354 with the death of Giovanni. The state this time was divided among his three nephews, and for thirty years the members of the family fought for control. In 1385 Giangaleazzo, a son of one of the nephews, overthrew and assassinated his remaining uncle, and the state was again reunited through the ingenuity and unscrupulousness of one member of the family.

The greatest of the Visconti, Giangaleazzo ruled from 1385 until 1402 and advanced Visconti fortunes in all three strands of their policy. In 1394 he bought the title of duke from the Holy Roman emperor, making the Visconti the first hereditary dukes in Italy and adding greatly to the legitimacy of the family's rule. His far-reaching administrative reforms included the institution of competitive examinations for government posts, a measure that made him one of the best-served rulers in Europe. He also created a standing army of mercenaries to free him from the limitations of the citizen militia.

Giangaleazzo is most noted for his foreign conquests. Using minimal force and relying mainly on diplomacy and bribery, he became lord of Verona, Vicenza, and Padua, bringing the lands of the Visconti to the frontiers of the Venetian republic. Then he turned south and took over Mantua in 1397 and Bologna in 1401. The Tuscan cities of Pisa, Lucca, and Siena surrendered to him, and he was encamped with his army before the walls of Florence in 1402, when he suddenly died of the plague. His achievements were striking, but they lacked substance and permanence. Historians now agree that he had little chance of actually defeating Florence. His treasury was depleted, and he had never conquered any major city by storm. When Florence remained united in opposition to his wiles and attempts at subversion, any plans he may have had to rule a united Italy were doomed.

When Giangaleazzo died in 1402, the state was divided among his children at a point when Milan's foreign policy dictated a firmly directed unified effort. The problem of unification was never solved, and it finally cost Milan its independence in 1500.

The Visconti successfully extended the rule of the family over the other cities of Lombardy. Milan's dependence on trade with the countryside was striking. Regimes tended to fall as a consequence of losing this countryside. In addition the Visconti strengthened their hold on the city of Milan by creating a Lombard state independent of the city; they always took title to the subject cities not as lords of Milan but in their own names. Territorial expansion was a slow and unsteady process during the fourteenth century: Pavia, only twenty miles away, was not finally incorporated into the state until 1360, and Bologna, whose position by the mountains made it a key to southward expansion, was won and lost several times.

Next to their failure to establish clear lines of succession and the vicissitudes of their territorial gains, the administrative achievements of the Visconti seem impressive indeed. During the fourteenth century there was a slow but inexorable erosion of the strength of communal institutions as these institutions were replaced by bodies controlled and appointed by the signore. Three bodies were created to administer the central government — a treasury that secured a constant source of income without having to request it from the communal councils, a court that had final rights of appeal in all cases, and a privy council that was ostensibly designed to try important crimes but actually dealt with foreign policy and matters of internal government. The Visconti appointed three foreign officials to rule each of the subject towns — a captain of the people, who was usually a member of the Visconti family; a vicar, who ran the administration; and a podestà, who acted as chief justice.

The lords of Milan created an efficient and obedient administration and formed a standing army even though they failed to solve several important problems. One hundred years of Visconti rule and the purchase of a legitimate title secured the family's hold on the city, but, lacking clear lines of succession, the family was always in danger of internecine feuding. Money to pay for the military campaigns necessary to secure Visconti rule was always in short supply, and at key points lack of funds prevented the signori from taking full advantage of their victories. Finally, the lack of citizen participation left the loyalty of the Visconti's subjects in doubt, and the line was plagued with conspiracies and attempts at assassination. Over the Apennines to the south, the republics in Tuscany developed institutions that did not suffer from these defects, but they encountered problems of their own that were equally deep-rooted and hard to solve.

The Republics

The city of Florence is central to the Italian Renaissance. The Tuscan republics, of which Florence is the most noteworthy example, have long been admired and studied as early representatives of the form of government that came to dominate Europe. The fame of Florence is partly the result of the excellent tradition of historical writing associated with the city. From the earliest years native Florentines sought to describe their past in ways that would reflect the glory of the commune. In the fourteenth century the merchant family of the Villani produced three chronicles that portrayed contemporary Florentine affairs in terms at once accurate, detailed, and adulatory. The humanist historians of the Renaissance enlarged upon these chronicles by creating a more coherent interpretation of the sources of Florence's greatness and of the inner workings of its politics. Machiavelli and Guicciardini in the High Renaissance developed the humanist tradition further by adding to their works an immediacy and narrative impact that humanist histories often lacked.

Florence's interest in its own past was carried on by later historians, but in the nineteenth century it became mixed with a desire to find the origins of the democratic movement in the city's institutions of that period. Romantic historians like Sismondi stressed the birth of the ideal of human liberty in Renaissance Florence, and many historians ignored the oligarchic aspects of Florentine politics in their search for modern democracy.

The constitution of Florence was established by the Ordinances of Justice in 1293 and changed little until the republic was transformed into the grand duchy of Tuscany in the middle of the sixteenth century. Three principles of government are found in the ordinances. First, Florence was governed not by a separate class of professional administrators but by the citizens themselves, who held office for brief periods of time. The short tenure of office, which was basic to Florentine politics, had a number of advantages. It permitted a wide participation from the citizen body in the affairs of government and prevented the monopolization of power by a single person. It also allowed the citizens to continue their business activities with minimal inconvenience. To maintain these advantages, restraints were placed on the frequency with which one could hold important offices.

The second basic principle of Florentine politics was the division of power among multiple governing bodies, a practice also important in early communal life in Lombardy. In Tuscany this division placed executive authority in the hands of six (later nine) priors, who oversaw the administration and made proposals to a variety of councils. The latter had the power to reject the proposals of the priors but could not amend them or initiate new legislation. After 1327, the priors, as well as the other high officials, were chosen by lot in a complicated process that left much room for manipulation. The power of the various councils to veto executive measures frequently produced a stalemate, and procedures developed for suspending the constitution in an emergency and appointing a group called a *balia,* with complete power to enact legislation and make fundamental reforms.

The third aspect of the Florentine constitution has attracted much attention and has been the cause of considerable misinterpretation. According to the Ordinances of Justice, election to the important offices was dependent on membership in one of Florence's guilds. Furthermore, the election was weighted so that the priors came almost exclusively from the greater guilds, made up of the owners of Florence's industry and trade, and not from the lesser guilds of artisans and tradesmen. (The seven greater guilds were the Calimala, which dealt in foreign cloth; the Lana, which dealt in wool; the Por Santa Maria, which included both retailers and silk merchants; the money changers; the judges and notaries; the physicians, who dealt in oriental spices; and the furriers.) Although the artisans were able to elect more priors at some times than at others, they were never able to dominate the government for long periods of time. The exclusion of the lower orders and artisans from the government is hardly surprising; the more striking feature of the Ordinances of Justice is the fact that they also excluded the magnates, or great noble families, from all important offices. It was a serious crime for a member of one of these families to accept such an office and could lead to his execution or exile.

The exclusion of a definite section of the upper class from political office has tempted historians into drawing overly simple pictures of the relations between social classes in Renaissance Florence. The magnates in particular have frequently been seen as landholding feudal aristocracy who were kept from power because Florence depended not on them but on the commercial classes. There is no doubt whatsoever that the economy of the city was based on international trade and banking. By the late thirteenth century Florentines had amassed much wealth by importing wool from England and silk from the East, weaving this material into fine cloth (rough cloth was largely made in Flanders), dyeing it, and selling the finished product to English and French noblemen. The money derived from this industry was either used for more trade or lent out at a good profit to the church or the cash-hungry rulers of northern Europe.

The Florentine economy was solidly based on commerce, but it is not so simple to identify the ruling class with those who managed this commerce. Recent students of Florentine social life have made clear that the wealthy families admitted to power under the Ordinances of Justice did not form a distinct economic class. These families, called *popolani,* as well as the magnates excluded by the ordinances, were all involved in the important commercial activities of the city. The Bardi, a magnate family, owned one of the leading banking houses in fourteenth-century Europe. Moreover, both magnates and popolani possessed large landed estates. Land was the fundamental form of wealth for all propertied classes in this period because only land was sufficiently stable to provide a safe means of passing the proceeds of commerce to one's descendants. Industrial establishments in the fourteenth century were too small to provide the stability we now associate with them, and banks were prone to disappear in the face of economic reversal.

The magnates excluded by the Ordinances of Justice constituted not an economic but a personal group. They represented the 150 families whose behavior had been most violent and least subject to regulation in the period prior to 1293. Some families were not included in the list because, despite their ancient feudal lineage, they had either weakened or had become peaceful and law-abiding. Others, like the Cerchi family, were not of noble descent but were designated magnates because they had consistently refused to use the judicial processes of the commune to settle their quarrels.

The political life of Florence was thus less of a struggle for power among different social or economic classes than a factional strife among members of a single social class itself held together by personal and family ties. During periods of great stress other classes occasionally managed to enter the political arena. In 1378, under the pressure of a war with the papacy, an internal political crisis, and a continuing depression, a group of weavers, the *ciompi,* briefly seized power, but they were quickly overcome and violently suppressed. The Florentine aristocracy was not completely closed even in normal times. Newcomers, called *gente nuova,* who amassed enough money in an honorable way (which is to say through international trade) found it possible to be elected to office and marry into the old families. During the period from the Black Death in 1348 until the ciompi revolt thirty years later, the fall in population together with the financial embarrassment of the old families created a political life particularly open to these new men, but even the reaction to the ciompi revolt did not completely close off access to power. The influence of the gente nuova continued into the fifteenth century.

A look at the actual workings of the government shows that the laws were administered to the advantage of this upper class, both magnates and popolani. The laws prohibiting magnates from holding high office were frequently circumvented, especially if the magnate desiring office attached himself to a guild in a formal way but did not actually take up the business for which the guild was formed. Not even the laws against violence were rigorously enforced against the magnate class. The court records show regular dispensations granted to magnates for infractions that brought the death penalty to artisans or industrial workers. Taxes were seldom collected in full from the upper classes, and the statutory obligation of noblemen to maintain the roads outside the walls was seldom enforced.

The Florentine constitution was operated by a narrow oligarchy in its own social and economic interests. It was rare for more than five hundred to be eligible for the priorate in any given election. Out of a population that fluctuated between fifty thousand and ninety thousand, this was a small number indeed. The total number of enfranchised citizens never grew larger than five thousand. Yet despite its narrowness the Florentine government did provide an arena within which citizens could compete openly for office and which required their services as a matter of duty. This ideal of citizen participation in government and administration had important effects on the attitudes of Florentine intellectuals. Most obviously it encouraged the creation of articulate and sophisticated citizens through education and technical training. Lawyers were essential for the prosecution of Florence's drive to dominate its countryside and for the administration of this control once secured. In addition, the republican form of government, however narrow its reality, gave impetus to the formation of an intellectual vocabulary that would stress the value of citizen participation and explain the strength that grew from such involvement. This vocabulary, created at the beginning of the fifteenth century, had an important influence in shaping the concerns of the Italian Renaissance, and proved relevant far beyond the confines of the Florentine republic.

Naples and Venice

At each end of Italy were two states that did not conform to the categories discussed so far in this chapter. The southern half of the peninsula lay under the suzerainty of the kings of Sicily. Despite that title the kings made their capital on the mainland at Naples, and during much of this period they had no control over the island of Sicily at all. Mountainous and agricultural, the kingdom resembled the feudal monarchies of the North rather than any of the Italian city-states. Control over the barons was intermittent at best; revenues were insufficient to develop the sorts of control wielded by the states of northern Italy; trade and industry never became dominant features of the economy. Yet the size, population, and legitimacy of Naples made it an important, if peripheral, factor in Italian politics. Sons of the ruling house frequently served as lords of cities in northern Italy, and in the early fifteenth century one of the most capable of the kings, Ladislaus, conquered the Papal States and threatened to unite most of Italy under his rule. After 1400 the kingdom exercised a constant influence in Italian diplomacy and played a large part in the crisis at the end of that century, but during the fourteenth century it was largely tied down by its own problems.

Equally involved in its own problems was Venice, the fifth major Italian state. Venice was built on a series of islands in the Adriatic Sea and completely separated from the mainland. This position protected the city from invasion by land and directed its attention to the East. During the fourteenth century Venice built up a chain of colonies in Dalmatia. At the end of that century it decisively defeated its Italian rival, Genoa, and became the dominant trading power in the Mediterranean. Its government was republican with a chief executive chosen by the council but serving for life. The executive, called a doge, occasionally sought to establish a control over the city that would compromise its republican foundations, but these threats were always forcefully met and defeated. The Venetian aristocracy was less open than the Florentine ruling class. After 1297 no new names were added to the list of families eligible to sit in the great council. In Florence the gente nuova came mainly not from the lower classes within the city but from the commercial classes in the surrounding towns dependent on Florence. The absence of a related countryside surrounding Venice explains much of the closed nature of Venetian society.

Toward the end of the fourteenth century, and partly to meet the growing threat of Milan, Venice began slowly to extend its influence onto the mainland. In 1405, Padua was secured for Venetian domination while the ruling Carrara house was hopelessly embroiled in conflict with Milan, and Verona was added to the Venetian sphere of influence in the same way. This foreign policy eventually brought Venice to the borders of both Milanese territory and the Papal States, and it made Venice one of the most unsettling factors in fifteenth-century diplomacy. But during the early Renaissance Venice's attention was concentrated on the East, and until its change in foreign policy the city played little part in the intellectual life of Italy.

Conclusion

The most significant fact of Italian life in the fourteenth and early fifteenth centuries is its urban nature. The city remained throughout the Middle Ages a far more important factor in Italy than in northern Europe and became the nexus around which political developments occurred. Except for the kingdom of Sicily, all major powers were based on the control of cities. Even the popes had to secure Rome before they could embark on the pacification of their states. The urban nature of Italian politics meant that many vexing problems of political administration in northern Europe were largely missing from the Italian scene. Most obviously, the difficulties of communication and transportation were diminished, and administration became more manageable. In Italy the subject cities could not defy Milan and Florence with the impunity enjoyed by distant parts of the French kingdom or the Holy Roman Empire, for the ruling city was only a few miles away and could respond rapidly.

The small size of the ruling classes in Italy also contributed to the ease of government. Within even the largest cities all enfranchised citizens were acquainted and often related. Devotion to the city was not an abstract feeling but an attachment to the very walls and buildings seen every day and to actual individuals who were a part of one's life in business and society as well as in government. Dangers to the city took on a similar immediacy. The frontier was close, and preparations for defense could not be entrusted to an impersonal administration. The citizens had to man their own walls or themselves raise the money to hire mercenary soldiers.

Political life in Renaissance Italy was more pervasive than farther north, but at the same time it was more directly influenced by the governed. This was especially true in the republics, but even in Milan the signori had to create an articulate citizen body to administer their territories. This pervasiveness gave to the intellectual life of Italy a civic cast that clearly distinguished it from the intellectual activity in the North during the same period. During the earliest stages of the Renaissance, concern with active political life was not conspicuous, but moral interests were clearly present that provided the ground for the political vocabulary that emerged in the fifteenth century. Before considering these early stages, the profound crisis that afflicted Italy during the fourteenth century must be considered, because this crisis formed the background against which the Renaissance was born.

Bibliography

The political history of Italy has been so diverse and fragmented, especially during the medieval and Renaissance periods, that the student will have great difficulty in finding a clear narrative account of it. Denis Hay, *The Italian Renaissance in Its Historical Background* (Cambridge: The University Press, 1961), has provided a good introduction to the problems of Italian history and is a good starting place. For a more comprehensive narrative, Luigi Salvatorelli, *A Concise History of Italy from Prehistoric Times to Our Own Day,* trans. R. Miall (New York: Oxford University Press, 1940), is still useful, as is the more recent *A Short History of Italy,* edited by H. Hearder and Daniel P. Waley (Cambridge: The University Press, 1963). For those who read Italian, volumes four and five of the Storia d'Italia series published by Mondadori — Nino Valeri, *L'Italia nell'età dei principati* (Milan, 1949), and Luigi Salvatorelli, *L'Italia communale* (Milan, 1940) — should be consulted.

Since Guillaume Mollat's classic study of the popes at Avignon, *The Popes at Avignon,* 1st French ed. 1912, trans. Janet Love from the 9th French ed. (London: Nelson, 1963), the strength and vigor of that period of papal history has been beyond dispute. Three recent studies of papal administration — Daniel P. Waley, *The Papal State in the Thirteenth Century* (London: Macmillan, 1961); Peter Partner, *The Papal State Under Martin V* (London: British School at Rome, 1958); and Partner, *The Lands of St. Peter* (Berkeley and Los Angeles: University of California Press, 1972) — have clarified many of the problems in that field.

Daniel P. Waley's *Italian City Republics* (New York: McGraw-Hill, 1969) provides a much-needed introduction to the communes of Italy, both republics and those that became lordships in the fourteenth and fifteenth centuries. John Larner, *The Lords of Romagna* (London: Macmillan, 1965), has stressed the complexity and uncertainty of communal developments even into the fifteenth century. Among cities studied, Tuscany boasts the most recent good literature. David Herlihy's *Medieval and Renaissance Pistoia* (New Haven: Yale University Press, 1967) and Gene Brucker's *Renaissance Florence* (New York: Wiley, 1969) are excellent studies and provide good bibliographies of the recent monographic literature. For Milan during this period, Dorothy Muir's *A History of Milan Under the Visconti* (London: Methuen, 1924) is still readable but is much out of date, and the seventeen-volume *Storia di Milano* published by the Fondazione Treccani degli Alfieri per la storia di Milano (1953–66) is hardly for the casually curious.

2 Crises of the Fourteenth Century

Urban politics provided the framework within which Italian intellectual life developed, but the Renaissance was born in the midst of an intense and profound crisis, or turning point, that affected every element of Italian life. The crisis was most obvious in its economic and demographic aspects, but it had political, social, and religious dimensions as well. It introduced new intellectual concerns and gave new uses to the classic and moral interests of Renaissance thinkers. Every dimension of Italian life was involved in the mid-century upheaval, and no one change should be considered more basic than any other. Each must be looked at on its own terms.

Economic Crisis: Depression

The wealth supporting the cultural and political activities of Italy was produced by the growth of commerce that dominated the thirteenth century and the first half of the fourteenth. The volume of trade, the value of goods transported, and the quantity and quality of industrial production all steadily increased during this period and made Italy the wealthiest country in Europe. In the mid-fourteenth century the growth came abruptly to a halt, and Italy plunged into a depression whose effects spread throughout Europe. After 1340 the signs of economic decline were clear. More people declared themselves destitute, and tax revenues declined. City walls, which had been steadily enlarged since the early thirteenth century, ceased to expand. Trade and industrial production fell off. Trade at one Genoese port plummeted from a value of 1,650,000 pounds in 1334 to 1,200,000 in 1391 and finally reached a low of 234,000 in 1423. Florentine cloth production, which stood at seventy-five thousand pieces in 1339, dropped to twenty-four thousand by 1378.

Recovery from the depression was slow and incomplete. Long periods of decline tended to follow brief spurts of economic growth, and even in the fifteenth century Italy apparently continued to lag behind its high point of the early fourteenth century. The Peruzzi, one of three leading Florentine banking houses of the early fourteenth century, counted ninety employees on its payroll and boasted a gross capital of 110,000 florins in the 1330s. By contrast, the Medici, which was the leading Italian banking house a century later, employed only sixty men and mustered capital resources of only 70,000 florins. While individual Italians were not necessarily poorer or more miserable, the scale of Italian economic activity was clearly reduced after 1340.

The origins of the economic crisis can be traced to the failure of the Florentine banking industry. In 1337, Edward III of England repudiated his debts in an attempt to raise money for an invasion of France. Most of the debts, about one million florins, were owed to two Florentine banking houses, the Bardi and the Peruzzi. Despite their wealth and Europe-wide resources, this sudden loss of assets proved too much, and they went bankrupt the next year, followed shortly thereafter by several lesser houses that had deposited money with them. By 1346 every major bank in Florence had failed, and the complex economy based on the banks' ability to make credit available and process international transactions ground to a halt.

While the immediate circumstances bringing down the Italian banking houses can be easily identified, the failure was actually part of a general economic pattern with far wider causes. The banking crisis occurred in the context of a decline in trade. Part of the reason for this decline was the fact that after a century and a half of expansion, the routes over which the trade was carried had become too narrow and too unstable to support the volume of traffic necessary to sustain the European economy. There were also specific impediments that interrupted the normal flow of trade, particularly from the East. The unification of Asia under the Mongols had formerly permitted the peaceful passage of goods across the Asian mainland, but Mongol rule collapsed during the fourteenth century and was finally destroyed by the Ming dynasty in 1368. The ensuing disruption of the mainland routes forced the great bulk of eastern trade through the Near East. To the ruler of Egypt this was a golden opportunity to levy tariffs, which raised the price of the goods so high that demand significantly decreased. At the same time, alternate trade routes through Constantinople became more difficult because of increasing Turkish pressure.

In addition to constriction of the trade route, the European economy was suffering from a contraction or disappearance of its normal markets. Edward III's invasion of France in 1337 was the prelude to a protracted war, now called the Hundred Years' War. The war went badly for France at first, and the French nobility, who had furnished the chief market for the luxury cloth woven in Florence or imported from the East, were impoverished by the costs of fighting. The French had an expensive tendency to be captured by the English and held for large ransoms. The English, on the other hand, instead of buying luxury cloth, sought to develop their own wool industry and enter into competition with the Italians.

Certain parts of the European economy ran against the general trend. English wool production, encouraged by the government, undoubtedly increased during this period. In Italy itself agricultural reforms led to a rise in food production, even though industrial activity was declining. But these advances could not offset the losses. England was not large enough to compensate for the reversals of Italy. The entire production of the English wool industry in 1490 was only forty thousand pieces, while in Florence alone annual production dropped by fifty thousand pieces in the space of fifty years. And although agriculture might advance in Italy, there was simply not enough arable land to offset the reduction in industrial activity.

It may seem hard to understand how the restriction of trade from the East, which consisted of luxury goods like silks and spices, could bring on a profound and lasting depression. We have to keep in mind that in a preindustrial society the cost of transportation made up a very large portion of total cost of a product. A load of grain traveling the fifty miles from Pisa to Florence tripled its price, and a bolt of silk increased in value many, many times between the Chinese weaver and the French count who finally bought it. In such an economy most liquid wealth was tied up in trade, and, when trade stopped, the wealth disappeared. Such was the case in most of Europe and particularly in Italy in the mid-fourteenth century.

Population Crisis: Plague

Historians were slow to see the full scope of the economic depression, because its effects were masked by another event of the mid-fourteenth century, one that struck the imaginations of contemporaries far more vividly than mundane trade figures. In 1347 a Genoese galley, returning from the East, landed at Sicily because sickness had broken out among the crew. The sickness soon spread to the inhabitants of the island. In 1348 another galley brought the disease to Pisa, and it rapidly spread throughout Italy, reaching into northern Europe by the end of the year. The disease, which was called the Black Death, seems to have been a mixture of bubonic and pneumonic plagues. It was not the first epidemic to hit Europe but was the most widespread and virulent since the great pandemic of the seventh century. Estimates of the dead ranged widely from a high of three-fifths of the population (Pope Clement VI counted 42 million dead) to a low of only one-fourth. It seems likely that at least a third of the inhabitants of western Europe succumbed to the disease. Cities were especially hard hit. The population of Florence dropped from 100,000 in 1347 to 40,000 when the plague finally abated. In Venice no fewer than fifty patrician families were completely wiped out.

The plague was related to the fourteenth-century decline in population much as the failure of the Florentine banking houses was related to the general depression. It was dramatic and obvious, but apparently it was not the only cause. It accelerated a trend already in progress. Recent studies of land cultivation in Tuscany show that the birth rate had been declining since the early years of the fourteenth century. The population of Europe had previously grown along with the economy, but by 1300 it was clearly straining the productivity of the land. The Black Death relieved this pressure in a violent and traumatic way, but the downward trend in population had already begun.

The Black Death made the general economic constriction that preceded it more difficult to see. Because of the scarcity of workers, wages rose when they should have been falling. Peasants could more often buy their freedom from seigniorial dues, and the money gave the landlords a purchasing power they would not normally have enjoyed and created an artificial market for goods. The plague also increased social mobility by elevating remote relatives to fortunes they never expected and by opening public office to new people who would not normally have been elected. All this gave an appearance of vitality to the society and masked the economic and social aspects of the crisis.

Political Crisis: New Politics in Florence

As the trading center of Europe, Italy felt the economic crisis most deeply; as the most urbanized area, it was also most devastated by the Black Death. The shock associated with these two events extended through all levels of Italian society — its political life, its thought, and its religious feeling. While the economic indicators leave room for doubt about the long-term effects of the depression, no one can seriously question the depth of the change in other aspects of Italian life after 1340. Yet the historian should hesitate to explain the general change solely as a result of the economic or demographic crisis. Tensions visible in other spheres of life certainly contributed to the reorientation of values and sensibilities at mid-century.

The attitudes and policies of Florentine government underwent a significant transformation in the early decades of the century. The constitution described in Chapter 1 should not be dismissed as a cynical alliance among the upper classes of the city to suppress and exploit the lower. If that had been the only motive, brute force would have been much simpler than the complex and unwieldy institutions that actually made up the Florentine state. The laws against the magnates were laxly enforced not simply out of favoritism arising from family and social ties among the ruling classes. The casualness also reflected an attitude toward the function of the state and its laws. For Florentines of the early fourteenth century, the state was not so fundamental and necessary an institution as it is commonly held to be today. The state was only one of several institutions that claimed a share of their loyalty, including the family, the church, and the faction or the guild. It was not even regarded as the basic institution that underlay and guaranteed all other institutions.

Limited in this fashion, the state was not expected to maintain the social order unaided; all institutions did this jointly. Its function instead was to make people better. Its laws were moral laws, to be obeyed not just because they were promulgated by the state but because they formed the basis for a better society. Strictly speaking, the state thus had no more right to enforce the law by retributive punishment than did the church. In both cases resort to punishment was admission of failure. Far better that the transgressors should be brought to see the error of their ways and repent. In fact the regular dispensations granted to the upper classes were always surrounded with religious ceremony. The transgressors marched solemnly to the Palace of the Signoria and then to the Baptistry, where a kiss of peace between enemies was required and solemn oaths of friendship were sworn in the presence of public heralds. The purpose of the state was moral persuasion rather than punishment, and the constitution of Florence assumed that citizens were open to such persuasion.

The relaxed attitude of the state made it reluctant to collect taxes rigidly, but the practice could be maintained only as long as expenses were kept down. By 1340 increased state expenditures had created severe problems. Florence had become embroiled in a long, costly, and eventually unsuccessful war with Lucca. At first Florence paid the lord of Lucca 250,000 florins in an attempt to buy the city without fighting, but later found that it had to take the city by force after all. To finance the military operations Florence resorted to forced loans paying high rates of interest. The collapse of the banks added difficulties to an already overextended system. By 1340 the public debt had risen to 1 million florins, on which an annual interest of 120,000 florins was due, while revenues declined to 400,000 florins. As the depression worsened, the city was compelled to seek further loans merely to pay the interest on the debt. The interest had to be paid because most of the Florentine families had invested heavily in state loans and were dependent on the interest for their income.

To deal with the situation the Florentines adopted a timeworn expedient: they called in a foreign lord. The lord was Walter of Brienne, and the remedy was disastrous. He arrived with universal approval, but within six months of his election he was driven from the city by universal hatred. The hatred long survived his death. Machiavelli, nearly a century later, considered him a weak and ugly villain with no understanding of Florence's problems. Recent studies have identified the source of Walter's unpopularity. Faced with rising expenditures, he began rigorously to enforce laws that had never been enforced. As a basis for taxation he established a new estimate of wealth that turned out to be fair and accurate. He unified treasury receipts so that those who had not paid their taxes could be plainly identified. He insisted on the performance of such services as upkeep of the roads and maintenance of the city's defenses, and he initiated prosecutions for peculation from the public treasury.

Walter introduced the Florentines to a new concept of political life — a state based on strict enforcement of the law as opposed to moral and personal persuasion, a state whose prime function was its own preservation. The existence and size of the public debt gave a new reality to the concept. Florentine citizens could understand that the state was a thing in itself because their livelihoods depended on it. Measures clearly had to be taken to preserve it. But Walter's implementation of this concept eroded ancient privileges and left him unpopular in every part of the city, despite his effort to win support outside the traditional oligarchy. His unpopularity, however, did not prevent his successors from continuing his strict measures. The lure of the added revenues was irresistible.

The political changes of the 1340s involved not only a stricter enforcement of laws and a new conception of the state. They reflected a new attitude toward man. Both before and after 1340 the state was deeply involved in fulfilling a moral function by making better men out of the Florentines. But after 1340 there was less optimism that men could be persuaded to be good and a growing conviction that coercing them into moral behavior was a regrettable necessity. A similar pessimism about man's natural goodness can be found in religious and intellectual activity after the 1340s.

Religious Crisis: Change in Popular Preaching

The new attitudes in religion were more closely connected with the Black Death than with the economic or political crisis. It is not surprising that the sudden death of a third of one's friends would lead to thoughts of mortality and questions about guilt and responsibility. In the fourteenth century the questions found their answer less in formal theology than in popular preaching. Preachers, whether resident in a particular place or wandering from town to town, were a major means of communication and played a large role in the formation of popular attitudes. They gave the people a vocabulary to use in dealing with their problems.

By its very nature popular preaching tends to be moralizing and emphasizes the necessity of bettering one's conduct and attitudes, but between the early years of the century and the period after the

Black Death important differences were apparent. The earlier preachers, exhorting their audience to prepare for the afterlife and the end of the world, stressed the redemptive power of love and the use of this power through existing social institutions. Men were urged to seek regeneration through inner renewal, to adopt the rule of love and charity. Social institutions could help in this effort; the church, through preaching, and the state by admonishment for transgression of laws. Patriotism and civic responsibility were exalted. In the words of the Dominican preacher Remigio di Girolami (1235–1319): "If you are not a citizen you are not a man, because man is naturally a civil animal."

Underlying this exaltation of civic life was a confidence in the natural goodness of human traits. The natural world, though imperfect, was thought to be good, and feelings, emotions, and social forms were considered basically consonant with God's will. Grace does not destroy nature; it only completes it. A constant theme among the early preachers was confidence in the ability of any individual, whatever his class, to perform socially useful acts without coercion. That confidence provided an important support for the casual attitudes toward law enforcement prevalent in Florentine government.

Preaching after the Black Death continued to be moral in tone, but the life to which sinners were called was a far different one. Gone after the 1340s were both confidence in man's ability to purify himself and faith in the goodness of his natural desires and feelings. Instead, religious figures pessimistically renounced life, and their pessimism found a strong echo in popular attitudes. One heard that the Anti-Christ had been seen among men and that the plague was a sign of judgment, caused by human corruption. One of the most popular tracts of this period was the *Mirror of True Penitence,* by Jacopo Passavanti (d. 1357). The *Mirror,* a systematic and finished version of the sermons Passavanti preached mostly in 1354, stressed the pervasiveness of sin and man's helplessness before it. Passavanti says that sin can be controlled only by complete submission to an external power — never by individual self-renewal. The institutions of the world only contribute to man's corruption and must be renounced. This reversal of previous religious attitudes is doubtless related to the trauma of the Black Death, but it is also part of a wider context. In political life the stricter enforcement of law introduced a new austerity and seriousness into Florentine life.

Moreover, in the cultural sphere, one of the more worldly writers of the early period began after 1350 to call for a renunciation of worldly pleasures. Neither of those changes was directly related to the Black Death, but both paralleled the change in religious attitudes, where indeed the plague played an especially prominent part.

Intellectual Crisis: Boccaccio

Accompanying the change in religious attitudes during the 1340s was a general reorientation in all forms of intellectual activity in Italy. This reorientation can be illustrated by the career of one man, whose interests and values were dramatically altered in the decade following the Black Death. Giovanni Boccaccio (1312–1375) was the illegitimate son of a Florentine merchant. He spent some time as a merchant and then studied canon law before deciding on a literary career. Though Boccaccio is most famous for the *Decameron,* his literary production was large, and he played a leading part in bringing the humanist attitudes and techniques of Petrarch to Florence. His career was clearly divided into two periods. Until the mid-1350s he lived alternately in Naples and Florence and wrote tales and fables in vernacular Italian. Thereafter he accepted regular employment as a Florentine diplomat, stopped writing in Italian, and began to produce treatises in Latin — to the detriment, unfortunately, of both languages.

The *Decameron,* begun in 1348 and largely finished by 1353, is the masterpiece of his earlier period. It is a collection of one hundred short tales, held together by the device of having the tales related by a group of young noblemen and ladies who have fled Florence during the Black Death and have shut themselves up in a country villa to avoid contagion. The stories cover a wide variety of subjects, including betrayed love, lighthearted romance, and casual priestly corruption. Some are ribald, and many are amusing. The author gathered his materials from many disparate sources, and he knew how to tell a good story.

Previous generations, particularly in the nineteenth century, have searched the *Decameron* for prurient material, but Boccaccio, like Chaucer, tells his tales in too straightforward a manner to be really salacious. He is a subtle and talented narrator who wants to convey certain values. Much has been made of his lack of moral sensitivity. De Sanctis, the great Italian critic of the nineteenth century, said that the world of the *Decameron* is one whose only law is nature and that Boccaccio reacted to medieval spiritualism and asceticism with an aestheticism where only art was serious. Recent critics, however, have stressed the medieval aspects of Boccaccio's work. Certainly the form of the work can be found in medieval sources, though Boccaccio's narrative is more complex and sustained. Another medieval influence can be seen in the ideal of courtly love, which forms the basis of many of the stories.

It is unfair to consider the *Decameron* morally insensitive, although its moral element depends on Boccaccio's transformation of medieval concepts of love. Courtly love in the medieval tradition of the Provençal poets was sublimated and beyond sensuality. Because love should remain unconsummated, its ideal object was a married woman, for a married woman was ideally unattainable and thus the love would never be sullied. This type of love was seen as a prototype of divine charity and categorically opposed to sensual love, which was a prototype of sin. Boccaccio joined the responsibilities of courtly love to the physical nature of sexual love. He saw love as an irrational instinct based on our appetites, but considered it nonetheless subject to moral rules and part of the moral order of nature.

The *Decameron* seems to call men to flee death and sadness by amusing themselves, but it also shows that health and well-being are maintained through the practice of restraint and decorum. The young people gathered to escape the plague amuse themselves according to an elaborate set of rules. Even the location in a Tuscan country villa involves a compromise between the activity of the city and the solitude of the countryside, and that compromise sets a tone of rational and moderate discipline throughout the whole work. Boccaccio felt that one could give rein to one's sensual desires without removing them from the area of moral concern. He said not so much "do what you want," as "what you want can be good." He displays, in short, the same confidence in man's ability to regulate and control his basically good natural drives that is found in preaching and political life in the early fourteenth century.

The confident faith in man's intrinsic goodness disappeared in Boccaccio's later writings. The mood of the *Corbaccio,* written in 1354 and 1355, is bitter and gloomy, and the author castigates love, calling its motives ignoble and its physical aspects revolting. Boccaccio never returned to his earlier attitude. He devoted much of his later life to such works as *On the Fates of Illustrious Men,* a moral discussion of the vagaries of fate. More than that, his change of heart involved an explicit repudiation of his earlier writings. In 1373, he wrote to a friend after hearing that the latter had a copy of the *Decameron:*

> I am certainly not happy that you have let the good women in your house read my trifles; in fact you must promise me you will not permit it any more. You know how indecent and immodest they are, how much they stimulate to wanton love and drive to lust even those most fortified against it. . . . My feminine readers will consider me a filthy pimp and an incestuous old man, shameless, foul-mouthed and malignant, eager to spread stories of the wantonness of others.

Boccaccio's was one of the most dramatic personal conversions of the century. It came shortly after the Black Death, but let us not imagine that event as the only cause. To do so would be to misunderstand Boccaccio as well as grossly oversimplify the problem of assessing intellectual influences. An individual's ideas are formed not by vague encounters with large historical events but by precise personal experiences. Although the historian can never hope to find exactly what these are, he can still keep in mind that he is dealing with actual human beings. Boccaccio in particular seems to have felt several influences that we can identify: the piety of Petrarch, his own advancing age and fears of death, and even the scorn of a young lady. The Black Death, however, does not seem to have been personally important. Unlike Petrarch, he lost no one close to him, and indeed the *Decameron,* which was his first and most direct reaction to it, reaffirms his earlier confidence.

In literature, then, the moral concerns of the earlier period were maintained and intensified after the 1340s, but the optimism about man's natural capacity to act morally disappeared. Human desires, which were means of growth in the *Decameron,* became in the *Corbaccio* obstacles to leading a moral life.

Conclusion

The crises of the fourteenth century deprived man of confidence in his own powers. Society seemed to falter. The economy crumbled, political life became harsher and more rigorous, literature ceased to entertain, and religious figures exhorted men to suppress their natural feelings. The moral concerns of the early years of the century remained, but they took on a new austerity and desperation. The Black Death, which struck in the midst of this crisis, intensified and perhaps prolonged its effects, but did not cause the upheaval.

It was in such an atmosphere that the Renaissance developed in Italy. The first stages of Renaissance humanism appeared in the earliest years of the fourteenth century, but Boccaccio was largely responsible for making the study of the classics popular in Florence, and that city rapidly became the center of Renaissance studies. But it is important to remember that as this study of the crises has shown, moral concerns continued to play a major role in all aspects of Italian life. They changed their form during the crises but not their importance. Moreover, the classics, which gave the Renaissance much of its vocabulary, were not necessarily a secular or worldly influence. Boccaccio's classical period in fact coincided with his conversion and repudiation of worldly naturalism, and he used his classical studies to support the unbending moralism of the *Corbaccio*. Deep and persistent moral concerns remained a fundamental feature of Italian thought and culture throughout the Renaissance.

Bibliography

The best introduction to the economic, social, and political aspects of the problems discussed in this chapter is the anthology edited by Anthony Molho, *The Social and Economic Foundations of the Italian Renaissance* (New York: Wiley, 1969). The articles and documents collected there provide a broad perspective on interpretations of the period together with an excellent bibliography for further reading. Marvin Becker's two-volume study of Florentine history, *Florence in Transition* (Baltimore: Johns Hopkins Press, 1967–1968), offers a stimulating if controversial account of the effects of the crisis on Florentine political life. The medieval aspects of Boccaccio have been discussed by Vittorio Branca, *Boccaccio Medievale* (Florence: Sansone, 1970). In the graphic arts, too, the crises of the mid-fourteenth century produced a major shift. Manifestations of the crisis in that field have been illuminated by Millard Meiss, *Painting in Florence and Siena at the Time of the Black Death* (Princeton: Princeton University Press, 1951).

3 Dante and the Medieval Tradition

The Renaissance was in part a reaction to certain aspects of the medieval world-view, and a picture of that world-view is essential to understanding the movement. Although this chapter will identify certain traits common to late medieval thought, the reader should not therefore conclude that the medieval period was more homogeneous than our own. Not only was the period too long to present such unity, but even in the thirteenth century, which produced the most unified and coherent statements of medieval values, men were not in unanimous agreement on intellectual matters. The most cursory glance reveals lively disputes over the basic issues. Still, Renaissance thinkers sensed a sharp difference between their own way of dealing with experience and that of the Middle Ages. This was partly because scholasticism, as the thirteenth-century approach is called, was still new in Italy. In northern Europe, and particularly at the University of Paris, much of the thirteenth century had been devoted to elaborating scholasticism, but that approach began to make significant inroads in Italy only at the beginning of the fourteenth century — precisely at the time when the earliest Renaissance humanists were beginning their careers. Part of the vehemence and coherence of the Renaissance reaction to scholasticism sprang from the fact that both movements were competing for the attention of the intellectual community at the same time.

A particularly eloquent statement of the scholastic approach can be found in the writings of Dante Alighieri (1265–1321). Dante is frequently ignored by Renaissance historians, perhaps because his major poetic work, the *Divine Comedy,* conveys his genius and individuality with a depth and force that make it impossible to treat the work as anything but unique. It is not a document, and historians are justifiably loath to consider it one. But Dante confounds the intellectual historian in other ways as well. The problem is suggested by the apocryphal student who wrote in his examination, "Dante stands with one foot firmly planted in the Middle Ages, and with the other he salutes the rising sun of the Renaissance." The statement is true though the metaphor is mixed. A transitional figure, Dante shared certain attitudes and values with early Renaissance thinkers like Petrarch, but he lacked the consciousness of participating in a revival, which was such an important part of the Renaissance. He conceived of human knowledge as did Thomas Aquinas and other thirteenth-century scholastics, but he introduced an intensely personal element into the pursuit of truth that Thomas would have found strange. While the ambiguity may account for the breadth of Dante's poetry, it also defies the historian who tries to place him too neatly into a historical context.

Historical Background of *De Monarchia*

A coherent statement of Dante's medieval assumptions can be found not so much in his poetry as in his prose treatise on world government, the *De Monarchia,* probably written in 1312 and 1313. In that work, Dante undertook a systematic investigation into the nature and function of government. He described the ideal form of government and assessed the rival claims of the church and the Holy Roman Empire to fulfill that ideal. The treatise stands among the most complete works of political theory of its time.

Historical circumstances combined to give the *De Monarchia* a more traditional cast than Dante's other writings. In the early fourteenth century new values and new politics were strongly challenging the conceptions of legitimate rule and universal jurisdiction that Dante defended. Dante himself actively participated in some of these challenges, but by the time he wrote the essay he had been hurt by his political activity and bitterly disillusioned by the weakness of traditional values. The treatise represents in part his response to defeat and disillusionment, and it cannot be fully appreciated without a brief consideration of Dante's own experience.

Dante was born in Florence into a family that became enfranchised by the Ordinances of Justice in 1293. He boasted in the *Divine Comedy* of the noble descent of the Alighieri, but in fact this is unlikely. All important members of the political faction to which his family belonged were in exile at the time of Dante's birth.

Since Dante was born in Florence, his father was clearly unimportant and had been allowed to remain. The Alighieri, while not a major political power, were entitled to serve on the legislative and executive bodies of the city and did so frequently whenever their faction was in control. From 1295 until his own exile in 1302 Dante took advantage of this opportunity. In 1295 he was a member of an executive council; in 1296 he sat on one of the major legislative councils and served on the electoral commission for the priorate. He also undertook several diplomatic missions for the city, including an important one to the papal court at Rome. In 1300 he was elected to the priorate and became one of the six chief executives of the city. Here his troubles began.

Dante came to grief from the factional strife that dominated Florence's history from its earliest years until the Medici domination in the fifteenth century. Feuding was endemic to all Italian cities, but men of Dante's age felt that Tuscany suffered more than most from this disease, and modern historians have found little reason to disagree. Neither Renaissance historians nor modern ones have found a very convincing explanation for factional strife beyond saying that it lay in the nature of the early city-state and the temper of its citizens, but all agree that it was a major cause of the foreign and domestic political problems of the age.

The particular feud that brought disgrace and exile to Dante broke out among the members of the Cancellieri family in neighboring Pistoia and would have attracted scant attention had the two branches of the family, the Blacks and the Whites, not been supported by the leading Florentine families. Two of these Florentine houses, the Cerchi and the Donati, were already rivals and took advantage of the Pistoian feud to bring the Black-White quarrel to Florence.

As Florence became embroiled in the feud, forces beyond Tuscany began to take an interest, in particular Pope Boniface VIII. Boniface, who meddled in the affairs of France until he brought the king's wrath and army down upon himself, could hardly ignore matters in a city only two hundred miles from Rome. Florence was a prime source of loans to the papacy, and Boniface sent a cardinal there with the charge of making peace — a euphemism for securing the interest of the church. The cardinal publicly sought to mediate the quarrel between the Cerchi and Donati families, but in secret he schemed to advance the cause of the church. A plot was conceived and directed by three backers of the Black faction to surrender Florence's independence to Boniface, but it was discovered during Dante's tenure as prior. Dante and his colleagues moved to protect the city by exiling the conspirators.

Boniface was furious that his plans had been balked, and he excommunicated the city's magistrates. Never one to rely wholly on spiritual sanctions, he also looked around for a more effective if less dramatic means of getting his way. He found one in the form of a French army that was marching down the peninsula on its way to Sicily. Boniface induced the commander, Charles of Valois, to stop briefly in Florence and restore the exiled Blacks. Ostensibly Charles was seeking to reunite the two factions, but the return of the Blacks by armed force could have only one result. Less than a week later, the Whites were driven out. Dante happened to be in Rome trying to make peace with Boniface when he learned that his faction had been expelled. He was destined never to see Florence again and spent the last two decades of his life in exile.

Dante showed an intense feeling for his native city in every part of the *Divine Comedy,* which he used as a vehicle for castigating the sins of his political enemies and extolling the virtues of his friends. For Boniface VIII, whom he blamed most of all for his troubles, he reserved a place in the eighth circle of hell, where the pope would spend eternity buried upside down in a grotesque distortion of the baptismal font while flames forever burned his feet. But Dante turned his bitterness not only against his enemies but also against the very political ambience in which he had suffered. Because Florence had been free from domination by the legitimate powers of pope or emperor, factions and social groups had freely competed without considering the abstract goals or justifications of government. Dante had participated actively in this world, had been a partisan politician. Now he had lost, and in losing began to wonder if a more stable government based on universal principles of justice and equity might be better than the free-for-all of an Italian city-state.

After a decade in exile, Dante saw a possibility that the traditional principles might still be workable. Henry VII, newly elected Holy Roman emperor, announced in 1307 that he was coming into Italy to be crowned at Rome and restore peace among the warring factions of Italy. The emperors for several centuries had been German princes, and many had done as Henry now intended. The last emperors to make the Rome journey, however, were the terrible Hohenstaufens, and they certainly had not come in peace. Henry VII promised much good, and Dante waxed enthusiastic. He excitedly addressed letters to the rulers of Italy exhorting them to welcome Henry:

> Behold now arise the signs of consolation of peace. For a new day grows brighter in its birth revealing the dawn that already dispels the shadows of our long-endured tribulation, and we who have kept a night-long vigil in the wilderness — we too shall see the long awaited joy. For a peace bringing Titan now climbs on high and Justice will once more glitter as soon as it receives his first ray.

How sad this sounds when compared with Henry's actual accomplishments. It was soon apparent that the emperor expected little more than the money to pay for his journey. He even had trouble in getting that because of his ignorance of the subtleties of Italian politics. Instead of bringing peace, his clumsy intervention in northern Italy served to exacerbate factional strife, and by the time he reached Tuscany his coming was dreaded by nearly all factions. Of all the Tuscan cities, only Pisa, Florence's bitter rival, opened its gates to him. Florence categorically refused even to acknowledge the legitimacy of Henry's title. Further humiliations awaited the emperor in Rome. He was forced to crown himself, and at the coronation banquet the revelers were driven under the table by a shower of rocks hurled through the window by angry Romans. When the emperor finally died of a fever in Tuscany in 1313, it was obvious to all how tenuous the exercise of legitimate authority had become in Italy. Dante, who had hoped to be restored, was still in exile, and in Florence his enemies, the Blacks, continued in power, undisturbed by the fulminations of imperial displeasure.

Dante's failure in Florentine politics convinced him that a worldview that saw government as legitimate, unified, and directed toward moral ends was preferable to the political life he had known. His disappointment at the inadequacy of Henry VII further convinced him that such a world-view had grown weak in his own day. These beliefs compelled him to write a coherent and forceful restatement of the values of an earlier age: the treatise on world government. With none of the rich variety of the *Comedy,* Dante analyzed political life from a unified and consistent set of assumptions, assumptions that men of the Renaissance — even Dante himself in various ways and in other works — sought to displace.

Scholastic Assumptions in *De Monarchia*

Dante argued that government has only one function: to maintain peace so that mankind can most fully develop itself. This function can best be carried out if government is unified. The most unified form of government is monarchy, and the best monarchy is a world monarchy. The Roman Empire exercised such authority, and its authority had now passed to the Holy Roman emperors. These emperors should exercise their control without interference from the church, which properly should have no political power.

Stated in its baldest terms the argument seems hopelessly naive. How could Dante maintain that government has only one function, when one can easily observe that medieval governments exercised a myriad of functions? Did he not realize that the Roman Empire never controlled the whole world? Did he not know that the Holy Roman emperors were not direct descendants of the ancient Romans, but petty, feudal German princes with no real title to the authority of the Roman state? Dante might have admitted the validity of these objections but would not have found them decisive, for they all depend on observations and judgment of historical fact. Dante's arguments depend on another process and imply other values and approaches to knowledge.

Above all Dante felt that knowledge is primarily deductive and rational. He believed that in order to understand experience we must abstract certain principles from our observations and reason from these principles to other principles until a conceptual system is created. The conceptual system permits us to see the structure and essential nature of the whole universe. It is obvious from the gross organization of the treatise on world government as well as from its minutest details that Dante relies on deduction. The treatise is divided into three parts. The first deals with the nature of the ideal government, the second with the Roman Empire as the concrete manifestation of this ideal, and the third with the claims of the papacy to temporal power. This organization strikes the modern reader as unusual. Twentieth-century discussions of political theory seldom begin with an abstract discussion of the ideal government. Nor did those of the Renaissance. Machiavelli began the *Prince* by describing all governments that had ever existed and kept as close as possible to actual governments. He believed that the workings of government could best be analyzed by studying existing governments, rather than by constructing governments from abstract principles of truth. The different approach of Dante should not, however, lead us to the conclusion that he was an idealistic dreamer or cause us to doubt his grasp of practical politics. Rather, the form he chose for his treatise is a reflection of his concept of how things are known. Particular political events can best be understood not by direct observation but by reasoning from first principles. We learn about existing governments by thinking about abstract, ideal governments.

Thus Dante begins more like a mathematician than a historian. He defines his terms: "By temporal government we mean a single government over all men in time." Before trying to answer the questions that arise from this definition, he states explicitly how he will proceed: "Since truth which is not itself an obvious statement is demonstrated as following logically from some truth that is an obvious statement, one must make clear what obvious statement is the source from which the subordinate statements are derived." This is simply the deductive process, and Dante first makes clear that he is using this process and then moves on to explain the fundamental principle on which his argument depends: that human civilization has the single goal of developing human potentialities to the fullest.

Deduction from first principles is used throughout the work. In Book One, Dante proves that a single world government is more likely to act justly than other governments. This argument could very easily be based on experience. Dante might have noted for instance that most wars are caused by the greed and ambitions of larger powers that prey on weak neighbors. If the temptation of weak neighbors is removed, the motives for war will disappear, and states will pursue justice instead of conquest. Since the world ruler would have everything, he would have no cause for greed or war and should act justly. This is a simple-minded argument, to be sure, but the line of reasoning is easy to follow and could be refined into a more sophisticated position.

Dante, however, does not take this path of argument. Instead of noting what has been the chief cause of past wars and injustices, he begins by analyzing the meaning of justice itself: "Justice is by its nature a kind of rightness or straight rule without deviation and therefore like whiteness justice in the abstract is not susceptible of degrees." In other words, the concept of justice has an abstract, absolute reality independent of its particular manifestations. From this premise he shows logically that justice can be weakened by two things: a will possessed by greed and a power whose effect is unlimited by external force. The only being whose will is free and whose power is unlimited is the world ruler. Therefore, Dante concludes, justice is most powerful in the world when it resides in a single world ruler. The entire proposition is thus a deduction from the meaning of justice — not an observation on the nature of human governments.

The use of deduction diminishes the importance of immediate experience and personal feelings as a path to knowledge. Though experience is a vital aspect of human understanding, it cannot be used alone as a path to genuine insight. In the *Divine Comedy,* Dante is attentive to the limited value of the senses. Dante the poet understands the nature of the judgment that has condemned men to hell. If he does not understand a particular case, he sees his ignorance as evidence that the mind of God is inscrutable, and he never feels that God lacks reason for His judgment. The source of this confidence lies in the wisdom he has acquired from his vision of God, which he describes in the third section of the *Comedy*. This vision of the first principle of all reality allows the poet to comprehend for the first time the particular things he has seen but not yet understood in the earlier stages of his journey, through hell and purgatory. His experience in hell, while important in preparing him for ultimate understanding, was not enough in itself to bring him true insight. Thus when Dante the pilgrim questions some of the judgments God has shown in hell, he is severely chastised for his failure to understand.

The use of deduction from first principles has certain implications for Dante's values — for his concept of what is good. First, he has a horror of ambiguity and paradox. If the real world is a series of ordered conclusions that follow by necessity from self-evident statements, real paradoxes or contradictions cannot be tolerated. Any that arise reflect defects in reasoning and must be eliminated. An example of his distaste for paradoxes can be found in the second section of the treatise on world government in which he discusses the Roman Empire. He wants to show that the Roman conquest of the world promoted justice and right. He does not, of course, do this by studying particular just laws that the Romans enacted. He proceeds deductively and demonstrates that world government implies by its very nature the ability to be just if it is seeking to be just. Any other conclusion would contradict his basic premise. Dante adduces proof that is logically sound, but he is not satisfied. He knew as well as we do that right at times seems to be done in the name of evil and evil in the name of right. To deal with this apparent difficulty he devotes some lines to considering the nature of paradoxes in general, showing that they cannot possibly exist and that opposite conclusions cannot be drawn from the same true premise. Paradoxes are explained either by false premises or false reasoning; they do not exist in nature. He makes utterly clear and explicit his conviction that to prove something paradoxical is to prove it false.

Second, Dante maintains that being one is the root of being good and being many that of being bad. This is the clearest value judgment in the treatise. The central thesis of the book is that one government leads to the good of mankind, whereas many lead to evil. A preference for the one over the many is found throughout the argument. Man is made in God's likeness. God is one; therefore mankind is most like God when it is unified. Dante makes the abstract point explicit at the end of part one when he shows that unity is basic both to good and to being itself.

Third, the use of deduction leads Dante to find the nature of a thing in its ultimate goal rather than in its present, ambiguous, and transitory state. This habit of thought is called teleological and is considerably removed from our own ways of thinking. Even the most abstract twentieth-century formulations of human nature usually emphasize the present, observable aspects of actual people — their physical, mental, and emotional characteristics. By contrast, Dante defines human nature in terms of its goals and proper fulfillment. Therefore, this nature is revealed not in the actual behavior of men but in their possible behavior. The central issue becomes one of values, for man cannot be understood without deciding what is best in him. Dante must establish what is good before he can know what is true.

Dante is strikingly confident that the true goal of man can be understood, and he even thinks this goal can be achieved. Man is created to realize his own ability to grow in intelligence. Individual men may fulfill a variety of other functions, but men as a race have only this one function, and Dante feels strongly that this end can be realized. The intelligence to which the race aspires depends on a grasp of clear and self-evident first principles devoid of all paradox and ambiguity. Although he is pessimistic about the state of political affairs in his own day, Dante feels that man will eventually know all that is good for him to know. Man's rational faculties are essentially pure and true; they give him an accurate picture of nature, which should be essentially the same for all men who use their intellect properly.

The Role of Analogy

This then is the world that Dante was defending in the treatise on world government. It is a world of orderly conclusions without paradox, discovered by reasoning from first principles; a world in which one will is better than many. It is a world man can hope to understand. Dante's way of looking at things seems very strange and uncongenial to us. Of all Dante's habits of mind, we are today most suspicious of the ease and confidence with which he moves from the world of abstract ideas to the world of concrete events. When he makes an analogy between the ideal world ruler and the historical Roman Empire, he treats the connection as real, not as loose and metaphorical. The analogy stems from the reality of both its parts, connecting them necessarily.

For Dante analogy is part of nature, and this is most obvious when he comes upon an analogy with which he disagrees. In the third part of *De Monarchia,* where he considers the church's claims to temporal power, he must deal with the traditional argument that the papacy is related to temporal governments as the sun to the moon, that kings and emperors derive all their power from the popes, just as the moon derives its light from the sun. Dante, a partisan of imperial government, rejects the argument, but instead of simply saying that the analogy is inappropriate, which would satisfy a modern reader, he devotes several pages to showing exactly why the analogy is false. He is compelled to do this, because if he cannot find improper reasoning, he is forced to accept the analogy as true.

Dante shared with most of his contemporaries a tendency to see everything as a sign, figure, symbol, or allegory of something else. This mode of thinking had a long tradition in the West and originated in a passage from Plato's *Timaeus,* the only significant dialogue of the Greek philosopher known and influential in the Middle Ages. In the dialogue Plato says that there are two worlds: one we can see, feel, hear, and live in — a world of change and uncertainty. The other can only be grasped by the mind through deductive reason; it is the invisible world of permanence and certainty — the world of true reality. The world of reason is a model or paradigm for the world seen by our senses, which in turn is only an imperfect reflection of the world conceived by the mind. Thus anything that man perceives with his senses, including other human beings, must be a copy of something else that is not perceptible. Sense objects, being copies, do not have a true reality of their own. Therefore, in looking at an object one should seek to understand the conceptual pattern that it copies and not dwell on the object itself. These ideas were elaborated in the centuries after Plato into a hierarchy of beings, each emanating from something more perfect above it and in turn creating a less perfect copy below it.

In this view the universe is a single, perfect, intelligible being that spreads and diffuses itself through descending orders of reality, becoming dimmer and dimmer until the black nothingness of formless matter is reached. Plato developed the moral implication of this cosmology in the *Theaetetus,* where he says that there are two moral patterns in the universe — one blessed and divine, the other godless and wretched. We must conform to the right pattern and do so by seeking to escape the visible world and become as much like God — which is to say, as intellectual — as possible. Lower forms should strive to imitate the higher forms of which they are copies. Thus there is a twofold movement in the universe: the downward flow of perfection from the top of the chain of being and the upward striving of morality toward its source.

This vision permeates Dante's works. The *Divine Comedy* is a literal journey upward informed by the vision of the light, which becomes clearer as the journey progresses. More important, particular points along the journey are seen as figures or symbols of points higher up in the world of pure ideas. Hence Cato, the Roman statesman, is found not in limbo but in purgatory, despite the fact that he was an unreconstructed pagan. He represents for Dante not just Cato but also an example of human liberty, and he is more real as an example than as a particular person. This use of figures or examples is also strong in the treatise on world government. Particular Romans become figures of abstract virtues and hence models for latter-day Christians.

The use of actual people as symbols is most obvious in precisely the aspect of the treatise that seems most untenable to modern readers. Dante treats the Holy Roman Empire of the fourteenth century as if it were the same empire that Augustus ruled, with the same rights and power. It seems patently absurd to reason from the Roman conquest of the world to the right of a German prince like Henry VII to exercise authority as world ruler, but let us avoid hasty conclusions about Dante's political blindness. He knew well enough that the world had changed radically since the days of Augustus and that the emperors of his own day were comparatively weak and ineffectual. When we read carefully we can find this awareness on almost every page. Dante treats the Holy Roman emperors as he does because he does not see them primarily as historical people dealing with a particular situation: he sees them instead as points on a ladder of perfection, a chain of being that draws its reality from the source of all being at the apex. Dante sees fully Henry VII's venality, his pettiness, his ineffectiveness, and the disparity between his pretensions and accomplishments, but these do not represent Henry's true reality. They only indicate his place on the ladder as a man, a part of the sensible and corruptible world. Henry's reality lies elsewhere. He is real only insofar as he symbolizes or figures the ideal world ruler, and that ideal gives reality to both Augustus and Henry. It is hard for us to take this hierarchic approach as seriously as Dante did. Modern historians see a world where the basic realities lie in social, economic or political relations. When they study Henry VII, they look for particulars that bear on these relations and consider his title as descendant of Augustus to be largely irrelevant. In Dante's world the basic realities are relations of lower forms to higher, and thus Henry's relation to Augustus is more real than the fact that he taxed Italian cities to support his imperial pretensions.

The Renaissance Reaction

This hierarchic world-view was fundamental to much late medieval thought. It developed during the thirteenth century, largely in northern Europe, and in the early fourteenth century began to appear in Italy. The early thinkers of the Renaissance, especially Petrarch, found important aspects of this view objectionable, and they boldly attacked the assumptions and values exemplified in Dante's treatise on world government.

The most striking aspect of the attack was its self-consciousness. Men of the Renaissance were aware that they were different from their predecessors to a degree that few other ages can match. And this awareness ensured that Renaissance values and modes of perception would be unified and coherent. Renaissance intellectuals became conscious of their identity only a few years after Dante's treatise on world government appeared, and they formulated their distinctiveness by criticizing the indifference to historical change that is so apparent in that work. Petrarch in the middle of the fourteenth century claimed that a new era had begun when the Roman emperors converted to Christianity in the fourth century, an era so devoid of culture and learning that he called it the Dark Age. Once he realized this, Petrarch was able to see the vast differences between Henry VII and Augustus, which to Dante were unimportant. Thinkers after Petrarch, like Boccaccio and Salutati, saw theirs as an age of revival, and finally in the fifteenth century Flavio Biondo divided history into the three periods that have since become conventional: the classical period, the Middle Ages, and modern times.

The consciousness of participating in a revival was particularly strong in the graphic arts. By the end of the fourteenth century chroniclers were already praising such painters as Giotto for abandoning the crudity of the Byzantine school and reviving classical art. This attitude found its fullest expression in Giorgio Vasari's sixteenth-century collection of biographies of artists. Vasari traced the progress of art from Giotto to Leonardo da Vinci and Michelangelo in the High Renaissance. He blamed the early Christians for allowing classical art to decay and credited the new interest in the classics with reviving an art that rivaled Rome itself.

But an impartial observer might not always agree with the evaluation the Renaissance made of itself. There were tensions and contradictions within the age that its participants only dimly perceived. Men of the Renaissance were least accurate in evaluating the immediate past. They stereotyped the thirteenth century as a period of monolithic scholasticism, a movement they defined by the emphasis on deductive reasoning, indifference to particulars, and insensitivity to historical change noted here in this chapter. In their attack on these attitudes, Renaissance writers often missed the variety of intellectual expressions and the positive features that had also characterized scholasticism. The scholastics' interest in deduction gave great power to human reason in man's efforts to understand his world and his God. Their association of unity and goodness provided a firm basis for moral values, and their analogical thinking offered a means of interconnecting all dimensions of experience into a single intellectually manageable system. To these virtues men of the Renaissance were often blind, but despite their imperfect perception they felt that they were participating in a true revival, and it gave them a sense of community and cohesiveness that profoundly influenced all of their thought. In Part Two we will look at how this community was established and outline the basic assumptions, values, scholarly techniques, and literary forms that defined Renaissance humanism.

Bibliography

The vast body of literature on Dante is not strictly relevant to the approach taken in this chapter. The student looking for a good recent introduction to Dante with a discussion of his historical background should consult Thomas C. Chubb, *Dante and His World* (Boston: Little, Brown, 1967). Joseph Mazzeo in *Medieval Cultural Tradition in Dante's Comedy* (Ithaca, N.Y.: Cornell University Press, 1960) has clearly shown the medieval assumptions in the *Divine Comedy*. The best English translation of the *Divine Comedy* has been done by John Ciardi (New York: Mentor Books, 1954), and the *De Monarchia* has been translated by H. Schneider, *On World Government* (New York: Liberal Arts Press, 1957).

An excellent historical account of how the concept of the hierarchy of being developed is Arthur Lovejoy's *Great Chain of Being* (New York: Harper and Row, 1960).

Part Two
The Growth of
Humanism in Italy

4 Petrarch and the Beginning of the Renaissance

The Renaissance is often identified with a revival of interest in the classics, but this by itself is misleading. It is true that during the Renaissance certain elements of classical culture became popular that in the Middle Ages were either unknown or ignored. Roman authors like Tacitus and Catullus, and virtually all of Greek literature, were essentially rediscovered after 1300. These facts do not, however, prove that the Renaissance was more interested in the classics than the Middle Ages was. Indeed, the entire period between the Fall of Rome and the fourteenth century was consciously dependent on classical ideas and deeply concerned with certain limited areas of classical literature and philosophy.

Early Humanism

What made the Renaissance different from the preceding period was that classical literature was approached and studied in a new way as men posed new questions and sought new standards of values.

This new approach had its origins in many parts of Europe and in many different intellectual activities. But the diverse origins were first tied together and incorporated into a coherent system by Francesco Petrarch (1304–1374), and for this achievement he was recognized as founder of the Renaissance both by his own contemporaries and by later scholars. The way in which Petrarch's predecessors reached toward a new understanding of the classics gives perspective to the magnitude of his own contribution and its continuity with earlier approaches to classical culture.

The earliest Italian scholar whose work with the classics seems to mark something new was a Paduan lawyer named Jeremiah of Montagnone (d. 1320 or 1321). Padua was a traditional center of legal scholarship and had produced many commentaries on Roman law. These doubtless formed the basis of Jeremiah's techniques of commentary on classical literature. His chief work was a collection of moral sayings and quotations from Roman authors called the *Compendium of Memorable Sayings*. Although medieval scholars frequently assembled the classics in this manner, Jeremiah's collection was characterized by certain important differences. None of the differences was overwhelming or even unprecedented in itself, but together they created a new form.

First of all, Jeremiah included a wider range of classical authors than usual. The Roman poet Catullus, virtually unknown in the Middle Ages, appears in the *Compendium*. More important, Jeremiah determined as best he could the authenticity of the quotations and developed more reliable critical techniques for discriminating true ones from false ones. He was clearly aware that previous centuries had included many questionable works in the canon of the classics. He rejected, for example, a spurious work of Seneca that had been accepted by previous commentators. Jeremiah's most significant contribution was his attempt to distinguish different periods of classical culture. He divided the *Compendium* into two parts, one consisting of quotations from authors of the period up to Augustus and the other of sayings from post-Augustan authors. The earlier authors he called poets, while the later were versifiers. Medieval commentators heretofore had seen a unity in the entire classical period. They had favorites, of course, like Virgil, but assumed that all classical authors were saying essentially the same thing. Jeremiah's chronological distinction was crude, to be sure, and did not connote any qualitative differences; but the mere attempt to separate parts of the classical period indicates a willingness to see classic authors in new ways.

Jeremiah of Montagnone was a transitional figure, hardly distinguished from his medieval predecessors, but Padua soon produced a circle of scholars whose work went far beyond simply collecting maxims from classical sources. These men, led by Albert Mussato (1261–1329), a contemporary of Jeremiah's and like him a lawyer, sought to recover the actual spirit of the classics and produce creative works informed by that spirit. They composed histories and poetry based on contemporary themes but conceived in a classical idiom. Mussato himself wrote a drama entitled *Ecerinis,* which was formally modeled on Seneca's tragedies but portrayed the life of a recently deceased Italian tyrant, Ezzolino da Romano. The subject was chosen with a view to current problems. At the time of composition Padua was under attack by the ruler of neighboring Verona, Can Grande della Scala, and the *Ecerinis* was clearly meant to stiffen the Paduans' hatred of tyranny and show them how to overcome their present danger.

The desire to give contemporary relevance to the classics was not the only element in early Renaissance humanism. Another circle developed in Verona along entirely different lines. The Veronese humanists pursued research for its own sake and devoted themselves to a rigorous criticism of classical texts. These antiquarian and scholarly interests were partly explained by the ready availability of manuscripts in the excellent library associated with the cathedral of Verona. The library, founded in the ninth century, contained Italy's largest collection of classical texts outside the seven-hundred-year-old monastery of Montecassino. Although they produced few original works, the scholars at Verona developed important techniques of commentary on classical texts and are credited with a number of significant discoveries. The Middle Ages had marveled that the Roman author Pliny had mastered both natural history and literature, but the Veronese showed that "Pliny" was actually two men: uncle and nephew.

Many elements of the revival of letters can be identified in the early fourteenth century, but as separate and uncoordinated trends. No one group or figure possessed all the interests and capabilities associated with the revival. In a sense the practical Paduans and the antiquarian Veronese were responding to particular aspects of their own environments. They blended dependence on medieval classicism with new concerns and critical techniques. The elements of critical scholarship and practical moral sensitivity were first synthesized by Petrarch, who created a strikingly new movement that can be truly identified as Renaissance humanism.

Petrarch

Petrarch did not come directly from the tradition of either Padua or Verona. He was not even primarily an Italian figure. He was born in Arezzo in 1304 to a Florentine family that had been exiled in the Black-White feud, but the family moved permanently to Avignon when Petrarch was only seven. Except for five years studying in Bologna, Petrarch did not return to Italy until he was thirty-five. His long exposure to the life of Avignon was clearly important. The city provided a bridge between French and Italian culture and gave Petrarch access to the rich store of manuscripts in northern Europe. Moreover, Avignon was a cultural center in its own right, exposing Petrarch to the rich Provençal literature that had flourished in southern France during the Middle Ages. Petrarch stood apart from the tradition of early Italian classicism in other ways, too. While most of the early scholars were secular lawyers, Petrarch was an ecclesiastic, making his living largely from the church. Indeed he had a great distaste for the law, having studied it briefly in Bologna. Petrarch's independence from the Italian tradition partially explains the uniqueness of his contribution to the classical revival.

As his first major work, an endeavor of his early thirties, Petrarch edited the first, third, and fourth decades of Livy's history of Rome. This history, which traced Rome from its founding to the reign of Augustus, was popular throughout the Middle Ages but had been circulated in separate, short sections or "decades" of ten chapters each. Petrarch's edition assembled three sections of the work for the first time in a connected narrative. More than that, Petrarch had compared different manuscript versions of each section in order to produce an edition that would correspond most closely to the original words of Livy. In the twentieth century many scholars begin their careers by preparing similar editions, and Petrarch's activity seems perfectly natural; but in the fourteenth century such endeavor was unusual. It is not immediately evident why a young man of vitality and imagination should have devoted so much time to the difficult and demanding task of collating manuscripts and producing a scholarly edition. In the first place, why was Petrarch so interested in an ancient Roman historian?

Petrarch did not consider the classics to be simply a repository of antiquarian facts or charming stories: they were sources of morality and virtue. They could teach men how to be more fully human. This attitude becomes clear when we examine Petrarch's other works. At about the time he finished the edition of Livy, Petrarch began to write a series of biographies of famous men, the *De Viris Illustribus,* drawing his material mainly from Livy's history of Rome. Here Petrarch stated his purpose plainly. By describing the great deeds and accomplishments of men in past times he hoped to stimulate his own contemporaries to deeds of equal merit. The same moral purpose informs his epic poem *Africa,* a verse biography of the Roman general Scipio Africanus, also written during this period.

The attitude that classical antiquity could instruct men in morality continued throughout Petrarch's life. Just four years before his death, he produced a work entitled *On His Own Ignorance,* to defend himself against the accusation of some scholastics that he was a good man but of little learning. Petrarch attacks the value of any learning that does not make him a better man. He maintains that he would rather be good than wise, but at the same time he uses his learning to help him be good. He reads the classics in order to better himself and guide others to emulate the virtues of the past. This motive, then, explains Petrarch's interest in classical authors, but not why he felt compelled to produce an accurate edition of Livy. Why must the exact words of the Romans be found in order to use the events of antiquity for moral ends? Are the great deeds of the Romans less instructive because they have been rephrased by later writers?

The answers to these questions underline Petrarch's assumptions about the nature of learning and the relation between words and knowledge. His attitude differed profoundly from the philosophy that informed Dante's treatise on world government. To Dante, as to most scholastic thinkers of the thirteenth and fourteenth centuries, the truth is unified and coherent, hierarchical and abstract. It is reached by a process of deductive reasoning. Words are of interest only to the extent that they point the way to unchanging truth. Thinkers who shared this attitude were relatively indifferent to the actual words used in a given work. It was important only that a work make sense, because insight into the truth could easily be found by any number of paths. Thus, when a medieval scribe came to a place in an ancient manuscript where the words had been blurred or erased, or even made no sense to him, he added his own words so that the passage would make sense and thus lead the reader to the preexistent and unchanging truth that lies behind all words.

The Renaissance concept of the relation between words and truth, first expressed by Petrarch, was less simple. The truth that lies behind words or particular events cannot be grasped directly and does not present a unified and unchanging appearance. Instead, it takes on different aspects depending on the people who are looking for it or the period in which it is expressed; each manifestation of the truth is unique and highly individual. Thus Petrarch studied a text not to find all truth but only the particular perspective that the person who wrote the text possessed. With this attitude the exact words become exceedingly important, for they provide the only means of finding the wisdom contained in a work. Their significance lies in the fact that they offer the insight of a particular person in a particular time using a particular mode of expression.

This attitude had a number of important effects on Petrarch's thought. Most obviously it resulted in a new sense that books are the direct emanation of personality rather than an abstract statement of truth. In a striking way, Petrarch felt that when he possessed a book he actually possessed the writer himself. Long before he had learned to read Greek, he secured a copy of Homer's epics. He tells of sitting and handling the book, seeking to get closer to the poet simply by looking at the words and phrases of which he did not know the meaning. Such an attitude was never encountered in the preceding centuries, for men set no value on words they could not understand. Petrarch's attitude found frequent poetic expression in his writings. In his metric epistles, he wrote:

> They come to me from every century
>   and every land . . .
> Sometimes they sing for me;
> Some tell me of the mysteries of nature;
> Some give me counsel for my life and death
> Some tell of high emprise, bring to mind
> Ages long past; some with their jesting words
> Dispel my sadness and I smile again.

Petrarch's new sense of the written word produced a new attitude toward the ancients. Thinkers of earlier centuries had virtually enshrined the classics and had eagerly sought to derive from them ultimate truth and wisdom, but their indifference to the exact words led to the feeling that differences among the various classical authors were not important either. Thus medieval scholars tended to miss the individuality of the writer, and they studied ancient works only as authoritative guides to general truth. By contrast, Petrarch and his successors considered the ancients to be wise but also human and limited; the classics contained much wisdom, but the insights were those of particular men with personal weaknesses and limitations growing out of their historical situation.

The idea that the ancients could be approached as fellow human beings came as a profound revelation. One of its most striking manifestations was the novel practice of writing letters addressed to the ancient Romans. This may seem strange to our sensibilities, but we must appreciate the delight that the fourteenth century took in the realization that men who for centuries had been revered as unquestioned authorities were merely human. It also had its practical effect, for it necessitated a reversal of some traditional methods of learning. The medieval scholar studying natural history, for instance, seldom read Aristotle's famous work on the subject. Instead he looked at a late classical summary of Aristotle and then read a medieval commentary on the summary. If he wished to know still more he might consult a commentary on the commentary. Though his efforts took him farther and farther from the source, he always felt that he was following the path to insight guided by Aristotle's wisdom. Men of the Renaissance pursued wisdom by moving closer and closer to Aristotle. They sought to know not what others had said about him, but precisely what the philosopher himself had said. To do this they had first to remove the many additions to the Aristotelian texts that had accumulated during the centuries when men cared only that the work mean something intelligible. Only then could they identify Aristotle's own personal biases and limitations and see how these influenced his thought. Through this critical process a scholar could truly appropriate the wisdom of the ancients to his own uses. Others had to be trained in the technique, and this training required new methods of education that could not be developed easily or quickly. Several generations passed before men of the Renaissance felt fully comfortable in the way way. The practice of writing letters to the ancients was, in fact, an important stage in the acquisition of the new learning. It provided one means of establishing the perspective that Cicero and Aristotle were human beings with passions and limitations like ourselves.

Petrarch's most important letters to the ancients were addressed to the Roman orator Cicero, whose philosophical treatises gave the medieval world its principal impression of classical thought. The background of the correspondence is well known. Returning from Naples in 1345, Petrarch stopped briefly at Verona to study the manuscripts in the famous library there. He happened to come across a collection of Cicero's letters to the philosopher Atticus. These letters are full of gossip and rumor current in the late Roman republic and even now are the source of most of our information about the political machinations of the period leading to the establishment of the Roman Empire under Augustus. Cicero himself had taken an active part in these maneuvers, and the partisan nature of his actions and feelings is evident on every page. Petrarch was dumbfounded and horrified to discover that Cicero, whom he had revered as an exemplar of style, reason, and philosophy, stood revealed as a petty, ambitious, and vain politician interested more in the transitory issues of the day than in the timeless philosophical wisdom described in his abstract treatises.

Petrarch never really recovered from this shock of suddenly discovering a man where he had previously seen a sage. He never fully forgave Cicero for letting him down. Yet at the same time he was strangely intrigued by the idea that the former sage was a person whom one could talk with, that Cicero had expressed his personality in relationships with others, and that these relationships could still be seen in writings like these letters to Atticus. Inspired by this notion, Petrarch wrote his first letter to the ancients. He castigated Cicero for personal and political inconsistencies. Quoting some of Cicero's own philosophical injunctions that the wise man should avoid involvement in politics, Petrarch asked how in the light of these beliefs he could treat his political enemies as he did. But it is the end of the letter that is most remarkable:

> In the upper world, on the right bank of the Adige, in the city of Verona in that part of Italy that lies beyond the Po, on the sixteenth day before the Kalends of July, in the year that is the 1345th since the birth of the God of whom thou hadst no knowledge.

Petrarch was explicitly concerned to describe the relation of both the recipient and the writer in time and place. He made a great effort to tell Cicero his own historical and geographical setting in terms that the Roman would have understood: he dated the letter in both the Christian and the Roman way and identified Verona's location in relation to Roman Italy. This deep awareness of differences in historical context is the central aspect of the Renaissance approach to the classics, and it played a vital part in the developments of the fifteenth and sixteenth centuries.

The new attitude that books and the classics are fundamentally human also increased in Petrarch's mind the importance of letter-writing. Inspired by his discovery of Cicero's letters, he decided to make a collection of his own correspondence, in order to express his own personality. The letters that he wrote are among his most important literary compositions. Despite the fact that they were intended from the first to be disseminated to the general public, it is significant that he chose the form of a personal letter as a vehicle for his ideas. There is a considerable difference between writing a general treatise on a subject and writing a letter to a specific person. Ideas can be expressed much more personally and intensely when they are directed to a particular recipient. Petrarch felt that this was true even though he was addressing the general public, because truth is best expressed through a series of personal perspectives. He succeeded in establishing the epistolary as a new form of discourse.

This interest in communication is one of Petrarch's most important traits. Rhetoric is a distinguishing concern of the Renaissance, setting it apart from both the Middle Ages and the seventeenth century. By "rhetoric," men of the Renaissance meant not simply graceful speaking or writing but persuasive power or eloquence. They felt that ideas must not only be logically consistent but must be phrased in such a way that people are moved to action. Rhetoric enjoyed great prestige in the classical world — Cicero was principally an orator — and Petrarch found in his studies of the ancients reinforcement for his own feeling that truth must be properly communicated in order to be effective.

Our search for an explanation of Petrarch's earliest scholarly activity has led us deep into his thought. His concern for the exact words of Livy reflected his conviction that knowledge can be acquired only through an understanding of the person who is speaking and can be communicated only in personal terms. Petrarch looked to the classical world for guidance in his own life and obviously considered it a wiser epoch than his own, but in this he was hardly different from his medieval predecessors. If anything, they revered the classics more than he. He departed from his predecessors by looking through the wisdom to see limitations and human feelings and by insisting that these personal elements must be understood before the wisdom of classical writings could be appropriated. In sum, Petrarch studied the classics not because of antiquarian interests or idle curiosity but because he wanted to enlarge his personal experience and deepen his moral awareness. He was not avoiding experience but seeking it directly, unmediated by systems or abstract formulations.

Petrarch's taste for direct experience found ample expression outside his literary and scholarly activities. He was an inveterate traveler in an age when travel was especially dangerous and wearisome. He journeyed frequently from his home near Avignon to the cities of northern Italy and even to Naples, seeking the same sort of understanding that he sought in books. Both books and travel brought him closer to the persons of antiquity. As he visited Padua, where Livy was buried, he was moved to write a letter to the Roman historian describing what the city was like thirteen hundred years after his death. Even more noteworthy is a metric epistle that Petrarch wrote to Virgil from that poet's birthplace in Mantua:

Here have I written what thou readest now,
In the dear peace of this thy countryside,
Wondering whither thou wast wont to roam,
What was thy path in darkling forest depths,
Through meadows fair, or by the banks of the stream
Or the bays of the curving lake; under what trees
Or in what glades remote thou didst find shade;
Upon what gentle hillside thou wast wont
To sit and gaze, or where in weariness
On the soft turf or by some lovely spring
Thou didst recline. And sights and scenes like these
Bring thee in very presence to mine eyes.

Petrarch sought experience not only in travel but in solitude. In 1337 he bought a small house in the wilderness of the Vaucluse to escape the noise and activity of Avignon. It rapidly became his favorite residence and until the last years of his life his writings displayed an acute sensitivity to his necessity for solitude and quiet in order to write, think, and digest his manifold encounters with the outside world.

It was from this house in the Vaucluse on the morning of April 26, 1336, that Petrarch set out on his expedition to climb Mount Ventoux. Petrarch was certainly not the first modern man to climb a mountain just to see the view, but the climb is significant because it became the occasion for one of his most famous works. Either shortly after he came down or some years later, he wrote a letter describing his experience to his old teacher, Dionigi of Borgo San Sepulcro. This moving letter contains all the themes of Petrarch's life and deserves a careful reading. Petrarch's climb up the mountain became an allegorical journey of his own soul in search of understanding. At the beginning of the letter, Petrarch describes his efforts to find a suitable companion for the expedition and explains that he finally settled on his brother because of their long personal relationship. Thus the concern for human companionship as a crucial aid in the search for understanding is explicit as well as implicit in the very form of the letter, for Petrarch was writing not a general treatise but a letter addressed to a person who had been unusually close to him. And other readers, even without knowing personally either Petrarch or Dionigi, are expected to understand Petrarch's message better in such a form.

At its climax, the letter recounts the moment when the two climbers reached the summit. An awesome view lay before them. Moved by the vastness of space Petrarch began to meditate on the vastness of time, considering his past life and what it had meant to him. Then, so that his spirit would raise itself up after the example of his body, he opened the copy of Augustine's *Confessions* that he had carried with him. Reading a passage at random, he found the words "And men go to admire the high mountains, the vast floods of the sea, the huge streams of the rivers, the circumference of the ocean, and the revolutions of the stars — and desert themselves." The relevance of these words stunned Petrarch. He closed the book and descended the mountain in silent contemplation of the vanity of his previous life, ashamed that he had pursued knowledge by outward experience and ignored the inward growth of his own soul.

The crisis Petrarch underwent at the top of Mount Ventoux is a significant indication of his doubts about the new path that he was traveling. Equally important is the identity of the man to whom he turned for spiritual guidance, for it was no accident that Petrarch was carrying Augustine's *Confessions* that day. The very copy he took with him had been given to him years before by his teacher Dionigi, the recipient of the letter, and was in turn given by Petrarch at his death to his closest friend and disciple. Another work of Augustine's, the *City of God,* was the first book Petrarch ever purchased, and his interest in the theologian was one of the most constant features of his life. In fact his longest and most sustained dialogue was not with an ancient Roman at all but with this early Christian thinker, and it is recorded in the three dialogues that Petrarch called the *Secretum.* How is this interest in a Christian figure who wrote long after the decline of ancient Rome to be explained?

Augustine (354–430) was one of a group of fourth- and fifth-century religious thinkers who established the basic lines of Christian orthodoxy and who are counted among the great early church fathers. Men in the Renaissance were fascinated by these thinkers, because the early theologians had faced problems very similar to their own. The men of Christian antiquity were concerned with reconciling the basic Christian texts with accepted philosophical and moral concepts of the classical world. Although a few of the very earliest Christian writings, notably the Gospel of John and the Pauline Epistles, betray a blending of Judaic and Christian notions with the concepts of Platonism, for the most part several centuries of work were required to integrate these two cultural traditions.

The early church fathers were usually thoroughly schooled in the classics, but they did not find the task of reconciliation easy. Many were themselves converts from paganism and were concerned that the classics were not really relevant to the new religion. Some even feared that scholarship after conversion might be impious. The men of the Renaissance were in effect imitating the church fathers by seeking to find in the classics a guide to moral life within a Christian framework. Finding doubts and difficulties similar to their own in men of unquestioned orthodoxy was a source of great comfort.

The early church fathers were also an invaluable guide to understanding the ancient world. Men of the Renaissance sought to learn by example, but examples are hard to appropriate directly from another age. Cicero or Scipio Africanus inhabited a world so different from the fourteenth century that it was hard to see them even as human beings. But the church fathers provided an important intermediary. They could be seen as individuals. They spoke a Christian vocabulary, but, more than that, many of them had left personal memoirs and letters. Augustine in particular left a full record of his spiritual development in the *Confessions* so that Petrarch could see him very clearly as a person. In addition, the church fathers had lived among the ancients and had seen their contemporaries from a perspective the early Renaissance could not hope to attain. The goal of the Renaissance to recognize the humanity of past ages was greatly aided by the example of these men, who were at once fellow Christians and members of the ancient world.

In spite of the example of the early church fathers, the crisis that Petrarch suffered on the mountain top seems to have bothered him throughout the 1340s and 1350s. It apparently grew out of his doubts about the value of the new learning, but was also related to doubts about his own personal values and the desire for glory and fame. It was not a question of a simple opposition between Christian values and those of classical antiquity, for indeed such opposition can hardly be found in Petrarch's writings. Neither Petrarch nor any other major Renaissance figure abandoned Christianity. The classics were expected to support and enlarge the basic truths of the faith, not supplant them.

Petrarch's doubts centered on the adequacy of the new way. On the top of the mountain he wondered whether one learned from experience or whether experience was only a hindrance to the true learning that came from contemplation. Petrarch's doubts found literary expression in the *Secretum,* written in 1342–1343 and probably revised in the 1350s. At the beginning of the work Petrarch pictures himself sitting alone meditating on the afterlife, when the figure of Truth appears to him. Although blinded by her light he gradually perceives a person standing next to her who is introduced as Saint Augustine. Truth explains that the saint will instruct Petrarch in his errors. Thus in its basic conception the *Secretum* fully embodies the new path of learning. Petrarch will come to understand the truth not through direct revelation but only through words of persuasion spoken to him by another person. As he has Truth herself say, "I would that some human voice speak to the ears of this mortal man. He will better bear to hear the truth so."

The rest of the *Secretum* is a long conversation between Petrarch and Augustine. This use of dialogue is another indication of Petrarch's indirect approach to truth. The dialogue, the letter, and the history were the favorite forms of Renaissance writers. Each permits the author to avoid direct and unqualified statement of a position. Dialogue in particular embodies the interchange between people that humanists felt so important for understanding the truth. It enabled them to express the ambiguities of knowledge, which they considered as changing according to historical context and personal perspective. Thus in Renaissance as well as in classical dialogues one is hesitant to identify any of the participants with the position of the author. Normally the author chose the form precisely because he felt that the truth was deeply ambiguous and could not be stated with consistency and directness; it could only be embodied in a number of various positions.

While the form and approach of the *Secretum* exemplify the new conception of knowledge and learning, much of its subject matter casts doubt on the validity of these avenues of understanding. In the first dialogue, where Augustine is presented as an example for Petrarch to follow, Petrarch admits that he is not really happy. Augustine replies that he can have happiness if he really wishes it and that he must achieve it by meditation and withdrawal from the world. The Augustine of the dialogue states that his own conversion was the result of prolonged meditation, in spite of the fact that the real Augustine of the *Confessions* experienced conversion as the result of a specific tangible experience. Petrarch here distorted the model to stress his own doubts about direct experience as a path to true understanding. The dialogue goes on to question but not reject the value of eloquence in bringing Petrarch to happiness. Augustine stresses that it must be used only in conjunction with silent meditation.

The second and third dialogues expand on the doubts Petrarch expressed in the first. In the second, where Augustine acts as a confessor, Petrarch claims to reject all worldly gain, such as position or wealth, in favor of spiritual goals. In the third dialogue, however, Augustine, this time more in the role of a friend than of a guide and confessor, tells Petrarch that he must give up both love and glory. Petrarch resists, saying that these two goals have been the source of all his most worthy achievements. An argument follows, and Petrarch seems to lose, but he never frankly admits that Augustine is right. Even at the end Petrarch still maintains the moral value of glory and earthly love. The three dialogues thus never firmly commit Petrarch either to rejecting experience and classical studies as paths to genuine knowledge or to considering pure contemplation to be inadequate without direct personal experience.

Petrarch's doubts do not reflect an inability to understand the classics. His personal success in applying the wisdom of the past to his own situation is remarkable and stands out most clearly in his Italian sonnets, for which he is most widely known today and which formed the basis of his reputation even by the sixteenth century. Despite the fact that they were written in the vernacular Italian rather than Latin, they are imbued with classical references and should not be regarded as an attempt to counterbalance his interest in the classics. Indeed, the classical references so effectively convey his deepest sentiments that they seem utterly natural and personal. The fifty-sixth sonnet, which begins "While I speak time flies," is actually a translation from Ovid. Another sonnet (number 35), beginning "Alone and thoughtful through deserted fields," speaks eloquently of the need for solitude and thus expresses one of Petrarch's deepest personal feelings; it is in fact a paraphrase of a passage in Cicero where the Roman author is quoting Homer. Despite its being a paraphrase of a paraphrase, the sonnet conveys its meaning with a depth and conviction that testify to the thoroughness of Petrarch's own understanding of classical literature.

Petrarch spent the last decades of his life revising earlier works, including his sonnets and the *De Viris Illustribus*. His essay *On His Own Ignorance,* written between 1368 and 1370, incorporated all the themes of his earlier career together with a strong sense of irony and humor that was often lacking in the serious young Petrarch. This work is more difficult to understand than the ascent of Mount Ventoux, but also more rewarding. Unlike his friend Boccaccio, Petrarch never decisively turned aside from the path he had followed from his early years. Toward the end of his life he began to buy more sacred than pagan books, but when Boccaccio decided to burn his own secular library, Petrarch offered to buy it to save it from the flames.

Petrarch died in 1374, having presided over a revolution in attitudes toward knowledge and letters. Though the details of his works showed continuities with preceding thinkers, the sum of his life represented a new man, who would be a model for generations that followed. Petrarch was the first Renaissance humanist. The term "humanism" is used to describe the major intellectual movement of the Renaissance. Because it covers such a wide variety of individuals its meaning is necessarily broad, and the next chapter will be devoted to the major perspectives modern scholars have brought to the term.

Yet Petrarch's chief interests suggest clearly three broad areas of humanist thought. His ability to see the ancients in a new light as people rather than abstract authorities shows a sense of history and a capacity to perceive historical change. Historical consciousness is the central trait of Renaissance humanism and underlies most of its thinkers' activities. Second, Petrarch developed a concern for rhetoric along with his sense of history. To see the ancients as people was to speak to them as people. The literary forms the humanists chose embody this sense of persuading particular people or groups through eloquence. Third, the rhetorical concerns of humanists made them place a more positive stress on an active life in society. If knowledge was acquired through communication, society became necessary. Petrarch himself was ambiguous on this matter. His taste for experience led him to seek an active life of travel and friendship, but he never engaged in political endeavors. Moreover, he clearly felt by the 1350s that the contemplative life of the monastery was the highest of human activities. Though Petrarch rejected the active life, his rhetorical and historical concerns implicitly demanded a consideration of the problem. The humanists who succeeded Petrarch developed his thought into a movement that was historical, rhetorical, and civic.

Bibliography

The early stages of Italian humanism have been studied by Roberto Weiss, *Il primo secolo dell' umanesimo* (Rome: Storia e letteratura, 1949). His researches are summarized for the English reader in a lecture he delivered in 1947 at University College, London, entitled *The Dawn of Humanism in Italy* (London: Lewis, 1947).

Our basic source for the life and career of Petrarch lies in his own rich correspondence. Unfortunately, Petrarch's tendency to revise his own letters at a later date has obscured much of his development. During this century Ernest Hatch Wilkins has undertaken the arduous task of editing and establishing a correct order for the letters. His *Life of Petrarch* (Chicago: University of Chicago Press, 1961) has established the basic events of Petrarch's life. For a more general study of Petrarch the student should consult Morris Bishop, *Petrarch and His World* (Bloomington: Indiana University Press, 1963), or Thomas G. Bergin, *Petrarch* (New York: Twayne, 1970). Varying interpretations of the consistency with which Petrarch developed his central ideas can be found in Hans Baron's *From Petrarch to Bruni* (Chicago: University of Chicago Press, 1968) and Jerrold Seigel's "Ideals of Eloquence and Silence in Petrarch," *Journal of the History of Ideas* 26 (1965): 147–174. See also Hans Baron's "Petrarch: His Inner Struggles and the Humanistic Discovery of Man's Nature," in *Florilegium Historiale: Essays Presented to Wallace K. Ferguson* (Toronto: University of Toronto Press, 1971).

A wide variety of Petrarch's writing in English translations is available in paperback editions. His letter on the *Ascent of Mt. Ventoux* and his *On His Own Ignorance* are found in *The Renaissance Philosophy of Man,* ed. Paul Oskar Kristeller et al. (Chicago: University of Chicago Press, 1948). Selected letters as well as other works of prose and poetry are also available. See *Petrarch: A Humanist Among Princes,* ed. David Thompson (New York: Harper and Row, 1971), and *Selected Sonnets, Odes and Letters,* ed. T. G. Bergin (New York: Appleton-Century-Crofts, 1966).

5 Humanism

Petrarch's lead was widely followed. His epistolary production testifies to a broad and varied correspondence with followers over much of Europe but particularly in Italy. There, where classical study had begun in the early years of the century, the new attitude toward learning and classical culture quickly took root. The presence of classical ruins, the continuing traditions of Roman law, the closeness of Latin to vernacular Italian, the similarities between the urban life of Italy and the urban setting of classical culture, all contributed to the enthusiasm with which Italian intellectuals greeted Petrarch's contributions.

The most important of Petrarch's disciples was Boccaccio, who was largely responsible for introducing Petrarchan humanism to Florence in the late fourteenth century. The intellectual circle grouped around Coluccio Salutati (1331–1406), the chancellor of Florence, quickly adopted humanism, and in their hands it began to take the form of a movement with clearly defined attitudes, interests, and techniques. In the fifteenth century the movement came to maturity and spread throughout Italy. Such people as Leonardo Bruni (1369–1444), Poggio Bracciolini (1380–1459), Pier Paolo Vergerio (1370–1444), and Vittorino da Feltre (1373–1446) developed and implemented a program for education based on the new learning, brought the values underlying the program to bear on the most pressing problems of the day, and reformed and gave a fresh conception to the literary and artistic tradition.

The dramatic growth of humanism in Italy raises a number of questions. What did the movement offer that proved so satisfying? What fresh perspectives did it bring to the personal experience not only of scholars but also of the statesmen and businessmen who supported and utilized it? What new values did it offer to the fifteenth century? Even the name of the movement presents problems. Today it is called humanism, but that term was devised only in the early nineteenth century to distinguish a type of classical education from the new scientific curriculum then being introduced. Men of the Renaissance referred to the movement most often as the *studia humanitatis,* the study of the humanities, but even this denoted more precisely the curriculum than the values that lay behind it.

The difficulties of describing and interpreting humanism are inherent in the nature of the movement. It was not a school of systematic thought but a loose association of men with common attitudes who contributed to a variety of activities. Primarily concerned with education and scholarship, the humanists eventually found themselves involved in politics, literature, law, and even philosophy and theology. No single perspective can fully illumine a movement of this variety and complexity, but in recent decades three important interpretations of Renaissance humanism have emerged. Each presents the phenomenon in a different perspective, and together they greatly augment our understanding of the movement.

The first interpretation, that of Paul Oskar Kristeller, is based on extensive research into the exact words used by the practitioners of the new learning in the fourteenth and fifteenth centuries. Kristeller discovered that although the word "humanism" cannot be found in the texts of this period, the word "humanist" occurs frequently. The term was used in a very precise sense to designate a teacher of a fixed cycle of subjects. The humanists primarily taught subjects concerned with human interactions. They taught grammar and rhetoric, because these improve men's capacity to communicate; but they did not teach logic, which merely provides techniques of analysis. They taught poetry and moral philosophy, which elevate the thought and actions of man, but not metaphysics and natural philosophy, which seek only to understand man and nature. Thus, the humanists were concerned with giving men techniques for dealing with their fellow men; they were not directly concerned with abstract speculation. Kristeller stresses these particular interests to explain why humanism was singularly devoid of philosophical innovation. In the eyes of many scholars the humanists were superficial, but Kristeller maintains that they did not intend to be partisans of tired philosophical notions. They were instead teachers of methods of expression without reference to a particular philosophical position. Kristeller's work laid to rest some standard clichés about the meaning of Renaissance humanism. He showed the inaccuracy of the long-accepted notion that the movement represented a Platonic reaction against the Aristotelianism of the Middle Ages. It is surprising that such a notion ever arose, because the humanists were clearly devoted to both Plato and Aristotle. To be sure, the open-ended nature of Plato's dialogues and his avoidance of systematic reasoning proved very attractive to the humanists, but many of the leading representatives of the movement were actively studying and translating Aristotle's writings, too. Leonardo Bruni, for example, translated works of both philosophers and probably would have considered himself closer to Aristotle. Kristeller's observations explain this mixing of philosophical trends. Because the humanists were teachers of rhetoric rather than philosophers, they can hardly be expected to have adhered to a single philosophical school.

To buttress his argument, Kristeller compared the Aristotelian and Platonic traditions both during the Renaissance and in the preceding period. He found that Aristotelianism, far from withering away under the new learning, remained a strong intellectual tradition into the sixteenth century. Furthermore, Platonism was not a novelty in the fifteenth century but had existed throughout the Middle Ages. In Italy Aristotelianism developed side by side with humanism and became stronger during the fourteenth century, precisely when humanism was also growing in Italian intellectual circles. Interest in Aristotle was stimulated by the humanist concern with translating and editing the texts in order to separate a classical author from his medieval commentators.

Aristotelianism and humanism, then, were not polar opposites; no more did humanism invent Renaissance Platonism. The Platonic tradition is so deeply ingrained in Western thought that there are few important movements not influenced by it. Not only that, but the nature of Plato's dialogues — literary, suggestive, and seldom coming to a clear conclusion — makes a rigid definition of Plato's philosophy impossible to achieve. The upsurge of Platonic ideas during the fifteenth century need not be related to a new movement, because currents of Platonic thought had been influential throughout the Middle Ages.

Kristeller's work has also cast a clearer light on the origins of the humanists. By defining them in terms of their functions, he was able to ask how those functions were served before the fourteenth century and thus could identify the antecedents of the humanists. He discovered a group of men called *dictatores* who were professional rhetoricians during the Middle Ages. They composed state correspondence and developed formal models for the writing of this correspondence. Humanists in the Renaissance were in a sense the professional successors of these men and fulfilled similar functions. Both groups were engaged in the eminently practical business of teaching people how to express themselves, but the dictatores relied on their own experience to develop techniques of expression. The humanists, by contrast, used classical models and insisted that only by studying the ancients could one learn to speak and write effectively.

Kristeller's analysis clearly and sharply defines the humanist movement but omits some broader problems of interpretation. By concentrating on technical aspects, it has difficulty answering questions about the more general attitudes of the humanists. Did they share values, attitudes toward learning, and conceptions of human nature that, taken all together, represent a fundamentally different perspective on experience from that of their predecessors? Is it likely that an intellectual movement of such duration and strength had nothing more in common than a commitment to certain techniques of expression? Kristeller himself does not maintain such an extreme position. He points to a common belief in the dignity of man that bound the humanists together, but he does not show in detail the connection between this faith and the humanists' professional work. Consequently many scholars felt the need of a broader definition of humanism that could relate all its component interests.

The Italian scholar Eugenio Garin identified in the philological concerns of the humanists a coherent set of values and assumptions about reality. These concerns, said Garin, spring from two assumptions: first, the ancients should be studied as men living in a certain historical time; second, human knowledge proceeds less by abstract speculation than by communication of personal perspectives and points of view. Garin felt that these assumptions are the defining characteristics of humanism from its very beginning until the end of the sixteenth century. They form a nexus that unites every humanist endeavor. Thus humanists could agree on certain important issues. In particular, because of their commitment to experience as a path to knowledge, they supported an active political life rather than one of contemplation and solitude. Garin saw the fourteenth century, when arguments were common over this issue, as a period in which the humanists were resolving their doubts about the value of an active life. Even solitude and withdrawal did not take the form of monastic isolation from the world. For the humanists of this period solitude was a means of rediscovering the richness of one's own inner life and a prelude to finding the richness in the lives of one's neighbors. The humanist approach to learning involved a positive encounter with the world.

Commitment to a life of activity inclined the humanists to favor republican government wherever possible, because only such states allowed broad groups of men to involve themselves in political affairs. This was most obvious among the Florentine humanists, who participated actively in the business of the city by holding state offices and by sitting on the legislative and executive councils. But the preference for republics was not universal. Some humanists worked in cities governed by a prince; others were associated with the papal curia, where fears of conciliarism evoked a strong distaste for republican forms. Even in Florence there was a falling away from political activity during the mid-fifteenth century, as the Medici family secured its grip on Florentine politics. In spite of these important reservations, Garin maintains that the humanistic method of argument from the particular to the general led to republican ideas, just as Dante's argument from deduction led him to favor a monarchy.

Garin's comprehensive approach to humanism is immensely satisfying, for it portrays the movement as a profound human experience, involving common values and conceptions as well as techniques of expression. At the same time, the very breadth of his approach obscures the inner workings of the humanists' minds and makes it difficult to relate the specific aspects of the movement to the general principles. Above all, the chronological development of humanism through the fourteenth and fifteenth centuries does not stand out sharply in Garin's work.

Hans Baron, the third major contributor to a contemporary understanding of the Renaissance, has been concerned specifically with the problem of development. His approach was to identify precisely the difficulties standing in the way of a mature expression of humanism and then to determine how these obstacles were overcome. His researches convinced him that a major change had taken place in the years around 1400, centered in the city of Florence. Humanism did not develop slowly and gradually but suddenly and dramatically. This realization permitted Baron to see in convincing detail the inner workings of the movement without losing sight of its larger significance. Because he identified so clearly the developing patterns of thought and values in this small period, Baron's work is crucial to understanding the entire humanist movement.

The change that occurred around the year 1400 has long been considered an important one, having ramifications in all aspects of intellectual life. In painting and sculpture the style of the late fourteenth century with its stress on formalization gave way to the naturalism of Masaccio, Brunelleschi and Donatello. Petrarchan humanism, by 1400 still clinging to the ideal of a quiet contemplative life and becoming vaguely antiquarian, was replaced by the more active humanism of Poggio Bracciolini, Pier Paolo Vergerio, and above all Leonardo Bruni. This generation of humanists pursued classical studies with a new vigor and intensity; they were aware of the unique position of Florence in fostering the revival and were firmly convinced of the superiority of the active life.

As a political backdrop to the sudden change, Florence experienced a major crisis in foreign affairs, although internal affairs during this period were relatively stable. The last years of the fourteenth century witnessed an expansion of the power of Milan under Giangaleazzo Visconti. He had seized the lordship of that city through the murder of his uncle in 1385 and begun a program of conquest that would bring him to the very walls of Florence in 1402. At first the citizens of Florence were undisturbed by the growth of Visconti power, considering the matter to be of more concern to the Venetians than to them. But by the 1390s, when Giangaleazzo had become lord of almost every city north of the Apennines except Venice, the Florentines finally realized the danger and initiated a period of intense diplomatic and military activity. They sought allies among the other powers threatened by Milan, such as Venice and even the Holy Roman Empire, and spent great amounts of money to equip armies that could resist Giangaleazzo's troops. As the power of Giangaleazzo waxed, city after city fell to him — Pisa, Siena, Perugia, and finally Bologna — and at last Florence and Venice were the only independent powers left north of the Papal States. Venice was relying for defense on its unique geographical position and offered Florence scant help. Small wonder, then, that Florence began to see itself as the sole defender of liberty in Italy and couch its diplomatic initiatives in those terms. When Giangaleazzo died suddenly of the plague while encamped outside Florence in 1402, many Italians thought that the hand of fortune had delivered the city, but the Florentines themselves were convinced that only their stubborn and determined commitment to liberty had held off the tyrant and saved Italy from enslavement.

In reality Giangaleazzo never posed a severe threat to the independence of Florence. Even if he had not died at such an opportune moment, he could hardly have sustained the siege of the city. Yet this is not to say that the threat looked small and unimportant to the Florentines who experienced it. Although some were aware of the weakness of Giangaleazzo's finances, the fears of most citizens were unquestionably genuine, and in consequence enormous quantities of money were spent to oppose him — a fact that was a source of pride to later generations of Florentines.

It is easy to see how this situation might cause Florentine intellectuals to become more inclined toward active political life, but Baron avoids making such a facile connection. After all, this was not the first international crisis Florence had suffered since humanism had come to the city. Foreign pressure had been common throughout the last half of the fourteenth century, especially during a long and bitter war with the papacy in the 1370s. Why had these pressures not brought forth the reaction that followed the Giangaleazzo war? How do the patriotic writings of Coluccio Salutati during the war with the papacy differ from those of Leonardo Bruni after the war against Giangaleazzo? The answer to these questions must be sought in the intellectual developments within the humanist movement itself.

Baron notes that by 1400 intellectual life in Florence had developed severe tensions arising from basic disagreements among the leading thinkers of the city. These disagreements divided Florentine intellectuals into two hostile camps. On one side were those who were interested in the new classicism but disdained participation in contemporary life. The most famous of these was Niccolò Niccoli, member of an established merchant family, who gathered around him a number of scholars sharing his views. These men showed no interest in Florence's political and intellectual heritage, looked down on Dante, and disparaged the vernacular tongue in favor of Latin. Their interest in the classics was antiquarian and seemed to have no connection with the problems facing their contemporaries. Niccolò's disdain for practical matters went to such an extreme that he bankrupted himself purchasing classical texts and had to ask Cosimo de' Medici to rescue him from his financial difficulties. Political effectiveness in Florence was dependent on wealth, and no act could show more convincingly Niccolò's refusal to participate in Florentine politics.

The classicists' rejection of the values and customs of Florence quite naturally provoked a reaction among the intellectuals who were more devoted to contemporary life. One of the most interesting documents of this reaction was the invective against classicists composed by Cino Rinuccini. The Rinuccini, like the Niccoli, were an important merchant family, but Cino had fully accepted the responsibilities of his position and led a life of active service in the Florentine government. Though well educated — he was trained in Latin and owned a copy of one of Boccaccio's most humanistic works — Rinuccini chose to write in Italian and reproached the classicists for their abandonment of traditional values. He denounced them not only for shirking civic duties but also for avoiding family life: Niccolò himself refused to marry and raise children for fear that it would interfere with his classical studies. Cino was particularly incensed by the classicists' distaste for Dante, even though the earlier humanists, Petrarch and Boccaccio, had admired the great poet. Finally, Cino accused the classicists of the impiety of abandoning Christianity for paganism. This last charge was untrue even for the most extreme members of the group, but their attempt to rehabilitate the pagan gods by showing that they had Christian elements lent some color to the accusation.

The classicists, however, were the dominant group among humanists in the last years of the fourteenth century. As a result, contemporary vernacular writers characterized all humanists as men who had abdicated their responsibilities, and society became increasingly hostile to the movement. The hostility was felt by the leading humanists of this period and led them to seek a way of making humanism more responsive to traditional Florentine values. The most important figure in this effort was Coluccio Salutati, whose life and work nevertheless displayed the deep-seated conflict between antiquarian classicism and civic involvement.

Salutati was born in a small Tuscan commune and had a varied career as a bureaucrat and professional diplomat before coming to Florence as chancellor in 1375. The post was an important one, involving management of the city's foreign affairs, and by its very nature it demanded active participation in civic life. But Salutati was also a noted humanist, who had begun classical studies in his twenties and by the time of his arrival in Florence had collected a large circle of friends and disciples both in the city and throughout Italy. Salutati maintained a large correspondence covering the whole range of topics that interested humanists in the late fourteenth century, from the discovery and analysis of classical texts to the relative merits of the active and the contemplative life.

Salutati's opinions on this last issue demonstrate the difficulty of reconciling humanism and political activity. Early in his career, three years before coming to Florence, he had begun to write a treatise on the active life, *De Vita Associabili et Operativa,* which disagreed with Petrarch's defense of the solitary and contemplative life *(De Vita Solitaria).* Although the work was never finished, it contained a consistent and compelling argument for the superiority of active political involvement as opposed to solitude and retreat from the world. Less than ten years later, in 1381, Salutati wrote another treatise entitled *On the World and Religion (De Seculo et Religione),* which adopted a very different point of view. Here he portrayed the life of the monastery as the highest moral ideal and made the secular world appear repulsive and undesirable. Salutati abandoned the unquestioning secularism of his youth and never returned to it. Although in later years he occasionally defended the active life, he always maintained that the contemplative existence was intrinsically superior. He seemed unable to reconcile the two values on which his own life was based.

The existence of inconsistency in a man's life is hardly unusual. Salutati, however, was such a central figure in early Florentine humanism that the difficulties he experienced exemplify the conflict within the movement as a whole. This fact becomes especially clear when we examine Salutati's most important work, the essay *De Tyranno (On Tyranny).* This essay has always puzzled scholars. It was written in the 1390s, when Florence was vigorously defending its republican liberties against the tyrannical ruler of Milan. Its author had previously produced several eloquent defenses of the republican form of government, but in this work he clearly and unambiguously maintains that monarchy is the best form of government, intrinsically superior to any government based on popular consent. In order to explain this remarkable inconsistency we must penetrate to the heart of the difficulties presented by the new learning.

Two disparate elements underlie the thinking of *De Tyranno*. The humanist element is clear, because the essay presents a significant advance in the realm of critical method. Petrarch used philological analysis to place an author in his historical context. Salutati went beyond this and critically examined the historical context itself. In the process he virtually rewrote Roman history. *De Tyranno* is overtly concerned with justifying Dante for placing Caesar's assassin, Brutus, in hell. Thus, Salutati had to show that the assassination was morally wrong. To do this, he first had to gain a deeper insight into the issues of the Roman civil wars that preceded Caesar's rise to power. Before Salutati, it was conventional to see Caesar's victory over his opponents as the triumph of order over anarchy and a necessary prelude to the Roman Empire. This victory was seen as desirable because the empire had brought peace and stability to the Mediterranean world and made possible the rise of Christianity. Salutati, however, was not content to read only the standard histories of the period but consulted other sources, such as the letters of Cicero. He discovered that in fact both Caesar and his opposition had been motivated by desire for power. There was no moral difference between the sides; Cicero in opposing Caesar was not championing liberty over tyranny, but simply choosing a faction in hope of political gain. Indeed, much of *De Tyranno* is an open attack on Cicero for cant and political expediency.

Salutati's judgment on the Roman civil war constitutes a remarkable achievement of historical criticism. Where formerly a clear moral pattern had been seen, he discovered an ambiguous situation in which conflicting goals and partisan strife gradually gave birth to the Roman Empire. Salutati might next have asked the vital questions of why people chose the sides they did and what Cicero's rhetoric about liberty meant. But he seemed unable to see Roman values through Roman eyes or ask if those values were appropriate to his own age. Instead, he rigidly adopted traditional medieval standards of value and subordinated the techniques of humanist criticism to medieval ideals. Caesar was justified, says Salutati, because it was God's will and God chooses only the right. Throughout *On Tyranny* the idea that temporal governments are divinely ordained intrudes on the historical criticism, and this faith becomes the basis of Salutati's belief in monarchy. His other arguments are equally deductive and not based on historical or philological issues. He argues, for instance, that monarchy is best because Aristotle considered it the ideal form of government. This unquestioning reliance on the authority of Aristotle's values stands in marked contrast to his refusal to make judgments on this historical authority of Cicero or Livy. Finally, the treatise contains a series of deductive arguments reminiscent of Dante's essay on world government that prove the ideal nature of monarchy.

The tension between the new critical technique and the traditional standards of value went unresolved in Salutati's work. In spite of his sophisticated and imaginative manipulation of humanist methods, he was unable to extend them to important matters involving his personal goals and values. The ideal of understanding the ancients as people remained unfulfilled, because their values remained closed and inaccessible. Salutati could criticize the details of the past but not its ideals. The impressive realism of his presentation of the details did not produce a realistic conception of the past, for the conceptual structure of *De Tyranno* remained formalized by medieval tradition.

It is Baron's argument that the impact of the diplomatic crisis facing Florence in the last years of the century forced a resolution of these increasingly severe tensions within the intellectual community. The pressures exerted by the necessity of defending the city brought together the values and techniques of intellectual discourse to create a new phenomenon: civic humanism.

The genesis of civic humanism can be seen clearly in the career of Salutati's successor in the Florentine chancery and his most distinguished disciple, Leonardo Bruni. The development of Bruni's thought has been hard to trace, because the dates of his key works are uncertain. For example, one important dialogue, which Bruni dedicated to his humanist friend Pier Paolo Vergerio, is divided into two parts that seem to embody two different attitudes. The first part seems to support all the attitudes of Florentine classicism that Rinuccini had railed against, while in the second part a new critical spirit can be found. Hans Baron has proposed a solution to this problem. His research indicated that the first part of the dialogue was written before the crisis of 1402, while the second was written afterward and thus bears the marks of a new attitude toward the classics. Baron's redating of the work provoked much criticism, but his suggestion makes sense out of Bruni's contribution, and at present there is no irrefutable evidence that the two parts of the dialogue were written at the same time.

An example will illustrate the attitudes found in the second part of the dialogue. Like Salutati before him, Bruni considered the question of why Dante had placed Brutus in hell, and in the process he arrived at a new critical perspective on ancient Roman history. Julius Caesar, Bruni stressed, was in fact the destroyer of Roman liberty, and therefore Dante could not have condemned his actual assassination. Instead, Brutus had been intended only as a symbolic traitor. Bruni then went on to criticize the Roman Empire itself, drawing his evidence especially from the Roman historian Tacitus. Tacitus, who is considerably more critical of the empire than Livy, had been recently rediscovered and was just becoming well known at the beginning of the fifteenth century. It was Bruni's contention that the empire had destroyed the greatness of Rome by stifling the free spirit of its citizens. In other words he equated Rome's strength with the vigor and energy of its citizen body and showed that that vigor was affected by political institutions. This observation was an insight much more profound than any Salutati had ever achieved, and it was also clearly relevant to the problems Florence was facing in Bruni's own day.

How did Bruni manage to put the classics to this new use? Clearly he learned to understand and criticize the values of the ancients. But to see the process by which he came to this new approach, we must turn to an earlier work, the *Laudatio Florentiae Urbis,* a panegyric or praise of the city of Florence that according to Baron was written very shortly after 1402. This work has usually been considered an unimaginative imitation of a second-rate panegyric by the Greek orator Aristides. Parts of it seem to be little more than a copy of the original. Aristides, for instance, included a long catalogue of human virtues that he ascribed to his city Athens, and Bruni simply copied the list for his own oration. But only a small part of the work involved literal copying of details. The most significant borrowing was the conceptual structure. Bruni exactly imitated the pattern and sequence of questions that were the foundation of Aristides' work.

Aristides considered Athens' greatness to lie in its defense of liberty, and he posed a series of questions designed to show how the city had acquired and maintained this greatness. Bruni adapted these questions to the condition of Florence. Thus, Aristides recalls Athens' historical defense of liberty as leader in the wars against the Persians; Bruni cites Florence's wars against Giangaleazzo. Aristides describes the political setting provided by Athens' mixed constitution; Bruni describes the particular institutions of the Florentine republic. The Greek orator voices his pride in Athens' support of culture; Bruni gives examples of the rise of Florentine humanism. In some cases Bruni went beyond Aristides to make his answers more convincing than those he found in the model. To Aristides, the significance of the geographical position of Athens was that it occupied the abstract golden mean between the plains and the mountains. Bruni, by contrast, analyzed Florence's location in terms of its precise military, economic, and psychological advantages.

Bruni, then, focused on the details of Florentine life but drew his form, his techniques of analysis, and even his values from the classical model. This appropriation of the classics for personal and contemporary use was the essence of the new civic humanism. It was not without precedent in the fourteenth century. We have already seen that Petrarch's sonnets were virtual translations of classical poetry even though they expressed his personal concerns and values. Petrarch's success, however, was a personal triumph of his own genius and was not effectively communicated to his successors. Bruni not only mastered a vital imitation of the classics but provided a method that others might follow.

Civic humanism, expressed in the new approach to classical imitation, embodied a new set of values that were clearly related to the pressures on Florence during the early fifteenth century. It was concerned for the vigor and energy of the citizen body, which was the true strength of the state. It was strongly and unequivocally convinced of the superiority of an active political life. It discarded such traditional medieval categories as the division between factions that were known as Guelph and Ghibelline and developed a new political analysis based on the manner in which institutions affect and are affected by the psychology of the citizen body. The civic humanists also had a vastly augmented respect for the vernacular as a tongue historically formed and adapted to the peculiarities of the Florentine experience. All these attitudes would find forthright expression a century later at the hands of Machiavelli, but they were adumbrated in the works of Bruni and his contemporaries.

Civic humanism was not a momentary response to the crisis of 1402 but a movement that persisted through the fifteenth century. This is evident in the tradition of historical writing. The humanist form was established by Bruni's major work, a history of Florence composed during the last thirty years of his life. Bruni analyzed the precise events of Florentine history in terms of the psychological motives of the participants — a notable innovation — but turned to the classics to strengthen his interpretation and provide an effective narrative form. Subsequent humanist historians of Florence continued Bruni's basic tools of analysis, even when they did not completely share his staunchly republican values, and they searched out further classical models as an aid to expressing their differing interpretations. Poggio Bracciolini, who wrote in the middle of the century when republican ideals were less prevalent among Florentine intellectuals, adopted Bruni's concern for human psychological motivation but used it to support his own historical perspective. Thus the central achievements of civic humanism survived even though the original values did not.

Baron, Garin, and Kristeller present the basic intellectual phenomena of the fourteenth and fifteenth centuries from contrasting perspectives. Kristeller sees humanism as a technical movement interested in using the classics as models of rhetoric to teach techniques of expression. He has eliminated much vague discussion about the attitudes and ideas of the humanists and has forced scholars to look more closely at the actual works. Garin insists that these works betray common values and attitudes stemming from a new emphasis on human communication and awareness of historical perspective. He has shown that the humanists could have common ideas without forming a definite philosophical school. Baron provides insight into the chronological development of humanist attitudes and approaches to the classics. Because of his work we can clearly see the actual problems confronting the humanists in realizing their goals. These three scholars have greatly expanded our understanding of the age in which humanism was the dominant intellectual current and have also opened new questions and avenues of inquiry.

In a sense each of these men has emphasized a different strain of the humanism found in Petrarch. Kristeller has shown how the rhetorical element of Petrarch's writings was related to the work of medieval rhetoricians. Petrarch differed from the medieval dictatores in drawing more directly from classical writings and in granting more explicit importance to eloquence as a means of teaching virtue. Garin has shown the breadth and comprehensiveness of historical consciousness in the Renaissance. Baron has probed the conflict between the active and contemplative life, showing how Florentine humanists resolved this conflict in favor of an active political life, using rhetoric, the classics, and historical study to support their civic concerns.

Bibliography

Kristeller, Garin, and Baron have presented their views in numerous books and articles. Kristeller's approach is most accessible in the two-volume set of essays published in Harper Torchbook, *Renaissance Thought,* 2 vols. (New York: Harper and Row, 1961 and 1965). For Garin see *Italian Humanism,* trans. Peter Munz (New York: Harper and Row, 1965), and *Science and Civic Life in the Italian Renaissance,* trans. Peter Munz (Garden City, N.Y.: Anchor Books, 1966). For Baron see *The Crisis of the Early Italian Renaissance* (Princeton: Princeton University Press, 1955; rev. ed. 1966). The revised edition contains an epilogue succinctly stating Baron's thesis. Debate over the issues raised by these men continues. Jerrold Seigel, *Rhetoric and Philosophy in Renaissance Humanism* (Princeton: Princeton University Press, 1968), has stressed the aspect of pure rhetoric in much humanist activity, while my own *Development of Florentine Humanist Historiography in the Fifteenth Century* (Cambridge: Harvard University Press, 1969) emphasizes the interdependence of rhetoric and values.

Several other perspectives on Renaissance humanism are worth consulting. Wallace K. Ferguson, *The Renaissance in Historical Thought* (Boston: Houghton Mifflin, 1948), has studied several centuries of varied interpretations of the movement. Erwin Panofsky, *Renaissance and Renascences in Western Art* (New York: Harper and Row, 1969), has offered an imaginative picture of the difference between the Italian Renaissance and previous revivals of classical culture. Finally, Giuseppe Toffanin, *History of Humanism,* trans. L. Gianturca (New York: Las Americas, 1954), has suggested the vital importance of religion and spiritual concerns to the Renaissance humanists. His interpretation, which brings to attention aspects of the movement that are often neglected, is controversial and has not won wide acceptance. Recently Charles Trinkaus, *In Our Image and Likeness* (Chicago: University of Chicago Press, 1970), has studied the religious ideas of the humanists and has presented a modified interpretation that may prove more acceptable.

An excellent summary of trends in Renaissance scholarship is William Bouwsma's *The Interpretation of Renaissance Humanism* (Washington, D.C.: Service Center for Teachers of History, 1973).

Important humanist texts will be noted in subsequent chapters. Of those mentioned here Salutati's essay *On Tyranny* is readily available in translation. It is found in Ephraim Emerton, *Humanism and Tyranny* (Cambridge: Harvard University Press, 1925; reprinted Gloucester, Mass.: Smith, 1964). The Latin of Bruni's *Laudatio* is found in Baron's *From Petrarch to Bruni* (Chicago: University of Chicago Press, 1968), and large sections of it are excerpted in his *Crisis of the Early Italian Renaissance*. Bruni's dialogue, the *Dialogi ad Petrum Paulum Histrum,* is translated in *Three Crowns of Florence,* edited by D. Thompson and A. Nagel (New York: Harper and Row, 1972).

6 Humanist Education and Scholarship

The humanists were clearly committed to the two basic activities of scholarship and teaching. As scholars they sought to develop and apply the tools of textual and historical criticism in order to illuminate human experience as well as recover classical authors unknown to their predecessors. As teachers they created an educational program based on critical scholarship that differed significantly from previous modes of instructing. Although education and scholarship will be treated separately in this chapter, these two activities were not separate in the humanists' minds. They insisted that an effective education depended on sound scholarship and that scholarship had to be used for moral and didactic ends.

Education

The general aims of humanist education are implicit in the humanists' approach to knowledge. Education was not instruction in particular techniques or skills but the creation of a consciousness or approach to the world that would form the foundation for all learning. This was achieved in two principal ways — the study of letters and the development of the whole man. Humanists saw literature as the tissue uniting all men and providing the basis for their mutual intercourse. Humanist writings on education spoke of the spiritual community to which the student was admitted by the study of letters. In this spiritual community, the student broadened his humanity and became aware of a greater variety of human feelings and aspirations than he could find in his own immediate experience. But awareness should not be limited to the mind. The student's body and emotions must also be educated by physical exercise, games, music, pleasant conversation — indeed, by the student's whole environment. With such educational ideals it is not surprising that even today the "Renaissance man" is synonymous with the well-rounded individual.

In a sense the very existence of an educational theory in the fifteenth century was an innovation. Treatises from earlier centuries commonly dealt with only limited aspects of education and were typified by moral and spiritual handbooks, studies of particular curricula, guides for rulers, or, rarely, treatises on the rearing of children. The absence of interest in general education during the Middle Ages is reflected in the paucity of words for describing the educational process. The terms we use today acquired their modern meaning during the Renaissance. Prior to the fourteenth century they were used only in a limited and technical sense. *Educo* had the literal sense of "leading out," as to lead out a horse from the stable; *doceo* meant to instruct, as in a technique or skill. There was not even a definite word for teacher. *Doctor* meant simply a learned man, while *magister* described a moral guide. The deficiencies of terminology point out the failure of earlier thinkers to connect learning and moral guidance in a deep and vital way. The leading moral teachers of the Middle Ages had deliberately used their own learning to enhance the value of moral instruction, but they had not abstracted a technique of instruction based on this combination.

The assumptions underlying humanist education developed slowly. Petrarch, in so many ways the founder of humanism, was uninterested in teaching and dissuaded his friends from becoming teachers. He seems to have felt that those who taught could do nothing else — an attitude known in other ages, too, but hardly conducive to the development of a mature educational program. By the end of the fourteenth century humanists were less embarrassed to be interested in education and became actively engaged in a fundamental dispute with traditionalists over the place of classical studies in teaching. One of these arguments erupted between the Dominican friar Giovanni Dominici and the Florentine chancellor Coluccio Salutati. Dominici wrote to Salutati denouncing the inclusion of classical literature in a curriculum on the grounds that such works were immoral and frivolous and that students should read only religious texts. Salutati replied with an eloquent defense of classical studies and clearly enunciated many of the attitudes and assumptions that informed subsequent humanist educational theory.

Salutati denied that there is any fundamental difference between sacred and profane letters. Both have the same goal: to create a good man. He firmly refused to acknowledge that the friar had a moral advantage and claimed that secular education had the same spiritual concerns that traditionally had been the exclusive province of religious training. To support the claim, Salutati introduced a concept central to all humanist educational theory, one thoroughly elaborated by his successors. To understand anything, he said — even the grammar that is the basis of both sacred and profane writings — one must first acquire the *scientia rerum*. Literally translated the term means "knowledge of things." For Salutati it meant specifically the knowledge of how all branches of learning and all aspects of humanity work together. It was a sense of something beyond technical knowledge, an attitude or consciousness that opened all branches of learning. Without it no particular subject could be understood. In other words, Salutati introduced the idea of a truly general education whose goal was not preparation for a particular profession but the creation of values and attitudes that would expand the student's awareness and fulfill his humanity.

Although Salutati thus justified secular education, he did not outline a systematic plan for that education. The earliest important treatise to provide such a plan was *De Ingenuis Moribus et Studiis Liberalibus (On Noble Manners and Liberal Studies)* of Pier Paolo Vergerio, written at the beginning of the fifteenth century. Vergerio was a typical wandering scholar of the Renaissance. He had studied at Florence and had been a part of Salutati's circle. After leaving Florence, he traveled widely in north Italy, teaching for a time at Padua, where he wrote *On Noble Manners* to aid in the education of Ubertino Carrara, the son of that city's lord. In 1411 Vergerio went north of the Alps to attend the Council of Constance. He remained in the North, and at the time of his death in 1444 he was in the service of the Holy Roman emperor Sigismund.

Vergerio's treatise on education was divided into two parts. In the first he defined noble character and how it is formed. Every individual, Vergerio maintained, has certain natural desires that must be guided and shaped in order to create a person of true nobility. In the second part he set forth an actual program of liberal studies designed to enlarge and form character in the desired fashion. Vergerio's definition of liberal studies is one of the most concise in Renaissance literature. He said, "I call those studies liberal which are fitting for a free man, through which one exercises and cultivates virtue and wisdom, and which lead the body and soul to their highest good." In part he was quoting a well-known classical definition by the Roman writer Seneca, who also had said that liberal studies are those proper to a free man. Vergerio, however, stressed that they are proper precisely because they form and fulfill the human personality. Liberal studies have an immediate value and are an end in themselves; they are not merely a preparation for further, specialized study.

According to Vergerio, a liberal education rests on three principles: methodology, the teacher's grammatical and philological expertise, and the student's personal interests and talents. The method through which a pupil is introduced to his subjects is crucial. The teacher must choose the books and their order of presentation carefully, for they must be read in such a way that their interrelations are fully and clearly understood. Here Vergerio himself explained the precise significance of each subject in the curriculum, its particular strengths, and its detailed relationship to the other subjects.

The stress on method was quite new and carried important implications. Only in a homogeneous society, or at least in one that perceives itself to be homogeneous, can a fixed curriculum be used to expose students to all aspects of human experience and values. Underlying humanist education was the assumption that all educable members of society share attitudes and values that could form the basis of the *scientia rerum*. This introduced a strong social element into education of the period. The pupil's education prepared him to be a member of his society and manifest his individuality through that membership. Indeed, humanist or liberal education has functioned most effectively in societies that have had a strong sense of their own cohesiveness. Twentieth-century Americans, by contrast, have difficulty agreeing on a common curriculum, and in our society liberal education is little more than an ideal.

How was the student to perceive the interrelations of the various subjects in his curriculum? Here, scholarly expertise on the part of the teacher was essential, for detailed analysis of texts formed the basis of training. The teacher led the pupil through his reading, pointed out the nuances of grammar and meaning, and showed him how to find these for himself. Thus the pupil learned the basis of human communication and became sensitive to the richness of human experience. By studying how the past communicates with the present, he would become better able to communicate with men in his own time. It is clear that this method of teaching texts could succeed only if the teacher himself was an expert philologist. Humanist educational theory stressed that scholarship and teaching are intimately related, and even today that relationship is important in university education.

The third aspect of liberal studies was the need to recognize the tastes and capabilities of the individual student. The student could not be expected to be expert in every field of his basic curriculum. Instead, he was to use the preliminary exposure to discover the areas in which he could best develop his own personal genius. The stress on the individuality of each student was a natural outcome of other humanist attitudes, particularly the belief that general systems of knowledge are subordinate to personal perspectives. The student was not being trained to grasp a single structured pattern of truth but to develop a consciousness of his own that would enable him to communicate with others and develop his own personal perspective. The particular subject matter he studied was less important than the attitudes and values he derived. Thus, individuals who specialized in music should be able to communicate fully with those who specialized in poetry or even metaphysics, because the same *scientia rerum* underlies all subjects.

Vergerio laid great stress on physical education as well. His treatise stressed that the whole person was to be developed, and exercises of the mind did not suffice to bring the individual to his fullest potential. The body, too, must be trained. He discussed how particular games develop particular parts of the body and create certain physical skills. Because he was concerned with the education of a future prince, he paid special attention to military training and its integration into the whole educational policy.

On Noble Manners and Liberal Studies was followed by several other important educational treatises in the course of the century. Leonardo Bruni wrote one of the most influential, entitled *On Studies and Letters (De Studiis et Literis),* intended for the education of a noble woman. Other Florentines wrote treatises for educating the citizen of a republic according to the values of civic humanism. The most important of these were the *Della Vita Civile* of Matteo Palmieri (1406–1475) and the *Della Famiglia* of Leon Battista Alberti (1404–1472). But the most famous of all was the *Courtier* of Baldassare Castiglione, written in the early years of the sixteenth century and destined to have a vast influence in northern

Europe. It elegantly and subtly presented all the themes of humanist educational theory and made them easily accessible to a wide variety of readers, outlining the qualities, skills, and knowledge that thereafter were always associated with the concept of a "gentleman."

These works had one important trait in common. None was addressed to the education of man in general. Instead each described an educational program for a particular sort of person: a prince, a noblewoman, a citizen, a courtier. This is a further indication of the humanist eagerness to see mankind in terms of particular men and not a general set of abstract characteristics. A man ought to be educated according to his particular genius and for his particular function in society. To achieve these ends, however, he had first to develop a consciousness of the *scientia rerum*, which would allow him to communicate with others who might manifest different talents and serve different functions. Humanist educational theory was permeated with the sense that something intangible lies behind particular things or events, something that can be seen only if one is educated to see it. Thus education lay at the heart of human personality and social intercourse.

The humanists were not content with theorizing. Many of them also established schools where theory might be implemented. The first humanist school was the Casa Giocosa, founded at Mantua in 1423 by Vittorino da Feltre. While a student at Padua, Vittorino had come under the influence of Vergerio's ideas on education. Later he joined the faculty at Padua and held the chair of rhetoric, until the duke of Mantua, Gianfrancesco Gonzaga, asked him to come to Mantua and tutor his three children. Vittorino agreed, on condition that he also be allowed to tutor poor children without charge. Thus was established the Casa Giocosa, where Vittorino remained until his death in 1446.

The curriculum of the school served three goals: religious discipline, classical scholarship, and knightly training. Vittorino believed that these were interrelated aspects of a single education and stressed the unity of all types of training received in his school. He taught no professional disciplines and sought only to make people fit for their social duties, whatever they might be. Unfortunately, Vittorino wrote little about the school, and not much detail is known about the curriculum. The school apparently trained its pupils from childhood until maturity. The Gonzaga children were from nine to thirteen years old when they entered the school, and some remained until they became twenty-one. Vittorino's instruments of training were classical and patristic texts, which were read, translated, and imitated. He was also concerned about the total environment in which the child was educated. Music was played at meals to give the child a sense of harmony and to emphasize that the entire curriculum was harmonious, and good physical development was encouraged through continual exercise, a Spartan discipline, and a strict diet.

Vittorino's fame spread, and soon other rulers in Italy wanted schools for their own cities. In 1429 Niccolò d'Este, the duke of Ferrara, hired Guarino of Verona to establish a school where the young duke, Lionello, could be educated. Guarino, like Vittorino, had studied at Padua and had come under Vergerio's influence. He eventually became a scholar even more famous than Vittorino and continued his own studies while running the school at Ferrara. He was seventy-nine years old when he completed his last scholarly work, a translation of the Roman geographer Strabo. Once again we see the intimate relationship between scholarship and the training of others even at the most elementary level. The men of the Renaissance clearly felt that the relationship was essential.

More is known about the nature of Guarino's curriculum, partly because he seems to have been more interested in producing scholars than was Vittorino. This is not to say that he favored an unbalanced education or neglected the less intellectual aspects of personal development. Games and physical exercises were an integral part of Guarino's program: for example, he organized snowball fights in which the students adopted the tactics and strategy of ancient Roman generals, thus preparing them for a subsequent military career while exercising their bodies. Imitating the classics even at play contributed to the full growth of the individual.

Scholarly instruction at Guarino's school was divided into three stages: elementary, grammatical, and rhetorical. There was no fixed age for promotion from one stage to the other, for individuals were not expected to progress at the same rate. In practice as well as in theory, the humanists laid great stress on adapting the course of study to the peculiarities of the individual pupil. In the elementary stage students practiced enunciation and pronunciation and were exposed to the rudiments of grammar. Guarino's assumption that simply pronouncing the words brought a student closer to understanding an author seems strange to us, but twentieth-century education has been deeply influenced by the printing press, which has vastly increased the number of books to be read. Before the sixteenth century only a few books were available to a student, and as a result these were perused intensively. In fact it was customary to read aloud even when reading only to oneself. One sought the author's meaning not only by the gross structure of his arguments but also in the cadences and nuances of his style, which appear most clearly when the text is read aloud.

In the second stage of education, the grammatical stage, the student learned close grammatical analysis, using Guarino's own manual. Medieval Latin grammars tended to be filled with obscure logical arguments designed to justify a particular grammatical usage. Guarino broke with tradition and abandoned the attempt to create a deductive grammar. He wrote a simple manual based on usage and eschewed elaborate explanations. "In addressing one person," he says in one passage, "you will write *te oro* and not *vos oro* because one is singular in number and all Latin authors follow this rule." The student was also given practice in oral composition through classroom conversations and recitations in Latin. In addition he memorized classical texts, so that the basic constructions of the language would become automatic and he could acquire a sense of style from the best Latin writers.

In the final rhetorical stage of Guarino's school the student began to compose his own works. He practiced the forms of classical composition — poetry, history, epistles, orations, dialogues — and he used the rules of Cicero and Quintilian to compose works in imitation of the Roman masters. Throughout the last two stages the manners, customs, and values of the classical authors were studied, and Guarino encouraged the student to think about the realities of his own life while studying the experiences of those who had gone before him. The acquisition of techniques of expression was pursued never for its own sake but always as a means of developing one's personality.

Guarino's school attracted a number of scholars to Ferrara, both as teachers and as students of his method. In 1436 the city created a studium or college in order to formalize their studies and appointed Guarino to the chair of rhetoric. In 1442 the studium became the University of Ferrara and the first university in Europe that was solely a faculty of arts. Earlier universities at Paris and Bologna had been professional schools designed primarily to teach law, medicine, or theology. Their arts faculties served only to give the students sufficient skill at reading and writing Latin to undertake professional studies. The innovation of founding a university liberal arts faculty that existed in its own right was the logical outcome of the humanist approach to education and its insistence that the fundamental purpose of education is the full development of the individual.

In summary, the humanists' deep concern for education was expressed both in educational theory and in the development of actual schools that put the theories into practice. Humanist education was distinguished from previous schools by new aims and new methods. Its goal was to create a consciousness, or scientia rerum, that would facilitate human communication and lead to the full development of the individual personality. It sought to create this consciousness by methodically exposing the student to a body of closely scrutinized texts and then encouraging him to select a special field best suited to his peculiar talents and inclinations.

Scholarship

The humanists directed their scholarly energies into two major channels: recovery of lost texts and critical analysis of existing ones. Several Latin authors were discovered during the fourteenth and fifteenth centuries — Catullus, large sections of Quintilian, and, most important of all, Tacitus — but the most notable achievement of the Renaissance was the revival of Greek. While continuing Byzantine influence in southern Italy had prevented the Greek language from completely dying out in western Europe, few medieval Europeans knew Greek or any significant element of Greek culture. Until quite recently historians believed that the Greek revival was caused by the Turkish conquest of Constantinople in 1453 and the subsequent arrival of Greek refugees in the West, but deeper research into the intellectual life of the fourteenth and fifteenth centuries has revealed that interest in Greek was growing gradually even before the fall of Constantinople. The West was exposed to Greek culture not only through southern Italy but also because of papal relations with the Eastern church, which took on new vitality during this period. Pressure from the Turks apparently drove the Eastern Orthodox church to ask for aid from the West in return for improved relations and several religious concessions.

Although Petrarch never acquired a firm command of Greek, he claimed to be deeply interested in the language. His enthusiasm had been excited by his connections at the papal court. It was a Byzantine envoy to Avignon who gave Petrarch the copy of Homer that first inspired him to learn the language. As his teacher for this effort he chose Barlaam, who was a Calabrian diplomat used frequently by the Eastern emperor in negotiations with the West. Barlaam was one of several Greek scholars active in the West during the fourteenth century, but the most influential of them all was Manuel Chrysoloras, who began public lectures on Greek culture in Florence in 1397. Chrysoloras was quickly received into the Florentine humanist circle and taught Greek to most of the early fifteenth-century humanists, including Bruni, Poggio Bracciolini, and Guarino of Verona. Guarino brought his knowledge of Greek to north Italy and began to teach the language in Venice and Padua after 1414. By the end of the fifteenth century Venice had become the center of Greek studies in Italy, partly because of the influx of Greek scholars from the East after 1453 and partly because of the establishment of the humanist press of Aldus Manutius.

An event of great importance in the development of Greek studies in the West was the Council of Ferrara-Florence, held in 1438–1439. As the Turks became more and more of a threat to the very existence of the Eastern empire, the Byzantine emperors showed greater willingness to compromise the independence of the Eastern church in return for immediate military and financial help from the West. Manuel II Palaeologus came in person to Italy in 1423 to solicit aid, but he returned empty-handed because of the Western demand for complete union of the churches under the primacy of the pope. By the 1430s the Turks controlled the whole empire except for Constantinople itself, and the Byzantines were more willing to compromise. They proposed a council to take up the matter of church union. It met in 1438–1439, first in Ferrara and later in Florence. The council attracted the leading scholars of both cultures and resulted in the most significant interchange of ideas between East and West in many centuries. The practical results were minimal, because the residents of Constantinople repudiated the council's plan for church union, and the city itself fell only a few years later. Despite this failure the intellectual effects of the council were far-reaching. Some of the leading Eastern scholars elected to remain in the West, among them Gemistos Plethon, a leading scholar of Platonism. Largely through his influence, a Platonic Academy was formed in Florence that was instrumental in the recovery of many Greek texts.

Of even greater significance than the recovery of texts was the critical apparatus the humanists developed to analyze and refine the classical tradition. It is hard for a twentieth-century reader to appreciate the importance of this, because with few exceptions the textual tradition of all important authors is now quite clear. We know enough of what Tacitus, Cicero, or Augustine said to be able to construct an accurate picture of their thought. Scholars may disagree on the interpretation, but they generally agree on the data. There was no agreement on data in the Renaissance. The textual tradition of even the most famous authors was clouded to the point that no one could be sure exactly what the original author had said. For instance, of 240 editions of Augustine printed before 1500, fully half are spurious and do not contain any of Augustine's work. Mistakes were made by good and bad printers alike. Boniface Amerbach, one of the most reliable early printers, published in 1495 an edition of seventy-six sermons of Augustine of which only two are accepted as genuine today. The other seventy-four included sermons written as recently as the fourteenth century and falsely ascribed to Augustine. The effects of this confusion on intellectual discourse were overwhelming. It was impossible to debate the real issues of interpretation when none of the participants could agree which were the author's works and which were not. The great contribution of the fifteenth century was to begin to resolve this problem. The existence of uncertainty about the works of key authors as late as the early sixteenth century shows that the humanists were not completely successful in developing critical tools, but they made a major advance.

The man who contributed most to the new scholarship, partly by pugnacious disposition but also by his solid and imaginative intelligence, was Lorenzo Valla (1407–1457). Valla was born in Rome and spent much of his life in the papal curia, but he studied at the Casa Giocosa in Mantua and was one of Vittorino da Feltre's most outstanding pupils. He thoroughly enjoyed controversy and spent most of his life starting quarrels or entering those of others.

Valla's first work appeared in 1430, when he was only twenty-three, and it initiated his first controversy. He had made a comparison of Cicero and Quintilian in order to show that the latter was the better model for imitation. In 1430 the full text of Quintilian had been known for only a decade, and Cicero was the preeminent model for style and thought. To suggest that Cicero was stylistically inferior to Quintilian constituted a major heresy and earned Valla the wrath of most major figures in Italian humanism. More important, the work revealed three themes that would characterize Valla throughout his career: (1) the refusal to accept the classics as unquestioned authorities, (2) the determination to find the exact strengths and weaknesses of each classical author by analyzing his actual works, and (3) the attempt to refine a critical method that could identify the classical authors in their full individuality.

The refinement of criticism was the principal concern of Valla's next work, *De Voluptate (On Pleasure),* which appeared only a year after his treatise on Cicero and Quintilian. This time Valla attacked the naive attempt to reconcile all intellectual traditions. Humanists like Petrarch and Salutati had been worried by charges of irreligion and met these accusations by showing that stoicism and Christianity closely resembled each other in their moral outlooks. Valla wrote *De Voluptate* as a three-way conversation among a Christian, a stoic, and an epicurean and playfully suggested that the hedonistic, pleasure-oriented morals of epicureanism better prepare a man for the eternal bliss of Christian paradise than does the gloomy self-denial of stoicism.

Less puckish but probably more infuriating to contemporaries was the attack that Valla launched against the legal profession in 1433. He accused Bartolus of Sassaferat, one of the greatest lawyers of the day, of completely misunderstanding the law. Valla maintained that the only way to grasp a particular ordinance is to discover the particular historical circumstances that produced it and then to deduce the larger principles of law behind its application. Bartolus, he complained, quoted uncritically from the law codes and missed their actual meaning because he ignored the fact that conditions had changed since the original enactment. Despite the personal invective, Valla's call for historical understanding of the law was eventually heeded, and French legists of the sixteenth century adopted it as an important tool of practical jurisprudence.

Valla moved to Naples in 1437 to enter the service of King Alfonso, and it was there that he wrote his most important works. In 1440 he published a sharp criticism of Livy's history of Rome, showing that the facts in the history cannot always be trusted but must be tried against the facts found in other sources. It was as daring to attack Livy's historical validity at this time as it had been to assault Cicero's style a decade before, but Valla's critical acumen was so great that few could legitimately object. He also finished the *Elegantiae,* which was an analysis of the style of the major classical authors. It clarified the meanings of obscure words and phrases and explained why certain usages were preferable to others. The work soon became a model for good Latin style and was used by most later humanists, including Erasmus.

Valla's most famous critical treatise was his investigation into the validity of the Donation of Constantine, also written during the years at Naples. The Donation of Constantine was a document that purportedly had been issued by the chancery of the Emperor Constantine in the fourth century. It endowed the papacy with wide temporal powers in Italy, and during the Middle Ages it was held to be the legal basis for many of the popes' territorial claims. Actually the document is a forgery produced in the papal chancery in the eighth century, but until the Renaissance it had been widely — if grudgingly — accepted as genuine. Valla attacked the document on many grounds and brought to bear all the critical techniques he had perfected over the preceding years. He analyzed the style and showed that the document was not written in fourth-century Latin or in any style used by the imperial court. He undermined the donation's historical pretensions by discovering evidence that the territory it supposedly granted to the pope had actually remained under imperial administration long after Constantine's death. Finally he argued that Constantine was not the sort of man to give away such powers, nor Pope Sylvester the sort of man to receive them. This last argument is a subtle and distinctively humanist mode of inquiry. Valla first established the personality of his characters by piecing together details found in the historical sources. Then, having established the personality, he used it to criticize certain of the very details in the sources on which it was originally based. Nothing shows more vividly the intensity with which the humanists pursued their goal of knowledge through insight into individual characters and personalities than Valla's confident use of this almost circular method.

In 1444 Valla returned to Rome to enter the service of the pope, and he remained there until his death in 1457. During this period he translated several Greek texts and undertook an edition of the Greek New Testament, which became the model for the two great editions of Erasmus and Ximenes half a century later. The New Testament edition raises a fundamental question about Valla and his work: did he have any strong convictions of his own, or was he merely a critic? His commentary on the New Testament lightly passes over passages that would provoke Luther into reformulating traditional theology. A famous passage in Saint Paul's Epistle to the Romans suggested to Luther the doctrine of justification by faith, but from Valla it only evoked the dry observation that Paul's grammatical structure had been mistranslated in the Vulgate. On the other hand Valla thoroughly understood the significance of his critical technique and must have seen its implications for subjecting the New Testament to the same criticism in depth that he had applied to Cicero and Livy. Modern-day historians of the Reformation regard Valla as the pure critic, lacking appreciation for the ideas he dealt with and possessing no firm commitments of his own. By contrast, Garin, who is more sympathetic to the deeper coherence of Renaissance humanism, perceives in Valla's works a fundamental commitment to a moral but natural life free from ascetic denial.

Valla's problem is, in a sense, that of the Renaissance as a whole. He was ironic, indirect, and distrustful of simple systematic statements of value. He also had what could be termed — out of politeness — a well-defined sense of his own interests. It is no accident that his treatise on the Donation of Constantine contained some of the most vitriolic attacks on the papacy ever written in the fifteenth century. It was written for Alfonso of Naples at a time when the king was at war with the pope and wanted arguments against papal claims. Yet within a few years Valla departed for Rome, where he dedicated translations to his papal patron in warm and enthusiastic terms. Valla clearly practiced expediency, and his wit was biting and often sarcastically negative, but it is hard to believe that his boundless energy had no commitments whatsoever except to incisive and elegant style. The critical apparatus that Valla developed and refined assumes the basic humanist attitudes toward value and epistemology. Valla seldom agreed with his fellow humanists on particular issues, but, in spite of the bitter quarrels, he shared with them the faith that human communication is the path to genuine insight and that human feelings and responses are fundamentally good. This was the scientia rerum that informed both scholarship and education.

Conclusion

This analysis of humanist education and scholarship shows clearly the movement's spread beyond Florence. Many of the men discussed here began their training in Florence but produced their most significant works in other parts of Italy. The princely courts in the plain of the Po between Milan and Venice, such as Padua, Mantua, and Ferrara, played an important part in the development of humanist education, while the kings of Naples and the popes supported scholarship. Much of this support was selfish. Alfonso was hardly disinterested in urging Valla to write his attack on the Donation of Constantine, but royal and papal patronage produced much of lasting merit. Finally, republican Venice, partly because its geographical location gave easy access to the East, became a center of Greek scholarship. By the end of the fifteenth century humanism was a major intellectual current throughout most of Italy.

The scientia rerum that educators sought to instill and that underlay Renaissance scholarship was a means to virtue and moral improvement. The aim of education was not knowledge itself but virtue. Moreover, virtue was not simply private and contemplative, but active and social. Even outside republics, men were educated for a life in society, where continual contact with one's fellow man made moral behavior as well as personal attitudes crucial. Scholarship, too, had practical ends, largely in the service of education, for it was to help the teacher produce virtue in his students. Thus education and scholarship brought together the central traits of Renaissance humanism and sought to create a society where values and behavior were founded on historical consciousness, rhetoric, and social commitment.

Bibliography

The classic study in English of humanist education is William H. Woodward's *Studies in Education During the Age of the Renaissance* (Cambridge: The University Press, 1906). This recently appeared in paperback with a foreword by Lawrence Stone (New York: Teachers College Press, 1967). Another excellent treatment of the subject, not yet translated into English, is Eugenio Garin's *L'educazione in Europe: 1400–1600* (Bari: Laterza, 1957). Salutati's letter in defense of liberal studies as well as parts of Vergerio's treatise can be found in Werner Gundersheimer's anthology of

Renaissance writings, *The Italian Renaissance* (Englewood Cliffs, N.J.: Prentice-Hall, 1965). Works by Vergerio and Bruni, as well as educational works of several other Renaissance thinkers, can be found in William H. Woodward, *Vittorino da Feltre and Other Humanist Educators* (Cambridge: The University Press, 1921). This too has been reissued in paperback with a foreword by Eugene Rice (New York: Teachers College Press, 1963). Charles Singleton has translated Castiglione's *The Book of the Courtier* (Garden City, N.Y.: Doubleday, 1959).

An interesting account of the confusion in sixteenth-century scholarly debate caused by the textual tradition and recently discovered works can be found in S. L. Greenslade, *The English Reformers and the Fathers of the Church* (Oxford: Oxford University Press, 1960). Deno J. Geanakoplos, *Greek Scholars in Venice* (Cambridge: Harvard University Press, 1962), has studied the Greek revival, while Kenneth Setton, "The Byzantine Background to the Italian Renaissance," *Proceedings of the American Philosophical Society* 100 (1956): 1–76, has traced the fate of Greek studies during the Middle Ages up to the beginning of the Renaissance.

Franco Gaeta's *Lorenzo Valla* (Naples: Instituto italiano per gli studi storici, 1955) has not been translated into English but is still the basic work on Valla. Hannah Gray's article "Valla's Encomium of St. Thomas Aquinas and the Humanist Conception of Christian Antiquity," in *Essays in History and Literature Presented by the Fellows of the Newberry Library to Stanley Pargellis* (Chicago: The Newberry Library, 1961), pp. 37–52, offers a remarkably sensitive interpretation of Valla's critical and rhetorical approach. For a larger perspective on Renaissance scholarship and its dilemma over pagan writings, see E. Harris Harbison, *The Christian Scholar in the Age of Reformation* (New York: Scribner, 1956). Harbison treats Valla as a pure critic whose activity was largely destructive. More recent work on Valla has stressed his serious religious ideas; see Mario Fois, *Il pensiero cristiano di Lorenzo Valla nel quadro storico del suo ambiente* (Rome: Libreria editrice dell'università gregoriana, 1969). Valla's *Donation of Constantine* can be found in *The Italian Renaissance,* the anthology of Werner Gundersheimer previously mentioned, and his *Dialogue on Free Will* is found in *The Renaissance Philosophy of Man,* ed. Paul Oskar Kristeller et al. (Chicago: University of Chicago Press, 1948).

7 Neo-Platonism

Neo-Platonism was a distinct philosophical tradition, which looked upon Plato as its source but developed its own peculiar interpretation of the master. Beginning near the birth of Christ, neo-Platonism was given its most authoritative expression by the Alexandrian philosopher Plotinus (203–270). He maintained with Plato that reality was abstract and immaterial and that it completely transcended the world of sense experience. This stance led him to stress the powers of the mind to know and control the universe through abstract understanding of its basic realities. Plotinus and subsequent thinkers of the neo-Platonic tradition elaborated far more thoroughly than had Plato the process through which the single source of reality — which they called the One — generated the visible, created world through a complex chain of intermediate realities. They saw all elements of the created world as related to one another through participation in a hierarchy of beings below the One. Man, both a part of the physical world and a part of the spiritual one, had unique powers to move up and down through the whole chain. A final characteristic of the neo-Platonists was a general commitment to reconciling all systems of thought. This eclecticism can be traced partly to their philosophical notion that reality is ultimately one and partly to the historical context in which the neo-Platonists arose. During the first centuries after the birth of Christ, a wide variety of philosophical systems competed for attention and raised acutely the problem of reconciliation. All these characteristic neo-Platonic traits — the notion of a reality transcending the senses, the exaltation of the mind, the picture of a created world drawing its being from a hierarchy of greater beings leading up to the one source of all being, and the desire to reconcile all systems of thought — were the defining traits of a neo-Platonic movement that dominated Florentine intellectual life in the last half of the fifteenth century.

The renewed interest in Greek stimulated this neo-Platonic revival by fostering a greater familiarity with Plato's writings. In Petrarch's day, few translations of Platonic texts were available and scholars seldom knew Greek. The civic humanists felt closer to Aristotle but were not generally concerned with the tension between the Platonic and Aristotelian traditions. But the middle years of the fifteenth century witnessed a dramatic upsurge of interest and sympathy for Plato. It exercised a decisive impact on the subsequent direction of the Renaissance, opening new areas of inquiry and bringing to the fore a new generation of thinkers. To appreciate the significance of Renaissance neo-Platonism and its relation to previous intellectual trends, we must look at the three areas of thought most deeply affected: philosophy, magic, and, in the next chapter, science. These subjects were the major concerns of Renaissance neo-Platonists but were so far from the interests of earlier humanists that some historians regard the two movements as distinct. Nevertheless, the neo-Platonists shared certain important values with their predecessors, and these must be identified in order to place the movement in its proper context.

The Birth of the Platonic Academy

There was an unmistakable break in Florentine intellectual life during the 1440s. Interest in civic life diminished along with active participation in politics. Until quite recently this change was generally believed to have been caused by the rise of the Medici. Cosimo de' Medici, the first of his line to wield great political power, returned from exile in 1434. For the next sixty years, the family played a major role in Florentine politics. Recent research has made clear that the development of Medici domination was gradual and tenuous. The Medici acquired only limited control of the actual political workings of the Florentine republic, and the citizens of Florence considered republican institutions and republican values to be strong and vital at least until the 1470s (see Chapter 9). Since the political change had barely begun in the 1440s, the sudden appearance of an intellectual movement that eschewed civic commitments cannot be solely explained by the rise of the Medici.

The new movement was partly due to changes within the intellectual community itself. By the 1440s the generation of humanists that had matured during the wars with Giangaleazzo was growing old. Some had died: Niccoli in 1439, Bruni in 1444. Others, such as Poggio Bracciolini, had left Florence after the Council of Ferrara-Florence and followed the papal court to Rome. Foreign affairs were unsettled during the decade 1445–1455, and many of the politically active humanists were continually absent on diplomatic missions. Gianozzo Manetti, who had been an important lecturer in the studium in Florence, served on embassies continuously from 1443 to 1455, mostly in Naples. Simultaneously the church launched the first serious attack on the humanist movement since the quarrel between Salutati and Dominici. Antoninus, the new bishop of Florence, determined to reform his flock, and shortly after his appointment in 1446 he delivered a series of sermons that castigated humanist culture for contributing to the moral decay of the city.

Under these pressures, traditional intellectual activity in Florence lost much vitality. Chairs in the studium vacated by death or resignation remained unfilled, and the college ceased to be a major center of intellectual life. The vacuum was partly filled by informal meetings in private homes to discuss intellectual matters and ways of dealing with the new situation. The most important of these gatherings met at the home of Alamanno Rinuccini, a member of an old Florentine family long active in both intellectual and political affairs. The group included members of other prominent families, and as meetings became more regular it took the name of the Florentine Academy. The name did not reflect a deliberate attempt to introduce Platonic thought into Florence but was chosen because the group felt that their association resembled Plato's informal "academy" in ancient Athens. Indeed, their concept of Plato's school was not even drawn from Plato himself but primarily from Cicero. The academy was at first only a discussion group, but gradually its members decided to broaden their influence and nominate professors to fill the vacant chairs in the studium. Here they encountered resistance from older, established humanists like Poggio, but they managed to place their most important candidate, John Argyropulos, a Byzantine refugee whose studies of both Aristotle and Plato had already given fresh philosophical insights to his Florentine hosts. Argyropulos assumed his chair at the studium in 1456.

This victory for the academy did not have direct philosophical significance: it was not the triumph of Plato over Aristotle. It represented simply the effort of a citizen group concerned to maintain the quality of intellectual life in Florence. The opponents of Argyropulos were not upset so much by his philosophical beliefs as by his foreign origin. He was a native of Constantinople who had fled when the city fell in 1453. Traditionalists maintained that it was not enough for a scholar to be technically competent; he should also understand Florentine civic values and be patriotically committed to the city's greatness. The defeat of the traditionalists revealed how much the civic aspect of humanism in Florence had weakened. By the 1450s intellectual concerns had become abstract and philosophical; men were not so preoccupied with making intellectual endeavor directly relevant to civic life as they had been earlier in the century. Internal and external pressures had made the academic community turn inward and limit its interests to relating ideas to one another.

But why the great interest in Plato? The new generation of intellectuals doubtless sought a fresh source of inspiration; but, more important in this case, Plato's works were becoming more widely available during the period when the academy began. Interest in Plato can be traced to the early years of the fifteenth century, when another Greek living in Florence, Manuel Chrysoloras, lectured on Plato and translated the *Republic* into Latin. Inspired by Chrysoloras, Leonardo Bruni made his own translation of several Platonic dialogues, thereby demonstrating that there was no intrinsic hostility between the civic humanists and the thought of Plato. When the first complete collection of Plato's dialogues arrived in Italy in 1423, there was already a growing interest in Platonic thought and a considerable familiarity with many of Plato's writings.

The 1430s and 1440s brought further stimulation. At the Council of Ferrara-Florence, called to promote unity between the Eastern and Western churches, Western intellectuals first met the great Platonic scholars of the East, and some of these men stayed in Italy instead of returning to Constantinople, because increasing pressures from the Turks were making intellectual activity more and more difficult. The decade before the fall of the city brought further refugees, many of whom were professional philosophers well versed in Platonic thought and thoroughly familiar with his works. Gemistos Plethon was one of the Eastern scholars who traveled to Florence for the council and never returned home. He interpreted Platonic philosophy to a generation of Florentine humanists. The ideas he set forth were not actually Plato's but more his own. They combined a core of Platonic thought with a large admixture of mysticism and evangelical reform. Plethon was sure that the great religions of the world were about to end, and the final apocalypse would usher in the Platonic state. His ideas were erratic, but he made a real contribution to the Platonic movement in Florence through his close friendship with Cosimo de' Medici. At the suggestion of Plethon, Cosimo decided to commission a translation of the complete dialogues of Plato, appointing Marsilio Ficino, the son of his private physician, to carry out the task.

Gemistos Plethon's role in the development of Florentine neo-Platonism is typical of the general impact of Eastern scholarship. Plethon was able to introduce the Italians to the full range of Greek literature, including many texts they had not known before. The actual ideas of the Eastern scholars, however, were either lacking in originality or, like Plethon's, so peculiar that they had little widespread effect in the intellectual community. Neo-Platonism, like other trends in Italian humanism, was therefore an indigenous movement and not an adoption of foreign ideas. Florentine intellectuals, faced at mid-century with new problems, devised a new vocabulary of their own to deal with them.

The rise of neo-Platonism was accompanied by bitter feuds that revealed important differences between the old and new generations in Florentine intellectual life. Traditional humanists disagreed with neo-Platonists on several substantive issues. Poggio and Bruni, for instance, were both hostile to the study of magic, which constituted a major interest of the neo-Platonists. Moreover, the younger humanists did not share the traditional concern for exact dating of documents, and as a result they made a number of careless but very serious errors that had a substantial effect on the thought of the movement. A large part of the problem was that many neo-Platonists had not been educated in the same manner as earlier humanists. Their older peers had been trained in humanist circles and carefully schooled in grammar, rhetoric, and history, but the younger men had frequently received narrow technical education at the hands of scholastics. Marsilio Ficino, the acknowledged leader of the group, had studied to be a physician like his father, and as late as 1455 he was still writing Aristotelian technical treatises without reference to the moral issues that preoccupied the humanists.

It is tempting to stress these differences and characterize neo-

Platonism as a fundamental reaction against humanist ideals. But such an interpretation raises more problems than it solves. The values and attitudes of civic humanism returned in the early sixteenth century and unquestionably dominated Florentine intellectual life. Machiavelli had little in common with his immediate predecessor Ficino but shared much with Bruni. It is more convincing to see mid-century neo-Platonism as a stage in the larger development of Renaissance humanism. Without ignoring the unique characteristics of neo-Platonism, we can also see that the movement clearly had forerunners among the civic humanists as well as successors among the humanists of the post-Medicean period.

Two external aspects of Florentine neo-Platonism link it securely to early humanism. Most obvious is the very structure of the academy. Although it began as a group of friends meeting informally to discuss Florentine intellectual life, Cosimo de' Medici later took it under his protection, richly endowed it with patronage, and turned it into the leading intellectual center of the city. Even then, the Platonic Academy, as it came to be called, never became a formal educational institution. Members of the academy never intended that it should compete with the studium, and they did not offer formal courses. The academy's only direct participation in the educational system were the attempts, already noted, to influence appointments to the faculty of the studium. Membership was drawn from all fields of endeavor. The academy welcomed the association of poets, rhetoricians, jurists, active politicians, priests, musicians, and physicians, as well as philosophers.

The academicians were held together largely by personal ties — especially their respect for Ficino — and the academy derived much of its influence and effectiveness from the friendship that existed between its members. Correspondence within the group shows that members encouraged each other to do independent work; Ficino especially took note of what everyone was doing, encouraging one member to complete his work on a historical translation, offering another advice on a medical treatise, and helping a third to clarify an obscure point of musical theory. The structure and daily workings of the Platonic Academy reveal that its members strongly distrusted institutionalized learning and assumed that direct personal relationships were more conducive to knowledge. These attitudes were clearly in accord with those of the earlier humanists.

The academy's sensitivity to its environment likewise carried strong humanist overtones. When Cosimo commissioned Ficino to translate Plato's dialogues, he made available to the entire membership of the academy the Medici villa at Careggi, where work could proceed unimpeded by the noise and distractions of city life. The members' correspondence shows that they sensed the importance of this villa in forming the attitudes and human relationships within the academy. The villa was set in the hills only a few miles outside Florence and made a happy compromise between the intense activity of the city and the excessive solitude of life in the remote countryside. This theme ran constantly through humanist thought; both Boccaccio and Petrarch stressed the need of an appropriate physical setting for contemplation and creativity. The civic humanists of the early fifteenth century had a somewhat weaker taste for villa life, but they too realized the connection between one's environment and one's thought. Now at mid-century the taste was turning toward leisurely contemplation.

Philosophy in the Platonic Academy

To consider the thought of the academy is to look at the work of its leading figure, Marsilio Ficino (1433–1499). All others deferred to him, and he was responsible for the two most famous accomplishments of the group — the translations of Plato's dialogues and the *Theologia Platonica,* which was a synthesis of Platonism and Christianity. While his early training had been technical and Aristotelian, he became interested in Plato under the influence of Gemistos Plethon and readily assented when Cosimo asked him to undertake the translation of Plato's dialogues. A copy of the dialogues was delivered to him in 1462, and Ficino immediately set to work, although the task had to be interrupted several times before its completion.

Ficino's interest in the personal elements of Plato's writings is striking. He noted in his own letters that Plato had personified the ideal of morality and religion and had intimately bound them together in a single conception that emphasized the power of human will. Significantly, Ficino felt this conception was most effectively communicated by glimpses of the personality behind the dialogues. In keeping with this feeling, he was acutely sensitive to the interaction of the characters in the dialogues through which Plato expressed himself. Ficino's concern for understanding the personality of the ancient thinkers was obviously deeply rooted in the humanist tradition and in turn supported his view that Plato's philosophy was a theoretical structure that expressed Plato's personal values.

Ficino's most famous work was the *Theologia Platonica,* written between 1469 and 1474 as an attempt to synthesize Platonic philosophy and Christian theology into a single system. The work is, to be sure, a cosmology — a study not limited to man but encompassing all existence. Thus it differed from the works of Bruni and Poggio, who were far more interested in subjects directly bearing on the human condition. The civic humanists never sought to create a systematic view of the world, because they felt it was less effective as a means of shaping human character than the study of particular men and particular problems. This is not to say that they did not have a coherent understanding of the world; such an understanding emerges unmistakably from a study of their works. They simply did not feel that the creation of a system based on this understanding was an effective educational tool.

Although Ficino clearly disagreed with his predecessors on points of method, there was no disagreement on basic values. Ficino posed his cosmological questions in ways that brought out spiritual and human problems more than issues of natural science. He asked how the ultimate realities of the universe were manifested in individual men, not how they could be seen in created objects. He avoided making a synthesis of all existence and answered questions that are fundamentally human in their orientation. The fundamental concept of the *Theologia,* as well as of the rest of Ficino's work, is that God is immanent or inherent in human personality. This concept, which reached the level of explicit mysticism, underlay many of his most important themes. It provided a theoretical basis for the creativity of the human spirit and especially for the glorification of the artist, for he used his own direct relation to God to create out of his own resources a thing of beauty. Before this time artists had generally been considered mere craftsmen. The prestige of the artist had been growing throughout the Renaissance, but Ficino provided the intellectual underpinning for the prestige by seeing the artist as a creator whose vision brought him close to God himself. Ficino also stressed in the *Theologia* the importance of desire and human will. According to him, God is will, and therefore his immanence in human personality makes being human more a question of willing than of knowing. Knowledge neither forms nor

Primavera *by Sandro Botticelli; Uffizi Gallery, Florence. Photo: Alinari-Scala.*

directs the will; it only provides aid. Hence Ficino considered the body not the prison of the soul, as the Platonic tradition had tended to picture it, but the soul's partner in a harmonious relationship. He valued direct experience, thus testifying to the depth of this harmony no less ardently than Vittorino da Feltre and the humanist educators. He exalted the mind, but not at the expense of the personality.

Concern for morality was the humanist value that most clearly permeated Ficino's work. Underlying all his writing was the assumption that piety and learning support each other. The concept of learned piety, *docta pietas,* was partly a response to the attacks made on humanism by the church in the 1440s, but it also reflected the strong piety of Ficino himself and other members of his circle. They all felt that true piety must be informed by genuine learning and that such learning fulfilled in and of itself a morally didactic role. The enthusiasm for moral education led the academy to support the reforming friar Savonarola at the end of the century. That preacher was far more extreme than Bishop Antoninus, and he attacked artists as frivolous and asked the Florentines to burn their art works. Despite these attitudes he offered the possibility of a reformed and righteous Florence, and this promise alone sufficed to win him several disciples from the academy, including Ficino's disciple Pico della Mirandola, who spent his last years in the cowl of a Dominican friar. For a while even Ficino himself supported Savonarola.

Tangible evidence of the neo-Platonists' interest in moral education is found in some of the most famous paintings of Botticelli. In particular, the *Primavera,* which has long puzzled its viewers, has been shown to be a part of a program of education prepared by Ficino for an adolescent Medici, Lorenzo di Pierfrancesco. The actual program Ficino drew up has been lost, but a letter the philosopher wrote to his young pupil shows Ficino basing his program on his cosmology, synthesizing astrological lore with moral allegory to provide Lorenzo with guides for his action. As its central theme the letter portrays beauty and humanity as gateways to the divine. Since words alone are not adequate to stimulate men to moral virtue, Ficino suggested the need for visual images.

The central figure in Botticelli's painting is Venus, whom Ficino used to represent humanity. In his letter Ficino described her in the following terms: "For humanity is a nymph of excellent comeliness, born of heaven and more than others beloved by God all highest. Her soul and mind are Love and Charity, her eyes Dignity and Magnanimity, the hands Liberality and Magnificence, the feet Comeliness and Modesty. The whole, then, is Temperance and Honesty, Charm and Splendor." The other figures in the painting also represent classical figures with allegorical significance.

The variety of traits Ficino saw in Venus is not capable of systematic expression and is best conveyed through a visual image, which can be concrete and moving, yet ambiguous and suggestive. In using classical images to express a classical moral allegory, Botticelli achieved an impressive synthesis of classical form and content by using the pictorial language of classical mythology to express the moral values of neo-Platonism.

Magic

Ficino's interest in cosmological speculation set him apart from the civic humanists. Nevertheless he shared with them an interest in moral reform through learning, a tendency to conceive reality in personal terms, and a thoroughly humanist approach to education. The humanist elements in his thinking become even clearer when we study Ficino's interest in magic. Modern historians are often embarrassed by the enthusiasm that the Renaissance had for magical studies, feeling that such superstition is unworthy of a reflective and self-conscious age. Magic is excused as a prelude to modern science, and the reader is left to conjure up the image of an alchemist in long white beard and star-speckled robe futilely mixing his chemicals to make gold out of base metals, who suddenly in a blinding flash of insight discovers the periodic table! Such an image unfortunately sheds little light on magic, on the origins of modern science, or on the human mind. To grasp the significance of Ficino's work, we must take magic a little more seriously.

In fact magic is a means of organizing and controlling experience. As such it can be as sophisticated or as primitive as any other means; its prescriptions as ordinary as, or far removed from, common sense. If a student suffering from tension and exhaustion goes to a twentieth-century doctor, he will most likely be advised to relax, take a vacation, get out in the country, perhaps have an affair. A fifteenth-century *magus* (as practicing magicians were called) would have hardly offered a different prescription, though the reasoning behind his suggested cure would be quite different. The magus would explain to the overworked student that his affliction was caused by the profound influence of Saturn, the planet associated both with intellectual activity and with melancholy. He should therefore avoid animals, plants, and people belonging to Saturn and instead surround himself with things belonging to the cheerful and life-giving heavenly bodies, which are the sun, Jupiter, and Venus. Among things associated with these planets are gold, green, flowers like roses and crocuses, and of course love. Therefore the patient should depart for the country to surround himself with green and flowers, take a vacation to spend some gold, and have an affair. (This analysis of melancholy and its cure is actually found in Ficino's own *Libri de Vita,* or *Books of Life.*)

Two major traditions of magic, the Hermetic and the Cabalistic, exercised a major influence on Renaissance thinkers. Ficino was primarily interested in the Hermetic writings, while the stronger, Cabalistic tradition was investigated by his brilliant disciple Pico della Mirandola (1463–1494). The Hermetic texts more easily blended with Christian thought because they were less ambitious and less explicit in their appeal to supernatural powers. They were brought to Florence in 1460 and caused such excitement among intellectuals that Cosimo asked Ficino to begin studying them at once. This intense interest, it must be admitted, was largely due to a crucial error in dating, for the texts were thought to emanate from the earliest Egyptian culture and to be the ancient sources of wisdom on which Plato himself drew. In actuality they were written in the second century after Christ and drew much of their own inspiration from early neo-Platonism. Although the Florentine neo-Platonists were wrong in dating the texts, it is still significant that they were interested in the writings primarily for their putative antiquity. The humanist search for the ultimate and most ancient sources of wisdom was vigorously if misguidedly carried on by Ficino and his friends.

The Hermetic writings, so called because of their association with the god Hermes, comprise the *Asclepius* and the *Corpus Hermeticum,* the latter being a collection of fifteenth-century dialogues. The *Asclepius* was known to scholars of the Middle Ages, but it had been thought to be simply a document of pagan religion, and those who made use of it were considered of questionable orthodoxy. Ficino undertook first of all to rehabilitate the texts for use in a Christian society. In introductions to the various dialogues, he noted important similarities between the myths found therein and the story of the creation from Genesis, suggesting that the texts supported the same basic truths as those revealed in Scripture and found in the writings of Plato. Ficino also noted that the tone of piety and religious conviction of the Hermetic writings made them suitable for his general program of moral education. The eclecticism of these remarks and his willingness to choose insights from a variety of sources must be kept firmly in mind as the distinctive trait of the Florentine neo-Platonists, for their interests were not limited to the body of Platonic writings. Instead, the members of the academy widely searched the thought of the past in an effort to stress that one Truth lies beneath the multifarious expressions of human wisdom.

The Hermetic literature contains two major themes. Parts of the writings are strictly philosophical and seek to give a systematic explanation of the world, but other parts are narrowly magical and deal with alchemy, astrology, talismans, incantations, and other apparatus of the working magician. The two interests are not clearly separated in the texts. The *Asclepius,* which conveys the most systematic philosophical view, also contains a long section on methods for bringing statues of the gods to life. More importantly, the philosophical sections picture the world in astrological terms that support the magical practices. The talismans and incantations are supposed to work because the dimensions of reality are interconnected in the manner described in the abstract sections of the writings.

The Hermetic world-view is based on certain key Platonic concepts, as developed and systematized by the early followers of Plato. Most important are the notions that all objects in the material world are modeled on higher forms existing in the spiritual world and that they draw their reality from these forms (see Chapter 3). If this is true, then it should be possible to reconstitute specific objects in the sense world even after degeneration by manipulating the higher images on which they depend. The magus tried to accomplish this indirectly by manipulating other material objects that depended on the same higher forms. The example given at the beginning of this section is a good illustration of this practice. A tense and depressed human being has degenerated by falling too deeply under the influence of a single higher form, or *spiritus,* as Ficino called it. His stability can be restored by invoking another spiritus. To accomplish this the individual is brought into association with other objects whose reality derives from the desired spiritus. The theory of Hermetic magic, stated so baldly and abstractly, is not likely to appeal to minds conditioned by the precepts and methods of modern science. But it is important to remember that the theory was applied by the best practitioners in a sufficiently complex and sophisticated fashion and with enough restraint so that respectable results were often achieved.

Hermetic magic was a natural magic, seeking to place the subject under the beneficent influences of objects and relations that exist in nature. Its aim was basically to help people find normal health, wealth, and happiness. Cabalistic magic, though based on the same neo-Platonic tradition, had far greater pretensions. Cabalistic magicians tried to tap spiritual powers beyond the natural ones invoked by Hermetic magicians and extend human consciousness into realms that completely transcend personal experience. Ficino, himself a physician and the son of a physician, never went much beyond the use of the Hermetic writings, but Giovanni Pico, the young lord of Mirandola, who joined the academy in 1484 at the age of nineteen, was more eclectic and more daring and became deeply immersed in the Cabalistic tradition.

Cabala is a mystical tradition purporting to have been handed down orally from Moses and to explain mysteries not made clear in Genesis. Practical, or operative, Cabala stems from these mystical revelations, and because of its stress on direct communication with higher powers it has a much stronger mystical aspect than Hermetic magic. Cabala rests on two basic doctrines: the doctrine of the ten *sephiroth* and the doctrine of the mystic power of the twenty-two letters of the Hebrew alphabet. The sephiroth are the ten names most common to God. They are laid down in the Book of Creation, and the universe is seen as a development of their creative force. In Cabalistic metaphysics the sephiroth are related to the ten spheres of the cosmos, and angels serve as intermediaries between these spheres and the world that we normally experience. The letters of the Hebrew alphabet are reflections of the fundamentally spiritual nature of the world and the creative language of God. Creation is thus an expression of the hidden self of God giving itself a name, and by contemplating the letters of the alphabet, in combination as the Hebrew names for the sephiroth, one is contemplating God himself. The Renaissance with its sense of language as an expression of reality was naturally attracted by this aspect of the Cabala, for here the importance of precise words was paramount.

Pico began his magical studies with the Hermetic texts, but soon he came to regard their natural magic as weak and ineffectual without the Cabala. His interest in the Cabala as well as some of his other speculations made him somewhat suspect among more orthodox thinkers, and in 1486, partly to combat the suspicion, he published a set of nine hundred theses that he offered to defend against all challengers. Only twenty-six of these were concerned with magic, but in them Pico, after carefully defending his religious orthodoxy by distinguishing between good and bad magic and by acknowledging that Christ did not perform his miracles with the help of magic, clearly drew from the Cabalistic tradition. *The Oration on the Dignity of Man,* which prefaced the theses and is Pico's best-known work, stressed man's role as intermediary between the created world and the world of the angels, able to participate in both if he would only train and develop his faculties.

Pico was attracted more to the contemplative aspect of Cabala than to its operative aspect. His goal was to expand his own imagination by dwelling on the letters and names. Operative Cabala, in which the angels are invoked by name to perform magical works, was of little interest to him and remained suspect throughout the Renaissance. In this connection it is worth noting that no comparison should be made between the serious magus and the parlor magician. The magus sought to reach realms of existence that ordinary human experience could not touch and thereby expand his own consciousness of reality.

Only in one realm did operative magic gain respectability — in the graphic arts. Here the desire of Renaissance artists to create living forms might well be related to the passages in the *Asclepius* that talk of living and breathing statues. Leonardo da Vinci and Michelangelo both were steeped in the magical literature. The unsurpassed vitality of their figures can be seen as the result of goals that may have been posed for them by that literature, and in this sense the true operative magi of the Renaissance were the artists.

Cabalistic magicians were fascinated by numbers and felt that the relations of numbers provided a key to the hidden meaning of the universe. Pico wrote in his *Oration on the Dignity of Man:*

> There is, furthermore, still another method of philosophizing through numbers, which I have introduced as new, but which is in fact old. . . . Plato writes in the *Epinomis* that, of all the liberal arts and theoretical sciences, the science of computation is the chief and most divine. Likewise, inquiring, "Why is man the wisest of animals" he concludes, "Because he knows how to count," an opinion which Aristotle also mentions in his *Problems*. . . . These statements cannot possibly be true if by the science of computation they mean that science in which, at present, merchants in particular are most skilled.

This belief in an ordered universe, whose basic structure could be explained in quantitative terms, is one shared by the founders of modern science. In this sense the magi were indeed precursors of Newton.

In summary, the fascination for magic found among the neo-Platonists had its roots in several humanist attitudes. The humanist cry *ad fontes* — to the sources — led the scholars of the academy in search of ever more ancient and pure sources of wisdom. In the magical texts they thought they had found the true sources not only of Plato's wisdom but that of the Bible itself. The stress on words and language, particularly in Cabalistic magic, reinforced the humanists' interest in textual criticism and provided the most complete justification for their continuing attempt to discover the precise word that a thinker had used to express his ideas. In a more general sense, the use of magic reflected the humanists' desire for effective means of knowledge and control; it was a part of their general exaltation of man's position in the universe.

At its most profound level magic reflected a belief in the priority of experience over system, a feeling that the formula that encompasses all reality is ineffable and beyond fixed expression. To the magus, experience that did not fit into an existing system was a sign of the inadequacy not only of that particular system but of all systems. He was skeptical about generalizations because the unity that underlies experience is too profound to be expressed by systematic generalizations; it must be sought instead in realms that completely transcend experience. Few humanists could accept such open and unashamed mysticism, but the values that underlay it and the methods adopted by the magi bore the unmistakable mark of the humanist approach to knowledge and to life.

Bibliography

For a good general introduction to Renaissance neo-Platonism see Nesca A. Robb, *Neo-Platonism of the Italian Renaissance* (New York: Octagon Books, 1968). Longer and more comprehensive is Arnaldo della Torre's classic *Storia dell'academia Platonica di Firenze* (Florence: G. Carnesecchi e figli, 1902). Paul Oskar Kristeller has presented an interpretation of neo-Platonism that differs from the one in this chapter, stressing its philosophy and difference from scholarly humanism. See his articles in the second volume of *Renaissance Thought* (New York: Harper and Row, 1965) and *The Philosophy of Marsilio Ficino,* trans. V. Conant (New York: Columbia University Press, 1943). Kristeller also disputes the importance that the neo-Platonists attached to magic, although recent studies by Daniel P. Walker, *Spiritual and Demonic Magic from Ficino to Campanella* (London: Warburg Institute, University of London, 1958), and Frances Yates, *Giordano Bruno and the Hermetic Tradition* (Chicago: University of Chicago Press, 1964), portray magic sympathetically against the broad context of Renaissance concerns. For a general treatment of magic and witchcraft in the Renaissance see Wayne Shumaker, *The Occult Sciences in the Renaissance* (Berkeley and Los Angeles: University of California Press, 1970).

On the neo-Platonic aspects of Botticelli see E. H. Gombrich, "Botticelli's Mythologies: A Study in the Neo-Platonic Symbolism of His Circle," *Journal of the Warburg and Courtauld Institute* 8 (1945): 7–60, and Edgar Wind, *Pagan Mysteries in the Renaissance,* new ed. (London: Faber, 1968).

8 Science

Though it is difficult to be open-minded about Renaissance magic, it is even harder to approach Renaissance science without condescension. We in the twentieth century tend to view science as the increasingly successful search for objective truth and to regard the scientific ideas of the past as mere steppingstones to our current wisdom. Moreover, we assume that the only path to objective fact lies in the patient and systematic observation of nature and that the validity of science is based on the empirical method. Thus we judge previous systems of science on the one hand by the extent to which they adopt this method and on the other by the degree to which they anticipate modern ideas. On both counts the humanists of the Renaissance left much to be desired. Their interests were primarily literary and philological — or, in the case of the neo-Platonists, speculative — and they seldom troubled themselves with scientific problems. Their scientific ideas were conventional for the day, and they had little interest in systematic observation. The overwhelming direction of their thought lay in attempting to observe life in all its personal peculiarities, rather than to organize it into a general system.

The humanists' direct contributions to scientific ideas and methods were few, and historians of science have seldom considered Renaissance humanism to be of much importance. Nevertheless, the humanist interest in recovering classical texts made the work of ancient Greek scientists available in a pure and usable form both in the original language and in Latin translations. The press of Aldus Manutius in Venice produced a Greek text of Aristotle in 1498. The works of other Greek natural philosophers, such as Theophrastus, Dioscorides, and Strabo, followed. Latin translations of Euclid's *Geometry* appeared in 1482, of Ptolemy's *Geography* in 1475, and of Ptolemy's *Almagest* in 1538. These all formed the basis of increasingly careful critical studies of the fundamentals of Greek science. In addition to textual studies, the humanists made two original contributions that stemmed from their interest in the graphic arts. The development of fixed perspective by Leon Battista Alberti and others led to a more refined optics, and painters' desire to depict the human body accurately stimulated an expansion of anatomical knowledge that culminated in Vesalius' treatise *On the Fabric of the Human Body* in 1543. But compared with the great scientific changes of the sixteenth century these efforts seem small indeed.

Technology

The most conspicuous scientific achievements of the Renaissance were technological: the voyages of exploration and the invention of printing. They reflected no new scientific notions and can be traced to the influence of humanism in only the most casual manner. The technological innovations that made the explorations possible were few in number and were available considerably before major expeditions to Africa and the New World began in the last decades of the fifteenth century. The compass and astrolabe as aids to navigation, a ship sturdy enough to withstand the weather of the North Atlantic and with a rigging sophisticated enough to make it maneuverable by a relatively small crew, guns small enough to mount on the ships for the protection of the expeditions — these were all essential to world exploration, and they emerged from slow and steady technological advances during the centuries before 1492.

Nor do we find a special impetus for the voyages in Renaissance attitudes. To be sure, the explorers openly expressed love of glory and desire to imitate the classical heroes. Some leaders used classical images to encourage their troops. But love of adventure is foreign to no age, and the basic motives for the explorations — religious zeal to convert the heathen and the timeless desire for quick money — are hardly unique to Renaissance humanism. Bartholomeu Dias, who first rounded the Cape of Good Hope and opened the passage to India, claimed he made his expeditions "to serve God and His Majesty, to give light to grow in the darkness, and to grow rich, as all men desire to do."

The sudden eruption of voyages of exploration at the beginning of the sixteenth century should be traced not to any particular intellectual movement or technological invention but to social and political developments in the Iberian Peninsula. There the last Crusade in Europe finally expelled the Moslems from Spain in the same year that Columbus set sail for America, and the newly united country turned the full measure of its religious zeal and political organization to support the expeditions. More prosaically, the end of the Moorish wars meant that there was no more land to be confiscated, and nobles who wanted to increase their wealth had to look to other parts of the world for new land and trade.

The invention of printing with movable type in the middle of the fifteenth century, associated with the name of Johann Gutenberg, represented a change in European attitudes even more momentous than the discovery of the New World. Here again the change was narrowly technological, but historians are still learning how profoundly the effects of printing changed basic Western concepts. New attitudes toward words, the structure of discourse, and the modes of argument, as well as new values and concepts of society — all can be traced to the ability to show large numbers of people identical copies of the same work. Even the relative permanence of the humanists' rediscovery of classical culture depended in part on the wide dissemination of classical texts through printing. But these changes, though important, did not appear overnight, and early printing differed little from manuscript except that it was more efficient and cheaper.

The invention of printing stimulated further technological change. Innovations in engineering could be widely disseminated and rapidly adopted. Mining and metallurgy were particularly affected. Among the most important writers on this subject were Vanocchio Biringuccio (1460–1539) and Georg Agricola (1490–1555), both of whom studied in Italy and worked near the mines of central Europe. They wrote popular treatises describing and illustrating the current practice of mining and added their own suggestions for mechanical and technical improvements.

Astronomy

Humanism was not a crucial ingredient in the technology of the period, but science is not to be equated with technology. Scientific ideas do not always spring from practical needs or even from systematic observation and experimentation. They are born from the matrix of values, attitudes, and preconceptions that are shared by society at large and that pose the questions for systematic observation to answer. No amount of observation can produce a basic change in science without a change in this matrix. Most would agree in a general way with this proposition, but fewer appreciate the extent to which even the most concrete scientific laws arise as much from their historical context as from empirical observation. A tale from the folklore of the scientific revolution illustrates this point dramatically.

Every student of elementary physics learns that any body in free fall accelerates at a constant rate regardless of weight, and thus a light ball will fall as fast as a heavy one. Yet Aristotle maintained that the heavier object falls faster, and for centuries the best scientific minds in the West agreed with him. Legend tells us that this erroneous theory was finally overturned when Galileo, instead of idly speculating on the problem, climbed to the top of the famous leaning tower of Pisa and confounded his opponents by releasing two balls of different weights. Aristotle's error crumbled, and scientific empiricism triumphed as the heavy and the light balls struck the ground simultaneously.

This particular legend contains more truth than most, but it confuses the roles. It was not Galileo who dropped the balls from the tower but his Aristotelian opponents, and it was their view rather than Galileo's that was vindicated, for the heavier ball hit the ground first. In nature a heavier object always falls faster than a lighter one of the same size and shape because the heavier more easily overcomes the resistance of the air. In fact no amount of experimentation from the tower of Pisa can establish the hypothesis of equal acceleration in free fall, because truly free fall rarely occurs in nature. Galileo certainly never saw it. His rule was an abstraction designed to describe ideal relationships between ideal objects in a theoretical absolute vacuum. However he discovered his law, it was not by systematic measurement of naturally falling objects, any more than Newton established the laws of gravity by measuring the way his apple fell from the tree.

If scientific revolutions cannot be simply explained by an improvement in the techniques of observation, then we must search for their causes in a larger context. From this perspective the humanist contribution to Renaissance science takes on new and more significant dimensions. An excellent example of the complexity of causes is furnished by the most revolutionary new theory of the sixteenth century — the idea that the sun and not the earth stands at the center of the universe. The history of this theory, first advanced by Copernicus and elaborated by Kepler, has been interpreted by Thomas Kuhn in a manner that makes clear how much the theory depended on contemporary sixteenth-century thought. Kuhn also shows that the Aristotelian world-view it replaced was in fact a sensible and sophisticated picture of the cosmos. His interpretation has not been universally accepted among historians of science, but it is adopted here because it illuminates the contributions of Renaissance thought to modern science.

When told that men once believed that the earth stood still while the sun revolved around it, we sometimes wonder how they could have remained ignorant for so long. Our sun-centered universe (or solar system) seems so natural that we tend to forget how our notions about astronomy were drilled into us from earliest childhood — through textbook diagrams and planetarium models. In fact, our personal experience does not suggest a moving earth. We watch the rising sun, and it moves, while the ground beneath our feet remains reassuringly solid and still. Observation alone did not produce a new astronomy in the sixteenth century. To understand its origin we must look at the strengths and weaknesses of the older view, keeping in mind that men of an earlier time were as comfortable in their earth-centered world as we are in our sun-centered one.

The most striking difference between pre-sixteenth-century cosmology and our own lies in the fact that men formerly saw the physical world, or universe, as divided into two distinct realms, celestial and terrestrial. We assume that the laws governing earthly movements also govern those in the heavens, but in earlier times men thought that earth and sky were fundamentally different and obeyed different laws. The earth was the solid, immovable center of the universe, but it was also the domain of imperfection, corruption, and decay. The heavens were perfect, incorruptible, and eternally cycling around the earth. The sun moved among the fixed stars in the celestial realm, whereas the moon moved below the heavens but above the earth, fully a part of neither realm.

By the fourth century before Christ this picture of the universe had emerged as the accepted theory, supplanting various alternative views, including one that postulated an earth revolving around a stationary sun. It had many advantages. For one thing, it supported a useful technology, being particularly valuable as an aid to navigation. Navigational textbooks even today direct the reader to picture the earth as a stationary object around which the sun and the stars move, and it is hard to imagine practical navigation based on any other assumption.

While cosmological theory is a practical framework for observation and allows us to apply complex data to useful ends, this is not its only purpose. It also serves to make man more at home in the world by offering a coherent explanation of a whole range of natural phenomena. Thus the simple system of two realms was elaborated to explain motion, cause, purpose, and many other aspects of both terrestrial and celestial existence.

The most complete and compelling statement of this cosmology sprang from the mind of the Greek philosopher Aristotle in the late fourth century B.C. Aristotle's goal was to integrate all human disciplines into his system, and many of his explanations and basic values depended on a division of the universe into two realms. He felt that physical motion could be explained by reference to the different properties of heaven and earth. He stated that in the absence of external force every object would come to rest in the part of the universe most natural to it. The solid earth rests at the very center of the universe and the fiery stars float at the periphery. Thus rocks fall because they seek their proper place at the center, and fire rises because it is returning to the realm of the stars. In this manner the natural motion of an object is determined only by its position in space and not, as is the case with Newtonian physics, by its relationship to other bodies.

Motion was not the only concept that depended on the organization of the terrestrial and celestial realms. Aristotle also postulated that the universe was full of matter, a *plenum* (from the Latin *plenus,* "full") without empty spaces. Beyond the celestial realm was nothing at all, not even a vacuum. Within the celestial realm all space was occupied. Aristotle suggested that a series of invisible crystalline spheres occupied the space between the earth and the stars. The principle that nature abhors a vacuum not only served astronomical theory but also explained common experience, such as the functioning of pumps and water clocks. The notion of a plenum implied that the universe was finite. If it was indeed finite, it had to have a center. Indirectly, then, the plenum reinforced Aristotle's laws of motion, which depended on the attraction of solid objects to an earthly center.

Aristotle's belief in two realms colored his system of values and introduced a religious note into his cosmology. The motion of the heavens in eternally repeating circles testified to their perfection, whereas on the corrupt earth everything was scrambling to get back to its natural place. Perfection was in fact a necessary attribute of the celestial realm, and it gave man an unchanging standard of value against which to measure the corruption of his own world. Thus the earth-centered system did not exalt the position of man. Rather it made him the inhabitant of the morally and spiritually inferior part of the universe. His centrality was a symbol of corruption and his low state, not his worth.

Natural motion, the plenum, nature's abhorrence of a vacuum, the perfection of the heavens — all these ideas were part and parcel of Aristotle's picture of reality. For almost two thousand years they were the framework within which Europeans saw their world, practiced their technology, and understood their religious and moral values. To be sure, Aristotle's system was not without flaws. According to his laws of motion an arrow, for example, should drop to the ground as soon as it is released from the bow. Aristotle himself was aware of this difficulty and suggested an unconvincing explanation, but clearly he did not consider the issue very important. Later ages disagreed, and by the fourteenth and fifteenth centuries criticism of Aristotle centered on the laws of motion. Nevertheless, the overwhelming weight of his system was consistent with individual experience and the moral and spiritual norms of European society. Its prestige was enormous. Considering these facts, that it persisted so long is hardly surprising. Instead, we should wonder why it was ever upset. What possible advantage could have led men in the sixteenth century to discard Aristotle's subtle, all-embracing cosmology in favor of a radically different sun-centered universe?

To appreciate the reasons, we must first look at certain astronomical phenomena that presented a severe challenge to the earth-centered cosmology. It is easy to account for the motion of the sun

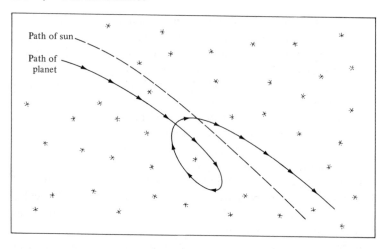

Figure 1 *The Path of a Planet in Retrograde Motion. The solid line represents the path of a planet as it goes through retrograde motion. The motion is viewed against the background of the fixed stars, seen as points. The planet does not follow the path of the sun, known as the ecliptic and represented by a dotted line, nor does it always go into retrograde motion at the same time of the year.*

and the distant stars by assuming that the stars are fixed to one sphere revolving around the earth and that the sun is fixed to another revolving just inside the first. Likewise the moon can be explained as riding on a third sphere intermediate between the heavens and the earth. But there are still other objects in the sky. They include bodies whose erratic movement led the ancients to call them "planets" (Greek for "wanderer"). Their motion through the sky follows no simple annual or daily pattern. What is more, at certain times they seem to stop, move backward, and then resume their original forward motion. This phenomenon is called retrograde motion, and we explain it today by noting that the earth and the planets are moving around a common center but at different speeds. (See Figure 1 for an illustration of the path of a planet in retrograde motion.) Any persistent star-watcher can observe retrograde motion, and the ancients were well aware of it. To fit it into their cosmology, however, was another matter, and it remained a problem for astronomical debate and speculation down to the sixteenth century.

Aristotle and his contemporaries tried to solve the problem by postulating that the universe was filled by a series of concentric crystalline spheres lying between the earth and the outermost realm of the stars. The sun, moon, and planets were fixed to certain of these spheres, while others bore no astronomical bodies at all. Each sphere was attached to the next outer sphere at two points, which determined its axis of rotation. Thus the motion of a given sphere was the resultant of its own rotation and that of all the spheres outside itself. Differences in the annual and daily paths of various astronomical bodies could be explained by assuming that the axes of successive spheres did not always coincide. This assumption, along with the belief in a multiplicity of spheres, was essential to account for the irregular motion of the planets. But the system was cumbersome (some planets required as many as four interdependent spheres to explain their behavior), and in the end it never succeeded in accurately predicting planetary paths.

A new solution to the problem was proposed in the second century A.D. by the great Alexandrian astronomer Ptolemy. He suggested that planetary motion cannot be understood in terms of simple circular paths about the earth. Instead, one should conceive

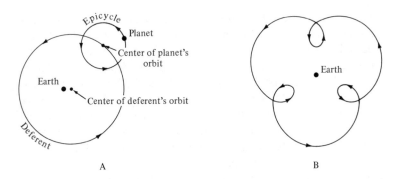

Figure 2   Ptolemy's Use of Epicycles to Explain Retrograde Motion. Part A shows a simplified picture of a planet with an epicycle and deferent. Notice that the planet rotates on the epicyle in the same direction that the epicycle itself rotates on the deferent. Part B shows the apparent path of the planet as it would be seen from the earth if it is moving on its epicycle three times as fast as the epicycle is moving on the deferent.

of a planet as revolving in a small circular orbit of its own, called an epicycle. The center of the epicycle traces out around the earth a much larger and slower orbit called a deferent. If it is further assumed that the earth is slightly off center inside the deferent, then retrograde motion as well as other irregularities of the planet's path can be explained. (See Figure 2.) The gross movements of the heavens thus become comprehensible in terms of five deferents, with epicycles for the known planets and two simple deferents for the sun and moon. Unfortunately for Ptolemy the actual paths of the planets through the skies refused to fit this ingenious system, and he was forced to put minor epicycles onto his major ones in an attempt to improve its accuracy. His followers in succeeding centuries added even more epicycles, and the complexity of the system grew enormously — while the inaccuracies remained.

The diffuseness and imprecision of the Ptolemaic system stimulated Nicholas Copernicus (1473–1543) to propose the radical new hypothesis of a sun-centered universe. It was set forth in his book *De Revolutionibus Orbium Caelestium (On the Revolutions of the Celestial Spheres)* published in 1543. Considering that this work would eventually destroy the Aristotelian world-view and revolutionize Western thought, its stated aims were amazingly modest. Copernicus was seeking mainly to help the process of calendar reform. By the sixteenth century the traditional calendar no longer corresponded to the actual seasons of the year. The church was especially interested in reforming the calendar, since the date of Easter is traditionally tied to the beginning of spring. Hence Copernicus dedicated his book to Pope Paul III and offered his system as a new working tool to develop a more accurate calendar. He did not attack the larger Aristotelian concepts, and in fact he specifically defended the laws of motion and idea of the plenum. Copernicus likewise retained the notion of a finite universe enclosed by the realm of the stars. The planets continued to move on crystalline spheres, but the sun, and not the earth, now stood at the center.

In the Copernican system the sphere of the stars was stationary. Its apparent motion was due to the combined effect of the earth's rotation on its axis and its revolution about the sun. (Actually, a third movement of the earth had to be introduced to explain the changing seasons — a conical movement of the axis within the crystalline sphere.) The new system explained the motion of the sun and stars no more accurately than Ptolemy's, and the earth's third move-

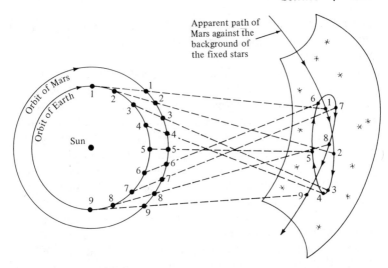

Figure 3 *Copernicus' Explanation of Retrograde Motion. As the earth and Mars move clockwise in their orbits, the earth, moving faster, will overtake and pass Mars. Consequently, when viewed against the background of the fixed stars by an observer on earth, Mars will appear to reverse for a while the normal direction of its motion (between points 4 and 6).*

ment made it even more cumbersome. But its great advantage lay in the simplicity with which it could explain planetary motions, especially retrograde movement, without recourse to major epicycles or deferents. (See Figure 3.) The elimination of these epicycles allowed Copernicus for the first time to measure the distances between the planets.

It is important to remember that Copernicus himself did not insist that the earth actually moved or that the sun was really the center of the universe. He simply maintained that his hypothesis provided a better method for making astronomical predictions than the Ptolemaic system. Yet in the next hundred years others used his work as a lever to overturn the entire Aristotelian world-view. What made his hypothesis so attractive to contemporaries that it produced a revolution? It was not a marked improvement either in scientific accuracy or in overall simplicity. Copernicus dispensed with the major epicycles, but he had to add about thirty minor ones to equal Ptolemy's precision in predicting the observed paths of the planets. Ptolemy himself had used no more, though by 1540 successive generations of astronomers had raised the number to seventy. Forty epicycles seem a small price to pay for being the center of the universe.

The impetus to overturn the old system did not spring from new empirical evidence. Systematic observation and the discovery of new data aided the Copernican revolution but were not decisive. The most careful observer of the century, a Danish astronomer named Tycho Brahe (1546–1601), actually made discoveries that led him to reject the ideas of Copernicus. Brahe developed techniques of observation that produced the most accurate set of data ever collected without a telescope. He was convinced that Copernicus was wrong, because if the earth actually moved around the sun, one should be able to see a shift in the angle between any two stars when the earth is at the opposite end of its orbit. Since he did not see this phenomenon, known as parallax (see Figure 4), he concluded that the earth remained stationary. Of course we now conceive of a far greater distance to the stars than Brahe or anyone else in the sixteenth century ever imagined, and parallax cannot be seen with the naked eye; it was first observed telescopically only in 1838. But the initial effect of increased accuracy in observation was actually to undermine the Copernican system and strengthen the Ptolemaic earth-centered universe.

Not all of Brahe's results were injurious to Copernicus, for Brahe finally emancipated astronomy from reliance on the data of the Greeks. These data were so flawed that no system could have explained them, and Kepler later depended heavily on Brahe's observations in working out his own solution to the problem of planetary orbits. In addition, Brahe helped break down the idea of the immu-

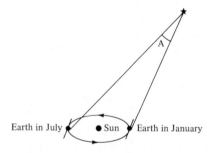

Figure 4   Parallax. As the earth moves around the sun, a given star should shift in position, from the viewpoint of a terrestrial observer, by the number of degrees in angle A at opposite ends of the earth's orbit.

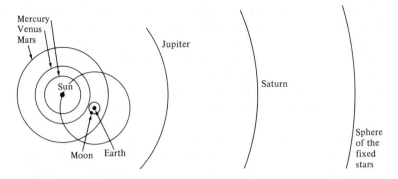

Figure 5   Tycho Brahe's System. The earth remains stationary, while the sun and moon revolve around it, as does the sphere of the fixed stars. All other planets revolve around the sun.

tability and perfection of the heavens, an important buttress of the two-realm system. In 1572 a new celestial body suddenly appeared in the constellation Cassiopeia and remained there for two years, gradually growing dimmer. In the past such a phenomenon had been dismissed as occurrences below the realm of the stars and near the earth, but Brahe's observational techniques gave him the confidence to conclude that it really was a star. Thereafter he supported the notion that important changes can occur in the celestial realm as well as on earth.

Tycho Brahe countered the growing dissatisfaction with the Ptolemaic system by proposing a modification of the Greek view, in which the earth was stationary but no longer the center of major celestial motion. (See Figure 5.) In the Tychonic system the sun and moon orbit around the fixed earth, as Ptolemy had pictured them, but most of the planets move around the sun. This system rapidly became the rallying point for conservatives seeking to defend the traditional view against the followers of Copernicus. It displayed mathematical simplicity and explained the data as well as a sun-centered system, but it did not require sacrificing the laws of motion or the plenum. Brahe's system was not without problems. It is hard to imagine what could cause the motions he described, and the center of celestial motion was certainly unbalanced. His cosmology, however, did not undercut the traditional values that supported the Aristotelian world-view.

It is puzzling why the sixteenth century did not widely support Brahe's system instead of that of Copernicus. The latter hypothesis was superior to Brahe's only from the perspective of two sixteenth-century attitudes. The first was the assumption that one can establish simple geometric regularities in nature. The second was the view that the sun is the source of all vital principles. Both of these are intimately bound up with the Platonic tradition. For the neo-Platonists, the triangles and circles of plane geometry were archetypes of Platonic forms and hence a reflection of the ultimate reality of the universe; they possessed a truth that irregular forms did not. This notion led the neo-Platonists to incorporate Pythagorean theories of music into their tradition. The Pythagorean school saw music as an exemplar of science, because strings or pipes whose lengths are in simple numerical ratios (1, ¾, ⅔, ½) produce harmonious sounds. This is one of the few pieces of empirical evidence for the numerical simplicity of the universe, and it has played an important role in Platonic thinking.

Light imagery is another prominent characteristic of Platonic thought. Although the association of light and the good has been common throughout the history of Western thought in both classic and Christian writings, the neo-Platonists were extreme in turning light imagery into a religious principle that bordered on sun worship. Ficino himself said that the light of the sun revealed the nature of God, that the sun was created first and placed at the center of the heavens. This attitude was clearly incongruous with the subordinate position of the sun in the Ptolemaic universe.

Because of the growth of neo-Platonism as an important intellectual movement in Europe, the Copernican universe seemed superior to the traditional world-view for reasons that were not empirical but aesthetic. The Ptolemaic system began to look ugly, and in contrast Copernicus' rules seemed beautiful. Thus the sixteenth century confronts us with a revolution in scientific thought based not on new empirical observations but on new aesthetic standards. The widespread acceptance of the Copernican system was correlated with the spread of neo-Platonism and humanism to northern Europe, events that will be treated at greater length in subsequent chapters. There is no simple way to explain the diffusion of the new standards. Neo-Platonism initially appealed to northern Europe because of its piety, but in the end its popularity depended on the entire fabric of social, intellectual, and cultural trends within sixteenth-century Europe.

The importance of the attitudes associated with neo-Platonism is nowhere more apparent than in the work of Johannes Kepler

(1571–1630), a disciple of Brahe's who finally banished epicycles from astronomy and drew the skies as they would be pictured by educated men in the West until Einstein. When one looks for the motives that impelled Kepler to overset the conclusions of his master, one is again struck by the absence of empirical or systematic considerations. Unlike Copernicus, who was barely aware of his debt to neo-Platonic notions, Kepler was an ardent neo-Platonist. He wrote in defense of Copernicus that the sun must be the center of the universe because it is the body "who alone appears by virtue of his dignity and power, suited to move the planets in their orbits and worthy to become the home of God himself, not to say of the first mover." Prompted by this feeling, Kepler set out to formulate laws of planetary motion based wholly on the assumption that they must conform to simple geometric shapes and ratios.

Kepler established three laws that accurately explained the movements of all the planets he could observe. The first law states that planetary orbits are not perfect circles but simple ellipses in which the sun occupies one of the two foci. (See Figure 6.) The second states that the orbital speed of the planets varies in such a way that a line drawn from a planet to the sun sweeps through equal areas in equal periods of time. (See Figure 7.) Both laws depend on simple geometric proportions, and the second suggests a radial force emanating from the sun and propelling the planets in their paths. In its original statement, the second law postulated that the planetary speed varies in inverse proportion to the distance from the sun, and Kepler always used the two statements interchangeably.

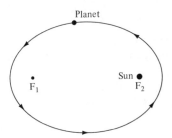

Figure 6   Kepler's First Law: The Law of Elliptical Motion. Each planet moves in a slightly elliptical orbit, with the sun at one of the two foci of the ellipse. F_1 and F_2 are the foci. The ellipse has been greatly exaggerated here. The actual ellipses traced by the planets are much closer to a circle.

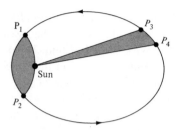

Figure 7   Kepler's Second Law: The Law of Equal Areas. Planets move faster as they near the sun and slow down as they move away from it. According to the second law, a line joining the sun to a planet sweeps out equal areas in equal times. That is, because the shaded parts in the ellipse have equal areas, the planet will travel from position P_1 to P_2 in the same time that it travels from P_3 to P_4.

The earlier formulation conveys more clearly than the final one the idea that the planets are moved by the physical force provided by the sun. Brahe's data were indispensable in confirming Kepler's laws. The inadequate data Copernicus had used would not have supported them. The laws themselves, however, undoubtedly arose from Kepler's neo-Platonic vision of the universe.

Even more revealing is Kepler's third law of planetary motion, which deals with the relationship between the periods of orbit of any two planets and their distances from the sun. The law is expressed by the formula $(D_1/D_2)^3 = (T_1/T_2)^2$, where D_1 and D_2 are the mean distances of planets 1 and 2 from the sun and T_1 and T_2 are their respective periods of orbit. The important point of this formula lies in the fact that the ratios are simple. Curiously, this is the only one of Kepler's laws that is still useful today: it allows us to predict the orbits of satellites and calculate the mass of galaxies. It was of no use to Kepler, however; it allowed him to make no calculations that he could not have made with the first two laws. Nevertheless, he considered the third law important because it expressed the harmony of the universe.

The Copernican revolution, one of the major changes in scientific thinking associated with the Renaissance, was far more deeply involved with humanist attitudes and values than is immediately apparent. Although the humanists themselves were not especially interested in systematic science, the standards of taste and approaches to knowledge that they formulated in the fifteenth century provided many of the underlying assumptions for the scientific ideas of the sixteenth. Neo-Platonism in particular offered a new aesthetic perspective that made existing scientific systems increasingly unsatisfying. This in turn stimulated the search for a new world-view and necessitated new laws of motion and a new explanation of other physical processes. The humanists' influence was indirect, but they prepared the way for Copernicus, Kepler, and Galileo.

Medicine and Chemistry

Advances in medicine during the Renaissance were partly practical and partly theoretical. They were based on new studies of the human body and new approaches to traditional alchemy and magic.

Vesalius' great treatise, *On the Fabric of the Human Body,* capped several generations of refined anatomical study. Physicians of the fifteenth and early sixteenth centuries had immersed themselves in the recently discovered texts of Galen, the second-century Greek anatomist, whose principal works had been unavailable through most of the Middle Ages. Galen was not always a reliable guide to the human body, however, because he had based his descriptions primarily on dissections of animals. By the 1540s men were beginning to go beyond Galen and dissect human cadavers themselves. But the process of correction was slow. Galen's prestige was great, and it was easy to see structures because he had described them, even when they did not exist. One famous example involved an intricate network of vessels at the base of the brain that Galen had observed in cattle, a frequent object of his dissections, but erroneously attributed to humans. In fact, man has no such network. Several important sixteenth-century anatomists claimed to have seen it in human cadavers and convinced bystanders at the dissection that they saw it too.

Vesalius had studied the anatomy of Galen and learned from the Greek master that experiments and observations on real bodies are more reliable than any textbook. He systematically tested Galen's descriptions by comparing them with his own dissections. The result of his efforts was the clearest and most comprehensive treatise on human anatomy the world had yet seen. Even today Vesalius' drawings are unsurpassed in their naturalness. The work promptly became an invaluable guide to physicians and surgeons, and an incentive to attempt more daring operations and cures.

A fresh approach to the use of medicines in the treatment of disease came from the work of the German physician and alchemist Paracelsus (1493–1541). Herbal remedies had long been used but seldom studied systematically. Paracelsus was a keen, systematic observer (he wrote a notable book on miners' diseases), but his real interest lay in mysticism and alchemy. The traditional concern of medieval alchemy had been to transmute base metals into gold. Paracelsus felt that an alchemist could better devote his energies to the preparation of drugs. His own research was guided by the neo-Platonic principle that the whole cosmos can be resolved into simple elements that can then be transformed into more complex ones. According to this theory, drugs owe their efficacy to the fact that they have the same elemental composition as the disease they are intended to treat. Thistles, for example, should be an effective remedy for internal bleeding because their leaves prick like needles. Such reasoning is far removed from today's experimental method, but it served to focus attention on the chemical properties of natural products used as drugs. The work of Paracelsus and his disciples led to a greatly refined and systematized knowledge of chemical substances, and it formed the theoretical basis for practical medicine and pharmacy until well into the seventeenth century.

As important as the work of Vesalius and Paracelsus was in their day, it is well to remember that neither the former's anatomical observations nor the latter's chemical studies produced a revolution comparable to the Copernican revolution in astronomy. Medicine would have to wait until the nineteenth century to find its Copernicus in Pasteur.

Bibliography

For an approach to the history of science more traditional than the one presented here see Charles Singer, *From Magic to Science* (New York: Dover, 1958), and Singer, *A Short History of Scientific Ideas to 1900* (Oxford: Clarendon Press, 1959). Thomas Kuhn has interpreted the new astronomy of the sixteenth century in *The Copernican Revolution* (Cambridge: Harvard University Press, 1957). In *The Structure of Scientific Revolutions* (Chicago: University of Chicago Press, 1963), Kuhn has broadened his approach and constructed a model for all major changes in scientific notions. Herbert Butterfield, *The Origins of Modern Science,* rev. ed. (New York: Macmillan, 1961), has also stressed the role of imagination in the development of modern science. For alternatives to Kuhn's interpretation, see I. Bernard Cohen, *The Birth of a New Physics* (Garden City, N.Y.: Anchor Books, 1960); Alexandre Koyré, *From the Closed World to the Infinite Universe* (Baltimore: Johns Hopkins Press, 1968), from a lecture series delivered in 1953; and Marie Boas, *The Scientific Renaissance* (New York: Harper and Row, 1962).

On the technological and political bases of the explorations, see John Parry, *The Age of Reconnaissance* (New York: New American Library, 1964), and Carlo Maria Cipolla, *Guns, Sails and Empires* (New York: Pantheon Books, 1966). The importance of printing in the Renaissance has been stressed by Walter Ong in *Rhetoric, Romance and Technology* (Ithaca, N.Y.: Cornell University Press, 1971) and by Elizabeth Eisenstein in "The Advent of Printing and the Problem of the Renaissance," *Past and Present* 45 (November 1969): 19–89. See also Theodore Rabb's comments on Professor Eisenstein's thesis in *Past and Present* 52 (1971): 135–140, and Professor Eisenstein's reply in the same issue, pages 140–144.

Italy in the Fifteenth Century

Part Three
The High Renaissance: Climax and Dissolution

9 Political Upheaval

The Renaissance in Italy reached maturity and came to an end with remarkable speed. Its greatest works were largely the product of the forty-seven-year span between 1480, when Leonardo da Vinci painted the *Adoration of the Magi,* and the death of Machiavelli in 1527. For more than two centuries modes of expression, techniques of art, and conceptions of humanity had slowly developed into an increasingly coherent perspective on life and experience, but in these two generations the Renaissance suddenly took on a fresh brilliance and, in a burst of energy, created the monuments that are the basis of its lustrous reputation to this day.

The achievements of the High Renaissance, as this period is called, are all the more striking in contrast with the period immediately preceding. We tend too often to imagine that any historical achievement is the natural result of gradual evolution, but the late fifteenth century does not, when seen by itself, seem to prefigure the magnificence of High Renaissance style. Machiavelli's play *Mandragola* opened areas of dramatic force that no fifteenth-century play had ever approached, just as his most famous work, The *Prince,* phrased the old truth of Florentine political life in a manner that no age has been able to ignore. Castiglione's *Courtier* transformed the humanist educational treatise into a vehicle that conveyed the deepest values of humanism to areas of Europe where humanism had been hardly understood. While some roots of the High Renaissance can be identified in the intellectual life of the fifteenth century, no study of that period has convincingly explained the range and brilliance of the achievements of the early sixteenth century.

The chapters in Part Three will eschew a broad survey of the accomplishments of the High Renaissance. Rather they will concentrate on three central aspects: first, an explanation of the political upheaval that dominated the entire period; second, an analysis of Machiavelli's *Prince,* the most famous literary and political work of the time and one of the few still commanding wide attention in the twentieth century; and third, a description of the achievements of the great painters of the High Renaissance, especially Leonardo da Vinci. By focusing attention on these three aspects a more precise idea of the period's character and significance can be acquired than by a fleeting list of all its manifold achievements.

The High Renaissance occurred at a time of swift and devastating political change. Italy had been immune from serious or prolonged foreign intervention since the early years of the fourteenth century, but beginning in 1494 it suffered a series of foreign invasions that by 1559 had robbed the peninsula of its political independence, its economic vitality, and its diplomatic influence. Established dynasties fell from power in many important areas; old alliances crumbled; and military techniques that had served Italy for generations proved unavailing before fresh challenges from the North. The suddenness and fury of the upheaval strongly tempts the historian to find in it an explanation for both the brilliant beginning and rapid demise of the High Renaissance. Like most temptations of its kind, this should be resisted. The political upheaval provided a major subject for the reflections of such contemporary thinkers as Machiavelli and Castiglione; Raphael gave relevance to his paintings by incorporating events from the upheaval into them. But the essential intellectual achievements of the period are more clearly understood by viewing them in context with preceding intellectual developments than by suggesting that they represent a simple and direct response to contemporary political events.

It is remarkable that the significance of the political crisis of the early sixteenth century was clearly and instantly perceived by contemporaries. Political developments seldom seem as clear to those who live through them as to those who study them long afterward, and some of the most profound eruptions of European history have passed nearly unnoticed by contemporaries. Such was not the case around 1500. Machiavelli and Guicciardini knew that the events of 1494 had ushered in a new age of Italian history in which traditional diplomacy and old political maxims were no longer applicable. Practicing politicians, too, especially in Florence, saw this revolution as rapidly and as clearly as the more detached and reflective members of their society. Florentine political life after 1494 was dominated by an attempt to reformulate traditional policies in light of the new situation.

These men were right in their assessment of events, but to a latter-day historian who looks only at the invasion of 1494 and the fall of the Medici, the magnitude of the change is not so obvious. Not until the 1520s does it become apparent that a sweeping and irreversible change has come over Italian life and that the trends of Italian political life in the fifteenth century are decisively broken. It appears that the perspicacity of thinkers and politicians during this period should be attributed less to the events themselves than to the intellectual tools with which they were analyzed. Humanism had stressed understanding problems through the precise historical context from which they emerge, and in doing so it equipped the Italians who suffered through the period of invasions with an unusually acute sensitivity to historical change.

A study of the political background of the invasions reinforces the notion that they were at the beginning no radical departure from the usual lines of Italian diplomacy. They grew out of traditional sources of instability and tension in Italy that underlay the veneer of peace and quiet during the last half of the fifteenth century.

Italy in these years was vexed with deep problems in foreign and domestic life. By 1455 new dynasties had taken control of Florence, Milan, and Naples. The new rulers sought to establish their control by means that gave them an appearance of greater power than their predecessors had wielded, but in fact the new dynasties had weak foundations and claimed only a superficial loyalty from their subjects. In the realm of foreign policy, disputed territories on the borders of each of the major states caused frequent quarrels, exacerbated by the far-flung interests of the major powers and their habit of intervening well outside their immediate spheres of influence. Naples, for instance, had a stake in the grain trade across the Tyrrhenian Sea and frequently tried to interfere with the Milanese protectorate of Genoa. Venice and the Papal States each adopted foreign policies that brought them into direct conflict with the other powers in a more intense and serious confrontation than had previously occurred.

Internal Problems in the Fifteenth Century

The most unstable of the new dynasties ruled at Naples. Ever since the thirteenth century two rival houses had contended for the Neapolitan throne. The first, the Angevin house, had descended from the younger brother of the French king Louis IX and claimed the throne by papal investiture. The second, the Aragonese house, was descended from the ancient Norman rulers of Naples. The latter family had conquered the island of Sicily from the Angevins in 1282 and had been adopted into the Angevin house in the mid-fifteenth century. Joanna II, the last Angevin ruler, died in 1435. An Aragonese claimant, Alfonso the Magnanimous, now appeared and after a seven-year struggle became effective ruler. Alfonso was a competent and imaginative king who experienced little trouble once he had secured his throne, but on his death the kingdom was again divided, leaving Sicily to his brother John, who was also king of Aragon, and Naples to his illegitimate son Ferrante.

Ferrante's illegitimacy provided an ever-present pretext for opposition, but he held the kingdom thanks to the aid of the other Italian powers, who were convinced that he would be weaker and less troublesome than the Angevin claimant. In 1480, the head of the Angevin house in France died without heir. His claims passed to the French king, reinforcing the general feeling in Sicily that the Aragonese were the safer ruling house but adding a new and potentially threatening element to the struggle for the Sicilian throne. As events were soon to prove, the French king could make a far more forceful bid for his claim in Sicily than his Angevin cousins ever had.

Meanwhile in the duchy of Milan, the succession had become clouded by the near demise of the Visconti line. Filippo Maria Visconti, son of Giangaleazzo and the last Visconti duke, raised the Milanese state left by his father to even greater heights but died without legitimate heir. He had given his illegitimate daughter, Bianca Maria, in marriage to one of his condottieri, Francesco

Sforza, in partial payment for services. A *condottiere* was the commander of a band of professional soldiers, the men who did most of the fighting in fifteenth-century Italy, and many of these commanders had taken over minor principalities. On Filippo Maria's death in 1447, his subjects formed a republic and sought to restore free institutions after a century and a half of Visconti domination. This policy ran against prevailing trends of the time and excited wide opposition from the other Italian powers. Even republican Venice moved to seize some Milanese territory. In this crisis the Milanese turned to Francesco Sforza, an unfortunate choice, for he soon claimed succession by virtue of his marriage to Bianca Maria and made himself duke in 1450.

Sforza attained his goal only after a protracted and bitter siege of the city, and his experience left him keenly aware of the strength of republican sentiment among his subjects. To win the allegiance of the Milanese he built on a magnificent scale, created a large and splendid court, and tried to cut taxes by relying on funds from outside his territory. These policies produced an appearance of strength and stability, but a current of opposition to Sforza rule remained throughout the century, and the support of the citizens was never assured. Francesco's elder son, Galeazzo Maria, was assassinated in a republican conspiracy in 1476, though the conspirators were unable to parlay their success into a permanent overthrow of the dynasty.

In Florence, the third city whose dynasty proved unable to survive the upheavel of the 1490s, the Medici exercised a control more subtle and complex than either the Aragonese in Naples or the Sforza in Milan. Later in the sixteenth century the Medici would be restored as hereditary rulers of Florence and grand dukes of Tuscany and would develop institutions and means of control more effective than any to be found elsewhere in Europe until the seventeenth century. Because of the later strength of the dynasty, some historians have looked at the family's position in the fifteenth century as if they dominated the city with means as sure and undisputed as in the later period. But scholars in recent years have looked more closely at the inner workings of Florentine political life in the period before the establishment of the Grand Duchy and have discovered certain crucial limitations in early Medici rule.

The factional rivalry endemic to Florentine government produced frequent shifts of power and expulsions of the losing faction from the city. In 1433, Cosimo de' Medici, the leading banker and the founder of his family's political fortunes, was exiled in such a shift. The following year the newly elected signoria proved favorable to Cosimo and invited him to come back. This turn of events reflected no deep change in the city's political alignments, but simply the operation of chance. Election to the signoria was by lot, and this time the lot brought in Cosimo's friends rather than his enemies.

The ease of Cosimo's return suggests how evenly the rival factions in Florence were balanced, but immediately after his return Cosimo set about to make sure that chance would never again take away what it had so freely given. Manipulating the lot was nothing new in Florentine politics. The signoria was drawn from an official list of names, and the complexity of eligibility rules made it relatively easy to control within broad limits the names that appeared on the list. Cosimo simply improved on the system that former factions had developed and created one that made it very difficult to elect a majority of anti-Mediceans to any major governmental body. The key to Cosimo's success was the creation of a commission (the *accoppiatori*) charged, during the confusion surrounding his exile and return, with drawing up a small list of eligible candidates for the signoria until a permanent — and constitutionally proper — larger list could be assembled. As long as Cosimo could keep the larger list from being completed, he could easily have the smaller one filled with his followers. The device was useful but could be continued only as long as Cosimo managed to convince the Florentines that the city faced an emergency. As soon as the city was at peace, threatened neither with foreign invasion nor internal conspiracy, even Cosimo's own supporters clamored for a return to normal, constitutional procedures and the end of the accoppiatori.

Cosimo's inability to subvert permanently the normal processes of Florentine politics sheds light on the limits of his family's control over the city. The Medici represented not a single family but a faction in which they played the most important part. The faction and not the family dominated Florence from 1434 until the expulsion of Piero de' Medici in 1494, and the family was never able to rule without its supporters. Even Lorenzo the Magnificent, who headed the family from 1469 to 1492 and brought his faction to the zenith of power, was able to change the traditional processes only by introducing new councils where members of the Medici faction outside the family sat by right and not by favor of the Medici.

Lorenzo's power lay largely in his ability to get along with the other families that formed the Medici party, not in his capacity to overawe them. The Medici's dependence on support from other powerful families — the weakness at the heart of Medici policy — led to the fall of the family during the invasion of 1494. Lorenzo's son, Piero, tried to rule only with the help of his close friends and ignored the powerful families his father had so carefully cultivated. It was the disaffection of these families that brought the Medici down.

Diplomatic Problems in the Fifteenth Century

Diplomatic tensions, too, added to the dynastic instabilities of the late fifteenth century. Officially, Italy was at peace. In 1454 the five major Italian powers met at Lodi to confirm Sforza's position in Milan, and in the following year they established the Holy League to bring their efforts into concert and check the growth of Turkish power. The fall of Constantinople in the year before the Peace of Lodi and the brief occupation of Otranto on the Italian mainland made the Turkish threat seem graver than it looks in retrospect. The league did indeed prevent wars of the type that formerly had torn Italy apart. During the late fourteenth and early fifteenth centuries, Giangaleazzo, Ladislaus of Naples, and Filippo Maria Visconti had launched vigorous aggressive thrusts that threatened the independence of some of the major powers. Giangaleazzo had died while laying siege to Florence in 1402, and Ladislaus had occupied Rome and most of the Papal States shortly afterward. Although the league could stop the outbreak of such major wars, it could not solve the problems of territorial expansion and economic conflict that underlay the disputes between the Italian states. Instead, it only succeeded in putting an end to minor wars before they could resolve any of these difficulties. Three such minor wars during the period between 1454 and 1494 illustrate not only the stubborn survival of long-standing tensions, but the growth of new diplomatic problems during the fifteenth century.

A conflict broke out between Alfonso of Naples and the Genoese in 1455, immediately after the signing of the Holy League. Alfonso had specifically excluded Genoa from the league because the two powers had for some time been quarreling over control of Sardinia, and when the general peace freed Alfonso from other worries, he turned all his fury onto Genoa. The city's pleas for help from the other signatories to the Holy League yielded much sympathy but little real aid. In desperation Genoa asked for protection from the French, who sent an army in the name of the Angevin pretender to the Neapolitan throne. The resultant turmoil in Naples lasted six years. Many aspects of this conflict foreshadowed the disastrous pattern of later invasions. It began with Neapolitan intervention in the North; it showed that the Italian powers, when hard pressed, were willing to call in foreign intervention; and it clearly demonstrated that the great Italian powers were vulnerable to even minor intervention by the European nation-states. But in 1455 Italians were in no mood to worry about these problems.

If the league could not prevent hostilities from developing over long-standing rivalries, it was even more helpless before two relatively new sources of tension: Venetian expansion onto the Italian mainland and the repeated attempts by the popes to establish on the borders of the Papal States territories for their own families. Both of these trends developed early in the century. After centuries of relative isolation from Italian diplomacy, Venice emerged as an active competitor for power and territorial possessions in the period of Giangaleazzo's expansion. At the same time, the end of the Great Schism in 1419 allowed the popes to reestablish control over the states of the church and led them to seek new possessions for their sons and nephews.

Papal nepotism was nothing new, but the pontiffs of the late fifteenth century pursued it with such vigor and openness that it was the cause of many of the period's wars. The most serious conflict in almost the entire century was the war of the Pazzi conspiracy, which began in 1478 as a direct result of Sixtus IV's attempt to secure land for his family on the border between the Papal States and Tuscany. Lorenzo de' Medici, naturally enough, opposed the pope's expansion into lands normally under the influence of Florence, and Sixtus retaliated by supporting an anti-Medici conspiracy led by the Pazzi family, owners of a Florentine banking house.

The conspiracy failed when Lorenzo narrowly escaped an attempt on his life organized by Sixtus and the Pazzi. The pope's attempt to assassinate Lorenzo so inflamed the Florentines that they hanged the archbishop of Pisa from the window of the Palazzo della Signoria. Sixtus, whether genuinely outraged by the hanging of an archbishop or simply glad for a pretext for open hostilities, placed Florence under an interdict and launched a surprise attack on Florentine territory in alliance with Naples. Lorenzo received some help from his allies, Milan and Venice, but was nearly overwhelmed until he suddenly took the risky step of traveling to Naples in person to negotiate with King Ferrante. This was regarded at the time as a courageous act, but Lorenzo had discreetly sought and secured guarantees from the French Court for his personal safety while in Naples. The war of the Pazzi conspiracy was settled without serious damage to any of the major powers, but it should have given the participants cause for concern about both their internal instabilities and the ever-present foreign influence in affairs of the peninsula.

Venice's expansion at first caused serious worry only for Milan, but by the middle of the century one after another of the smaller cities in the eastern plain of the Po had become Venetian dependencies, and all Italy began to show signs of disquiet over the possibility of Venetian domination. A general war broke out in 1482. It began when Venice attacked the duchy of Ferrara in league with Pope Sixtus IV, who wanted some Ferrarese territory for his family. Florence, Milan, and Naples banded together to prevent the duchy from being overrun, and Venice was limited to taking only some small pieces of Ferrarese territory.

By 1494 Italian politics and diplomacy bore a façade of stability and relative peace that only hid the numerous possibilities for tension and disruption. Venice and the Papal States, both intent on increasing their territories, found themselves arrayed against Florence, Milan, and Naples; each of these three powers was governed by a dynasty less than a century old and still insecure. The minor skirmishes among the Italian powers, despite the Holy League, both reflected and exploited the diplomatic tension and the potential instability of internal politics. The precarious quiet could never survive a major crisis, and such a crisis broke with the French invasion of 1494.

Invasions

The French invasion was triggered by an innocuous ceremonial dispute among the women of the court of Milan. Giangaleazzo Sforza, son of the preceding duke, had been only a child when his father was assassinated in 1476. Giangaleazzo's uncle, Ludovico, assumed the ducal functions during his nephew's minority. But in 1494 Giangaleazzo was twenty-four years old, and his uncle still had not relinquished possession of the duchy. Giangaleazzo's wife, Isabella of Aragon, found herself taking second place in court ceremony to Ludovico's wife, Beatrice d'Este, and was particularly incensed. Isabella complained to her grandfather, Ferrante, king of Naples.

This petty court intrigue gradually involved the intricate mesh of Italian diplomacy in ways that none of the participants could have imagined. Ferrante, wishing for a pretext to further his state's interest in the North, threatened to intervene in Giangaleazzo's behalf. The other Italian states, glad to see Milan embarrassed, refused to guarantee Ludovico's position, To save his alliance with Naples and Florence, Ludovico suggested that the three powers make a show of unity by sending a single delegation to the coronation ceremonies of the newly elected pope, Alexander VI. Such an act might have dispelled the tension, but the new head of the Medici family, Piero, refused to take part. Piero, who had succeeded his father only two years before, was twenty-two years old, vain and indifferent to the nuances of diplomatic practice. He turned down Ludovico's suggestion not out of any sinister motives but simply because he wished to make the biggest possible impression on the rest of Italy by staging a splendid show of his own. Ludovico was a master of the subtle arts of Italian diplomacy and could not believe that Piero's refusal was motivated solely by vanity. It seemed much more likely that Piero wished to abandon the alliance.

Fearing that both his allies were deserting him, Ludovico adopted a familiar course of action: he called for intervention by the Angevin claimant to the throne of Naples. He, like the other Italian powers, was playing a war of nerves, for no one wanted or expected a foreign invasion. Appeals to the North had never provoked serious military action since the early years of the fourteenth century, and there was no reason to believe that there was danger of such action now.

But conditions had changed radically in the decade before 1494. First, the passing of the Angevin claims into the French royal house meant that the pretender was no longer a minor French lord but the king of France himself, who could draw on the resources of the whole kingdom to pursue his claim. Furthermore, the power of France had grown remarkably in the last half of the century.

Freed from the long war with England, France developed a standing army, a solid tax base, and a vigorous economy. Louis XI (1461–1483) had brought large pieces of territory under royal control, and now his son, Charles VIII, was eager for an adventure that would make him as famous as his father.

The young king was urged on not only by his own advisors but also by some Italians who had lost out in the feuds and quarrels of the fifteenth century. Chief among these were the Pazzi, who had transferred their banking business to Lyon after being exiled from Florence in 1478. They offered Charles the money to finance an expedition. The papal election of 1492 had been especially bitter, and the losing contender, Cardinal della Rovere (who in 1503 would become Pope Julius II), had fled to France to avoid being imprisoned or killed by Alexander VI. Della Rovere offered his full support to Charles and promised to confirm him as king of Naples — if the king would call a general council to depose Alexander.

Under these influences Charles decided to go to Italy with a large army and secure his claim to Naples. Now, however, the Italian powers began to realize their mistake. Charles crossed the Alps in 1494 with an army of thirty-two thousand men, and Ludovico, who had first invited him, could do nothing but greet him at the Milanese frontier. The passage of the army from the Alps to Naples was swift and calamitous. Charles' attitude toward war shocked the sensibilities of the Italians, who were used to relatively bloodless contests in which the fates of major states were decided in battles where only one or two soldiers died. The king's army butchered the first garrison that offered serious resistance, and after that no army in Italy was eager to face the French. Piero de' Medici, completely overawed and terrified, surrendered the key passes in the Apennines and permitted Charles to pass easily into the South. For his diplomatic ineptness as well as for his political mistakes, the Florentines drove Piero from Florence and reestablished a free republic. The French also won Alexander's permission to pass through the Papal States and reached the outskirts of Naples itself without fighting a major battle. Charles crossed the Alps on the ninth of September, and on February 21 he entered Naples.

For two centuries, the Italians had considered themselves the most cultured, sophisticated, diplomatically astute, and politically advanced people of Europe. The humiliation of Charles' invasion was intense. After the initial shock, the major powers banded together to expel Charles. A new Holy League was formed, this time including Maximilian, the Holy Roman emperor, and Ferdinand, king of a newly united Spain. In the meantime disease and discouragement had begun to spread in the ranks of Charles' army, and, threatened by the league, the king began a retreat from Naples. The army of the league actually caught Charles at Fornovo, but he managed to escape. In October of 1495, little more than a year after entering Italy, Charles arrived again in France. He had nothing to show for his expedition but a huge debt and a humiliating defeat. Italy had managed to unite and recover its independence.

But in throwing off the French, the Italian states sought the help of an even more dangerous ally. Spain was now involved in Italian affairs and, because of its strength, could defend the Aragonese claims to Naples better than France could prosecute those of the Angevins. Italy was for the moment free from foreign domination, but the twenty years after 1495 made clear that both France and Spain intended to make their influence felt and that Italians could hope for nothing better than a precarious balance between those two powers, whose military and economic might overshadowed Italy.

Charles' successor, Louis XII, was the great-grandson of Giangaleazzo Visconti and thus had claims on Milan as well as on Naples. In 1499 Louis invaded Italy and seized Milan from Ludovico Sforza, who had recently assumed the ducal title after the mysterious death of his nephew. Simultaneously King Ferdinand of Spain dispossessed his Neapolitan cousins and took the southern half of the peninsula for himself. Louis' brief attempt at protest ended in defeat at the battle of Garigliano in 1503. Both ends of Italy were now under foreign domination and would remain so for centuries.

Next it was the turn of Venice. The Venetians had been quietly taking Milanese territory while Milan itself fell to the French. In 1508, however, the pope, the dukes of Ferrara and Mantua, Louis XII, Maximilian, and Ferdinand allied against Venice and formed the League of Cambrai; later they were joined even by England. Venice was by far the most wealthy and powerful state in Italy, but even Venice could not prevail against the combined strength of so many foreign powers. Decisively defeated at Ghirad'adda, Venice displayed a wisdom in adversity unusual among great powers and agreed to give up all claims on the mainland in order to keep its overseas influence and commercial wealth intact. Venice survived in the sixteenth and seventeenth centuries, chastened and poorer, but with greater independence than any other Italian power.

When the war of the League of Cambrai ended in 1512, it was apparent that Italy's fate no longer lay in the hands of Italians. The next two decades determined that Spain, rather than France, would be the victor. Both Louis XII and his successor Francis I attempted to resist the steady growth of Spanish influence but failed. In the Treaty of Cambrai (1529), France gave up its claims on Milan and allowed the Sforza to return under the protection of Spain. In 1535 the last Sforza died without heir, and Spain assumed direct control. All French claims in Italy were definitively abandoned by the Treaty of Cateau-Cambrésis in 1559, and the Italian wars ended.

The invasions left Italy bankrupt, subjugated, and decadent. By 1600 Italy's economy had become predominantly agricultural, and little remained of the commercial and industrial activity that had made the region so important since the eleventh century. Spain governed Milan and Naples directly through a vicar; the Medici were restored to power in Florence by Spanish troops and given the title of dukes, but they ruled at Spanish sufferance; and the popes were preoccupied by fears of Protestantism. Under Alexander VI (1492–1503), Julius II (1503–1513), and Leo X (1513–1521), Rome had been the intellectual and artistic center of Italy. But in 1527 the city was sacked by unpaid and mutinous troops of the emperor. Italian cultural life never recovered from this calamity. Remarkably, however, the period from the first French expedition in 1494 to the final peace in 1559 was one of the most artistically and intellectually productive periods of Italian history. This will be the subject of the next chapters.

Bibliography

The best introduction to late fifteenth- and early sixteenth-century politics and diplomacy is Peter Laven's *Renaissance Italy: 1464–1534* (New York: Capricorn Books, 1967), which contains an excellent bibliography for further reading. Felix Gilbert has studied the Florentines' perceptions of the significance of the invasions in *Machiavelli and Guicciardini* (Princeton: Princeton University Press, 1965). Nicolai Rubinstein has shown the slow and tenuous development of the Medici domination in *The Government of Florence Under the Medici* (Oxford: Clarendon Press, 1966). See also his *Florentine Studies* (Evanston, Ill.: Northwestern University Press, 1968) for a collection of articles on various aspects of Tuscan history covering the entire period of the Renaissance. The classic work on diplomacy is Garrett Mattingly's *Renaissance Diplomacy* (Boston: Houghton Mifflin, 1955).

10 Thought and Letters: Machiavelli

Painters and writers of the High Renaissance shared to a large extent the values and the interests of their humanist predecessors but conveyed them with an impact that has excited the admiration of generations ever since. The source of this lasting appeal cannot be simply identified. In part, of course, it is the personal genius of individual creators, but they worked within the context of mechanical techniques and intellectual formulations that had been developed and refined by two centuries of artists and thinkers. The brilliant culmination in the High Renaissance can best be appreciated by a direct look at those works subsequent ages have most admired.

Ironically, none of these works is purely literary. The humanists were keenly aware of the meaning of words and the virtue of rhetoric, but they never produced a literature of really lasting appeal. Several fine poets of the sixteenth century did exercise a profound influence on their contemporaries in northern Europe. Ariosto's *Orlando Furioso* and Tasso's *Jerusalem Liberated* provided much of the thematic material for the Northern Renaissance. Baldassare Castiglione, mentioned earlier in connection with humanist education, described in elegant and well-turned phrases the educational ideals and courtly life of the Italian Renaissance and shaped the manners and schools of all Europe. But today we have little interest in Italian literature of the sixteenth century. Tasso and Ariosto are relegated to specialized courses in Italian literary history, and Renaissance playwrights are studied only because of their influence on Shakespeare.

The writer who is the major exception to their general neglect is seldom thought of as a literary figure. No Renaissance writer occupies a more secure place in the pantheon of great Western thinkers than Niccolò Machiavelli (1469–1527), but he is primarily known for his political thought rather than for his plays, poems, and novellas. Machiavelli is justly famous for his political maxims, but they are not found in any systematic treatise. They appear in common literary forms: commentaries on classical works, biographies, histories, and dialogues. Only the *Prince* is not a literary form typical of the period, but it too is unsystematic, indirect, and artful.

Machiavelli's avoidance of systematic statement has led to widely divergent interpretations of his thought. Beyond universal admiration for his originality and insight there is little agreement. Even his contemporaries found him puzzling, and his own friends disagreed sharply over the meaning of his words. To some he appeared as an open advocate of blatant immorality in the use of power. In Elizabethan England he was a personification of the Devil. In the eighteenth century such pragmatic rulers as Frederick the Great of Prussia wrote scathing attacks on his works — and thus were excused for closely studying his formulas for political success.

In the nineteenth century Machiavelli became the hero of the Italian independence movement, but under a different guise. He was viewed no longer as a diabolic schemer but as an ardent nationalist whose seemingly unscrupulous maxims were inspired by a desire to see Italy unified and strong. Most of the evidence for this interpretation comes from the last chapter of the *Prince,* where Machiavelli calls for a strong ruler to unite Italy and rescue the country from the grip of foreign invaders.

This romantic vision gave place to the twentieth-century image of a political realist, not advocating immorality but simply facing the political facts of life. In this guise Machiavelli became the founder of political science, the first to devise rational rules explaining how power functions. The various faces of Machiavelli tell us more about the ages who saw them than about the man himself, but they do suggest the breadth and subtlety of Machiavelli's mind. A man who could be one century's romantic nationalist and the next century's dispassionate analyst was at the very least a thinker of some complexity and probably did not wish to fit into a simple and systematic mold.

Machiavelli's distaste for abstract theory stems partly from his bent for practical politics. After the fall of the Medici in 1494, he served the Florentine republic in several capacities, but on the return of the family in 1512 he was tortured and exiled. Though he eventually returned to Florence, he never again held an important political post. He turned to writing only after his political interests had been frustrated, and he carried to his writing the active man's impatience with abstruse theorizing.

His political experience was not the only factor contributing to the practical wisdom of his works. Writing to an audience of Florentines thoroughly accustomed to humanist attitudes, he combined their interest in the ancient world with a conviction that the ancients could be made to speak more clearly to the problems of his own day. "When we consider the general respect for antiquity," he remarked at the beginning of the *Discourses,* his commentary on the first ten books of Livy's history of Rome,

> and how often . . . a great price is paid for some fragments of an antique statue, which we are anxious to possess to ornament our houses with . . . and when we see on the other hand the wonderful examples which the history of ancient kingdoms and republics presents to us, . . . more admired than imitated or so much neglected that not the least trace of this ancient virtue remains, we cannot but be at the same time as much surprised as afflicted.

The absence of a single, coherent political system is an integral part of Machiavelli's humanism. He is determined to see in detail the strengths and weaknesses of all governments and political policies. Thus he concentrates on particular cases rather than on abstract political forms. Machiavelli avoids a definite position even on the basic issue of whether a monarch or a republic is the better form of government. His two most important works, the *Prince* and the *Discourses,* seem to offer different answers. In the *Prince* he extolled the ability of a single ruler to make rapid decisions and carry out forceful policies, especially in foreign affairs. In the *Discourses,* without contradicting these advantages, he stressed that a republic has greater continuity and can command the energies of a committed and active citizenry in time of trouble. Most of his works are republican in sympathy and his own political experience testified to a deep republican commitment, but he still knew the weaknesses of a republic and was unwilling to construct a rigid system that would obscure them.

Machiavelli's greatest work and the basis of his fame is the *Prince.* Short, pithy, quotable, even outrageous, the book deals with the nature of princely governments and explains how a prince, by understanding the power he exercises, can survive its dangers and pitfalls. Few Renaissance works have remained so readable, and the *Prince* is indispensable for anyone who wants to understand the genius — as well as the limitations — of the period. The analysis presented here is intended as a guide to the book and not as a substitute.

The *Prince* was the first product of Machiavelli's fall and exile, written just after his release from prison while he was still adjusting to the inactivity and loneliness of his new life. In a touching letter to a friend still in favor with the Medici, he told how he consoled himself by working on his farm and reading the classics:

> When evening comes, I return home and go into my study, and at the door I take off my daytime dress covered in mud and dirt and put on royal and curial robes; and then decently attired I enter the courts of the ancients where affectionately greeted by them, I partake of that food which is mine alone and for which I was born. . . . I have written down what I have learned from their conversation in a short work "On Principalities."

A superficial glance at the *Prince* gives the impression that the book is full of hard-hitting, cynical, and thoroughly pragmatic maxims for seizing and holding power. But Machiavelli seeks to direct the reader's attention to more subtle issues. In his dedication he considers problems of perspective and viewpoint, noting that a prince is most clearly understood by a lowly subject, just as a landscape is more clearly seen from a distance. The issue of perspective is in fact crucial, for an analysis of many of the book's insights hinges on the ability to distinguish appearance from reality and understand the context of one's perceptions.

Just as the dedication only indirectly reveals the theme of the work, so the opening chapter suggests obliquely the novelty of Machiavelli's approach to political forms. He begins, "All states and dominions which hold or have held sway over mankind are either republics or monarchies." To modern ears this twofold division sounds overly simple, and Machiavelli's sixteenth-century readers would have felt it equally strange. Conventional wisdom accepted Aristotle's division of states into six types: monarchy, aristocracy, and democracy; and their corrupted counterparts, tyranny, oligarchy, and anarchy. Machiavelli himself uses this sixfold division in the *Discourses,* and by naming only two simple categories in the *Prince* he suggests that here he is talking about something new and different, something that transcends the traditional way of looking at governments. But he does not say so directly, only by implication. The reader must keep constantly alert for these implications to understand the author's true intent.

Again and again in the *Prince,* Machiavelli makes observations and generalizations that cannot easily be taken at face value. In a famous chapter on the Papal States, he notes that ecclesiastical governments, being maintained by God, do not follow the rules of normal states:

> These princes alone have states without defending them, have subjects without governing them, and their states, not being defended, are not taken from them; their subjects not being governed do not resent it, and neither think nor are capable of alienating themselves from them. Only these principalities, therefore, are secure and happy. But, as they are upheld by higher causes which the human mind cannot attain to, I will abstain from speaking of them: for being exalted and maintained by God, it would be the work of a presumptuous and foolish man to discuss them.

This seems clear enough, though such piety sounds strange on the lips of a man wise in the world's ways. But he does not stop there. He goes on to discuss the Papal States in detail and to discover that popes who acted like astute princes strengthened their dominions, whereas those who relied only on God weakened them. These details belie the chapter's thesis, but in so doing they confirm the rest of the book.

The ironic use of concrete details to convey the real point and contradict the ostensible rule is a favorite device of Machiavelli's. Because of it, at least one scholar has suggested that the *Prince* is really a satire, intended to castigate the Medici, who had ruined the author's political career. According to this thesis, suggested by Garrett Mattingly in 1955, Machiavelli sought to embarrass the Medici by showing that the rule of even the most brilliant and forceful princes could be short-lived. This argument has aroused little enthusiasm among Renaissance scholars, but it does emphasize the obvious importance of irony in Machiavelli's writing. When he wrote plays or histories, the forms themselves encouraged indirect and ambiguous expression, because the interaction of characters or the flow of narrative easily masked the author's opinion when he did not wish to reveal it. Even when writing in a form not so adapted to indirect expression, as in the case of the *Prince,* Machiavelli regularly forced the reader to find the true sense without the help of direct statements.

Machiavelli was not uncertain of his opinions or afraid to take definite positions. But like his humanist predecessors he felt that the truth was best found in particular perspectives, that its expression varied with time and historical circumstance, and that no systematic and abstract statement of reality could be complete and meaningful. The complexities of life demanded a subtle and flexible approach that could fully convey the contingent and varied color of life. Machiavelli sought to arrive at conclusions that by their tentative nature and lack of complete consistency more accurately expressed the truth. Thus his contribution to political thought does not lie in the pithy maxims that seem to be derived from first principles; his true thinking is a series of related insights, applied differently in different situations, but unified by a single humane perspective.

The viewpoint expressed in the *Prince* was novel for its day. The state, said Machiavelli, is a secular body, governed by rules that are not the same as those governing individuals. Dante had asked: what is the purpose of government and how does it fulfill the will of God? Machiavelli eschewed these questions and asked only how government was organized, how power was wielded, who made decisions, and who enforced them. His avoidance of teleological and moral questions completely undercut the conventional wisdom of his own day. Machiavelli was not indifferent to moral issues, but he was evidently convinced that they too should be approached indirectly through concrete, real situations. Therefore he turned to a practical consideration of how power is actually seized and held.

Of the twenty-seven chapters that comprise the *Prince,* the first fourteen describe how various states function. The author omits republics because he has treated of them elsewhere, presumably in the *Discourses,* and concentrates on monarchies. He carefully distinguishes different forms of monarchies — established ones, mixed ones in which new territory has been recently added to an established rule, and wholly new ones. He further distinguishes between states acquired by the prince's own arms and ability and those acquired by fortune or the help of others. The author is mainly concerned with the ease or difficulty of maintaining rule in these different sorts of monarchies, and in discussing the problem he also reveals the true basis of political power.

All states derive their strength and stability from the allegiance of the people, and allegiances differ in predictable ways among different kinds of states. Old and established monarchies are the easiest to maintain because the people have not experienced a change in their rulers and are not likely to think of one. Mixed monarchies are less stable, but if the newly acquired territory speaks the same language and observes the same laws and customs as the prince's own state, it will be easier to hold, because the subjects will not so much perceive that they are being governed by a new prince. A prince should in any case minimize changes made in the lives of his subjects. As might be expected, states that have lived under a former prince are easier for the new prince to rule, because the subjects are not accustomed to making their own laws, than are states that were formerly republics.

After showing how the attitudes of the people vary, Machiavelli next considers how power can be acquired and how it affects the stability of the prince's regime. If a ruler comes to power by his own strength, his state is more likely to be permanent; any prince who has the qualities necessary to seize power can probably keep it by the same qualities. By contrast, a prince raised to power by chance or the help of others is likely to be lacking in native talent and will fall at the first turn of fortune. These rules seem simple enough, but Machiavelli now says that there are two special cases — those who seize power by crime and those who are given it by their fellow citizens.

The purpose of the chapters on these two special cases is not immediately clear. In the first place, there is an apparent contradiction: those who became princes through crime have nevertheless achieved their goal through their own ability, while those raised up by their fellow citizens have received their power from others. Thus the special cases should fall into the categories already discussed, but Machiavelli says no. Their power is different and cannot be attributed entirely either to fortune or to ability. Of those who attain their states through crime he says, "It cannot be called ability (*virtù*) to kill one's fellow citizens, betray one's friends, be without faith, without pity, and without religion; by these means one may indeed gain power, but not glory." Of civil monarchies, in which the prince is elected by his fellow citizens, he observes, "To obtain this position depends not entirely on worth or entirely on fortune, but rather on cunning assisted by fortune." He explains that the cunning involves realizing that stable power must be based on the support of all the people and not just the nobles, for the people want only to escape oppression, whereas the nobles want power for themselves and will overthrow the man they have made prince as soon as an occasion arises.

Thus these exceptions to the earlier rules actually reinforce the notion that the strength and reality of the state rest on the allegiance of the people. The prince can use any means he likes to achieve his ends, but if the means do not bring him glory among his own people, his power will not be secure. Princes who rise by their own ability generally enjoy stable rule, but crimes committed in the process damage their reputation. Princes who depend on others usually rule precariously, but if they owe their position to their subjects, they should be safe. A prince who receives his power from the people is supported by the essential basis of the state.

Machiavelli is certainly not trying to elaborate a systematic theory of the general will or popular sovereignty. He is simply trying to show that in all types of states changes in the exercise of power can be traced to underlying changes in the attitudes and desires of the people who inhabit the state. He presents this position by implication rather than by direct statement, dealing with particular problems that arise in each kind of state and giving historical examples of the way these problems have been worked out.

In chapters ten through fourteen of the *Prince,* Machiavelli considers the relative strength of states. Again he insists on a strictly practical analysis. Strength is measured not by transcendental standards such as justice or the moral guidance of citizens but by economic wealth and military might: "I consider those capable of maintaining themselves alone who can, through abundance of men or money, put together a sufficient army, and hold the field against anyone who attacks them." But this definition is not so simple as it seems. Machiavelli discusses the various forms of military strength, noting that weak states include not only those that depend on stronger powers for protection but even those that use mercenaries to fight for them. A state that is really strong is defended by its own willing citizens. Thus a prince is strong and secure when his subjects are ready to fight for his cause. Military as well as political power ultimately rests on the people.

With this discussion Machiavelli completes his treatment of the nature of states, how they are acquired and maintained, and how their power is measured. In chapter fifteen he shifts his attention to the virtues characteristic of an effective prince and introduces the topic with one of his most famous passages:

> As I know that many have written of this, I fear that my writing about it may be deemed presumptuous, differing as I do, especially in this matter, from the opinions of others. But my intention being to write something of use to those who understand it, it appears to me more proper to go to the real truth of the matter than to its imagination, and many have imagined republics and principalities which have never been seen or known to exist in reality; for how we live is so far removed from how we ought to live, that he who abandons what is done for what ought to be done, will rather learn to bring about his own ruin than his preservation. A man who wishes to make a profession of goodness in everything must necessarily come to grief among so many who are not good. Therefore it is necessary for a prince, who wishes to maintain himself, to learn how not to be good, and to use this knowledge and not use it, according to the necessity of the case.

This passage has shocked or intrigued generations of readers, and it needs to be understood with great care. Machiavelli, who always maintains extraordinary control over his style, refrains from explicitly stating that the prince should act evilly. Instead he notes that the prince should learn *how* not to be good and *how* to use this knowledge. Likewise he does not say that anyone who is good will fail but that anyone who always professes to be good will fail. To be sure, these observations could lead to the conclusion that a prince should act without considering moral issues, but they can also mean that a prince should base his actions on a clear grasp of the real situation and place moral issues in the context of these realities. In order to see which conclusion is Machiavelli's own, we must look closely at the author's values and the intellectual tradition in which he was writing.

In the above passage Machiavelli makes a point of criticizing his predecessors for failing to understand what a state really is: "Many have imagined republics and principalities which have never been seen or known to exist in reality." When he noted that many have written on the subject of princely virtues, he was referring to the so-called mirrors of princes, the medieval handbooks for statesmen that listed the qualities of an ideal prince. These manuals paid little attention to the nature of the state over which the prince ruled and concentrated on his personal characteristics, stressing generosity, kindness, honesty, and fairness. Machiavelli, by devoting more than half of his book to an analysis of the state, could hardly have shown more clearly his feeling that the nature of the state is as important as the personality of the ruler. Now, having analyzed the state and come to some novel conclusions, he is prepared to write on the well-worn subject of princely virtue.

It should come as no surprise that Machiavelli relates personal virtue to the context in which it is implemented, for this mirrors the basic humanist approach to historical and philological criticism. Words, values, and maxims for the humanists had meaning only in particular contexts and could be understood only by searching out that context. Machiavelli claims to have identified politics as a new context, and because of this discovery traditional political virtues and vices must be reinterpreted. In other words, Machiavelli was developing a new morality that he thought superior to the old one because of its being based on reality and not just imagination.

This approach is closely related to the humanist concept of knowledge. If the reality of the state resides in the attitudes and desires of the people who inhabit it, then the prince is only as powerful and secure as he seems to his subjects. The reality of his rule lies in its appearance to those who are ruled. Just as the humanists sought the truth as it was perceived by particular people in a particular time and place, so Machiavelli understands power not as something absolute but as something perceived by particular people that shifts as their perceptions change. This is the central insight of the first part of the *Prince,* and in the second part Machiavelli brings it to bear on his reevaluation of the traditional princely virtues.

He begins with generosity, always considered a desirable trait in a prince. Machiavelli agrees, but he cautions his readers against the usual meaning of the term. Generosity, as the world understands it, will injure the prince. True inner liberality will not be known, and people will think the ruler miserly. Outer generosity, manifested in extravagant display, will force the prince to raise taxes, and his subjects will hate him. Machiavelli warns:

> A prince, therefore, not being able to exercise this virtue of liberality without risk if it be known, must not, if he is prudent, object to being called miserly. In the course of time he will be thought more liberal, when it is seen that by his parsimony his revenue is sufficient, that he can defend himself against those who make war on him . . . so that he is really liberal to all those from whom he does not take, who are

infinite in number, and niggardly to all to whom he does not give, who are few.

Machiavelli constantly shifts perspective here between the real and the imagined to bring his point home. Generosity is still a virtue but is real only when apparent to the people. Lavish expenditure might at first seem to be generosity, but in the long run it will make one appear — and hence be — a tyrant and a miser. The virtue remains; its meaning changes with context.

Next Machiavelli analyzes cruelty and kindness, and here too the appearance forms the reality. If the prince acts firmly at the beginning of his rule, keeping his subjects united and faithful by means that might otherwise be considered cruel, the ensuing stability of the state will engender less bloodshed and the prince will come to be considered merciful. In the end he is kind to his subjects by sparing them the disorders that might otherwise occur. The prince's initial cruelty will make him feared, but as long as the cruelty is not indiscriminate or prolonged, he will not become hated. Here again the virtue remains. The prince should be kind, but Machiavelli finds that the meaning of kindness changes when placed in context with the realities of political power.

The next virtue is good faith, and here Machiavelli explicitly introduces the problem of change, which underlies his treatment of states earlier in the *Prince*. The prince cannot truly keep his word without understanding the difficulties he faces and the fact that these difficulties are in constant flux. Machiavelli illustrates the point with one of his most striking metaphors. "A prince . . . must imitate the fox and the lion, for the lion cannot defend himself from traps and the fox cannot defend himself from wolves. One must therefore be a fox to recognize traps and a lion to frighten wolves." To keep one's word in all situations is to break faith with life. Because the prince is faced with a continually shifting challenge — now a subtle stratagem, now brute force — he must not keep his word when the context in which he gave it no longer exists.

The prince who breaks faith for these reasons will be understood and trusted, whereas the one who breaks it indiscriminately without regard for his own interests will be distrusted. The one who invariably keeps his word no matter what the situation will find that his faithfulness leads to ruin; he will never be able to develop a successful strategy. "Alexander VI," Machiavelli points out, "did nothing else but deceive men, he thought of nothing else and always found subjects for his deceptions. Never was a man so good at giving assurances and affirming promises with the strongest oaths. In spite of this his deceits always worked, since he knew this part of the world well." The last phrase is typical of the richness and ambiguity of Machiavelli's style. It implies that Alexander knew the rules for when to break faith and that he had also mastered the political realities of Italy. The maxims in the *Prince* cannot be applied in a vacuum. They all depend on the prudent assessment of a concrete situation. Nowhere does Machiavelli make this clearer than in this chapter. If the prince keeps faith with his own interests through an astute understanding of the problems he faces, and if he changes his word as these interests change, then he will appear to be faithful.

Machiavelli summarizes his account of princely virtues with a direct statement of his theme:

> It is not, therefore, necessary for a prince to have all of these qualities, but it is very necessary to seem to have them. . . . He must have a mind disposed to change as the winds of fortune and the variations of life command and, as I have said above, to stay with the good if he can but to know how to enter into evil if he must.

This passage by itself seems to justify Machiavelli's reputation as an advocate of blatantly immoral conduct, but in context with the previous discussion of the ambiguities of the traditional virtues and the subtle relationship between appearance and reality, it cannot be interpreted so simply. Machiavelli is dealing with different levels of morality, advocating conduct that traditionally would be considered evil but that in Machiavelli's transvaluation becomes virtuous.

The concluding chapters continue to stress the importance of the prince's reputation among the people. He must at all costs avoid being despised or hated, for hatred will make him vulnerable to conspiracy. His best fortress is the love of his people. Machiavelli briefly explains how a prince can gain a good reputation, why he should take counsel, and why he needs wise ministers. Finally he suggests that the princes of Italy who have lost their states have fallen because they were ignorant of the rules he has set forth.

In the next to last chapter of the *Prince* Machiavelli treats the subject of fortune and assures the reader that the foregoing maxims are not meant as a systematic and inflexible prescription for seizing and holding power. He refers to the power of fortune throughout the book, but here he makes himself quite clear. The prince will avoid many difficulties by following the author's precepts, but he must still be alert for those cases where the rules do not apply.

Circumstances beyond his control can bring all prudence and foresight to naught. Machiavelli has previously demonstrated the importance of taking particular circumstances into account, and in this chapter he stresses the point. At the same time he is quick to observe that although one cannot foresee everything, intelligent planning based on political insight will redound to the advantage of the prince:

> I would compare [fortune] to an impetuous river, that, when turbulent, inundates the plains, casts down trees and buildings, removes earth from this side and places it on the other; everyone flees before it, and everything yields to its fury without being able to oppose it; and yet though it is of such a kind, still when it is quiet, men can make provision against it by dikes and banks, so that when it rises it will either go into a canal or its rush will not be so wild and dangerous. So it is with fortune, which shows her power where no measures have been taken to resist her, and directs her fury where she knows that no dikes or barriers have been made to hold her.

The *Prince* is unquestionably Machiavelli's most powerful and effective work. Scholars may point to the greater complexity and depth of the *Discourses,* the maturity and balance of his *History of Florence,* and the dramatic excellence of the play *Mandragola,* but it is the *Prince* that has attracted avid readers ever since the sixteenth century and even today epitomizes Machiavelli for most people. Yet the *Prince* raises many questions it does not answer. The problem of human desires in particular is not really faced. Machiavelli bases the reality of his state on the desires of its citizens, but he scarcely comments on what basic human needs are, how they are formed, or how they may be manipulated. To pursue Machiavelli's thinking on these subjects we must turn to his other works.

Machiavelli slights these issues in the *Prince* not because he thought them unimportant but because the brevity of the book did not permit an adequate investigation. His conception of human nature would not have been satisfied by the tracing of every manifestation of human desire to one or two basic needs that express themselves invariably and inflexibly. Desires arise out of particular circumstances and are as varied as the circumstances that produce them. The *Prince* contains a number of aphorisms that seem to simplify the problem, but they lack universal applicability. For instance, the author says that the people want only not to be oppressed. This is too abstract to be very useful, and it immediately raises the question of what constitutes oppression. Machiavelli suggests a partial answer when he says people will tolerate losing their relatives and friends but not their property. We cannot be expected to take this literally, however, and furthermore the statement is contradicted at many other places in Machiavelli's works.

Because Machiavelli was unwilling to provide an abstract hierarchy of desires, he was constrained to analyze them in detail, showing the multiplicity of desires revealed by history and the varied means by which they can be manipulated. He found an excellent vehicle for this in the *Discourses,* a commentary on Livy's history of the early years of Rome, most of which Machiavelli wrote after the *Prince.* In it Machiavelli deals with such factors as religion, law, customs, greed, and avarice, all in the context of particular historical examples. His last work, completed shortly before his own death, was a history of Florence down to the death of Lorenzo de' Medici; it too afforded an opportunity to analyze how human needs manifest themselves. Machiavelli's comedies are also rich in insights. His most successful play, the *Mandragola,* involves a net of desires — an old man's desire for a son, a youth's desire for the old man's young and beautiful wife, a priest's desire for money, and a go-between's desire to serve the youth for reasons that never become quite clear. Machiavelli subtly develops the plot and interweaves these desires — each of which is satisfied in the end — to show his audience how human needs arise and how they may be fulfilled by stratagems or pure chance.

Machiavelli gave Italian Renaissance letters their finest expression. His epistemology and values came from his humanist predecessors, but he expressed them more cogently. Earlier humanists, less sure of the exact means for putting their critical method into practice, tended to write elaborate discussions of the method itself. Ironically, the humanist distrust of abstract truths was often expressed in cumbersome abstractions. But Machiavelli grasped the method and the viewpoint so thoroughly that he could confidently write of specific problems in concrete terms and still convey the deeper ambiguity of life. Thus instead of writing an abstract treatise about the impossibility of a systematic view of politics, he wrote the *Prince,* which is both precise and ambiguous. The impact of his writing clearly depends on his abandoning abstract and technical discussion in favor of vivid and concrete insight.

Through his concrete insights Machiavelli conveyed several ideas that have exercised a profound influence on later ages. First and most important, his picture of a secular state whose fundamental structure could be analyzed formed the basis of modern European political theory. Second, because in his view the basic realities of the state are psychological, he evaluated all social institutions by probing their psychological significance. This stance opened a new perspective on religion. Instead of asking whether the precepts of religion are true or false, Machiavelli asked what effect religion has on the strength of the state. Without denying the validity of Christianity, he looked at it in secular terms, criticizing its otherworldliness and praising the civic value of paganism. Third, Machiavelli showed his successors how to use history as an effective means of inquiry. The humanist search for a usable past culminated in his works.

Machiavelli also reminds us how important it is to look behind superficial meanings. It is easy to interpret the *Prince* as a simple recognition of political pragmatism and nothing more. But there was no need for Machiavelli to point out what was obvious in the sixteenth century as well as in our own. Nor was Machiavelli an extraordinary authority in the field; his political career, like Dante's, was a dismal failure. Machiavelli was profound not because he understood the ordinary side of life but because he looked at life and posed new questions. We in turn can understand his questions only in context with the intellectual tradition of which he was a part. Grasped in this framework, his ideas give us insight into dimensions of political experience that are not apparent in the ordinary course of life, and thereby they fulfill one of the most important functions of ideas. Ideas should enlarge our experience, not simply fit into our preconceived notions.

Bibliography

Roberto Ridolfi has written an excellent, readable biography of Machiavelli, *The Life of Niccolò Machiavelli,* trans. Cecil Grayson (Chicago: University of Chicago Press, 1963). Federico Chabod, *Machiavelli and the Renaissance* (New York: Harper and Row, 1965), has made the classic analysis of Machiavelli against the political background of Renaissance Italy. More recently J. R. Hale, *Machiavelli and Renaissance Italy* (New York: Collier Books, 1963), has discussed Machiavelli in this context, as has Cecil Clough on a more monographic level in *Machiavelli Researches* (Naples: Instituto universitario orientale, 1967). Herbert Butterfield, *The*

Statecraft of Machiavelli (New York: Collier Books, 1962), has analyzed the political elements of his thought, while very recently Sydney Anglo, *Machiavelli: A Dissection* (London: Gollancz, 1969), has questioned his originality. Felix Gilbert in *Machiavelli and Guicciardini* (Princeton: Princeton University Press, 1965), has studied Machiavelli's relationship to Florentine intellectual circles. In a stimulating but highly controversial article, Garrett Mattingly suggested that the *Prince* has to be understood less literally than has been the tendency among scholars: see Garrett Mattingly, "Machiavelli's Prince: Political Science or Political Satire?" *The American Scholar* 27 (1958): 482–491, reprinted in *Machiavelli: Cynic, Patriot, or Political Scientist?* ed. De Lamar Jensen (Lexington, Mass.: Heath, 1960).

The best translation of Machiavelli's basic works is Alan Gilbert's *Machiavelli: The Chief Works* (Durham, N.C.: Duke University Press, 1965). The *Prince* and the *Discourses* are more readily available in the Modern Library edition with an introduction by Max Lerner (New York: Random House, 1950). The *Prince* alone, translated by Thomas G. Bergin, is available in the Crofts Classics series (New York: Appleton-Century-Crofts, 1947). Machiavelli's plays and novellas have been translated by J. R. Hale, *Machiavelli, The Literary Works* (London: Oxford University Press, 1961). The *Mandragola* is available in *Eight Great Comedies* (New York: Mentor Books, 1958).

Douglas Radcliff-Umstead's *The Birth of Modern Comedy in Renaissance Italy* (Chicago: University of Chicago Press, 1969) provides an introduction to that field.

11 Graphic Arts

Patronage

The graphic arts are the most famous and long-lasting of Renaissance achievements. In no other age do they so clearly outstrip literature, philosophy, history, or music to stand in the minds of men as the symbol of an age's greatness. The very nature of the graphic arts explains in part this phenomenon. They may tell a story, yet need not commit themselves to a single unequivocal moral. They portray man in all the complex activities and moods of which he is capable, but the artist need not spell out the mood or evaluate the activity in precise hierarchical relationship to other moods. The artists of the High Renaissance took full advantage of this ability to communicate without systematic statement. In works of art they captured the full range of general humanity.

The aptness of painting, sculpture, and architecture for expressing humanist values is not the only factor contributing to the stature of these fields in the Renaissance. No discussion of Renaissance art can ignore the willingness of rulers and wealthy men to pay for works of art and support the many artists who produced them. Patronage is a vital aspect of Renaissance art.

The earliest patrons of the arts probably supported artists and writers to buttress their own shaky thrones or consciences. The della Scala of Verona, who supported Dante, or the early Visconti of Milan and the early Angevins of Naples, both of whom supported Petrarch, doubtless welcomed the adherence of famous intellectuals. Wealthy bankers, worried about the damage their commerce had done their souls, built churches and shrines so that their money would be spent to good end. But such negative reasons were not the only ones. Acceptance of personal glory as a worthy goal also encouraged men to want their names remembered. What better way than to commission an altarpiece that would bear the donor's name, or even contain in the corner of the painting a representation of him kneeling and worshiping, to be seen by all who would ever visit the altar?

Such simple reasons as the desire for glory, guilt, or concern for a recent, unstable title cannot explain the great outpouring of patronage that sustained artistic activity after 1400. In fact the early Medici, who were among the greatest of patrons, took pains to funnel their patronage through existing social institutions. Cosimo contributed through guilds and parish organizations. He supported the building of such monuments as the sacristy of San Lorenzo and the monastery of San Marco, but only as part of a collective venture. He gave heavily, as befitted a man of his wealth, but did not flaunt his affluence or seek to patronize as an individual. Art was a social phenomenon, expressing the values of society. Consequently society as a whole should be its patron. Cosimo gave from feelings of duty, but also out of a more positive, secular feeling that his wealth should serve the glory and beauty of his city. His descendants engaged in more individual patronage, but the scale of their contributions to art in Florence did not approach Cosimo's.

Another important center of patronge was Rome. The monuments of the Renaissance papacy — the Raphael rooms of the Vatican Palace, the frescoes of Michelangelo, the great Basilica of Saint Peter itself — are so well known that papal patronage seems entirely natural. But until the mid-fifteenth century the resources of the popes had gone for self-defense, administration, and charity. Nicholas V (1447–1455) was the first pope to maintain that the papacy should spend its money for its own worldly glory and in support of humanist ideals. He founded the Vatican library, financed numerous scholars — including Valla — and laid down a plan for the rebuilding of Rome. While few of the great Roman monuments can be traced to him, his is the vision that later and more famous popes carried out.

Three great popes of the High Renaissance are the most noted of papal patrons. All scandalized the religious reformers while making Rome the artistic center of Europe. Alexander VI (1492–1503) began this work by enlarging the Vatican Palace and commissioning several painters to decorate its rooms. The greatest of the patrons was the warrior pope Julius II (1503–1513). The man who led his own troops in battle also began the construction of Saint Peter's Basilica. He hired the greatest sculptors, painters, and architects to implement his grand design. His successor, the Medici pope Leo X (1513–1521), carried on Julius' work, decorating the Vatican Palace with some of the finest frescoes of the Renaissance. In addition to these major efforts in the Vatican, all three popes built lavishly throughout the city and surrounding countryside.

The most obvious motive for papal patronage is a plain, strong faith in the inherent value of art and letters. The popes could hardly feel guilty about the source of their money. Nor were they using spare capital. The money to patronize Renaissance artists was sought out with great vigor at no small cost. Saint Peter's was indirectly financed in part by the indulgence that aroused Luther's ire in 1517.

A final center of patronage was the republic of Venice. Even more than Florence, Venice regarded patronage as a civic duty. The state itself commissioned for its public halls frescoes that commemorated and glorified the great deeds of Venice's past and symbolized the historic independence of the republic. Lay patrons, religious communities, even courts in the towns subject to Venice, commissioned artists who made sixteenth-century Venice such a showplace of art.

Painting

In Machiavelli's writings the concerns and analytical perspectives of the Italian Renaissance were cast in a new light. During his career, painting achieved a similar breakthrough to a new style.

Because painting is visual, the transition from the old to the new can be seen with particular force. In fact, it is embodied in a single work. Verrocchio's *Baptism of Christ*. Verrocchio was a popular fifteenth-century painter and sculptor who, in accordance with common practice, designed the painting and executed the major figures, Christ and John the Baptist, but left the minor figures and peripheral details to his pupils. Thus, the two angels were done by students, and one of them gives us the first glimpse of High Renaissance style.

The angel on the left is subtly different from the other figures in the painting and appears to live and breathe in a way that the others do not. The angel is hardly more accurate; Verrocchio himself was a good student of human anatomy, and his paintings depict the

Baptism of Christ *by Verrocchio; Uffizi Gallery, Florence. Photo: Soprintendenza alle Gallerie, Florence.*

human body in all clarity. In part, the painter of the angel avoids bold outlines; he uses light and shade to suggest the form of the face — a technique known as *chiaroscuro.* Nevertheless, the genius of the figure cannot be simply explained by this technique or any other. This angel introduced a new era in Renaissance painting, and it is said that when Verocchio saw it he vowed to paint no more.

The pupil whose talent drove his master into retirement was Leonardo da Vinci (1452–1519), and the promise that Verrocchio discerned in him was fully realized. In the course of his long career Leonardo created a series of paintings still considered among the finest products of Western art. Leonardo's first full-scale work was the *Adoration of the Magi,* and, like many of his endeavors, it remained incomplete. Leonardo was so interested in solving new problems and exploring fresh subjects that he seldom had the patience to finish a painting down to the last detail. Even though the *Adoration* was displayed in Florence when it was still a sketch, its impact could hardly have been greater. Not only practicing artists but many citizens of the city came to study and admire it. For generations, painters from all over Europe, as well as Italy, copied it to absorb Leonardo's technique.

In order to grasp the true significance of Leonardo's achievement, we must examine the development of Italian painting during the fifteenth century. Giorgio Vasari, a sixteenth-century painter and historian of Renaissance art, identified a single major trend in Renaissance painting from Giotto in the early fourteenth century to the High Renaissance of the sixteenth. He felt that painters had discovered better, increasingly sophisticated techniques of physical description. The process culminated in the sixteenth century with an abundance of means for creating works of art that copied nature precisely. Until recently Vasari's interpretation was commonplace, but art historians now tend to see a more complex process at work

Adoration of the Magi *by Leonardo da Vinci; Uffizi Gallery, Florence. Photo: Soprintendenza alle Gallerie, Florence.*

Virgin and Saint Anne *by Masaccio; Uffizi Gallery, Florence. Photo: Soprintendenza alle Gallerie, Florence.*

in the early Renaissance. Where Vasari saw only increased realism, present-day historians note two important poles of artistic development, only one of which was concerned with exact naturalism.

The so-called monumental school was indeed devoted to the accurate description of nature, and especially of the human body. Masaccio's (1401–1429) *Virgin and Saint Anne,* the earliest and probably the greatest representative of the school, provides an interesting contrast to the works of Leonardo. Masaccio was clearly more schematic, and thus he seems less penetrating and personal than Leonardo. The techniques by which painters in the monumental style sought to achieve a convincing naturalism were more conceptual than directly sensory. Instead of describing nature by realistic details, they sought to depict a framework that related the figures in the painting to one another in a way that convinced the viewer that he was witnessing a three-dimensional scene. The monumentalists devised mathematical rules to govern the placement of objects and the proportions of parts of the body. These were first concisely stated toward the middle of the fifteenth century by Leon Battista Alberti (1404–1472), but early in the century Masaccio displayed a taste for conceptual naturalism that antedated Alberti's theory of fixed perspective. In the *Saint Anne,* he systematically foreshortened the throne and the figures' limbs to create a sense of real space in which the various parts of the painting could be related to one another.

Masaccio not only used the technique of perspective more rigidly than Leonardo; he also seemed overwhelmed by an interest in physical description. In his paintings, spiritual realities take second place, though this is not to say that Masaccio lacked power. Most of his works testify to the power that a physical description of nature can convey, as do the works of other great painters in the monumental style. In the hands of lesser artists, however, the monumental style became an empty exercise in technique, a dull pattern of architectural forms framing blandly accurate renditions of the human form.

But a style that lacked a conspicuous interest in physical description thrived by the side of the monumental style during the fifteenth century. Because it was influenced by the art of northern Europe, it has been called the international style. Vasari considered painters who practiced this style reactionaries who impeded the progress of Renaissance art and contributed nothing of significance to its development. Modern historians find that these painters intended to convey and embellish spiritual values the monumental painters ignored, and thus their paintings have qualities the more naturalistic paintings lack. Gentile da Fabriano's (1370–1427) *Adoration of the Magi,* for instance, is not concerned with uniform perspective or accurate physical description. Instead, Gentile used both human and animal forms as decorative ornaments to emphasize the spiritual significance of the scene. He was content simply to indicate the figures through established conventions, so that we merely recognize them as men, dogs, or horses. His real interest lay in rich colors, graceful lines, and intricate designs. Whereas Masaccio accurately models the human body by the draping of the robes, Gentile's robes are almost purely decorative. He conceives of the Adoration not as a physical meeting between the Magi and the Virgin and Christ Child but as a glorious, miraculous event in which the rich and powerful of the world adore the humble infant who is the heavenly king. If we concentrate only on Gentile's literal accuracy as compared to that of the monumental school, we lose the spiritual strength of his style.

These two poles of artistic style, the monumental and the international, seldom fused during the fifteenth century, and most painters can be readily identified with one side or the other. On the eve of Leonardo's *Adoration,* both styles coexisted in Florence. Domenico Ghirlandaio (1449–1494) provides an excellent example of the mature monumental style. For him the simple description of the human body and its physical surroundings constituted a sufficient reason for painting a picture. The figures in his *Adoration* are virtually without flaw or distortion; they are grouped in regular geo-

Adoration of the Magi *by Gentile da Fabriano; Uffizi Gallery, Florence. Photo: Soprintendenza alle Gallerie, Florence.*

Adoration of the Magi *by Domenico Ghirlandaio; Church of the Innocents, Florence. Photo: Alinari-Scala.*

metrical patterns; the perspective is drawn with mathematical precision. But unlike Masaccio, Ghirlandaio did not use these techniques as a means to study the shapes and interrelationships in nature; they became mere conventions that helped him organize his material without the strain of having to invent a unique, personal organization for each painting.

Sandro Botticelli (1444–1510), a contemporary of Ghirlandaio and also active in Florence, painted in the international style. His *Adoration* is more fanciful than Ghirlandaio's. The lines of perspective are broken. Although the central figures are grouped in a triangle, the painting as a whole does not fit into a simple geometrical form. Botticelli, like Gentile da Fabriano, was striving to communicate the emotional and spiritual significance of the scene. He clearly had a greater command of the tools of physical description than did Gentile, but when he felt the need to express intense emotion he abandoned accurate physical description and distorted or decorated his figures to make them more expressive. He evidently felt that the spiritual impact of his painting was lessened by rigid adherence to physical description as dictated by the conceptual rules of the monumental style.

These trends in fifteenth-century art give significance to Leonardo's achievement. Leonardo managed to convey the spiritual and emotional intensity of Botticelli without sacrificing the accuracy of physical description exemplified by Ghirlandaio. Leonardo's *Adoration,* unlike Botticelli's, immediately conveys its geometrical simplicity: a triangle imposed on a semicircle. Yet the painting is not mere physical description. Leonardo used his mastery of perspective to impose a clear structure on the work yet simultaneously distort the details and figures in such a way that the viewer is moved to awareness of the intangible dimensions of the scene. Spiritual values are not sacrificed; they are heightened and stressed.

Adoration of the Magi *by Sandro Botticelli; Uffizi Gallery, Florence. Photo: Soprintendenza alle Gallerie, Florence.*

Virgin and Saint Anne *by Leonardo da Vinci; Louvre, Paris. Photo: Réunion des Musées Nationaux.*

Leonardo combined the vitality and spiritual awareness of the international style with the rational order of the monumental style in order to study human communication. His interest in this problem is hardly surprising. Communication was a constant source of fascination at every stage of the Renaissance, from Petrarch's attempt to converse with the ancients to Machiavelli's concern for how the prince communicates his power to his people. Leonardo's interest is clearly expressed by the intimacy with which the central figures of the *Adoration* interact. It is even more unmistakable in his *Virgin and Saint Anne.* Here again the picture does not convince of its reality through physical accuracy. No human bodies could actually assume these poses. Instead Leonardo has subordinated physical details to the conceptual structure binding the people together. Within the structure he has portrayed the emotions of each figure in a way that is individual and yet expresses feelings common to all mankind. Leonardo's Virgin is not an abstract symbol of motherhood but an actual woman who leaves no doubt about her individuality, yet Leonardo conveys through her a sensitivity to the universal values and emotions associated with motherhood. By exalting the passions of particular people he identified the general canons of human feeling and touched the common humanity that is the basis for all communication.

Leonardo's achievement inspired others to imitate him, and in the generation following the *Adoration* his style was taken up and developed by several artists of genius. Among them were two of the greatest painters of the High Renaissance: Raphael (1483–1520) and Michelangelo (1475–1564). Michelangelo, a pupil of Ghirlandaio, maintained the definite lines and massive forms of Ghirlan-

School of Athens by *Raphael; Stanza della Segnatura, Vatican Palace, Rome. Photo: Archivio Fotografico delle Gallerie e Musei Vaticani.*

daio's monumental style, while introducing an energy that his master had never had. Raphael was the broadest and most catholic of the great painters of the High Renaissance. His works depict a wide variety of human emotions — the deep religious feeling of the Madonnas, the intense personal individuality of the portraits, the complex discourse of the murals, such as the *School of Athens,* in the Vatican Palace. These three great painters, Michelangelo, Raphael, and Leonardo, though they differed in personal interests and even in the way they solved the problems of design and execution, all had one characteristic in common: they subordinated physical detail to the overall structure of their paintings. They portrayed the human spirit in general terms that could be easily seen in their subjects, who are idealized even while they remain individuals.

Part of the genius of High Renaissance art lay in the ease with which lesser painters could imitate the style without sacrificing their individuality. Earlier, the lesser fifteenth-century painters who modeled themselves on the great practitioners of the monumental style produced works in which the personality of the artist was completely lost, and their paintings seem to be the mechanical product of a set of rules rather than the result of human creativity. High Renaissance style did not exact such a toll of its followers. The early sixteenth century abounded in painters who produced works of technical excellence that nevertheless convey the unmistakable stamp of the artist's personality.

The power of High Renaissance art also lay in the fact that it attacked problems of general and long-standing concern to men of the age: human communication, the inner structure and order of nature, the meaning of mankind. It shunned solutions that were abstract and generalized. Instead it depicted particular individuals so real that they seemed to live and breathe, but whose individuality was suffused with a sense of universal humanity. Leonardo achieved this goal by departing from his predecessors just as Machiavelli had departed from his. Both men could be vivid and concrete without sacrificing their awareness of underlying principles. Both were so confident of their technique that they felt no need to explain principles abstractly and directly; they knew how to make the particular speak for them.

Architecture and Sculpture

Architecture and sculpture passed through a development similar to that of painting. The fifteenth century seemed to move toward certain goals and to strive for the solution of definite problems, while the sculptors and architects of the early sixteenth century felt a sense of achievement and synthesis. Renaissance sculpture and architecture were aided by the availability of classical models: while no Roman painting survived into the fifteenth century, Roman ruins and some late Roman sculpture could be used for direct imitation. The relative precocity of sculpture and architecture can also be explained in practical terms. Just to make a building or a piece of sculpture support itself requires insight into the essence of the medium. These arts presented immediate, stimulating problems beyond the purely decorative or expressive ones.

The aims and achievements of fifteenth-century architecture are best illustrated by Filippo Brunelleschi (1377–1446) and Leon Battista Alberti (1404–1472). Brunelleschi was trained as a goldsmith and approached his work as a craftsman. Without much of an education (he could not read Latin) Brunelleschi immersed himself in the practical details of construction, not only designing the form of the edifice but also inventing machines for more efficient movement of the building stones. He clearly perceived also that classical architecture was based on simple proportions among all the dimensions of a building, from the diameter of a column to the length, width, and height of the whole structure.

His most famous achievement was the dome of the Florentine cathedral. This was the first dome since ancient times constructed without using a wooden skeleton for support during the building. Brunelleschi applied to the problem both his practical genius and his study of the Roman Pantheon, the only such classical dome still standing in the fifteenth century. The Florentine dome is more pointed than classical domes, because of structural problems, but Brunelleschi understood and liked classical decorative motifs. He used them in the churches and chapels he constructed throughout Florence. These, such as the churches of Santo Spirito and San Lorenzo, are built according to the classical rules of proportion and use such classical motifs as columns, rounded arches, and hemispherical domes.

If Brunelleschi was a practical craftsman, Alberti was a highly educated theorist who "built" some of his most famous monuments by correspondence, without either visiting the site or talking with the masons doing the work. Alberti developed an architectural theory (he also developed a theory of fixed perspective for painters) in his work *De Re Aedificatoria* (1452). By studying the recently discovered architectural classic of the first-century Roman Vitruvius, Alberti produced a complete statement of Roman architectural theory, including a sophisticated discussion of proportion. Yet his own buildings are often tied to earlier, medieval forms and lack the great daring of Brunelleschi. Alberti did not understand all the principles of classic architecture. Like all men of the Renaissance, he had never seen a Greek building. Consequently, he thought that columns were only decorative additions to a straight wall that bore the weight. Thus the church he designed at Rimini, which was the first Renaissance attempt to use classical principles for the façade of a Christian church, used columns only for decoration. The church

Saint Peter's Church in Montorio designed by Bramante. Photo: Alinari-Scala.

was classical only in the sense that its dimensions were proportional to one another.

In the High Renaissance, classical motifs and classical proportions were synthesized by Bramante (1444–1514), who, after an early career in Milan, did his finest work in Rome. His most famous building is a small circular church called Saint Peter's in Montorio. In that work Bramante fully evoked the classical style. Its proportions are simple and visually satisfying (the height is exactly the same as the width). The classical columns are accurately reproduced, and the building has a monumental power that belies its size. Saint Peter's in Montorio became for architects what Leonardo's *Adoration of the Magi* was for painters. Men came to Rome to study and imitate it, and the great architect Palladio of the late sixteenth century used it as the only Renaissance structure other than his own fit to illustrate the highest principles of classical architecture.

In sculpture, the early and mid-fifteenth century was a period dominated by the Florentine Donatello (1386–1466), who produced the first free-standing statues Europe had known since antiquity. A free-standing statue must not only balance a vertical mass of stone; it must do so in such a way that the body looks as though it is actually standing at rest. To solve these problems Donatello recovered the position known as *contrapposto,* in which the weight is more on one knee than on the other and the hips are slanted slightly in an opposite direction from the shoulders. Statues successfully sculpted in this form have a presence that few other stone or bronze figures can have, and Donatello's works stand with the most vital sculptures of any age. He is probably the artist of the fifteenth century who most successfully recaptured the greatness of the ancient world.

Sculptors after Donatello, particularly Antonio del Pollaiuolo (1431–1498) and Verrocchio, concentrated on deepening their detailed knowledge of the human anatomy. Pollaiuolo may have been the first artist to dissect human bodies. Their works tend to portray every vein and muscle as clearly and accurately as possible. Verrocchio, who was more famous as a sculptor than as a painter, sculpted a condottiere on horseback in imitation of an earlier one by Donatello. Verrocchio's possesses the grace and balance of Donatello's but shows the anatomical features of both horse and man in greater detail.

Again, the High Renaissance witnessed a synthesis of fifteenth-century achievements and interests. Michelangelo, the greatest sculptor of the High Renaissance, studied anatomy, like Pollaiuolo, but considered the concept or style of the work to be more important. For him sculpture was a branch of design, and the most challenging work of sculpture lay in the solution of conceptual problems. Thus, like Leonardo, he finished few of his works. As soon as he had arrived at a conception of his work, he grew bored with it and looked for new worlds to conquer.

Michelangelo was even more authoritative a model in his field than Leonardo and Bramante were in theirs. His early works, the *Pietà* in Saint Peter's Basilica (1498) and the *David* (1504), were the models for nearly all subsequent sculpture of the High Renaissance. They combined anatomical accuracy with classical rules for proportion and posture. In them Michelangelo produced an idealized, living humanity and captured the goal of exalted human communication as surely as Leonardo had captured it in the *Virgin and Saint Anne.*

Michelangelo was the true universal artist of the Renaissance. Though sculpture was his forte, he was also a superb painter and architect. After the death of Bramante, the architect originally chosen by Julius II to design Saint Peter's Basilica, Michelangelo took up the work and constructed the dome, modeling it on Brunelleschi's Florentine dome. All means of human expression — even poetry — gave him opportunity to convey his personality and his genius, both to his own contemporaries and to all who followed.

Bibliography

D. S. Chambers has put together an interesting collection of documents relating to patronage — *Patrons and Artists in the Italian Renaissance* (Columbia: University of South Carolina Press, 1971). For a good discussion of Medici patronage see E. H. Gombrich, "The Early Medici as Patrons of Art," in *Italian Renaissance Studies*, ed. E. F. Jacob (London: Faber and Faber, 1960), pp. 279–311.

H. W. Janson's *History of Art* (Englewood Cliffs, N.J.: Prentice-Hall, 1965) is a good starting place for those who want a general history of art. For more specialized studies on the art of the Renaissance, Bernard Berenson's classic *Italian Painters of the Renaissance* (London: Phaidon Press, 1953) is still readable and gives a sensitive appreciation of the field (a less lavishly illustrated edition is available in a Meridian paperback). See also Andre Chastel's *The Flowering of the Renaissance,* trans. J. Griffin (New York: Odyssey Press, 1965). The interpretation of artistic developments presented both here and in the following chapter owes much to Sydney Freedberg's *Painting of the High Renaissance in Rome and Florence* (Cambridge: Harvard University Press, 1961). See also Freedberg's *Painting in Italy, 1500–1600* (Harmondsworth, Middlesex: Penguin Books, 1971). The relationship of art and society has been treated by Arnold Hauser, *The Social History of Art* (New York: Vintage Books, 1961), and with more particular reference to Florentine art by Frederick Antal, *Florentine Painting and Its Social Background* (London: K. Paul, 1948). The classic study of Leonardo da Vinci is still Kenneth Clark's *Leonardo da Vinci: An Account of His Development as an Artist* (Cambridge: The University Press, 1939).

For a clear and readable account of Renaissance architecture, see Peter Murray, *The Architecture of the Italian Renaissance* (New York: Schocken Books, 1963). John Pope-Hennessey's *Italian Renaissance Sculpture* (London: Phaidon Press, 1958) and his *Italian High Renaissance and Baroque Sculpture* (London: Phaidon Press, 1963) are excellent guides to sculpture. The classic study of Michelangelo is Charles de Tolnay, *Michelangelo,* 5 vols. (Princeton: Princeton University Press, 1943–1960).

12 The End of the Renaissance in Italy

The Italian Renaissance was an outlook on the world. Beginning in the city-states of the Po valley, the Renaissance was shaped by Petrarch and Boccaccio into an identifiable, conscious movement. Renaissance humanists were bound together by common concerns and interests: history, philological criticism, and the classics; and underlying these concerns was their shared belief in the moral and practical worth of their learning. To some, like Petrarch, the value of learning was personal, but more commonly the humanists were committed to the moral uplift of society and politics.

During the fifteenth century humanists devoted their efforts to creating techniques for implementing their concerns. They learned to interpret accurately the writings of the past, and they refined the techniques of imitation as a means of bringing the insights of the past to bear on the problems of their own time. They established an educational program to make this new wisdom available to future generations. The culmination of their efforts was the High Renaissance, which drew on the achievements of its predecessors and created a powerful synthesis out of the manifold elements of earlier humanism.

The Renaissance sensed that human experience has coherence and unity, unity that could be perceived in the details of history and personal relations. This unity was at once too simple to need elaborate abstract formulation and too complex to be fully comprehended by any possible philosophical system. The painters of the High Renaissance expressed this outlook most graphically in their forceful portraits of individuals, portraits that also conveyed an exalted and generalized humanity. One might expect such an achievement to be long-lasting, but it was not. At precisely the point when this long-sought goal was reached, a new style appeared that appropriated the techniques of the High Renaissance without sharing its sense of

Deposition from the Cross *by Rosso Fiorentino; Museo Civico, Volterra.
Photo: Soprintendenza alle Gallerie, Florence.*

common humanity. This new style, called mannerism, or more
accurately anticlassicism, appeared in Italy shortly after the death
of Raphael in 1520. It signified more than just the arrival of a new
generation of painters, and indeed some of the foremost mannerists
were also the great artists of the High Renaissance, notably Michelangelo, who led the way in mannerist sculpture and architecture.

The peculiar way painters in this style turned away from the High Renaissance casts light on how the Italian Renaissance came to an end. One of the earliest mannerist painters was Rosso Fiorentino (1494–1540), who was trained by one of the lesser painters of the High Renaissance. Despite this background Rosso introduced tension and distortion into his paintings that contrast strikingly

Deposition from the Cross *by Pontormo; Santa Felicità, Florence. Photo: Soprintendenza alle Gallerie, Florence.*

with the balance and harmony of the earlier style. The distortion was not due to lack of technique but was deliberate. Rosso's masterpiece, the *Deposition from the Cross,* depicts anatomical details accurately enough; in fact the individual figures are no more distorted than many seen in Leonardo's paintings. What is unnatural and strained in Rosso's work is the design and conception. Leonardo distorted the bodies of Saint Anne and the Virgin to give unity and balance to the work. Rosso altered his figures to destroy the sense of harmony and prevent the viewer from seeing the painting as a clear and simple whole.

As the harmonious balance of Leonardo generalizes his work, so the distortion of Rosso makes each of his works seem unique and individual. The conceptual structure of his paintings does not manifest accepted geometrical forms, like the triangle that unites the figures in Leonardo's *Virgin and Saint Anne.* Instead, Rosso expresses his individuality through a structure that has no simple point of reference. In this he is typical of mannerist painting, where the unnatural poses, violent movements, and distorted forms all reinforce the disharmony of design. By themselves the details might fit into any High Renaissance painting, but taken together they express a new style in which the painter is seeking to convey his own personality in all its subjective nuances rather than portray the universal canons of humanity.

The subjective and intensely individual nature of mannerist art is even plainer in another *Deposition from the Cross* painted by Rosso's contemporary Pontormo (1494–1556). Once again we see the tension of line and the artificiality of form that contrast strangely with the descriptive naturalism of the details. Pontormo evidently felt unduly constrained by the harmony and geometrical simplicity that was so liberating to the artists of the preceding generation. Although the figures in his *Deposition* can be almost grouped into a circle, Pontormo breaks the lines of the circle to force attention on the stark poses of the individuals. It seems that they are interacting with one another less than trying to speak to the viewer. The painter even depicted himself on the far right-hand side of the painting looking out at the viewer, as a final measure of subjective identification. Pontormo sought to communicate without using intermediaries of form or convention. He did not give us a general reality through a particular perspective; he supplied only the particular perspective. Refusing to communicate through common humanity, he expressed his own soul as his closest approach to reality and as the most effective way of reaching the viewer.

Vertumnus and Pomona *by Pontormo; Poggio a Caiano. Photo: Alinari-Scala.*

Accompanying this heightened subjectivity was a new sense of the painting itself. Painters had striven for generations to create the illusion that the two-dimensional surface was really three-dimensional, that the viewer was looking at a real scene rather than at the canvas and wood on which it was drawn. With the advent of the mannerist style painters cast that goal aside. They began to regard the picture as a two-dimensional plane whose only reality lay in its expression of the painter's soul. In Pontormo's *Vertumnus and Pomona,* painted in a lunette at the Villa Careggi, the artist took great pains to reduce the sense of depth by filling the open spaces with leaf patterns and drawing bodies that seem to be confined to the two-dimensional world defined by the architecture rather than by conceptual space. The aestheticism of this approach reached its high point with the frescoes that Giulio Romano (1499–1546), a pupil of Raphael, painted in the Vatican Palace. Painting on a flat wall, he drew a battle scene on a simulated tapestry within an architectural frame. By this device he presented his viewer with the exaggerated artificiality of an art imitating another art within the form of a third.

The fine arts were not the only area in which Renaissance sensibilities and values were abandoned in the mid-sixteenth century. A similar change can be discerned in one of the most enigmatic literary works of the period: Francesco Guicciardini's *History of Italy*. The Guicciardini family was an established Florentine house, and Francesco (1483–1540) was active in Florentine politics before entering the service of the Medici popes. He was a close friend of Machiavelli's, though wealthier and more successful. Guicciardini's chief work was a history of Italy from the French invasions in 1494 to the death of Clement VII in 1534. It was a vast work comprising many volumes and occupied most of Guicciardini's attention during his last years; many have compared it in scope and execution to the great histories of Thucydides and Tacitus.

Despite these flattering comparisons, the *History of Italy* has never attracted the wide readership that Machiavelli's works have enjoyed. This is due in part to its overwhelming length, but that is not the only reason. A reader interested in the Italian wars is likely to want not only an account of the events but also an interpretation of their significance. Therein lies the difficulty of Guicciardini's work, for although he provides a wealth of meticulous detail, he fails to present a unified, coherent explanation of either the war's causes or its results. The reader cannot clearly grasp why Italy lost its independence or what lessons for future generations might lie in the Italian experience. Indeed, Guicciardini seems hardly to have cared whether similar disasters could be prevented; he was concerned only with describing this particular one. It is as if his consciousness of the larger world had been destroyed along with Italy's independence, and thus the prospect of future repetition was now meaningless for him. In other words, Guicciardini's perspective was as purely personal and subjective as Rosso's or Pontormo's.

In analyzing the disaster, Guicciardini focused not on underlying patterns of change but on change itself. His history begins on a note of unpatterned and uncontrollable movement:

> It will appear from countless examples how unstable are human affairs — like a sea driven by the winds; how pernicious, nearly always to themselves but invariably to the common people, are the ill-judged actions of rulers when they pursue only vain error or present greed. And forgetting how often fortune changes, and converting to other people's harm the power vested in them for public good, they become through lack of prudence or excess of ambition the authors of fresh upheavals.

Guicciardini's reference to the general instability of human affairs was merely conventional in the sixteenth century, but the way he illustrates that instability is remarkable. Although he immediately pulls the reader into specific examples that suggest causation through guilt and error, he does not stop to assess the relative importance of alternate causes and refuses to pass moral judgment.

Guicciardini habitually announces important events by listing a series of related events. For instance, he describes the first entry of French troops into Italy by saying,

> The king entered Asti on September 9, 1494, bringing with him into Italy the seeds of innumerable disasters, terrible events, and change in almost everything. His invasion was not only the origin of changes of government, subversion of kingdoms, devastation of the countryside, slaughter of cities, cruel murders, but also new habits, new customs, new and bloody methods of warfare, diseases unknown until that day.

The disease referred to was an epidemic of syphilis, the first ever in Europe, that began among the French troops besieging Naples. Guicciardini uses it as a metaphor for the foreign invasions, and the appropriateness of the metaphor is evident in the short passage that describes its outbreak:

> After our account of other matters, it does not seem unworthy to report that at this period — when it was Italy's fate that all her ills should originate with the French invasion or should at least be attributed to them — the disease which the French called "the Neapolitan sickness" and the Italians commonly called *buboes* or "French sickness," made its first appearance.

The French caught this disease in Naples, and they spread it all over Italy on their way home to France. It was either quite new or until this time entirely unknown in our hemisphere except in its most remote parts and was for many years so horrible that it deserves to be mentioned as a grave disaster. It showed itself either in hideous boils which often became incurable sores, or with intense pains in the joints and nerves all over the body. The doctors, who knew nothing about the disease, did not employ suitable remedies but quite often wrong ones which made the symptoms much worse. Many people of every age and sex died from it, and many others were hideously deformed and became helpless and subject to almost continual agonies of pain. Indeed most of those who appeared to have recovered in a short time fell again into the same misery. However, after many years the influence of the stars which had made the disease so virulent was mitigated or the appropriate cures for it became known through long experience, and it became much less malignant.

It had of its own accord also produced several types different from the first form of the disease. This was a calamity of which the men of our age might the more reasonably complain if it had fallen upon them without any fault of their own: for it is agreed by all those who have closely observed the characteristics of the disease, that it never, or hardly ever, occurs save by contagion in coitus. Yet one should rightly remove this smirch from the French name, because it was later seen that the disease had been brought from Spain to Naples and was not characteristic of that nation but brought in from those islands which, as we shall narrate at some more appropriate moment, began to be known to our hemisphere during those years through the voyages of a Genoese, Christopher Columbus. In those islands, however, this malady finds a prompt remedy through the benevolence of nature; for they cure it easily, simply by drinking the juice of a tree distinguished for its many remarkable properties.

Despite the intricate detail of this passage, the reader finds it impossible to come to a clear understanding of the causes of the epidemic. For every explanation of its origin, course, or disappearance, Guicciardini cites an alternative that negates the first. Either it was brought by the French, or it was simply blamed on them; either a cure was discovered, or it disappeared of its own accord. Guicciardini is unqualifiedly certain only that those whose profession it is to understand diseases could not deal with it and only made it worse. Otherwise he avoids deciding among the possible causes and instead concentrates on describing the incidence and symptoms. These raise no problem of causality and hence can be discussed without suggesting larger patterns. Even his moral stand is ambiguous. He observes that the disease is apparently transmitted by sexual contact, but carefully qualifies the statement to allow for exceptions.

Like the ravages of syphilis, the affliction of the foreign invasion has complex origins, and its causes are manifold and ambiguous. The historian feels that the French brought disaster with them, but admits that the diplomatic situation that permitted them to enter the country so easily was a long-standing fault of the Italians. He cannot decide whether the foreigners finally left because of their own mistakes or because the Italians had united to expel them. Although he does not blame the Italian rulers for losing their states, he is nevertheless sure that most of them had been playing the dangerous game of diplomacy — except for some who had not. In short, Guicciardini cites a myriad of possible causes for the invasions but can point to none that was fundamental. He narrates events in the most concrete terms possible without indicating a framework for understanding them or a morality for judging them.

Guicciardini's ambiguity is totally unlike that of Machiavelli, whose warning that the prince should look well to circumstances and be mindful of fortune was not due to doubt about the fundamental structure of the prince's state. Machiavelli was sure that he understood the rules of politics, but realized that one cannot apply general rules to every particular case. Nor does Guicciardini share the suggestive ambiguity of Leonardo da Vinci. The most sophisticated art critic would find it impossible to state every emotion and inner relation expressed by Leonardo's *Saint Anne*. Nevertheless, even the casual viewer instantly recognizes that the figures in the painting portray feelings and behavior common to all mankind. Guicciardini, by contrast, seems unaware of the existence of general canons; he can see no coherence in experience beyond the superficial relations of one event to another.

We search his works in vain for the hallmark of Renaissance humanism, the sense of general principles and common humanity tying together the complexity of particular events. Turning away from general rules, he bent his energies to a thorough research into the documents so that the past could be recorded accurately in its minutest detail. Guicciardini's public life shows that he shared the belief of his social class in the value of political action. But he did not express that belief in his intellectual life. Indeed, he came to doubt the existence of any of the general rules bequeathed to him by the labor of generations of humanists. He was left with only his own personal vision to communicate directly to his reader.

The absence of the basic humanist notion of universality in the work of the mannerists and Guicciardini casts a light on the Italian Renaissance not heretofore apparent, and it bears significantly on the period's sudden end. The High Renaissance in its greatest monuments had achieved a perfect expression of universal values and general concepts through concrete details and specific events. But the achievement by its very nature was volatile and could not be prolonged. It had been the goal of generations of artists and thinkers to synthesize the general with the particular, but as soon as that goal was reached, it passed into a preoccupation with individuality and a fascination with the particular for its own sake.

Viewed from this perspective, it is unnecessary to search for external causes to explain the sudden demise of High Renaissance style. To be sure, the Counter Reformation and the sack of Rome played a part, but the church did not turn its repressive measures against Renaissance taste and secularism until well after Guicciardini's death, and anticlassicist painting was already established before the sack of Rome. External events confirmed the rejection of humanist values in Italy, but by looking at them alone we miss the intrinsic element that was both the strength and weakness of the Renaissance. Its genius was to bring together two divergent poles of life — the general and the particular — into a single coherent statement; the goal was too fragile, and impermanence was the price of success.

Bibliography

For a discussion of mannerist painting see Sydney Freedberg's *Painting of the High Renaissance in Rome and Florence* (Cambridge: Harvard University Press, 1961).

Roberto Ridolfi has written an excellent biography of Guicciardini, *The Life of Francesco Guicciardini,* trans. Cecil Grayson (New York: Knopf, 1968). For an interpretation of Guicciardini against the background of Florentine politics see Felix Gilbert's *Machiavelli and Guicciardini* (Princeton: Princeton University Press, 1965). Guicciardini's works are available in the English translations: *The History of Italy and History of Florence,* trans. Cecil Grayson (New York: Twayne, 1965); *History of Italy,* trans. and ed. Sidney Alexander (New York: Macmillan, 1969); and *History of Florence,* trans. Mario Domandi (New York: Harper and Row, 1970).

The Reformation

Part Four
Introduction and Background

13 Introduction

All too frequently studies of the Reformation begin on the last day of October in 1517, when Luther allegedly nailed his ninety-five theses to the door of the Wittenberg cathedral. But it is dangerous to interpret the history of an age in terms of a single event. To understand the Renaissance it was necessary to trace common attitudes and values, as well as divergent interests and modes of expression, that stretched over a span of 250 years. The Reformation, too, makes more sense if it is seen in a context broader than the sixteenth-century revolt against the church of Rome.

What began on that day in 1517 was not so much the Reformation as a split in the institutional structure of Western Christendom, an event far-reaching in its effects but not without precedent. During the eleventh century Christianity had split into Eastern and Western churches in a schism that has not been healed to this day. Just a hundred years before Luther, at the Council of Constance, the assembled leaders of the Western church had mended a papal schism of forty years' duration that had spread to the outer reaches of Europe. Nor had that been the only problem. The Bohemian church broke away from Rome and launched a heretical attack on the sacramental priesthood after its leader, John Hus, was burned at the same Council of Constance. This church survived despite the best efforts of popes and emperors to subdue it. Despite these precedents, however, the institutional crisis precipitated by Luther at Wittenberg was more serious than the Great Schism healed at Constance or the establishment of the Hussite church. Luther broke with Rome on doctrinal as well as institutional grounds, and Luther's church was more successful than the Hussite church in gathering support from large areas of Europe.

Although the institutional upheaval that created Protestantism began in the early sixteenth century, the attitudes and values underlying it were not limited to just a few decades. The sixteenth-century reformers felt that the late medieval church had ignored a variety of human needs, and their central goal was to formulate a more personal religion that would satisfy the deficiency. This aim was not entirely new; the search had begun long before the sixteenth century. Early in the fourteenth century, thinkers and religious figures manifested similar concerns, and the Reformation, considered as a moral and intellectual movement, includes these earlier critics of society as well. Conceived along these broader chronological and thematic lines, the Reformation, while lacking the coherence and the self-consciousness of the Renaissance, is a discernible movement parallel to and contemporary with the Renaissance and sharing with it some important values. The Reformation differed sharply from the Renaissance, however, in seeking an abstract statement of truth unchanged by personal or historical perspectives, and this explains why Renaissance humanists failed to communicate effectively with the leaders of the Reformation.

Many distorted interpretations of the Reformation arise from an overly narrow focus on the events of the sixteenth century. Catholic historians at the time usually blamed the origin of the Protestant churches on the personal weaknesses of Martin Luther. They charged that Luther, as a monk unable to maintain his vow of chastity, had split the church in order to take a wife. Luther's language, colorful and anything but prudish, lent some credence to the argument, but the superficiality of the argument was immediately obvious to sensitive and thoughtful people, and it has long been discredited among reputable Catholic historians.

Protestant historians during the sixteenth century saw Luther's revolt in the context of the corruption of the Renaissance church. According to their view, the church had become increasingly worldly during the fourteenth and fifteenth centuries and had abandoned any real attempt to satisfy the religious needs of its flock. This corruption climaxed in the sixteenth century with the building of Saint Peter's Basilica in Rome. To obtain money for the construction, the pope sold an archbishopric to Albert of Hohenzollern and permitted him to recover his costs by selling indulgences in Germany. Tetzel, the salesman chosen by Albert, outrageously claimed that by buying an indulgence the sinner could be forgiven all his sins, past, present and future. He told peasants that as soon as their coins dropped in his box, the souls of departed relatives would come flying out of purgatory. So preposterous were his claims and so offensive were his tactics that they caused widespread revulsion against the church in Germany. Luther mobilized the revulsion into a campaign against clerical corruption, and an open break became inevitable when the church refused to reform. Only afterward did the church undertake to recover its spiritual mission in what was known as the Counter Reformation, which was characterized as nothing more than reaction against the Protestant threat.

This Protestant interpretation, being less scurrilous and somewhat more plausible than the early Catholic one, has lasted into our own day, but it must be rejected just as firmly. It is impossible to show that clerical corruption had significantly grown during the period just prior to Luther. The practices that caused scandal in the sixteenth century — multiple benefices, clerical concubinage, political involvement among the higher clergy — existed throughout the Middle Ages. Nor were complaints against these abuses anything new. Attacks on the morals of the clergy have been commonplace since the days of the early church and will doubtless continue as long as laymen expect superhuman purity in the priesthood to compensate for their own moral lapses. Feelings probably ran higher on these issues in the sixteenth century than in the thirteenth, but that intensity reflected a general religious revival during the fourteenth and fifteenth centuries. The revival touched the clergy as well as the laity and the institutional church had responded with considerable sensitivity. Even the most worldly of the Renaissance popes took measures to reform the church and satisfy the more intense religious needs of their congregation. In fact, the great reformers did not display the overriding concern for corruption that the Protestant interpretation assumes. Luther willingly used the issue to embarrass the papacy, but his real argument with the church involved issues far deeper than worldly priests or improper selling of indulgences. Erasmus, who stayed with the church, was far more vexed by corruption than Luther. In other words, to look on the Reformation primarily as a protest against clerical corruption is to misrepresent its significance and obscure all its basic attitudes.

More recent Roman Catholic historians, influenced by the ecumenical movement, have seen the religious crisis of the sixteenth century as part of a long tradition of self-reform going back to the earliest years of the church. Because the reforming impulse is at the heart of orthodoxy, Luther's reform was not intrinsically heretical. Consequently these historians feel that the Roman church must bear much of the blame for the intransigence that drove the reformers out of the traditional institutional structure. This is more subtle than earlier Catholic interpretations and brings out important elements of the Reformation, but at the same time it tends to blur the distinctive characteristics of the reforming movement during the fourteenth, fifteenth, and sixteenth centuries.

Recent secular interpretations have explained the institutional break by referring to social, political and economic trends. Max Weber, the great sociologist of the early twentieth century, suggested that the Protestant concept of "calling," which holds that service in secular occupations is just as sacred as service in the priesthood, might underlie the rise of capitalism. Weber, trying to propose an alternative to Marx's economic explanation of capitalism, suggested that psychological factors, such as the attitude toward work for its own sake that he saw implicit in Protestant theology, led to the acceptance of unlimited gain that underlay modern capitalism. Unfortunately, Weber's brilliant hypothesis has now become a tired theory, and generations of historians have combed the evidence and exhausted their imaginations trying to explain the relationship between Protestantism and capitalism. It is becoming clearer and clearer that the relationship resists explanation because it does not exist, except in a much later period, and no meaningful correlation has been drawn between Protestantism and the rise of capitalism. It is equally hard to identify the Reformation with any particular social trends. Some social groups were attracted to particular aspects of the Reformation. The radical reformers, for instance, found support among weavers and miners. But attempts to show that the Reformation appealed to the "rising middle classes" have foundered on the fact that it also appealed to peasants and aristocrats, and that the aristocracy was rising in the sixteenth century as fast as the middle classes. The social and economic history of the sixteenth century presents complex problems that are best approached through economic and social documents. These problems are not significantly illuminated by reference to the theology of the reformers. Conversely, the Reformation is first and foremost a religious movement and cannot be explained by reference to particular social and economic trends.

In the chapters that follow the Reformation will be treated neither as an adjunct to the social history of the sixteenth century nor as a moment in the age-old reforming impulse within the church itself. It will be seen as a distinct movement whose origins lie in the early fourteenth century and whose spokesmen share common concerns based on a common reaction to certain aspects of the late medieval experience. They worked with a vocabulary that was thoroughly religious, but they sought solutions to the fundamental human problems of identity, meaning, and purpose. The importance of the movement cannot be grasped without looking behind the theological language for the new perspective on basic human feelings.

To provide a background to the intellectual movement of the Reformation, three topics will be treated in this introductory section. First we will examine the political setting, since certain broad trends originating in the twelfth and thirteenth centuries continued into the period of the Reformation and affected the lives of contemporaries in significant ways. These trends are more clearly related to the Reformation than either the social or economic forces associated with the rise of capitalism. Second will be the institutional setting, for developments within the structure of the church during the fourteenth and fifteenth centuries brought it more forcefully into the lives of individuals and stimulated many of the complaints of the sixteenth-century reformers. Third, we will look at the intellectual setting, because thinkers of the Reformation were also reacting against many of the values and attitudes of their predecessors, and thus we need to understand the chief intellectual concerns of the period from the thirteenth to the fifteenth century.

Bibliography

For a modern Catholic interpretation of the Reformation see Joseph Lortz, *How the Reformation Came,* trans. O. Knabb (New York: Herder and Herder, 1964), and *The Reformation in Germany,* trans. R. Walls (New York: Herder and Herder, 1968). See also John Dolan, *History of the Reformation* (New York: Desclee, 1965), where many recent Catholic interpretations are synthesized. For an excellent modern Protestant interpretation see Roland Bainton, *The Reformation of the Sixteenth Century* (Boston: Beacon Press, 1952), or Owen Chadwick, *The Reformation* (Harmondsworth, Middlesex: Penguin Books, 1964). For a secular interpretation that places the religious movement against its social, economic, and political background, see G. R. Elton, *Reformation Europe: 1517–1559* (Cleveland: Meridian Books, 1964). Elton, himself an administrative and political historian, convincingly lays to rest simplistic attempts to relate the rise of Protestantism to capitalism or the rising middle class, but those who wish a more detailed study of the problem should consult Kurt Samuelsson, *Religion and Economic Action,* trans. E. French (New York: Basic Books, 1961), on the Weber thesis, and J. H. Hexter, *Reappraisals in History* (Evanston, Ill.: Northwestern University Press, 1962), for an assessment of the middle class in the sixteenth century.

14 The Rise of Territorial States

By 1500 the state throughout most of western and central Europe had begun to intrude into the lives of individuals in an impersonal and purely administrative way. This process, which had its origins as early as the twelfth century, has been called the rise of the territorial state. Feudal society, which dominated the Middle Ages, was not territorial. Instead it was organized largely on the basis of personal ties and loyalties. Men were judged, taxed, and governed less according to where they lived than according to the personal relationships that they or their ancestors had entered into. In practice, personal ties were most important among the upper classes. Four knights who were vassals of the same count might owe widely differing individual duties, while four peasants who were serfs of the same count would usually have the same obligations. They would be treated more as members of a social group than as individuals. Despite these discrepancies, feudal society was tied together in theory by a complex web of personal bonds.

To such a society the rights of political sovereignty could not be clearly established. Maps of medieval Europe show boundaries of empires, kingdoms, and counties that are mere approximations, for at this time there were no frontiers. Political power was not the control over a specific area but the right to exercise certain functions — to collect the toll over a bridge, to appoint the prior of a monastery, to collect a portion of the produce of a manor, or to try specific types of criminal cases. These rights formed no coherent or logical pattern. They were simply the functions that a particular count, abbot, or king had accumulated in the past. They could have come to him by custom, purchase, or outright conquest. Most of the rights that adhered to the lord's domain were usually located in a particular geographical area, because jurisdiction was personal and travel was difficult, but no one, not even the king, could claim to have intrinsic rights over a piece of territory. The kings of France, for instance, whose rights were concentrated in the area south of Paris, did not for several centuries possess control over the bridge that connected their personal domain with Paris. They acquired control only by marrying into the family that held the rights to it.

Ownership of property was similarly confused and fragmented. Title to land did not carry with it all of the rights we now associate with ownership, since rights to the use of land did not always remain with a single owner. The lord who resided on a given manor and managed it might claim 30 percent of its produce; his overlord, the count, might take another 30; the peasants who farmed the crop still another 30; and the king 10. Even this mathematical division is only a rough approximation of the actual sharing. The count's 30 percent might consist of all the fruit of certain trees on the manor, all the fish from a specified section of the stream, and the grain from one of the fields. As a further complication, many of the rights were not permanent. When the original trees died, the count might lose his claim on the fruit from any new trees; after three generations the rights to the fish might revert to the family of the local lord, or even to the king.

The effects of this fragmentation were considerable. First, power tended to be localized, for the rigors of travel made it unfeasible to wield feudal rights over the far-flung domains. Because functions and privileges were more a matter of personal fortune than rational organization, a lord could continue to exercise his rights only if he was willing to travel constantly. If he was absent when it was time to make an appointment that was his to bestow, others would make it for him. If he did not regularly visit a bridge to make sure that the tolls were being properly collected, others would collect them in his place. If he was not present at harvest time, he might never see his share of the grain. No lord could rely on a bureaucracy of overseers. His rights were his personal property and required his personal presence to be claimed. The kings of France during the tenth and eleventh centuries spent most of their lives on horseback, traveling to and fro in their domains to maintain the rights that they had inherited and to recover those that had lapsed.

In addition, the fragmentation of rights posed severe obstacles to the transfer and sale of property. It was virtually impossible for one person to assemble all claims to a piece of property so that he might own it in the modern sense. Thus it was risky to purchase property, for the rights purchased might have been only temporary and might have to be surrendered in the next generation. Obviously this made it hard to accumulate capital and hindered the development of the aspects of the economy that depend on liquid wealth.

Law

Little distinction existed during the feudal period between the ownership of property and political power. The rights that we now consider to indicate sovereignty belonged to persons and were regarded as personal property. In the realm of law there was no distinction between public and private spheres. Rights to try certain types of cases were possessed in the same way as rights to the produce of a manor. Generally the local lord tried minor cases involving disputes or criminal offenses among his own people, whereas his overlord held the right to try all cases involving bodily punishment. Jurisdiction over the latter, called high justice, was an important indication of who wielded the most political power within a region. Consequently, the terms "royal domain" or "ducal domain" usually meant the territory within which the king or the duke exercised the power of high justice over the inhabitants. It is also used as an index for drawing maps of the period, but the right of high justice did not necessarily indicate possession of any other types of official power.

The procedures of feudal law dramatically illustrate the great role played by personal relations in medieval society. A man accused of crime and brought to trial could defend himself in a number of ways, but none of these involved a systematic and rational investigation of the facts. Most commonly he assembled several of his social peers who would swear under oath that he was not the type of person to claim innocence falsely; they did not testify whether they had actual evidence of his innocence. This means of trial, called compurgation, seems a far cry from our notions of rational evidence, but it worked well in a small, relatively stable society where people were well known to their neighbors. Moreover, in feudal times, as in our own, the majority of crimes never came to trial; often this was because the evidence of guilt from eyewitnesses was so overwhelming that the criminal could only plead guilty. Cases were tried by compurgation only when the facts of the matter were in doubt, and the accused had sworn his innocence.

Other procedures of feudal law were equally personal. If the accused could not assemble the requisite number of oath helpers to testify to his character, he could purge himself either by submitting to an ordeal or by combatting his accuser. The ordeal took a variety of forms. The accused might hold a piece of hot iron in his hand. The hand was then bandaged and, if the wound had healed a number of days later, the accused was found innocent. Or he could be thrown into a tank of water. If he floated, the water was refusing him and he must be guilty; if he sank, he was innocent. These means of trial were not simply primitive superstition, but an attempt to exploit the conscience of the guilty. Trial by combat, in which the accused and the accuser faced each other in open fight, had this function, too. None of these means was completely accurate, but neither were they completely arbitrary. Feudal law should not be dismissed as more primitive than modern law; it had a different goal — to assess personal character rather than to determine the objective facts.

Like the trial procedure, the appeal process in feudal law was based on personal considerations. Inasmuch as the trial court had not decided questions of objective fact, the accused could not appeal on the grounds that the facts were established incorrectly. Instead, his only appeal was to claim that the court had deliberately rendered false judgment. Because it challenged the character of the judge, the appeal was settled by physical combat between the accused and the judge. This was thoroughly consistent with feudal legal assumptions, but in practice it was unsatisfactory to the accused, for the judge was usually his lord and possessed the wealth to hire a stand-in for the combat.

Before territorial states could emerge from feudal society, institutions and practices had to be established to modify the dependence on personal relations and personal character. As early as the twelfth century in England and the thirteenth in France, there appeared new forms of law based on Roman rather than feudal concepts. In Roman law, equity rather than precedent was the determining consideration. Law was supposed to be based on rational principles of right, and particular ordinances were deductions from these principles. Thus, it was important to determine fact in order to decide a case. What this meant in practice was that a jury would be picked to make an inquest into the facts and establish whether the evidence pointed to the guilt of the accused. If so, he was tried by the normal feudal procedures; if not, he was released and not required to purge himself further.

This procedure of inquest, which was the ancestor of our own grand jury, originated in royal and ecclesiastical courts. The church's canon law had always been based on Roman law, and the kings of the twelfth century began to adopt the institutions and practices of Roman law in their own courts. This was partly due to a brief revival of interest in classical culture during the twelfth century, and partly due to the fact that Roman law provided an excellent vehicle for extending royal power at the expense of the feudal barons. Soon the kings offered to conduct an inquest into the guilt or innocence of anyone who was about to be tried in a feudal court.

The attractiveness of royal justice is obvious. The accused had nothing to lose by appealing to the royal inquest, for even if the inquest found him guilty, he might still exculpate himself by compurgation, ordeal, or combat. As a result the royal courts became very popular. By the end of the thirteenth century in England or France a case from the feudal courts might be revoked to the royal courts at any time before judgment was given, and the kings of these countries had become the chief dispensers of justice within their realms. Royal justice was more impartial, rational, and reliable, but it also lessened the personal nature of law. Character and personal reputation were no longer relevant, except to evaluate evidence before the jury. Despite the manifold advantages of the new legal system, it subjected the individual to a more abstract and impersonal apparatus than he had experienced before.

The expansion of royal justice fostered the growth of a professional and specialized administration, which in turn encouraged the king to exercise his other political rights on a regular basis. Again England led the way, followed by France. Royal judges began to make regular rounds of the kingdom to preside over inquests, and royal officials followed them to oversee the king's territorial rights. These officials were at first local notables who exercised power largely through their own personal positions, and this continued to be the case in England. But elsewhere they soon became functionaries of the king without personal connections or position within their districts. Here again, making administration more rational also made it more impersonal.

Taxation

The growth of the king's territorial power required new sources of income. Traditionally, the lack of distinction between personal property and political power precluded the concept of public finance. The king was expected to live off his own personal income. As defense and administration became more expensive, these revenues became inadequate and had to be supplemented. Medieval kings had at their disposal few recognized sources of revenue. They had the right to coin money, and thus could raise funds by debasing the coinage. Though popular, this practice was of limited usefulness because it tended to interfere with trade and commerce. Another recognized source of income was the feudal dues that the king could claim by virtue of his position as suzerain or liege lord of all other lords in the kingdom. The lords were expected to make an offering to the royal coffer when the king knighted his eldest son; they were required to ransom the king's person when he was captured in war; and they had to contribute to the defense of the realm. Finally, the king could levy duties on imported goods.

Money for defense was the most common source of revenue, and kings often abused the right by insisting on contributions when the threat of invasion was not obvious, a practice that understandably aroused opposition. King John of England (1199–1216) frequently used this pretext to raise money, and finally provoked a revolt by his barons. The barons forced John to accept the Magna Carta (1215), forbidding taxes for foreign wars without their consent. This constraint gave the nobility an interest in royal power and proved in the long run a blessing for it, because the intervention of the nobles helped establish a regularized system of taxation. The French nobles, partly because of France's greater area and partly because of interference by the French kings, never acquired enough of a sense of community or organization to impose such restrictions or offer such assistance. As a result, the kings had no regular means for taxing the wealthier elements of the kingdom. This was a severe problem in France during the Hundred Years' War in the fourteenth century. Although the French kings were desperately fighting the English and frequently suffering defeat on their own soil, they were unable to secure adequate revenue for defense, even by pleading legitimate need. They had to rely on extraordinary contributions from the clergy and nobility. Two regular taxes were instituted successfully during the century only because they fell almost exclusively on the poor and left the powerful undisturbed. In the early 1340s, Philip VI (1328–1350) imposed a tax on salt, the *gabelle.* It was easy to collect, for no one could claim that he did without salt and therefore owed no tax. Another royal tax was created when the English captured King John II at the battle of Poitiers in 1355. The king's right to collect money to ransom his own body was a recognized feudal due, and John's son, the future Charles V (1364–1380), imposed a hearth tax, or *taille,* to pay the ransom. John died in captivity and the ransom was never paid, but Charles and all subsequent kings continued to collect it. Both the gabelle and the taille were still in force in 1789 at the time of the French Revolution.

Regionalism

The difficulties experienced by the kings in securing adequate income (even the kings of England were unable to get a share of the national wealth that any modern state would consider sufficient) reveal an aspect of the development of the territorial state that is often overlooked — the continuing independence of the regional units within it. Nineteenth-century historians often equated the growth of territorial power with the rise of national feelings. In reality, nationalism had little if anything to do with the growth of the state as a territorial entity rather than as a collection of personal loyalties and obligations. And in all areas of Europe there is ample evidence that smaller-scale regional loyalties continued to be strong through the entire period of the Reformation. England came the closest of any political unit of the time to being a centralized nation-state, but even there regionalism persisted. Many of the issues in the fifteenth-century English civil wars, the Wars of the Roses, were based on the resentment of regional units against interference by the crown. Likewise in the sixteenth century much of the opposition to Henry VIII's Reformation stemmed from regional feelings.

In France the force of regional loyalties was masked by the king's practice of bestowing parts of the country, called *apanages,* on his younger sons so that he could pass the crown undivided to the eldest. This practice was a major factor in keeping peace within the royal house, which never experienced the bitter fraternal wars that plagued the English kings, but at the same time it endangered the power and even the independence of the king. In the eleventh and

Europe in 1526

Hapsburg Dominions

Boundary of
Holy Roman Empire

twelfth centuries the titles given to the younger sons — Count of Anjou, of Burgundy, of Flanders — meant little, for power was not exercised on a territorial basis. But by the fourteenth and fifteenth centuries the situation had changed. The title now carried power, and its holder could wield independent influence. One of the most disastrous gifts was an apanage bestowed by the same John II who was captured at Poitiers. The son to whom he gave Burgundy founded a line that eventually allied with the English and brought the French crown to its knees. As a result, the French king Charles VI (1380–1422) in the Treaty of Troyes of 1421 was forced to make the English king Henry V heir to the crown of France.

The disastrous effects of the apanages during the fifteenth century made it imperative to bring them back under royal control. Louis XI (1461–1483) finally managed to reunite all of the territories by a combination of plotting, conquest, marriage, and sheer luck. The count of Anjou, for example, died without heir, allowing his apanage to fall back to the royal family. Considering all the trouble it created, the practice of bestowing apanages seems foolish. Yet in addition to the already noted advantage of keeping peace within the family, it also served to placate strong regional feelings. The apanages were not arbitrary units but traditional regions of France that had maintained a strong sense of cultural and political integrity throughout the period of the growth of the national state. The inhabitants were more willing to accept the increased demands of the state when they came from a man attached to and living in their own land rather than from a remote king for whom they had little feeling.

In Germany, regional loyalties were even more obvious. There the territorial state developed not under the central control of the Holy Roman emperor but under numerous regional princes. The emperors were hereditary lords of Austria and by 1500 had organized their own domains in a manner that resembled the territorial states of the West. Outside Austria they were almost powerless to tax, and their right to hear judicial appeals from the princely courts was severely limited. The weakness and poverty of the empire spawned attempts at reform in the late fifteenth century, but neither the territorial princes nor the imperial cities were willing to support a centralized imperial administration. By the mid-sixteenth century the empire was incapable of any concerted institutional action.

The weakness of the empire does not mean that the state did not grow in Germany as elsewhere in Europe. On the contrary, there was a great augmentation in the power of regional rulers — the seven electoral princes who elected each emperor (the archbishops of Mainz, Trier, and Cologne; the duke of Saxony; the count palatine of the Rhine; the margrave of Brandenburg; and the king of Bohemia), the dukes of Bavaria, and the archdukes of Austria and of great imperial cities like Nuremberg. In the course of the fifteenth century they strengthened control over their citizens, developed legal procedures based on Roman law, increased their power to tax, and secured dominance over individuals and social groups within their territories. This development was essential to the later success of the Protestant Reformation. If the elector of Saxony had lacked independent political strength, Luther, as his protégé, could not have founded a lasting institutional church against the opposition of the emperor. Furthermore Frederick the Wise, elector of Saxony in 1517, and other princes supported Luther only partly out of religious conviction. However much they sympathized with Luther's attacks on the medieval church, they were above all determined to resist every imperial attempt to interfere in their own internal affairs.

Thus the growing power of the German princes on the eve of the Reformation was an important factor in the immediate success of the Lutheran movement, but the broad political background was equally important because of its effect on the intellectual concerns that dominated the period from 1300 to 1500. Society had been developing in ways that diminished the role of personal relationships and personal status. Political leaders throughout Europe successfully created administrative and judicial institutions that dealt with their subjects impartially, rationally, and impersonally. The new order made possible a wealthier, more complex, and more efficient society than had existed in medieval Europe, but at the same time it imposed new burdens and values on the citizenry. The fourteenth and fifteenth centuries were not peaceful years in Europe, and much of the unrest, both internal and external, was founded in resistance to the new political system. It is not surprising that men also began to search for a more personal form of religious expression.

Spain, which later had such a great impact on sixteenth-century Europe, both through its conquest of Italy and through its control over the gold and silver from the New World, faced unique problems. By the fifteenth century the Iberian peninsula had been divided into four major historical regions: Navarre, Portugal, Castille and Aragon. The eventual kingdom of Spain was created when two of these were joined by the marriage in 1469 of Ferdinand, heir to the Crown of Aragon, and Isabella, heiress to Castille.

The two regions differed in many ways. During the late Middle Ages, Aragon had been an active commercial power with a large Mediterranean empire. The power of its kings was sharply limited by the assembly, the Cortes, whose approval had to be sought for new taxes or any significant innovations. Aragon was in economic and political decline during the fifteenth century but still contributed to the union a wealth of administrative and diplomatic experience.

Castille was by far the largest region on the peninsula, occupying 65 percent of the area and claiming nearly three-fourths of the population. The single most important fact in its history was the *reconquista,* or recovery, of the country from the Moors, who had occupied all of Spain during the early Middle Ages. The reconquest, which was nearly complete by 1469, had created large landed estates for the nobility, who acted as independent lords under minimal royal control.

The reconquista also had important spiritual effects. The prolonged period of military operations served to glorify the soldiering profession and create an ideal of the *hildalgo,* who was brave and honorable but who, as part of his code of honor, valued wealth won by conquest and plunder over earned riches. Second, the reconquista, since it was directed against a non-Christian people, took on the aspects of a crusade and gave religion a vitally important place in the hearts of Castillians. Problems of orthodoxy were far more seriously treated in Spain because of this long struggle against the Moors.

The differences between Castille and Aragon were not reconciled by the union, for the two regions retained their own institutions, having only a common head. Ferdinand and Isabella made no important change in either state. They strengthened royal power not by creating a new state but by insisting on the historic rights of the crown.

Significantly, the only institution common to all Spain was the Inquisition. Begun in 1478 to make sure that Moors converted to Christianity did not surreptitiously return to their old faith, the Inquisition was at first a Castillian phenomenon, but by 1487 it was imposed over bitter opposition on Aragon as well. With the rise of Protestantism the Spanish Inquisition turned its attention to the new heresy and rooted out the Protestants with such fervor that it has become a symbol of intolerant repression. Yet its activities were inspired by more than simple religious zeal. The Inquisition was among the few institutional means allowing the Spanish kings to deal with all of their subjects under a single heading.

Spain's use of the church points up an important tension that grew out of the systematization of political power. In attempting to regulate the lives of their citizens, the territorial sovereigns sought to draw on all available social institutions. Yet some of these institutions were not wholly under their control. The church was itself seeking the same rational order in its own institutions. Inevitably the church and territorial state would collide. In the next chapter we shall look at the growth of the church during this period and show how the intrinsic tensions between church and state were worked out.

Bibliography

The personal aspects of feudal society have been demonstrated in Marc Bloch's classic work *Feudal Society,* trans. L. A. Manyon (Chicago: University of Chicago Press, 1961). For English constitutional and legal developments see John Jolliffe, *The Constitutional History of Medieval England from the English Settlement to 1485,* 4th ed. (London: Black, 1961), and Bertie Wilkinson, *Constitutional History of Medieval England,* 3 vols. (London: Longmans, 1960–1963). For the development of the French territorial state, see Robert Fawtier, *The Capetian Kings of France,* trans. L. Butler and R. J. Adams (London: Macmillan, 1960). Problems of taxation have been discussed by Joseph Strayer and Charles Taylor in *Studies in Early French Taxation* (Cambridge: Harvard University Press, 1939) and more recently by John Henneman in *Royal Taxation in Fourteenth-Century France* (Princeton: Princeton University Press, 1971). Russell Major, *Representative Institutions in Renaissance France, 1421–1559* (Madison: Wisconsin University Press, 1960), has analyzed the assemblies. Hajo Holborn, *A History of Modern Germany,* vol. 1 (New York: Knopf, 1961), has written an excellent introduction to the history of Germany during this period. For more specialized regional studies see Henry Cohn, *The Government of the Rhineland Palatinate in the Fifteenth Century* (London: Oxford University Press, 1965), and Gerald Strauss,

Nuremberg in the Sixteenth Century (New York: Wiley, 1966). Cohn provides a particularly interesting analysis of the powers enjoyed by the regional rulers, at least in the Rhineland palatinate.

The best treatment of the Spanish monarchy is J. H. Elliott's *Imperial Spain: 1469–1716* (New York: St. Martin's Press, 1963). See also R. Trevor Davies, *The Golden Century of Spain, 1501–1621* (New York: Harper and Row, 1954). For a picture of the later history of Spain in context with the Mediterranean world see F. Braudel, *The Mediterranean and the Mediterranean World in the Age of Philip II,* trans. S. Reynolds (New York: Harper and Row, 1972).

15 The Church Before Luther

By 1500 the territorial state was victorious but not unchallenged. Traditional, nonterritorial groups in society that had enjoyed considerable autonomy during the Middle Ages still maintained some independence and insisted that the territorial sovereign deal with them in special ways. The nobles, the guilds, even some towns, formed legal corporations and demanded rights and privileges that most subjects of the sovereign did not enjoy. By far the largest and most influential of the nonterritorial institutions was the church. Possessed of vast lands and wealth and claiming the allegiance of all the souls of Europe, the church constituted a potential barrier to the growing power of the prince and threatened to compete with him for control of the wealth and the allegiance of his own subjects.

Because the church was so important, we sometimes believe that men in the fourteenth and fifteenth centuries were more pious than they actually were. In fact the church filled functions besides the religious one. Its primary responsibility was of course to minister to the spiritual needs of its flock; without fulfilling this role the church had no justification for wielding power and wealth. Every pope and prelate, however worldly and cynical, was aware of this fact and had to be in some measure concerned with how the church carried out its spiritual mission. But strictly religious activity was neither its only nor even its most obvious social contribution. The church took care of the sick and poor and was responsible for many other aspects of welfare nowadays assumed by the state. Education was a church monopoly. The leading universities operated under ecclesiastical privileges, and both students and teachers were clerics. Because the land possessed by the church was a significant portion of all land in Christendom, the church was a major economic force. Indeed, the medieval church played a major role in developing agricultural technology and new ways of organizing and administering the land. Thus the church was visible in many activities of the secular world. Monks cleared land and drained swamps. Teaching clerics educated scholars and lawyers and supplied much of the administrative and legal talent that ran the territorial states. Even the ecclesiastical courts were involved in society, for they adjudicated not only religious matters, like heresy and clerical crimes, but also cases that involved swearing an oath or a sacrament. On the latter grounds the church assumed jurisdiction over international treaties, marriages, and even business transactions.

In short, many of the functions assumed by the modern state were carried out by the church, and its role in society cannot be overlooked. But the territorial state gradually acquired competence in these areas and grew more willing to assume the costs of welfare, education, and land management. By the end of the Reformation the church played a far less important role in both Catholic and Protestant countries than it had in 1300, and the period marks a clear watershed in this regard. In 1600 we first glimpse the secular society of modern times, where the church itself regards its function as primarily moral and spiritual. But secularization had only begun; events in the sixteenth century clearly accelerated the trend, but they neither initiated nor finished it.

The Growth of Papal Government

During the two centuries before Luther the church was actually increasing its power and influence in much the same manner as the territorial states. Previously, despite its vital role in medieval society, the church had been no more centralized or efficiently administered than the secular powers. Its chief leaders had found their authority limited and fragmented by entrenched personal rights and special privilege. A series of great thirteenth-century popes, beginning with Innocent III (1198–1216), streamlined the administration of the papal bureaucracy and forced most European sovereigns to acknowledge, at least temporarily, the spiritual leadership of the pope. Nevertheless, even these men did not manage to acquire control over the entire workings of the church. For example, in 1300 there was still no central authority to hear appeals from local ecclesiastical courts. Appointments to clerical positions were made by a bewildering variety of powers, both secular and ecclesiastical, and escaped any systematic control by the pope. The latter, lacking any broad-based income, had to live like a territorial lord off the revenues of his own property, in this case the diocese of Rome. Finally, he even had difficulty controlling the forms of religious expression. The thirteenth-century popes managed to limit the proliferation of religious orders, but there existed extreme local variations in the liturgy as well as in the moral guidance offered by the clergy. In short, the medieval church manifested considerable toleration for varieties of religious life, because the central hierarchy was too poor and politically too impotent to do otherwise.

The fourteenth century witnessed a remarkable change in this situation, as the papacy gradually evolved a sophisticated adminis-tration and brought much of the church under its direct control. The popes at Avignon, freed from the constant disturbances that drove them from Rome, established a permanent administrative structure (see Chapter 1), and they extended their powers of ap-pointment, taxation and jurisdiction over most of Europe. The key to the new power was increased papal control over appointments to benefices. The benefices were major ecclesiastical offices carrying control of land or other sources of wealth. Because most of them were monastic, involving no responsibility for the cure of souls, the holder of the benefice had little to do but oversee the land attached to his office. Originally the appointments were made locally: the bishop was elected by his people, abbots and priors by their brother monks. But in the thirteenth century popular election was a thing of the distant past. Bishops were most often appointed by the canons, the priests residing in the cathedral. The canons in turn might be appointed by the bishop, by the local lord who had donated the land to support the canon, or even by the other canons. Monastic benefices were commonly filled either by the family that endowed the post or by the local bishop.

Late in the thirteenth century the popes revived an old rule that gave them the right to appoint the successor of any beneficiary who died in Rome. This was originally a common sense rule designed to prevent the murder and mayhem that might result as rumors of the holder's decease filtered vaguely back to his benefice, prompting plots for the succession. Gradually the popes expanded the rule, first claiming the right of appointment within fifty miles of Rome, then within the vicinity of Avignon, then wherever the holder of a benefice died violently; finally the pope declared that any benefice that fell to his appointment for whatever reason would forever remain subject to papal provision. Thus the right of papal appointment spread to every major benefice in Europe by the end of the fourteenth century.

Control over benefices was a boon to the papal treasury. The benefice was the basic economic unit of the church, and from the early fourteenth century the pope demanded one year's revenues as the price of appointment. This tax, called an annate, had to be paid before the appointee was formally invested with his office. Moreover, the popes claimed a number of other taxes, including the so-called loving aid — one-tenth of revenues, collected on special occasions. Bishops and abbots were very heavily taxed. They were expected to make annual visitations to each parish in their dioceses or each monastery under their supervision, but could avoid the actual visits by paying the pope the equivalent of the travel cost. They were also required to make periodic trips to the papal curia, but could avoid them in similar fashion. For added income, the popes collected the revenues from any see that was vacant and soon began to sell expectatives, or future appointments to benefices, even while the holder was still living.

As the papacy extended its control, the administrative machinery of the curia increased in size and complexity. The papal *camerarius,* or director of the treasury, became the most important official, and special tax courts were instituted to hear appeals arising from papal assessments or other fiscal matters. The papal collectors traveled all over Europe to assess taxes, estimate annual revenues, and oversee the disposition of a dead beneficiary's personal property, which the pope claimed as the final tax. Simultaneously the papal courts proliferated and regularly heard appeals from all over Christendom. Until the fourteenth century, the popes appointed a judge to hear a case but gave the final sentence themselves after hearing the judge's advice. Soon this practice became unwieldy, and a system of permanent courts was established to hear each type of case that came before the Holy See. The most important of these was the Rota, established in 1336 to hear suits arising out of appointments to benefices. Although there was no appeal from the Rota, its procedures were so intricate that a determined litigant could delay his case indefinitely, hoping to get a more favorable hearing from another judge, and soon the popes had to create another court just to hear the delaying maneuvers.

Opposition to Papal Power

The popes did not extend their power without opposition, and indeed, there were three distinct challenges to papal power during the fourteenth and fifteenth centuries. First, within the curia itself, the college of cardinals constantly sought to bring the pope under its control. Second, the church as a whole resisted papal centralization through the mechanism of general councils. Finally, the territorial magnates by their own centralizing efforts ran counter to the growing central authority of the church. All three were significant, but the last was formidable.

The college of cardinals, originally a select group of bishops, priests, and deacons from the area around Rome, had secured for itself in the eleventh century the right to elect the pope. During the Avignonese period the college was a wealthy and influential body of about twenty-five ecclesiastics. Its members were the obvious people to help the pope with his administration, and in return they had sought with some success to share in his power. The pope published his decrees in consistory — that is, in company with his cardinals, only with the consent of the college. At each papal election the college sought to exact concessions from the nominee, but, once crowned, the new pope usually forswore the concessions and placated the college by giving them wealthier appointments.

The dangers implicit in this tension at the center of the church became obvious in the papal election of 1378. Meeting in Rome for the first time since the beginning of the century, the college was pressured by the Roman populace into electing an Italian pope. Immediately after his election, Pope Urban VI (1378–1389) imprisoned and tortured some of the cardinals who had opposed him. The rest of the opposition hastily fled, declared Urban's election null and void, and elected a new pope. Their choice, Clement VII (1378–1394), was a Frenchman who promptly returned to Avignon. The result was the Great Schism that lasted forty years. Although it was probably not so damaging as has been commonly thought, the spectacle of two, and after 1409 three, popes excommunicating each other and their followers can hardly have strengthened the allegiance of the faithful. Not only that, but the recently augmented influence of the papacy made the schism more appalling. Schism in twelfth-century Europe involved little more than theoretical issues, but by 1400 it created concrete problems of who should collect taxes, make appointments, and hear cases.

The college had split Christendom but could not put it back together. Lacking broad popular support, the cardinals could not move decisively against either of the rival popes. A group of cardinals from each rival college joined together at Pisa in 1409 to elect a single pope, but their action only served to divide the allegiance of Christians by three. Thus it became increasingly plain that only a general council, one of the oldest and most respected institutions of the church, could mend the schism. The council finally met at Constance in 1414 and proceeded to elect Martin V as the first pope of a united Christendom in forty years. Having succeeded in its primary mission, the council then turned to reform so that such schisms would not recur.

The council represented a far more serious threat to papal authority than the college of cardinals had ever posed. It was composed of a broad variety of bishops and abbots who resented the heavy burden of papal taxes and papal encroachment on their traditional rights of appointment. Furthermore, the secular rulers of Europe, including the Holy Roman emperor and the kings of England and France, looked on the council as a means of limiting papal power. The Council of Constance sought to capitalize on this support by reducing papal taxes and insisting that a general council should meet at regular intervals in the future to oversee the course of the church.

Had the reforming decrees of Constance been carried out and the councils continued to command support, the pope's control over the church would effectively have dissolved. But the conciliar movement arose in Europe at a time when republican attitudes were not in the ascendant. The monarchical aspects of the papacy accorded more closely with prevailing trends. Equally important, the growing particularism of European states prevented them from cooperating with one another in a united front against the papacy. In the decades after Constance, the papacy maneuvered the councils into a position that seemed to foster schism rather than prevent it. In 1460 Pope Pius II, himself a former conciliarist, declared an appeal from a pope to a council to be heretical, but by then few remained to mourn the demise of the conciliar movement. This experience with conciliarism helps explain the popes' later reluctance to call a council in response to the Lutheran threat.

The most serious threat to papal policy came from the kings and territorial princes who had actively supported the conciliar movement. The popes and the princes were competing to control many of the same aspects of society. No king wishing to be sovereign in his own territory could permit unrestricted papal taxation, or appeals from his courts to the Roman curia. These were the two major areas of contention from the fourteenth century onward. The English parliament in the 1350s, for example, enacted measures to limit the papal prerogative: the statutes of Provisors and Praemunire forbade the appeal from any of the king's courts to a foreign court and prohibited popes from appointing to benefices within the kingdom. Nor was England the only country to react against the growth of papal power. In 1438, the Pragmatic Sanction of Bourges, under the guise of supporting the reforming decrees of Constance, imposed the same restrictions in a somewhat milder form on the church in France.

These measures, had they been enforced, would have hamstrung the papacy's policy, impoverished its treasury, and effectively prevented the centralization of the church. But kings seldom used the laws except to threaten the pope and extort concessions. Both the king and the pope were eager to destroy local power and had no wish to return the right of appointment to local chapters and monasteries. In the campaign toward centralization, the king usually found the pope less of a threat and far easier to accommodate than the local churchmen.

Just before Luther first appeared in Wittenberg, the territorial sovereigns in most of Europe had come to an understanding with the papacy. The most famous settlement was the Concordat of Bologna, signed in 1516 between King Francis I of France and Pope Leo X. The king granted to the pope the right to invest individuals with benefices, but the pope acknowledged the king's right to nominate candidates for all important benefices in France. The revenues were to be split between them. The concordat thus overrode the pretensions of local lords or prelates who had traditional rights of appointment. It made available part of the local revenues to the papal treasury, and also satisfied the king because he could prevent the appointment of unacceptable candidates and benefit from the flow of wealth within his own borders.

The Concordat of Bologna shows that an institutional break was not necessary in order to make the church yield its wealth to the territorial monarch. Henry VIII in England suppressed the monasteries and confiscated their wealth as part of his reformation, but the Spanish kings and, to a lesser extent, the French kings tapped the same wealth without destroying the traditional church. The popes generally understood their own strengths and weaknesses and realized the impossibility of directly opposing the territorial states. In Germany, for example, no formal accommodation as broad as the Concordat of Bologna had been reached by 1500, but the popes adopted the expedient of overturning local elections to benefices and then ostentatiously appointing the very man whom the local authority had chosen. In this way they managed to keep their theoretical claims without sparking open resistance from local power.

The tension between the growth of papal power and the rise of the territorial state was certainly a factor in the Reformation. But in addition, church policy during the fourteenth and fifteenth centuries independently added another element of rational and impersonal organization to the lives of Europeans. Beneficiaries found themselves subject to rules promulgated by distant bureaucracies. They were judged in courts by men they did not know and taxed by officials from far-away parts of Europe. Laymen sensed the growing intervention in their lives as the parish system became more intrusive and formalized. The practice of regular confession before the parish priest, for example, was an innovation that appeared during this period. But there were also advantages. Papal appointees were almost uniformly more competent, pious, and generally interested in religion than those chosen locally. They probably served the general populace more capably and efficiently — whether in educational, social, or religious functions — than their counterparts in previous centuries. Nevertheless, the new shape of the church was less personal and therefore less responsive to individual needs than it had been in the early Middle Ages. Far from acting as a counterpoise to secular society, the church became a part of the trend, closing off avenues of personal religious experience at the same time that opportunities for personal expression in society, politics, and law were constricting.

Bibliography

For an excellent and readable introduction to the history of the church during the Middle Ages and just before the sixteenth century, see R. W. Southern, *Western Society and the Church in the*

Middle Ages (Harmondsworth, Middlesex: Penguin Books, 1970). A more detailed account can be found in volumes twelve to fifteen of Augustine Fliche and Victor Martin's *Histoire de l'église depuis les origines jusqu'à nos jours* (Paris: Bloud and Gay, 1934–). For a Catholic history that sees many of the weaknesses of the late medieval church see Philip Hughes, *A History of the Church,* 3 vols. (New York: Sheed and Ward, 1947–1949). Guy Mollat, *The Popes at Avignon,* has shown the strength of the papacy during that period. On the development of papal control over the church, see also Walter Ullman, *The Growth of Papal Government in the Middle Ages* (New York: Barnes and Noble, 1956). For the German church see Joseph Lortz, *The Reformation in Germany,* trans. O. Knabb (New York: Herder and Herder, 1968).

The classic assessment of the strength of corporations during medieval and early modern times is still Emile Lousse, *L'état corporatif au moyen âge et à l'époque moderne* (Louvain: I. Wijnants, 1938).

16 Intellectual Background

Politics and church organization were not the only areas in which men sought to make the existing order more rational. Scholars and intellectuals of the thirteenth century bent their efforts toward organizing all human knowledge in a uniform, coherent scheme, and they succeeded in producing the most comprehensive and satisfying philosophical system to appear in the West since Aristotle. While it was not immediately accepted and in fact was held in suspicion by many contemporary authorities, the system provided succeeding generations with an intellectual orthodoxy at once more coherent and more narrow than any that had been established in earlier centuries.

Augustine (354–430)

The eleventh and twelfth centuries were a time of intellectual ferment in which the dominant Christian philosophy was Augustinian. In particular, thinkers of this period were relatively unsystematic; they stressed the primacy of faith over reason; and they regarded the basic religious question to be the problem of personality and personal adjustment to life. These characteristics are hallmarks of the thought of Augustine himself as well as of the Christianity of the eleventh and twelfth centuries, but it is difficult to explain their meaning and how they are interrelated. It appears that lack of system is merely an unwillingness to organize; primacy of faith, on the other hand, is a doctrine; and concern with personal problems is only a question of subject matter. Yet when examined more closely all three characteristics are parts of the same way of looking at the world, and together they form Augustine's basic contribution to Western thought.

First, why the avoidance of systematic thought? Augustine himself never wrote a comprehensive philosophy but addressed himself to particular problems, changing his emphasis according to the particular issue that confronted him. When he considered ethics and behavior, he emphasized the importance of personal effort and man's ability to determine values by his own reason and follow them in his conduct. When he considered salvation and personal justification, however, he stressed the importance of divine grace and said that without aid man is unable to choose his ultimate values. Toward the end of his life Augustine attempted to reconcile some of the tensions in his thought, but apparently he felt that human experience could never really be categorized in a single logical system. Thus he tolerated a wide variety of perspectives on faith, and his medieval followers used this tolerance to advantage. Twelfth-century theologians, instead of teaching a strictly systematic theology, used as their basic text the *Sentences* of Peter Lombard, a collection of sayings from all the major church fathers.

The doctrine of the primacy of faith over reason at first appears hard to understand. In essence, though, it is not a demand for unquestioned belief but a way of stressing the limitations of human reason. Ultimately it springs from Augustine's efforts to incorporate Plato into Christianity. Plato, as we noted in Chapter 3, saw the visible world as real only to the extent that it participated in an invisible world of ideal forms. These forms remained invisible because the senses gave only a distorted picture of reality, but they could be understood by mental intuition apart from normal experience. Because Plato affirmed that true reality is spiritual and totally transcends human experience, his writings furnished an appropriate support for Christianity, at the same time that they diminished the importance of the senses and the patterns and abstractions that reason creates out of raw experience. In Augustine's view, the intuition of reality that forms the basis of true knowledge can come only from divine grace — in other words, never through our own efforts but only through an infusion of faith. Therefore, said Augustine, faith stands higher than reason. In fact, unguided natural reason yields not merely an incomplete picture of reality but one that is actually distorted and leads us further and further from the truth.

The third element in Augustine's thought was his stress on the central importance of human personality. Augustine was largely responsible for interpreting the full implications of the doctrine of the Incarnation. Christ, who was fully God, became fully man, thereby demonstrating that nothing in the universe is more real than a human person. Augustine devoted a large part of his *Confessions* and his more formal theological works to elaborating this doctrine. For Augustine, knowledge was uniquely personal and individual. We know a thing not because of the external evidence of our senses that is shared by others, but because of inner intuition, which represents the infusion of grace into our persons. The intuition is uniquely our own, however much it may seem to be shared by humanity at large in the form of generally accepted notions. Because Augustine conceived of knowledge in this way, it is hardly surprising that he distrusted systematic reason. The clarity and coherence of formal logic was deceptive, whereas the complexity of personal experience represented true reality.

Aristotle (384-322 B.C.)

The twelfth century felt comfortable with Augustine, but the thirteenth century seemed to feel a need for a more systematic theology. The attempt to create such a theology was related, moreover, to a growing interest in the works of Aristotle. Aristotle was known in the early Middle Ages. His logic had always been the basis of systematic thought in the West; his observations of nature were the basis for medieval natural science, and his rules for individual behavior informed medieval ethics. Aristotle's metaphysics, however, could not easily be assimilated into Christianity. He had tried to refine Plato's philosophy by explaining how we acquire knowledge. Knowledge, he said, depends on the evidence of the senses — that is, on observation — rather than on direct intuition; but in making this claim he encountered many difficulties. He could not logically postulate a source of being that transcended the senses but that also caused the senses to perceive, for the senses could not know it. He therefore maintained that there was no efficient "cause" of existence. Instead, all material and spiritual species — that is, all types of things and classes of notions — were eternal and necessary, requiring no explanation for their existence; thus they could be fully known by the senses. Aristotle's concept of the eternity of things and ideas could hardly be reconciled with the biblical doctrine of creation revealed in Genesis. Worse yet, Aristotle had no real sense of personal immortality and maintained that the essence of the soul was its ability to grasp abstractions and had nothing to do with its personal nature. In other words, we draw our being from our ability to calculate and think correctly, rather than from any desires or feeling that we may have.

Plato had separated "being" from the sensible world and firmly established the reality of the metaphysical world, but evidently he was unconcerned with how we come to understand metaphysical reality in the first place. Aristotle, attempting to devise an epistemology and overcome these difficulties, sacrificed Plato's clear explanation of what properties a thing must have in order to exist, or, in other words, his ontology. The medieval Latin world paid little attention to this problem, but Arab scholars from the mid-eleventh century onward sought to reconcile the two streams of thought. They were induced to undertake the reconciliation partly because they believed that certain neo-Platonic texts actually belonged to the Aristotelian corpus, an apparent fact giving the impression that Aristotle had devised two conflicting philosophies. The Arabs felt it was their task to find an underlying meaning that would comprehend them both.

The Thirteenth-Century Synthesis

By 1200 most of Aristotle's writings, and several major commentaries, were available in Latin. Thirty years later new and more accurate translations appeared, together with the works of Averroes, the greatest of all Arab commentators on Aristotle. These texts spurred the Latin world to try to relate Aristotle to Christian truth. At first the efforts were negative, simple refutations of those parts of Aristotle or Averroes that were clearly contradicted by Christian teaching. But by the middle of the century Aristotle's central notions had been carefully but firmly incorporated into Augustinian Christianity. The man responsible for the synthesis was Saint Thomas Aquinas (1226–1274), a Dominican friar whose two chief works, the *Summa Contra Gentiles* and the *Summa Theologica,* stand among the great monuments of Western thought.

Thomas fully accepted Aristotle's doctrine that all knowledge comes directly or indirectly from the senses. Before anything can be known, something has first to be perceived by the senses. But he based this epistemology on the Christian-Platonic conception of creation in which God is the continual creative cause of the universe, which in turn draws its reality from participation in God and which is totally dependent on the creative influx of the supreme being. Thus, from God's perspective the universe is a reflection of his own being and derives its reality from direct participation in his own ultimate reality. From its own perspective the universe appears to be composite, made up of finite beings perceived by the senses and understood as causing one another to act.

This perspective casts a new light on faith and, in contrast to Augustine, Thomas said that reason informed by the senses is true, even though incomplete. In its own sphere it leads to correct conclusions, but in matters beyond its reach it must yield to faith based on revelation. In all of his works Thomas sought to identify clearly the limits of reason, to find postulates that could be derived from reason, and to show that postulates based on faith were not contrary to reason. His interest was to harmonize and reconcile seeming contradictions and to fashion a synthesis of all experiences based on the twin pillars of faith and reason, each operating in its own sphere.

In claiming that reason and revelation were sufficient paths to knowledge, Thomas Aquinas was not denying the validity of direct intuitive insight through mystical experience. Being eager to incorporate everything into his synthesis, he recognized that special insight could be valid. He simply insisted that it was not necessary, because the knowledge gained by direct intuition could equally well be gained by reason and revelation. Therefore personal knowledge was based on evidence available to all. Anything that is known and true can be traced either to the Bible or to the evidence of the senses and is thus objectively demonstrable. The uniqueness of subjective insight is an illusion.

The thirteenth century's search for a systematic, empirical understanding of experience had produced a splendid result. Thomas' system was subtle, flexible, and brilliantly comprehensive. It had a universality and objectivity that Augustine's more personal theology lacked. But its strength was also its weakness. By eliminating the necessity for direct personal knowledge, Thomas greatly reduced the importance of individual peculiarities, and encouraged the construction of a uniform code of social ethics. Because norms of human conduct were rational and objective, variants that did not fit the norms were implicitly less meaningful and less true. Consequently, Thomistic social ethics necessarily left some intense personal dilemmas unresolved.

The work of Thomas Aquinas typifies the intellectual concerns of the thirteenth century. Pursuing an essentially philosophical goal, men narrowed their field of view, and the rich variety of scholarly curricula that had flourished in the previous century became submerged in the single-minded pursuit of systematic philosophy. But soon Thomas' system lost favor, together with the Aristotelian philosophy on which it was based. Aristotle was condemned at Paris in 1277, and Thomas did not regain a dominant position in Catholic thought until the Council of Trent, three hundred years later. The intervening centuries, the centuries of the Reformation, saw the rise of new questions, new interests, and new approaches to knowledge. Men were seeking a more personal basis for knowledge and religious expression and a greater variety of paths to these goals. The reason for the quest becomes apparent when we realize that its backdrop was the thirteenth century, which sought with remarkable success a different goal, attractively rational and clear but narrow in its appreciation of personal needs. The following three chapters will discuss movements beginning in the fourteenth century that offered alternatives to Thomas' system — Rhineland mysticism, nominalism, and humanism.

Bibliography

For a good introduction to medieval thought see Gordon Leff, *Medieval Thought: Augustine to Ockham* (Harmondsworth, Middlesex: Penguin Books, 1958), Fernand Steenberghen, *Aristotle in the West,* trans. L. Johnston (New York: Humanities Press, 1970), shows the brilliance of Thomas' incorporation of Aristotle into Augustinian Christianity. For a slightly different interpretation, see Etienne Gilson, *Reason and Revelation in the Middle Ages* (New York: Scribner, 1959). For more detailed discussions of Augustine and Aquinas by the same author, see *The Christian Philosophy of St. Augustine,* trans. L. Lynch (New York: Random House, 1960), and *The Christian Philosophy of St. Thomas Aquinas,* trans. L. K. Shool (New York: Random House, 1956). Charles Haskins in *The Renaissance of the Twelfth Century* (New York: Meridian Books, 1957) has given a picture of the variety of interests among twelfth-century intellectuals.

Part Five
The Building of the Reformation Vocabulary

17 Mysticism

The institutional reformers of the sixteenth century drew on three intellectual traditions. One of these, Renaissance humanism, was largely imported from Italy and became important in northern Europe only during the last half of the fifteenth century. The other two traditions, Rhineland mysticism and late medieval nominalism, were native and can be traced back to the early fourteenth century. All three were attempts to find a basis for understanding human experience that was more personal than the system of Thomas Aquinas, but they differed in significant ways. Each must be understood in its own terms if we are to appreciate its appeal to the great thinkers of the Reformation.

The essence of mysticism is the notion that individuals can have direct experience of ultimate reality unmediated by the institutional church or by the evidence of the external senses. As a serious philosophy it is much more than simple emotional religiosity. Nevertheless, the possibility of direct personal knowledge does pose a potential challenge to the institutional regulation of religious life, for a mystic can claim insights not available to society at large or susceptible to normal means of investigation.

The church cannot easily deny the validity of mystical knowledge. Saint Paul, who propagated the Gospel to the gentiles, owed his own conversion to a mystical experience. Paul clearly and explicitly claimed that he had received a direct communication from God on the road to Damascus. He emphasized that the encounter was ineffably and unquestionably outside normal experience. Paul's testimony, in context with the long prophetic heritage of the Old Testament, plainly places mysticism in the biblical tradition. Many of the early church fathers themselves claimed to have had mystical insights, and Saint Augustine owed his own conversion to a mystical experience, which he explicitly compared to Paul's. In order to disavow this path to knowledge in the interest of orderly religious life, the church would have to abandon its own heritage.

Mysticism is equally hard to deny on the basis of psychology. Most people, at some time in their lives, are aware of feelings and insights that they cannot trace directly to sensory or "objective" investigation. Any number of natural causes — from indigestion to hallucinogens — can be adduced to explain these feelings, but their precise content cannot be rationalized so easily. To many people they indicate dimensions of reality beyond daily existence, and to the true mystic they may be more real than life itself. These experiences lie so close to the heart of the religious impulse that no religion can afford to ignore them.

Practicing Mystics: Catherine of Siena

The church has seldom objected to the principle of mysticism and has generally accepted the fact that human experience is sometimes enlarged by means outside normal ecclesiastical channels. But it has sought to control it by adopting clear standards of judging and criticizing genuine mystical experience. The fruits of such experience, if properly understood, ought to be kept within the bounds of orthodoxy and made available to Christians in general. The church in the fourteenth century was no less sympathetic to mystical insights than in other periods, and its attitude can be illustrated by the career of Saint Catherine of Siena, a strange woman who was personally unpleasant and socially embarrassing but who was tolerated and eventually canonized.

Catherine was born in 1347, the youngest of a Sienese dyer's twenty-five children. She had her first vision at the age of seven, while walking in the country with her brother. Describing it in later life, Catherine wrote:

> Raising her eyes toward heaven she saw in the air, not very high above the ground, a *loggia* [porch], rather small and full of light, in which Christ appeared clothed in a pure white garment like a bishop in his cope, with a crozier in his hand; and he smiled at the young girl and there issued from him, as from the sun, a ray which was directed at her; and behind Christ there were several men in white, all saints, among whom appeared St. Peter and St. Paul and St. John, just as she had seen them painted in churches.

The reference to contemporary art suggests an obvious source for her vision, and it was a recurring theme in her experience. A few years later she had a vision of Saint Dominic, who prompted her to join the Dominican order, and she said that on this occasion, too, Dominic appeared like a painting in the local church. Catherine's inspiration by contemporary painting appeared dramatically on still another occasion. As a young teenager Catherine had a vision in which she became the bride of Christ. She seems to have been influenced by the example of an early Christian saint, Catherine of Alexandria, who was commonly depicted as wedded to Christ. The marriage of Catherine of Alexandria was a popular theme of painters in the fourteenth century, but the way they drew the ceremony changed markedly in the course of the century. Before 1350 the saint was usually depicted with an infant Jesus, whereas in the last half of the century Christ is usually shown as an adult man. Catherine of Siena's accounts of her own marriage reflect this change exactly. In her earliest descriptions she claimed to have wedded the infant Jesus, but later she said it was the adult Christ. Clearly her visions reflect the impact of contemporary painting on an impressionable young girl.

We should be careful, however, not to dismiss a mystical experience just because a natural explanation can be found for certain details. Catherine's own contemporaries were doubtless aware that her imagery came from the art about her, but the visual originality of a mystic's visions is not the criterion of a valid mystical experience. Instead we must assess the mystic's entire life and contribution, for it is much easier to counterfeit imagery than to feign an inspired way of living. By any standard, Catherine's career was remarkable. An uneducated and socially obscure citizen of a small Italian town, she annoyed and terrified in the course of her brief life the greatest powers of Europe and influenced the conduct of pope and emperor alike.

As a result of her first vision Catherine took a vow of perpetual chastity. This hardly seems of much account at the age of seven, but, supported by subsequent visions, she confirmed and strengthened her original vow and expanded it into a resolve to lead a wholly ascetic life. When one of her sisters who had tried to moderate her asceticism died of the plague in 1362, Catherine took it as a divine command to increase her determination. Indeed, willingness to interpret even the death of her sister as a personal message indicates the degree to which Catherine believed herself to be in direct communication with God.

Shortly thereafter, Catherine acquired a confessor and spiritual advisor, the monk Tommaso della Fronte. Tommaso supported her ascetic vows, suggesting that she cut off her hair to frustrate her parents' attempts to arrange a marriage. Under his influence she began long fasts and lived for days on end eating nothing but the Host while depriving herself of sleep. She also began exposing herself to diseases with the intent of disfiguring her body. Tommaso also began to guide Catherine's spiritual development and help her explore the meaning of the visions and how they revealed God. He began to focus her attention on the problems of the world and suggested that she might use her asceticism and visions to influence men toward a solution to their problems.

Under Tommaso's guidance Catherine's fame spread rapidly, first in Siena and then throughout Italy and the rest of Europe. Although her family had been excluded from power by a recent revolution, Catherine's person became so inviolable that she could lead her brothers through hostile quarters of the city in safety. She acquired a reputation as an arbiter as people came to her for help in resolving their quarrels. In all these activities the influence of Tommaso can be detected. Just as her visions were governed by the paintings she saw, the purposes to which she put the visions were guided by her confessor. Her contemporaries must have known this, too, but the power and influence lay in her person and asceticism, not in his social conscience.

Around 1370 Catherine had her most celebrated vision, in which

God appeared and instructed her to leave her contemplative and introspective pursuits and become a messenger of peace and righteousness among men. She immediately began to send letters all over Christendom calling for the reform of the church, the pacification of Italy to permit the return of the pope, and the pacification of Europe to permit a crusade. But years of asceticism and self-inflicted discomfort had left their mark on Catherine's disposition, and the unpleasant result is evident in every letter. She castigated the curia as a stinking cesspool and Pope Gregory XI as the keeper of a brothel, while threatening him with all manner of afflictions unless he returned from Avignon to Rome and cared for his flock as he should. Similar abuse was heaped on the secular rulers of Europe. Catherine was a woman without compassion, tact, or understanding of anyone less single-minded than herself — in other words, nearly all of Europe. It is hard to see why her contemporaries put up with her as they did, but she clearly burned with a fire that none could ignore. Her power to convince and put to shame is the strongest testimony we have of the genuineness of her mystical experiences.

Not surprisingly, Catherine's letters attracted the attention of the Dominican order, which she had joined in the 1360s, and she was called to Florence to be examined. When the order could find no heresy in her, she was assigned a new spiritual guide, Raymond of Capua, a sophisticated theologian under whose direction Catherine's letters became more precisely phrased but no less vigorous. In 1375 she received the stigmata, or marks resembling the wounds Christ received on the cross. These further enhanced her message, and in 1376 she went to Avignon in person to demand that Pope Gregory return to Rome. He did return shortly thereafter, though only partly in response to Catherine's prodding, and Catherine followed him there to found a religious house in 1378. But not even a saint could long endure the rigors Catherine demanded of herself, and two years later she died at the age of thirty-three.

Catherine's career shows that the church was not uniformly hostile to mystical knowledge. Catherine was a practicing mystic who claimed direct revelation from God and supported the claim by the power of her life and words. Furthermore, she sought to reveal her experience to all Christendom, including the pope himself. No present-day critic of society could be more abrasive than this acerbic girl in her twenties, who denounced the great men of Europe in the most offensive language possible. The temptation to have her silenced must have been strong. Yet the church sought instead to guide her visions to useful paths. Thanks to the efficient organization of religious life during this period, the means of supervision were readily available. The confessional system brought her into contact with an advisor early in her career, and her monastic order was able to provide more sophisticated guidance when the time came. As long as these avenues of regulation were maintained, the church accepted her strictures along with her insights, however trying they might have been.

Catherine's popularity and influence point up the widespread interest in mysticism during the centuries before Luther. Part of this interest can be traced to a general intensification of religious practice during that period. Cults of the Virgin flourished in the fourteenth and fifteenth centuries, which also saw the appearance of popular belief in Mary's immaculate conception, later adopted as a dogma by the church. The rosary took on a new importance, new religious observances appeared, and new devotional societies were created.

Supported by such religious sentiments, several mystics founded communities where the devout could pray and live together. Most famous of these communities was the Brethren of the Common Life, founded by Gerard Groote (1340–1384). Groote intended the Brethren to encompass laymen and clergy in an organized society of small communities living a sort of monastic life, but he died before carrying out his plans. The Brethren remained loose in organization, serving mainly to supply boarding for boys attending city schools and to copy manuscripts. They were conservative in religious outlook and failed to support the sixteenth-century reformers. By the seventeenth century they had ceased to exist.

The Brethren also ran a few of their own schools, although Deventer, where the noted humanist Erasmus received his early education, was not among them. The Brethren's association with teaching and learning attracted a number of the leading religious figures of the fourteenth and fifteenth centuries to the order. Thomas à Kempis (1380–1471), whose *Imitation of Christ* was one of the most widely read religious tracts of the late Middle Ages, worked as a copyist for the Brethren and drew much of his inspiration from the example of Groote.

The Theology of Mysticism: Meister Eckhart

Practicing mystics like Catherine and Groote actually posed less of a problem to the church than the speculative mystics, whose goal was to formulate a theology based on mystical experience. The generation before Catherine produced one of the most important and creative speculative mystics of the Western tradition — the German monk called Meister Eckhart. Eckhart attempted to incorporate direct and unmediated experience of God into systematic religious life. Ironically, he was responding in part to the same desire for regulation and organization that had motivated Thomas Aquinas a few years earlier.

Meister Eckhart was a contemporary of Dante. Born about 1260, he became a Dominican friar in 1278 at the Saxon town of Erfurt. The Dominican order, like the Franciscan, had been founded a few decades earlier in response to a widely felt need for a more intense, personal devotion than was available in the older monastic orders. The Dominicans were particularly charged with the elimination of heresy. Because of this task they sought to clarify the lines of orthodoxy through intellectual inquiry; they were from the beginning the more learned of the two orders and tended to attract scholars and intellectuals, who gave the order a leading role in formulating the thirteenth-century theological synthesis. Thomas Aquinas was himself a Dominican. Because the order provided an outlet for more personal religious experience and also developed an intellectual synthesis of that experience, it is not surprising that the Dominicans became the focus of speculative mysticism as well.

Eckhart rose to a position of responsibility in the order. He became prior of Erfurt some time before 1298 and then went to Paris to study for a degree in theology, which he received in 1302. Two years later he became provincial, or regional overseer, of all the monasteries in Saxony. In this capacity he undertook to reform several houses within his province, a task that required frequent visitations. On these occasions he preached to the members of the houses and developed his considerable talents in this field. In 1311, he was sent back to Paris to teach theology, and there he wrote his systematic theological treatise, the *Opus Tripartitum* or *Three Part Work*.

In 1325 a general meeting of the Dominican order at Venice raised doubts about the speculations of certain unnamed German friars. Whether this first sign of theological difficulties involved Eckhart or not cannot be said, but in the next year the archbishop of Cologne opened heresy proceedings against him. Eckhart appealed to the pope, and the trial became enmeshed in jurisdictional disputes. In 1327, after Pope John XXII had revoked the case to Avignon, twenty-eight statements found in Eckhart's writings were condemned as heretical. Eckhart disavowed the statements and returned to his province where he died shortly afterwards.

The church did not object to any claims of personal mystical insights that Eckhart himself made. In fact there is no record that he had ever had visions similar to those of Catherine of Siena. Nor did the language of his sermons ever indicate such experience; it was always based directly or indirectly on abstract and systematic analyses of mysticism. While not seeking to communicate a personal mystical experience, Eckhart wished to awaken scholastic theology to the possibility of regular, direct, and personal revelation. In a sense Eckhart expressed the rationalizing trends of his age. He wanted to generalize and organize the mystical experience, and in so doing he came into conflict with others seeking to organize experience in a different way.

Eckhart was a theologian who wrote and thought in the tradition of Thomas Aquinas but who differed from Thomas on the important issue of how God is known. Thomas saw two pathways: reason and revelation. Reason, operating on data provided by the senses, understands the laws of things and raises itself above nature to grasp from its own perspective the essence that underlies all nature. Revelation provides what man cannot attain by reason. It comes from outside his own experience, convincing him by the pattern that it imposes on humanity and nature. Eckhart accepted both these paths to knowledge but wished to add a third: the inner sense, God's direct revelation of himself to the inner soul independent of all senses or external guides. He maintained that the impression we have of this revelation is in fact valid and reflects essential attributes of the deity that cannot be otherwise acquired. Thomas recognized the existence of this type of knowledge but considered it special and not necessary. He thought that anything acquired in this way could also be gained from reason and revelation.

A theology of speculative mysticism must deal with two important problems: how mystical knowledge is acquired, and how it is communicated to others. In other words, how can a finite creature gain direct, personal insight into ultimate reality, and, having received such insight, how can he convincingly express it to others who have not shared the experience? Eckhart was most interested in the latter problem and suggested that the solution lay in the use of three techniques: negation, emanation, and the argument from cause. The first of these is the most striking because it seeks to define God by what he is not. Eckhart maintained that because God is outside all experience, he is not anything within human experience. Thus, attributes like "good," "just," or "merciful" only drag God down to the level of human nature. It would be more accurate to say he is none of these. "If anyone said that God was good, he would do him as great an injustice as if he said that the sun was black." In essence, negation cleared the mind of all preconceptions regarding God's nature. The technique of emanation was based on the notion that God is the perfection of all things; therefore all perfections emanate from him, and he can be defined partly as the perfect reality behind all virtues. In this sense God can indeed be described as perfect goodness, because whatever goodness we find in the world ultimately comes from God, the source of all goodness. Both negation and emanation were standard arguments in scholastic discourse, and Eckhart used them with equal frequency, but his use of negation was so striking and so extreme that one recent scholar has characterized his thought as "negative theology." Eckhart's third means of communicating God's nature is the argument from cause, which seeks to describe God in terms of the effects of which he is the cause. This, too, was common among scholastics, and Eckhart found it least useful because it implied a close relationship between God and creation. Eckhart maintained that God is so utterly different from his creatures that he can be truly known only outside of nature and ordinary experience.

Eckhart was not so much concerned about the means of acquiring mystical knowledge. He felt that to prepare oneself for mystical insight one should empty the mind of all content by withdrawing as far as possible both from experience and from all feeling related to experience. He called that process *Abgeschiedenheit,* meaning disinterest, solitude, or withdrawal. The concept is related to negation and Eckhart described it in those terms. One should not love one's fellow man or even God, because this is creaturely love and a part of the world. He cited, as an example of true understanding, Saint Paul, who renounced God for the sake of God.

Meister Eckhart's works describe mystical insights and the path by which the soul may be prepared to receive them in a way that stresses the distance between God and his creatures. God is so different and so far removed from the world that human nature could not be used as a path to discover as much about him as we should know. But Eckhart was careful to note that the world, too, was necessary for the soul's self-knowledge, and he never advocated complete renunciation; he simply insisted that the world did not provide the fullest possible insights. Yet in trying to incorporate mysticism into the systematic view of God, he broke apart the careful synthesis of natural and supernatural that formed the basis of the church's claim to mediate between God and man. The sentences that were condemned in 1327 were those that tried to show the otherness of God by saying that he is not good or that he should be renounced and not loved. Such ideas strained Christian orthodoxy to the breaking point.

Eckhart had little direct influence in the two centuries that followed his death. The condemnation of his key propositions placed his thought in the shadow of heresy and discouraged a popular following. In addition, the abstract and austere nature of his writings closed their full impact to all but the literate and sophisticated. Although his sermons were appealing and even earthy, Eckhart expressed his most central insights in terms that were hard to grasp. But he should not be seen as an isolated or uninfluential figure. Indirectly, he had a widespread and pervasive influence. Largely because of him, both popular piety and learned discourse during the fourteenth and fifteenth centuries were deeply aware of the possibilities of direct personal knowledge of God.

German, or "Rhineland," mysticism achieved its greatest popularity and influence through the efforts of two followers of Eckhart, Henry Suso (1300–1366) and John Tauler (1300–1361). By largely by-passing the lofty question of the nature of God and instead showing, by word and deed, the way to mystical knowledge, these men managed to avoid the odor of unorthodoxy and appeal to a wider segment of Christendom than Eckhart had reached. Suso in particular became very popular, both during his lifetime and afterward. His most famous work, the *Book of Eternal Wisdom,* was among the most popular books of the day, eclipsing even Thomas à Kempis' *Imitation of Christ.* Over five hundred manuscripts survive, including versions in German, Latin, French, English, and Dutch, and it was among the earliest works to be printed.

Through the *Book of Eternal Wisdom* and other writings Suso had a significant effect on devotional practice. He argued that the way to understand God was through the humanity of Christ. Men should piously meditate on the latter and live in such a way that they are constantly reminded of it. Suso himself carried personal piety to remarkable lengths. When he ate an apple, he would cut the fruit into quarters, eating three in honor of the Trinity and the fourth in honor of the love with which the Virgin Mary fed the infant Jesus. Since infants cannot peel apples, Suso would eat the last quarter with the paring on, and immediately after Christmas he would not eat the last quarter at all, for the newborn Jesus was too young to be fed raw fruit.

Johan Huizinga, one of the greatest modern historians of the late Middle Ages, sees the behavior of Suso and his contemporaries as a love of ritual for its own sake. To be sure, much late medieval devotion was purely formal and lacked deep feeling, but Suso's piety unquestionably had a spiritual base. His life was devoted to showing others the path that he had found. He claimed that midway in his life he had experienced God with mystical clarity and that words alone were inadequate to express this ineffable insight. After his vision, he gave himself over increasingly to preaching and pastoral care. He had never been deeply preoccupied by theological issues. Except for some passages in his early works where he sought to find an orthodox interpretation for Eckhart's condemned statements, Suso eschewed theological speculation in favor of describing the joys of direct mystical knowledge of the divine. Nature, he said, is a metaphor for the richness and fertility of the world beyond our senses, and he brought the message home with all the lush imagery of literature. His popularity is easy to understand.

Suso's contemporary, John Tauler, was, by contrast, far more interested in developing a mystical theology. Tauler was also a practicing mystic, though he was reticent about describing his own experiences. Like Suso, his goal was to show the way to mystical insight, and unlike Eckhart, he did not become embroiled in an attempt to describe the nature of God. His great concern was to identify the aspects of human nature revealed by mystical insights. Austere and demanding in his preaching and writing, Tauler never acquired Suso's popularity.

Tauler believed that human nature consisted of an animal-sensual component, a rational component, and a spiritual component; the last was the innermost and highest part of the soul. In one sense the spiritual component is the most stable and solid, for it constitutes the ground of our existence; but in another sense it is constantly moving upward and is the means by which we join ourselves to God. It is both the place and the energy of our spiritual life. The spiritual component, which Tauler called the *gemüte,* can be seen as a sign that each individual existed in the mind of God before creation. The fall of Adam corrupted man's will but not his gemüte, for the latter continues to bind man to God and offers him a path to regain lost intimacy with the divine. Indeed, God could not destroy the gemüte even if he wished to, because it is part of his own being as well as of man's. The last doctrine trembles on the brink of heresy, for it seems to question God's omnipotence and to obliterate the distinction between God and the soul. Some of Tauler's works were in fact questioned, but he escaped the fate of Eckhart. His works continued to be widely read throughout the fifteenth and sixteenth centuries without any taint of unorthodoxy. Luther read Tauler's sermons just before he published the famous Ninety-Five Theses, but he did so only because Tauler was a respected mystic who had pointed the way to a deeper and more immediate knowledge of God.

A third important figure in the tradition of Rhineland mysticism was Nicholas of Cusa (1401–1464), a thinker of such breadth and originality that he defies categorization. Some historians have regarded him as a founder of modern science and philosophy, because a century before Copernicus he maintained that the earth moves, and his philosophical concept that God is the reconciliation of opposites seems to anticipate nineteenth-century German idealism. But Nicholas expressed his notions in the language of medieval scholasticism, and it would be as fair to call him the last of the old as the first of the new. Nicholas had read Eckhart with great interest, though with caution, for in his manuscript copy we find marginal notes in Nicholas' hand pointing out the places where Eckhart could not be followed with safety. But Meister Eckhart's description of God in terms of paradoxes clearly had an impact and helped Nicholas formulate his own central doctrine — namely, that God within himself reconciles all opposites: God is simultaneously the most and the least, the brightest and the darkest, the fastest and the slowest.

The Rhineland mystics have often been considered forerunners of the Reformation. We know, for example, that Luther was interested in their thinking. But more than that, the mystics shared many traits with the sixteenth-century reformers. They were deeply committed to personal religious experience and distrusted the formalized and ritualistic practices of the established church; they were sincerely and deeply pious, and, like Luther himself, many of them practiced asceticism for a time and then reacted against it. Suso in his youth wore hair shirts and iron chains, tied his hands at night so that he could not scratch his sores, and deprived himself of food and drink. These practices ruined his health but failed to soothe his soul, and he gave them up suddenly and decisively in order to explore gentler, more spiritual means of solace. The mystics were also concerned with institutional reform and clerical corruption. Suso and Eckhart both actively campaigned to bring the Dominicans back to the purity of their original rules, and Nicholas of Cusa, who became a bishop, made his diocese of Brixen a model of honest administration and intelligent devotional practice.

These concerns illustrate the links between the mystics and the later reformers, but beneath them lay an even deeper community of values and ideas. Eckhart and his followers believed that knowledge of ultimate reality was intensely and unavoidably personal and did not easily fit into a well-ordered world. It was this vision that inspired Luther and led to the rupture of the institutional church. But mysticism was not the only force for reform active in the fourteenth and fifteenth centuries. It coexisted with two other important intellectual movements, nominalism and humanism, that were largely unconcerned with direct experience of God and in fact tended to distrust the mystics' claims. But all three movements were equally dissatisfied with late medieval rationalism, and that is the common theme that gave them their influence on the sixteenth-century Reformation.

Bibliography

The three chapters in Part Five stress the fourteenth- and fifteenth-century antecedents of the Reformation. An excellent collection of recent essays in this field can be found in *The Reformation in Medieval Perspective,* ed. Steven Ozment (Chicago: Quadrangle Books, 1971).

For a broad study of mysticism see Evelyn Underhill, *The Mystics of the Church* (New York: Schocken Books, 1964). For more particular studies of the Rhineland mystics see James Clark, *The Great German Mystics* (Oxford: Blackwell, 1949), or Jeanne Ancelet-Hustache, *Maître Eckhart et la Mystique rhénaine* (Paris: Editions du Seuil, 1956). Millard Meiss, *Painting in Florence and Siena* (New York: Harper and Row, 1973), gives a brief sketch of the career of Catherine of Siena. See Vladimir Lossky, *Théologie negative et connaissance de Dieu chez Maître Eckhart* (Paris: Vrin, 1960), for an analysis of Eckhart's systematic theology, and Steven Ozment, *Homo Spiritualis* (Leiden: Brill, 1969), for a discussion of Tauler's concept of man in comparison with Luther's. For Nicholas of Cusa see Paul Sigmund, *Nicholas of Cusa and Medieval Political Thought* (Cambridge: Harvard University Press, 1963).

The best collection of Eckhart's writings in English is Raymond Blakney's *Meister Eckhart* (New York: Harper and Row, 1941). Although this contains none of the *Opus Tripartitum,* it does include many sermons and short essays. For Tauler's works see his *Spiritual Conferences,* trans. E. Colledge and Sister Mary Jane (St. Louis: Herder, 1961); for Suso see *The Exemplar,* trans. A. Edward (Dubuque, Iowa: Priority Press, 1962).

The Brethren of the Common Life have often been credited for much of the rise of humanism in northern Europe. The most famous statement of this interpretation is Albert Hyma's *The Brethren of the Common Life* (Grand Rapids, Mich.: Eerdmans, 1950). More recently, Regnerus Post, *The Modern Devotion* (Leiden: Brill, 1968), has sought to show that they played less of a role and limited themselves to the activities mentioned in this chapter.

18 Nominalism

Mysticism stressed the otherness of God, but at the same time it offered a way to reach out and experience God directly. A part of each man's soul was in some way part of God himself, and men could use this channel to gain direct access to the divine. By contrast, the theological school called nominalism separated God from the world and denied even this means of reaching him. Creation, said the nominalists, does not reflect God's nature, for God is pure, unlimited will. God might easily have created other worlds and other values, and no study of this world can provide us with insight into his true nature.

In one form or another nominalism had existed among medieval thinkers at least since the eleventh century. From its inception, nominalism had been an abstruse doctrine, but its statement in the fourteenth and fifteenth centuries was especially extreme and presents the modern student with a considerable challenge to his understanding. William of Ockham (1285?–1349?), the leading figure in late medieval nominalism, turned the world inside out in order to provide a new outlook on experience, and he gave us notions of truth, certainty, and reality totally unlike our ordinary definitions. Ockham intended to undercut the ordinary picture of the world and force us to think in extraordinary ways. Although the abstractions of Thomas Aquinas are not easy to grasp, they were intended to structure our daily experience; Ockham's method was to destroy common sense in order to give us new insight.

Little as we may question them in everyday life, the assumptions of common sense clearly do not represent accurately the minute detail of our experience. As we look down a straight railroad track, for example, our eyes see the rails meeting at the horizon, but our common sense "sees" them continuing parallel to the end of the line. Without the operation of common sense we could hardly ride trains with confidence, because there is nothing in our actual visual perception of the track to tell us that the rails are parallel. Thus we allow our common sense to overrule our sight.

We in the twentieth century are accustomed to the idea that there are many things in the abstract world of science and mathematics that defy common sense. We accept, even if we may not understand, non-Euclidian geometries — geometries that define worlds of more than three dimensions, worlds where parallel lines do meet or the size of solid objects literally decreases as the distance from the observer increases. We cannot use non-Euclidian geometries to drive trains, but we can use them to open up avenues of thought and cast our experience into new perspectives not available within the confines of conventional geometry. Like such geometries, nominalism violates "common sense" at every turn because it seeks to show that what we regard as obvious and everyday truth is actually an abstract and arbitrary construction superimposed on raw experience.

The Philosophy of Nominalism: William of Ockham

The leading nominalist of the fourteenth century was William of Ockham, an Englishman and younger contemporary of Meister Eckhart. He became a Franciscan friar and studied and taught at Oxford, where he developed some of his most important ideas, expressed in a series of commentaries and treatises on particular philosophical and theological problems. His most important work was a commentary on the *Sentences* of Peter Lombard. The chancellor of the university in 1323 accused Ockham of expressing heretical ideas in his commentary, and in the following year he was summoned to the papal court at Avignon to answer the charges. After four years, with the case still undecided, Ockham fled from Avignon and took refuge at Munich with the Holy Roman emperor, Lewis IV, and there he remained for the rest of his life supporting the emperor's struggles against the pope. Ockham died in 1349, probably from the Black Death, finally condemned by the church not for heresy but for refusing to submit to papal authority.

Ockham's works divide human knowledge sharply into two separate types. The contrast between Ockham and Thomas Aquinas is striking. Whereas Thomas tried to unify and synthesize aspects of life that seemed irreconcilable, Ockham broke them apart and drew sharp, impenetrable boundaries. For Thomas and most other thirteenth-century thinkers, a contradiction or paradox was a challenge to find a means of reconciling the opposing terms and show that there was an underlying unity. But for William such a tactic was a sign of muddled thinking, which mixed concepts that sharper analysis would prove irreducibly opposite. For example, Thomas carefully integrated the operations of faith and reason, showing that each was reliable in its own sphere of inquiry and that the truths of one could never contradict those of the other. Ockham, by contrast, felt that they were radically different ways of knowing, and that the truths of faith and reason need not coincide. To appreciate the impact of late medieval nominalism we must keep in mind that William of Ockham could not be more different from his thirteenth-century predecessor Thomas Aquinas; a gulf separates their basic attitudes.

Ockham's basic categories of knowledge are the intuitive and the abstractive. The distinction is simple: intuitive knowledge allows us to establish whether a thing exists; abstractive knowledge does not. Intuitive knowledge is derived from sensory perceptions; it comes from the raw data of experience. Moreover, it includes a capacity that many previous thinkers denied it, but that is necessary to make the absolute distinction Ockham intends. Intuitive knowledge includes not only the sensory perception of an object but also the process of identifying it. Thus, intuitive intellect tells us that we are facing an object of a certain size, color, and shape, and moreover that the object is a chair or the child next door. Aquinas and most other thinkers said that identification is the result of abstraction and that knowledge therefore results from a combination of abstraction and perception. Ockham insists that the faculty of perception inherently contains the power to identify objects; its province is to establish truth, and it needs no help whatsoever from abstraction.

The abstractive intellect forms concepts; its province is not to demonstrate truth but to understand the truths discovered by intuition. It does this most obviously by classifying the objects we perceive into general categories, which allow us to grasp relationships and remember whole groups of individual perceptions. Thus, we can see an object for the first time and still recognize it as a chair, because our abstractive intellect has grouped the characteristics of other such objects into the general category "chair." But this is not a demonstration of truth, and there is no way to show that the general concept "chair" has any real existence. The denial of existence to universal categories is the source of the term "nominalism, because it holds that general terms are mere names (*nomen* is Latin for name) and not objects in their own right. The extreme view among early nominalists maintained that the terms "chair" and "man" have no more reality than the breath with which they are pronounced. Ockham does not go so far. He says that the general concepts formed by the abstractive intellect have a logical status that prevents them from being completely arbitrary and unrelated to the objects they seek to describe.

By separating logic from the existence of things, Ockham sought to create sharper tools of analysis and clearly identify the limits within which logic and mathematics can operate. In particular, he insisted that the only way to construct a tautology — a statement that is necessarily true — is to make the statement hypothetical. For instance, most would consider the statement "A triangle with all angles equal has all sides equal" to be a necessarily true statement, for this is basic geometry. Ockham would say that the statement is necessarily true only if rephrased. To construct a tautology we must say, "If there is a triangle such that all angles equal imply all sides equal, then a triangle with all angles equal has all sides equal."

All general terms must be similarly analyzed. The term "man," for instance, implies certain characteristics abstracted from all men that allow us to identify any particular man as a member of the species. Most of us would agree that when we encounter particular individuals we can easily recognize them as men, but we would be reluctant to identify all the necessary characteristics — particularly moral or psychological ones — that a particular human being must show to be considered human. Ockham maintains that this reluctance is fully justified; no necessary attributes can be found, because all necessary statements must be hypothetical. The statement "A man is human (that is, belongs to the species of man)" is not necessarily true unless it is stated, "If there is a man who is human, then he is human." Only by postulating the existence of a particular man with perceptible traits can we say that these traits are necessarily human ones. Ockham's reasoning can also be applied to railroad tracks, despite the fact that he never saw them. We can construct logical proofs that the tracks will never meet because they are parallel, and we can prove that parallel lines do not meet. Nevertheless, we cannot make a necessary statement that any particular tracks will not meet unless we walk down them to their terminal. Even in that case we can only say that the tracks we have tested do not meet.

For Ockham, then, only particulars can be said to exist, because the faculty with which we perceive particulars is the only one that permits us to make statements about existence. The world of general concepts is a world where only conditional statements can be made, statements that depend for their veracity on perceptions of the physical world. And indeed, individual events cannot truly be said to depend on physical laws, for the laws of physical motion are products of the abstractive intellect and have no necessary existence. Thus everything in the universe is contingent to its roots; that being the case, everything could have been made differently, and anything could change in any respect at any time. None of the apparent regularities in the universe, neither the daily rising of the sun nor the values of human life, is necessary; any of these could change without a moment's notice.

Firmly, categorically, and without compromise, Ockham maintained that the structure of the human mind can tell us nothing about the essential nature of the universe. Insofar as our mind is particular, it is contingent, and insofar as it is part of the world of universals and ideas, it can tell us nothing about existence. This limitation applies not only to our grasp of the physical world, where Ockham requires us to operate through observation rather than deduction; it also applies to the moral world. We know that love is a virtue, both from an analysis of our own minds and from revelation, but that does not mean that God's nature is love. He could have just as easily created a world in which malice was a virtue, without changing any of his own essential attributes. He did not create such a world, and from revelation we can be sure that he did not, but we cannot reason from creation to an understanding of the creator.

The implications of Ockham's epistemology become more surprising the further they are followed. His statements that there are no necessary regularities in the universe, or that we may change our essential natures at any time, seem to defy experience and offend common sense. Certainly he was aware of the regularities of experience that the rest of us base our lives on. Why did he go so far out of the way to assert that these laws are unreal? Did nominalism have anything to contribute beyond abstract and unreasonable formulations? To answer these questions we have to shift our perspective from the purely philosophical aspects of nominalism to some of the ways it came to be used in society.

The Pastoral Effects of Nominalism: Confession and Gabriel Biel

Nominalism had a widespread influence. The empiricism that underlies modern science is akin to the nominalist notion that objects exist in and for themselves, not as reflections of higher realities. Furthermore, Ockham formulated the logical principle that the simplest possible explanation for a phenomenon should be adopted. This principle too, known as Ockham's razor, is congruent with the assumptions of contemporary science. These two ideas give Ockham's thought a modern flavor, even though, as we have seen, science actually developed in the sixteenth century more directly from the neo-Platonist tradition.

In addition to this long-range significance, Ockham's ideas played a crucial role in the genesis of Luther's thought. During the fifteenth century Ockham's followers made of his ideas the principal alternative to Thomas Aquinas' theology. The Modern Way, as Ockham's theology was called, was taught in many of Europe's leading universities, particularly those in Germany. Erfurt, where Luther studied, was an important nominalist center. Gabriel Biel (d. 1485), one of Ockham's most important followers, had taught there after 1451, and Luther studied deeply in his works before coming to his own theological position.

Biel was more interested than Ockham in the practical and pastoral implications of nominalism. In particular, he posed a new view of the sacrament of penance, the practice of regular confession to the parish priest. Biel sought to eliminate from this sacrament some of the problems that bothered many devout Christians in the fifteenth century. To understand Biel's contribution and to illuminate the general significance of nominalism for religious questions, we must first look more closely at how the sacrament developed during the period before Biel.

Among the means chosen by the church to organize religious life, few had a more direct effect on the lives of Christians than the practice of regular confession to the parish priest. The advantages of the institution are clear. First, it strengthened the parish system.

Second, confession gave the priest greater awareness of the concerns and behavior of his flock, and also greater control over their shared values. Third, in conjunction with an efficient hierarchical organization within the clergy, the priest's knowledge could be made available to all levels of the church. At the same time policies adopted by the bishops or the pope could be translated effectively into popular attitudes and behavior. The practice of private aural confession can be traced back to the early Middle Ages in certain parts of Europe, particularly Ireland, but it did not become a widespread custom backed by sophisticated administrative techniques and theological underpinnings until 1343, when it was codified by Clement VI in the bull *Unigenitus dei Filius*.

Actually, the church conceived of penance as a four-step process, of which confession, or acknowledgment that a sin has been committed, is only one. The first step in the sacrament of penance is contrition. One must feel genuinely sorry for his sin, and the sorrow should be more than simple fear of punishment. The latter is called "attrition," and because it makes the repentance of the sinner imperfect it destroys the efficacy of the sacrament. Confession is the second step in the sacrament. Normally, confession must be made to a priest, but in the fourteenth century the church did not insist so strongly on this point as it did after the Council of Trent. Contrition and confession wipe away the guilt of the sin and bring about the third step in the sacrament: absolution bestowed by a priest. By recognizing a sin and truly repenting, the sinner has saved himself from the eternal punishment that would otherwise be his due and has removed the effects of the sin from his soul. The fourth and last step in the sacrament is actual penance; its concern is no longer with the sinner as a private person, but with the social effects of the sin. A sin inevitably causes damage to others, as well as to the personality of the sinner, and that damage is hard to assess, for it may continue long after the sinner has repented and even after his death. Some sins, like gossiping, are likely to have short-lived effects, while others, like murder, are likely to continue indefinitely, for no one knows what the murdered person might have accomplished had he lived. To deal with the relative effect of specific sins the church has devised standards that assess the probable time necessary to work out the effects, and those standards are expressed as numbers of years in purgatory.

Several factors determine the length of time needed to resolve the effects of a particular sin. This time can be shortened if the sinner, or even a third party, does good works to offset the effects of the sin. If someone takes over the task of rearing a murdered man's children, the effect of the murder is less severe than if they had been left alone. In the eyes of the church, all mankind is interdependent, and the church itself administers this solidarity; thus it can oversee a treasury of the good works of all men, which collectively help to alleviate the effects of specific sins. Thus a sinner can reduce the effect of his own sin by doing penance and by relying on the good works of others to offset the full temporal punishment that would otherwise be due.

Indulgences originated in the concept of penance as a substitute for punishment. At first the penitent was required to make a pilgrimage or perform an act of charity; but inasmuch as these were only substitutes for the real punishment due, it was a simple step to make further substitutes for the original ones. The sinner could make his penance by paying the cost of going on a pilgrimage in lieu of actually making the trip. In an age when travel was both expensive and dangerous, saving one's soul could easily cost one's body, and the monetary substitution was sensible. The sinner suffered financially, and the church could use his money in acts of charity to build up its spiritual treasury of mankind. Thus indulgences were born. The opportunities for abusing the practice of giving money for penance are legion, and many churchmen practiced them all. Indulgences were frequently criticized, and Luther's famous attack is only one among many. Yet the principle is sound, and difficult to attack without undermining the entire theology of penance.

The confessional system was designed to provide comfort for the large majority of Christians. It assured them that their sins could be absolved in such a way that neither they nor the society around them would be irreparably harmed. There is every indication that the system served its purpose and that most of the faithful found it completely satisfying. But some found it distinctly upsetting. Martin Luther's well-known difficulties in finding solace in the sacrament of penance will be treated in another chapter, and he was certainly not alone.

The strength of the confessional system lies in its ability to satisfy certain religious sensibilities. It deals with the sins of society, and it promises, through the accumulated wisdom of the church, to absolve more sins and match more sins with their proper punishments than any other system. Yet sin is a personal as well as a social problem, and such probable judgments will not satisfy everyone. The intellectual conviction that most sins are absolved may assuage most people's fears for their souls, but others will insist on absolute assurance that their own personal sins have been absolved. The latter assurance the sacrament cannot provide and does not pretend to provide. The assurance of absolution that the sacrament of penance offers is of the type that we in the twentieth century call statistical. It is irrefutably clear that airplanes are much safer than other forms of transportation, and most people are satisfied with the statistical assurance that they are less likely to die in an airplane than in an automobile. Some, however, despite their intellectual awareness of this fact, are still afraid to fly. They feel the need for personal assurance of survival, and that the statistics do not pretend to give.

The sacrament of penance applies probable judgments at two key points. First and most obviously, in assigning the penance it judges the probable seriousness of the sin. In actuality a minor sin can sometimes have far-reaching and disastrous consequences. From a social point of view this is not so important, since over the long run these inequities will balance out against one another. From the point of view of a sensitive person worrying about a particular sin he has committed, however, the possibility that the effects could be unusual might prove deeply disturbing.

The second point at which probable judgments are applied can be even more unsatisfying. The efficacy of the sacrament of penance depends on a perfect act of contrition — being truly sorry rather than simply being afraid of punishment. Since everyone is afraid of punishment, it is not easy even for the individual himself to know exactly his real motive toward repentance. One of the advantages of confession before a priest is that the priest, drawing on the church's experience, can try to reassure the sinner that external signs — like willingness to redress the wrong, to apologize, to give back stolen money — suggest that his act of contrition is perfect. But the priest can never be completely sure, since he sees only the external signs and not the internal feelings. Here again the church is only claiming statistically that most people who manifest these signs are truly sorry, not that each person necessarily is. To a sensitive and introspective conscience such assurance is inadequate.

This weakness of the confessional system was in the eyes of the church more than counterbalanced by its social usefulness and its success in satisfying the great majority of the faithful. The late medieval period, which placed a high value on social, intellectual and political organization, was more impressed by what we would call statistics than a less peaceful and less systematic age might have been. But the fact remains that the confessional system as originally constituted could not satisfy everybody.

Nominalism, however, offered a fresh perspective. By bringing out some important implications of the Ockhamist division of knowledge, Biel offered a means of stressing the psychological aspects of the sacrament and making it more personal. Biel, like Ockham before him, maintained that just as there are two separate types of knowledge, so are there two separate orders in the universe. The first is the order according to God's ordained power. This is the world that God has freely chosen to create and the laws he has chosen to follow. We deal with this first order through intuitive knowledge. But God's nature is not limited by his creation, nor is his world an indication of his nature. He might have created any other world, any other laws, or any other values. In fact the only limitation on the possibilities is the law of noncontradiction. God cannot both create and not create something; he cannot make virtues of both malice and love. The worlds that God could have chosen to create belong to the order established according to his absolute power. This second order may be investigated only by the abstractive intellect.

Before Ockham, Christian thinkers had conveniently divided the universe between nature and supernature. Ockham and Biel suggested another division. In their view God and all supernatural values permeate both orders; God makes himself manifest in both experienced and nonexperienced reality. The only difference lies in the fact that he has actually chosen one sphere — the order according to his ordained power — though he could have chosen any other — the order according to his absolute power. The sphere he has chosen can neither be discovered by reason nor can it be predicted; it can only be observed. Physical aspects of this sphere must be seen by looking at events; its spiritual aspects and values emerge from revelation. In the nominalist view, revelation itself should be considered a particular datum of experience that can therefore be studied through the intuitive intellect.

The division of the universe between two orders according to God's ordained power or his absolute power contains important implications for the sacrament of penance, which the division renders more effective in dealing with personal guilt. First, only the unbeliever need trouble himself with the order of absolute power; that is the realm where judgments are made by abstract thinking, which of course makes them only probable. The believer *knows* the laws that God has ordained and that judgments based on those laws are certain because God has freely committed himself to them. Thus concern is shifted away from the probable effects of sins, about which certainty is intrinsically impossible, toward personal obedience to God's commands, about which a person *can* make a certain judgment.

Biel tells us that God's laws are not mere rules of conduct; they are commands to love, and the highest law is to love God for his own sake. Moreover, we have within us the capacity to obey this law. Original sin has not corrupted the will; it has simply robbed us of the pleasure that Adam felt in loving God naturally for his own sake. The pleasure can be reacquired through personal effort. We can learn through reading and observation that the love of God is its own highest reward. Like revelation, this is a particular fact to be observed and appears in the examples of others who loved God for his own sake, especially Christ. Since the Christian's own efforts are so important as he strives toward salvation and seeks to love God for his own sake, the nature of the sacrament of penance is changed. Penance becomes less a sacramental act, whereby the church bestows sanctifying grace through its apostolic powers, than a psychological confrontation, whereby the sinner is assured that his sin is forgiven.

How can the sinner acquire a personal assurance of forgiveness? Not from any deduction from the nature of God, for deduction only produces probable conclusions. Assurance must come from observation. By looking at the Bible, says Biel, we see that God has ordained the world as the place in which man can sanctify himself and, more important, we see that man can satisfy the requirements for sanctification. The command to love God for his own sake should not be taken as an injunction to look deeply within ourselves and speculate on all the motives for our acts. Instead it is a command to do the very best that is in us, to use our own natural powers. We can have confidence in the efficacy of those powers because of two commitments that God has made to men. First, God has promised to reward those who do the best that is in them by granting them the habit of grace; that is, he promises to restore in us

Adam's primal pleasure in good acts for their own sake. The habit of grace will lead to further meritorious acts and bring us at last to the love of God for his own sake. Second, God has promised to infuse with saving grace and reward with salvation those who manage to love him for his own sake. From time to time he may extend his mercy even to those who have not earned salvation, but he has promised with certainty that those who achieve his command through their own merits will never be denied salvation.

This doctrine comes very close to the early church heresy of Pelagianism, the doctrine promoted by a rival of Saint Augustine's who denied original sin. Though Biel laid remarkable stress on man's unaided efforts, he was not trying to revive ancient heresies. He was trying not to overturn but to understand the basic Augustinian Christianity that had prevailed through the millennium before him. He affirmed that God's general assistance is necessary for the performance of any good work, and in this sense God's grace precedes and supports the Christian at all stages of his journey to salvation. Nor, when he spoke of the order of God's ordained power, did Biel intend to summon up the image of God as a clockmaker who merely created the world and then let it run according to its own laws. God's creation of the ordained world is never finished at any point in time, for time itself is part of his creation. God sustains the order at all points and all moments by his totally unconditioned will. His promises assure us that the order will continue, but because of *him* — not because of itself .

Biel's pastoral theology was likewise orthodox in that it never offered Christians *absolute* assurance of their own personal salvation. No theology within the mainstream of Christianity has ever offered such assurance. What Biel promised was not subjective assurance of being saved but objective assurance of the conditions for salvation. By limiting the Christian's concern to the sphere of God's ordained power, Biel intended to eliminate fruitless speculation on the infinite possibilities that might hypothetically affect the sinner's soul. Instead he drew attention to God's clear and explicit laws, which show God's mercy but in no way limit his nature. We are certain of the requirements that will bring salvation because the evidence is open to our intuitive knowledge, which in turn produces necessary and certain statements.

In short, Biel says that the Christian need not speculate about the nature of God or about his own salvation. Instead he is called to love God for his own sake. The church can give psychological help in this task. It brings hope to the believer through the Incarnation and the sacraments dependent on it, and fear through the Last Judgment promised in revelation. The Christian can never achieve subjective certainty that he is saved, but in wavering between fear and hope he can have some confidence that he is on the right path. Thus nominalism, without weakening the sacramental position of the church, related it more directly to personal needs for assurance.

The nominalists of the fourteenth and fifteenth centuries sought an understanding of orthodox Christianity that would comprehend dimensions of human experience that they felt had not been adequately understood by earlier theologians. They endeavored to clarify Christian orthodoxy, not undermine it. Both Ockham and Biel considered themselves in the mainstream of Christian thinking. Neither the sharp logical distinctions of Ockham's epistemology nor Biel's innovations in pastoral theology attracted in their own day the disapproval that later Catholic theologians have expressed for nominalism. Although some of Ockham's statements were condemned by an ecclesiastical body, he never suffered papal condemnation, as did Eckhart. Many of Biel's observations on the sacrament of penance were later accepted by the Council of Trent. Nominalism remained throughout this period a respectable alternative to Thomistic theology.

The nominalists divided faith from reason and reason from experience in a manner antithetical to the fine blending achieved by Saint Thomas. Biel's concentration on the world of God's ordained power greatly enhanced the personal element in the sacraments, but by dividing reality into two worlds Biel implicitly called into question the church's ability to join them together and administer their union. None of the major nominalists during the period before the sixteenth century faced this implication squarely, partly because orthodoxy was still sufficiently flexible to allow a diversity of approaches to religious truth, and partly because the nominalists did not think of themselves as radicals. But in the sixteenth century a stronger and narrower sense of orthodoxy forced the incompatibility of Ockham and Thomas into focus, and a bolder and more forceful thinker in the person of Martin Luther would derive from the logic of nominalism a fundamentally new statement of religious life.

To summarize the contribution of the nominalists, they introduced new radical dichotomies into experience. These dichotomies sprang from the unlimited sovereign will of God. The nominalists used this notion to stress the importance of human actions, maintaining that God has chosen to reward our efforts even though they have no merit apart from his will. This stance in turn gave new force to the sacrament of penance. The doctrine of the absolute sovereignty of God's will, however, could be used to deny man's ability to work for his own salvation. The sixteenth-century reformers agreed with Ockham on the *absolute* power of God but dissented from the nominalist emphasis on our ability to act freely within the realm of his *ordained* power.

Bibliography

For a clear and readable introduction to nominalism the student should probably start with Meyrick Carrée's *Realists and Nominalists* (London: Oxford University Press, 1946). A more specialized study is Paul Vignaux's remarkably lucid study of Ockham's philosophy, *Nominalisme au XIVe siècle* (Montreal: Institute d'études médiévales, 1948). See also the same author's *Philosophy in the Middle Ages,* trans. E. C. Hall (New York: Meridian Books, 1959). For Gabriel Biel see Heiko Oberman's difficult but penetrating study, *The Harvest of Medieval Theology,* rev. ed. (Grand Rapids, Mich.: W. B. Eerdmans, 1967). Oberman stresses the similarity between Biel and Ockham and gives a good account of varying schools of interpretation.

A figure related to the nominalists who expressed himself in the field of political thought is Marsilio of Padua, whose writings give a different perspective on nominalism. See his *Defender of the Peace,* translated with a good introduction by Alan Gewirth, 2 vols. (New York: Columbia University Press, 1956).

The nominalists used such technical language that it is hard to get much out of their own writings. Some of Ockham's writings are available in English for those who wish to try. See *Philosophical Writings,* trans. P. Boehner (Indianapolis: Bobbs-Merrill, 1964), and *Predestination: God's Foreknowledge and Future Contingents,* trans. M. Adams and N. Kretzmann (New York: Appleton-Century-Crofts, 1969). Some of Biel's treatises have been translated by H. Oberman, D. Zerfoss, and W. Courtenay in *Defensorum Obedientiae Apostolicae et Alia Documenta* (Cambridge: Harvard University Press, 1968). A more manageable selection from Biel is found in Oberman's edition of *Forerunners of the Reformation,* trans. P. Nyhus (New York: Holt, Rinehart and Winston, 1966).

19 Northern Humanism

Early Humanism in the North

Humanism offered a third alternative to Thomistic philosophy, less systematic and abstract than mysticism or nominalism but equally concerned with the personal elements of life. Humanist philosophy was largely imported into northern Europe from Italy, and its influence was especially felt in the last half of the fifteenth century, as growing contacts with Italy culminated in the invasions. Although Italy supplied the decisive impetus, the movement was not entirely dependent on Italian models. During the fourteenth century a significant number of northern scholars, without any outside influence, used the classics and looked for the moral value of learning in a manner that might earn them the title of humanists. Avignon in particular was a center of intellectual activity where humanist concerns could be found, and in the opinion of some modern historians it was an important source even for Italian humanism. The town became the site of the papal university early in the fourteenth century and later the residence of the popes themselves. Petrarch resided there much of his life, and his influence remained even after he left for Italy. Nicholas of Clemange, the secretary to Benedict XIII, and Jean Muret were both interested in humanist scholarship. The Holy Roman Empire also had centers of humanist learning, notably the court of Charles IV (1347–1378) in Prague. Charles founded the city's university in 1348. The scholars who were attracted to study at Prague, unlike those at most other European universities, devoted themselves more to the use of the classics and the perfection of their Latin than to systematic philosophy. Charles' chancellor, Johannes von Neumarkt, wrote a book on forms for official documents and letters used in diplomacy in which he drew on classical models.

These early humanists expressed themes and values different from those of the first Italian humanists. Guillaume Saignet, for example, wrote a tract in which Nature laments against clerical celibacy. His use of the dialogue form, his personification of ideals, and his classical references all suggest a humanist approach, but his theme would hardly have interested the Italian humanists. Petrarch was deeply concerned with religion but seldom with clerical or ecclesiastical matters. Saignet in fact cited Petrarch as an example of how wretched priests became under their vows of chastity. Petrarch would certainly have been surprised, since he neither observed the vows nor seriously worried about the problem until middle age, when he took up chastity for quite personal reasons. The superficiality of humanist techniques among northern thinkers can be seen further in Johann von Tepl's *Ackerman aus Bohmen,* which recounts a dialogue between a peasant and Death after the latter has taken the peasant's wife. Both the theme and its treatment are quite traditional, and the only influence of humanism is Tepl's familiarity with Plato, Seneca, and Boethius.

This tentative period of humanism came to an end as Italian influences asserted themselves in the North after the Council of Constance (1414–1418). Many of Italy's leading humanists attended this council. They were impressed both with the variety of manuscripts available in northern libraries and with the opportunities for employment among northern rulers, who were eager to have learned and cultured men in attendance at their courts. Poggio Bracciolini went from Constance to England in 1418 to serve as chancellor to Henry Beaufort. Poggio was mainly interested in investigating the English libraries and stayed in England four years, before the lack of kindred spirits drove him back to his homeland. Poggio seems to have had little direct influence, but another Italian, Piero del Monte, served as papal tax collector in England from 1435 to 1440. During his tenure he influenced the brother of Henry V, Duke Humphrey of Gloucester, to promote humanist studies. Humphrey patronized Italian humanists, founded a famous library at Oxford, commissioned Leonardo Bruni to translate Aristotle for him, and kept several Italians as residents in his household. More importantly, he encouraged English scholars and formed the first circle of English humanists.

Exposure to the new scholarship led to much curiosity about Italy and a desire to find out how the Italians became so well educated.

Early in the 1440s a few Englishmen began to travel to Italy to enroll in humanist schools. They came especially to Guarino of Verona's establishment at Mantua, which they regarded as more scholarly in its orientation than Vittorino da Feltre's Casa Giocosa. The most important of these students was William Grey, chancellor of Oxford, who resigned in 1442 to study under Guarino. The willingness of a mature man, the head of England's great university, to go and study among children at Guarino's school clearly indicates how superior Italian education was considered to be.

England was not the only country of the North visited by Italians. Poggio, Vergerio, and Aeneas Sylvius Piccolomini, the future Pope Pius II, all visited Germany, although they left little lasting impact. In France, too, Italians initially made little impression, largely because of France's protracted war with England, which lasted until 1453. But as soon as the war was over, Italians arriving in Paris discovered an intense interest in their work. Tifernate, a minor humanist from Città di Castello, lectured on rhetoric in 1456 to large crowds of students who were more interested in improving their Latin than in learning humanist critical techniques. George Heronymous began to teach Greek to the Parisians in 1476 and continued until 1508. He was succeeded by an even better Greek scholar, John Lascaris. Throughout the last half of the century numerous minor Italian humanists attracted wide audiences by lecturing on subjects that would have been considered obscure and pointless only a generation before. Beroaldo lectured on Lucan in 1478, and Aemilio on historiography in 1483. These are subjects that might seem more appropriate to a university curriculum, but the university at Paris was largely indifferent to the new learning. Most of these humanists taught outside the university community and without its cooperation.

The French invasions of Italy that began in 1494 brought northern Europeans into even closer contact with humanism. To be sure, the invaders did not always appreciate the true achievements of the Italian Renaissance. Charles VIII and his advisors were far more impressed with the exotic colored marble of the Venetian palaces than with the proportion and harmony of Bramante's churches. But the invasions only intensified the impact of humanism on the North. The ground had long been prepared by Italian visitors to northern intellectual centers as well as by northerners who had come to Italy to study the new learning.

Ca' D'oro in Venice. Photo: Alinari.

The character of humanism in Germany, France, and England was strongly influenced by its foreign origins. Humanism was accepted at first because it provided a vocabulary that satisfied an existing need or spoke to a vital concern growing out of indigenous problems. For this reason the humanists of the North did not simply copy their Italian models but selected the values and intellectual tools appropriate to their interests. For this reason the various aspects of Italian humanism are not always absorbed together; in particular, philological and rhetorical interests were not always closely tied to social and moral concerns.

The intellectuals of northern Europe could not accept the secular language that the Italians had developed by the end of the fifteenth century. In their view, all important problems still had religious dimensions and had to be dealt with in religious terms. Machiavelli especially horrified them, and even civic humanists like Bruni seemed to offer little that they could directly assimilate into their intellectual vocabulary. Only the neo-Platonism of Ficino and his school seemed to offer direct help. Ficino's attempt to incorporate Platonic philosophy into Christian theology manifested a clear religious concern, and he explicitly assumed that learning and study by their very nature led to greater piety. This *docta pietas* (see Chapter 7) gave the thinkers of the North a solid justification for their studies. Consequently, many great northern humanists came to Florence to visit the Platonic Academy, where they felt more at home than among the less overtly religious movements of humanism.

French Humanism

Each country in the North differed in the way its intellectuals drew on humanism. In France a strong current of moral reform, frustrated by the indifference of the University of Paris, found much of use in the humanists. Many elements of French society were drawn to espouse a more austere morality. Two popular preachers of the late fifteenth century, Maillard and Menot, attacked with impunity members of the royal court for their lax conduct and political venality. In addition, many of the religious orders and colleges were reformed along stricter lines during the period. Gaguin (d. 1501), for example, one of the greatest French humanists of his day, brought the Trinitarian order back to the strict principles of its foundation. Because moral issues were so close to the heart of humanism, the French boasted many humanist thinkers whose sophistication and breadth are worthy to be compared with the Italians'.

Two of France's most impressive scholars were Lefèvre d'Etaples (1450–1536) and Guillaume Budé (1468–1540). Lefèvre's career showed the French preoccupation with moral reform, for he combined a number of diverse influences around this central concern. Early in his life he came under the influence of the thirteenth-century Spanish mystic Ramond Lull, who tried to convert the Arab world to Christianity by a combination of rational argument and ascetic mysticism. Lefèvre encountered Lull's works in the early 1490s and remained attracted to them throughout his life. He also read the works of Tauler and Suso. He found the asceticism of these mystics very appealing and on many occasions in his life considered withdrawing to a monastery.

In 1491 Lefèvre traveled to Italy and studied under Ficino at the Platonic Academy. There he was impressed by Pico della Mirandola's syncretism and his effort to find the central truth in all philosophies and religions. Just as he had previously been deeply affected by the mystic who withdrew from the world in order to convert it, so was he now interested in the humanists who placed their studies directly and clearly in the service of religious truth and piety.

The editions and commentaries Lefèvre produced after returning from Italy showed that he had learned to apply the techniques of humanist scholarship to his own concerns. In 1494, he published a commentary on Aristotle's ethics, which he called the *Moral Art (Ars Moralis)*. In Italy he had met the noted Aristotelian scholar Emolao Barbaro, who had convinced him of the importance of understanding Aristotle. Lefèvre's commentary set out to separate the philosopher from his scholastic commentators and find the essence of his teaching. Significantly, the first of Lefèvre's works concerned the problem of ethics.

He next turned his scholarly talents to Christian texts. In 1505 he produced an edition of John of Damascus, showing the same interest in the early church fathers that characterized so many Italian humanists. Four years later, in 1509, he finished his most famous work, the *Quintuplex Psalter,* in which he presented five versions of the Psalms side by side to make the text as clear as possible. This was followed in 1512 by a commentary on Saint Paul's Epistles, which contained Lefèvre's own translations with frequent references to the Greek text, and finally in 1522 he published a commentary on the Gospel and a complete translation of the New Testament. But Lefèvre was also interested in mysticism and edited the works of Nicholas of Cusa.

In 1521, Briçonnet, bishop of Meaux, invited Lefèvre to help reform religious life in his diocese. Reform had always been one of Lefèvre's prime concerns, and he accepted with alacrity, joining a group of moral reformers whose fame spread throughout Europe. The group not only sought to abolish the traditional abuses of venality and corruption among the local clergy of the diocese but also instituted educational programs to raise the level of piety among laymen. They emphasized spiritual life rather than ritual observances and published simple French translations of biblical passages to bring the people closer to the simple and pure truths of Scripture. At Meaux, Lefèvre was able to combine all his interests into a coherent program for moral reform. He understood how useful the scholarly methods of humanism could be in support of his values.

His own scholarship, however, did not quite measure up to Italian standards. He accepted, for instance, the validity of an alleged correspondence between Saint Paul and Seneca that Italian humanists had discovered to be false seventy-five years earlier.

Guillaume Budé, by contrast, developed a scholarly expertise in no way inferior to Italian standards and became the finest Greek scholar in all Europe. But even his career demonstrates how greatly the French humanists were preoccupied with moral and practical matters. In his earliest work, a commentary on Justinian's law code published in 1508, he tried to separate the pure principles of Roman law from the scholastic interpretation that had accrued over the preceding centuries. His method was to identify the historical circumstances in which specific laws had been promulgated and thereby uncover the underlying principles. Similar interests led Budé to a study of Roman coins and in 1514 to write the *De Asse*, which established criteria for classifying and dating them. Such a work required the considerable historical sophistication that was at the heart of humanism. It is clear evidence of Budé's firm grasp of the principles of the new learning.

Nevertheless, Budé felt uncomfortable unless his learning was put to practical use. Both the commentary on the Justinian code and the book on coins were filled with asides that drew lessons for his own day. His subsequent works were even more overtly practical. He wrote a treatise on philology in 1525 that showed how the government could profit from the new learning, and in another work, the *De Transitu Hellenismi* (1532), he explained how Greek philosophy had been morally improved by being Christianized. Clearly the best French humanists did not regard knowledge as antiquarian or irrelevant; the pursuit of wisdom was the pursuit of a good and fruitful life in society. They sensed the concrete connection between learning and morality and discovered particular lessons in every area of humane study.

François Rabelais (1494?–1553?), although he is best known for his bawdy humor, must also be counted among the French humanists. His tale of the giants, *Gargantua and Pantagruel,* embodies many of the moral and educational concerns of Budé and d'Etaples. Rabelais' account of Pantagruel's education satirizes scholastic learning and holds out as an educational ideal the curriculum introduced by the Italian humanists. In the work Rabelais creates a monastery where the single rule is "Do what you will." Yet the monastery is not given over to license. Instead, Rabelais uses it to exemplify a simple piety, untrammeled by elaborate rules, whose aims resemble strikingly those of the reforming group at Meaux. In his commitment to moral education over scholastic, technical training, as well as in his critique of the ritualism of late medieval religion, Rabelais shows himself to be one of the most fully humanist of sixteenth-century French writers.

English Humanism

English humanists did not so fully appropriate the Italian tradition. English humanism never fully broached the issue of fundamental human values until very late — the middle of the sixteenth century; instead it was confined to a more or less superficial application to traditional intellectual problems. This happened in part because the earliest humanists were accepted in the established structure of university life. (Remember, for example, that the chancellor of Oxford was one of the first Englishmen to travel to Italy for humanist education.) Thus they accepted the traditional forms of university education and inquiry, unlike their French colleagues, who were forced to operate outside the university and frequently in opposition to it.

The superficiality of early English humanism can be seen in the career of John Whethamsted (d. 1465), the abbot of Saint Albans. One of the first Englishmen to come in direct contact with Italian humanism, Whethamsted produced a number of works influenced by Italian models and indicating that he had access to many classical texts. Nevertheless the works themselves showed little real understanding of Italian humanism. Whethamsted's Latin style was clumsy, and he used his textual sources without regard to historical context and only to substantiate points arising from systematic argument. His writings are diffuse and disorganized collections of information, seemingly untouched by the humanists' desire for clarity and elegance.

The most famous humanists who followed Whethamsted, John Colet (1466–1519) and Thomas More (1478–1535), understood humanist critical techniques better. But they, too, used the techniques chiefly to support traditional values and failed to investigate the relevance of values implied in the classical experience. On a journey to Italy in 1493, Colet was impressed by Ficino's and Pico's researches into the connection between Platonism and Christian theology. After returning to England, he gave a series of lectures at Oxford on Paul's Epistle to the Romans. The lectures were published and became the most famous explicitly religious humanist works in England. They eschewed the allegorical interpretation of Scripture so common among scholastics, and in good humanist fashion held fast to the literal meaning of the text. But Colet's humanism was not wholly consistent. He had no real philological interests and never attempted to question the Vulgate version of the Epistle by comparing it with the original Greek version. Furthermore, Colet's emphasis on sin and grace almost led him to deny the worth of the natural world — a most uncharacteristic position for a true humanist. And indeed, his enthusiasm for Ficino's neo-Platonism markedly waned in later years. Colet's most important contribution to the growth of humanism in England was the founding of Saint Paul's School in London. He became dean of Saint Paul's in 1505 and established a school on humanist principles that influenced much later English education.

The most famous of the English humanists was Thomas More, best known to posterity as the author of *Utopia* and as a saint of the Roman Catholic church, who went to the block rather than support his king's divorce. More was a man of wit and charm who could appreciate the company of Erasmus, and at his own execution he could remove his beard from the block, telling his executioner that it had not sinned and should not suffer for the sins of its owner. If wit is a trait of humanism, it can be amply found in More's most famous work, *Utopia*. The book is cast as a dialogue between a questioner and a traveler who tells of a far-off land where there is no private property and in which most of the ills that beset European society are unknown. In the first section More presents a conversation about the aspects of European society that need correction; much is made of the king's need for good advice to enable him to reform his kingdom. More also raises the issue of the active versus the contemplative life, of such concern to fifteenth-century Italian humanists. Many of the approaches and issues dealt with in this section of *Utopia* indicate the growth of humanist ideas in England. More's concept of a state that can intervene strongly and programmatically in social affairs recalls the political ideas of the Florentine civic humanists.

Yet beside More's humanism lay attitudes more common in an earlier age. His very martyrdom for his faith suggests a confidence in the absolute truth of the specific doctrines of the church that is hard to reconcile with humanism. Humanists often possessed a firm and unshakable faith, but they seldom identified their faith with any particular doctrines, regarding it instead as ineffable and capable of being expressed in a variety of ways. More's confidence in the truth of orthodoxy took other forms as well. Just as he was willing to die for his faith, he eagerly persecuted those who did not share that faith. As chancellor he intervened in heresy trials and persuaded the judges to render harsher judgment for heretics.

Indeed, humanism is not central to More's writings. His letters show that he could correspond with humanists in their own terms, but most of his writings except *Utopia* are theological and orthodox. At its heart the values of *Utopia* itself are very much those of the medieval Christian commonwealth. More objected to private property not so much because it resulted in social inequities but because he saw in it a manifestation of the sin of pride. He rejected as irredeemably evil both private acquisitiveness and calculating statecraft and pictured in *Utopia* a society where the abolition of private property made it easier to follow the traditional pattern of a Christian moral life. Many details that make the modern reader uncomfortable, like the suppression of religious liberty and the harsh treatment of those who will not accept the laws, do not foreshadow the modern totalitarian state; they reflect More's acceptance of medieval values. He, like Colet, used the tools of humanism principally as a means of inculcating those values.

German Humanism

In comparison to the rest of Europe, humanism in Germany was distinctly antiquarian; the Germans seemed more delighted in studying the past and the classics for their own sake. The antiquarian cast can be partly explained by the breadth and vitality of the German universities. As the preceding two chapters testified, intellectuals who felt a need to explore human experience and morality in a deeply personal way could turn to nominalism or even mysticism and still be welcome in the scholarly community. Germany, unlike France, did not need a new movement outside the university to satisfy its humane concerns. Thus those who were attracted to the new learning tended to be those who were simply curious rather than those who were dedicated to discovering through the study of the classics new means of dealing with social and personal problems.

The German humanists, like the English, frequently failed to grasp the Italian achievement of bringing classical scholarship to bear on contemporary problems. One of the earliest, Rudolf Agricola (1444–1485), went to Italy in 1469 and stayed for ten years, becoming a master of Latin style, and was asked to lecture at the University of Pavia. His Latin must have been truly excellent, for Italians were usually contemptuous of northerners, and even the best northern humanists shied away from public exposure in Italy. Despite these accomplishments, Agricola seemed untouched by the philosophical aspects of Italian humanism and viewed the movement as basically a revival of the classics. For example, in 1474 he wrote a life of Petrarch, condensed from a longer biography by the fifteenth-century Italian humanist Filelfo. Whereas Filelfo's biography displayed an appreciation of Petrarch's total contribution to the new learning — his concern for morality, his attack on scholasticism, and his new concept of knowledge — Agricola omitted these considerations and concentrated exclusively on Petrarch's revival of the classics as an end in itself.

Agricola was aware that the issue of moral reform was stirring his contemporaries. The influence he exerted on his students and his own writings testify to his interest in this issue. Compared with Lefèvre or Budé, however, he just did not find a meaningful connection between classical studies and the promotion of moral or practical ends. Echoes of the works of Bruni and Guarino can be found in his writings, and he even noted Guarino's association of letters with moral education; but there was a basic difference. Guarino saw that the new approach to letters implied attaching new values to human experience. By contrast, Agricola saw no contradiction between humanism and the categories of medieval scholasticism; he agreed that humanist education had moral value but expressed this view in only the most general and tired terms.

After Agricola, many German humanists became more aware of the philosophical trends of Italian humanism. Johann Reuchlin (1455–1522) made two voyages to Italy, meeting Ficino in 1482 and Pico in 1490. He subsequently became the greatest Hebrew scholar in Germany, publishing in 1506 the first adequate Hebrew grammar in Europe. Reuchlin explicitly claimed to be interested in abstract thought, but little trace of this can be seen in his grammar. For instance, although Reuchlin included an edition of the Psalms, giving himself ample field for interpretation, he refused at every disputed point to consider the philosophical and theological implications and said that he was interested only in the grammatical context and meaning. Even more surprising, Reuchlin wrote a study of Cabalistic magic in 1517, but he claimed not to accept the validity of magic. Since magic is an essential part of the Cabala, Reuchlin's denial suggests a failure to appreciate the true meaning of the texts. His refusal to face the question also got him into considerable trouble with the authorities. Pico had understood and accepted the magical basis of Cabala but directly sought to bring it within orthodox religion. Reuchlin, by ignoring the issue, left himself open to the charge of supporting magic and undermining orthodoxy.

Other aspects of Reuchlin's treatise suggest that he did not fully grasp the significance of the new learning. He sought to create a synthetic and systematized philosophy based on the Cabala. Pico had avoided this both because he found rigid systematizing unsympathetic and because the Cabala itself assumed that the essence of life defied all systematization. Reuchlin not only tried to force an antisystematic mode of thought into a rigid mold but presented it as a Renaissance dialogue, ignoring the fact that the latter form, as the Italian humanists used it, was totally inappropriate. The very purpose of a dialogue was to suggest the ambiguities and ironies of life that resist comprehensive and systematic philosophy.

Part of the problem facing German humanists was that classical culture was foreign to Germany. Agricola wanted his countrymen to know Latin better than the Italians, but Latin culture could hardly have the impact in Germany that it had in Italy, where the ruins of ancient Rome were part of everyday experience. But Germany was not devoid of a cultural heritage of its own, and the spread of humanism soon awakened German scholars to their own past. Conrad Celtis (1459–1508), one of the most imaginative of the humanists, developed early in his life a sharp distaste for things Italian. He was the first of the German humanists to be educated before traveling to Italy, and when he did make a brief trip there in 1487 he was unfavorably impressed with the pretensions of Italian intellectuals and their scorn for the North. But he liked some aspects of Italian thought, especially neo-Platonism and the Cabala, though he seemed even less sure than Reuchlin of their significance.

Celtis was most important in the revival of German history and culture. He published Tacitus' *Germania* and discovered a manuscript of the works of the tenth-century German woman poet Roswitha. His own major work, though unfinished, was a history and geography of Germany that frequently dwelt on his love for Germany — and hatred for the Italians. His enthusiasm tended to be romantic, vague, and uncritical. He talked about the purity of early German religion in comparison to the corruption of his own day, but could give no explanation for this. Despite the fact that he taught at the imperial court at Vienna, he made no attempt to use the past to illuminate the political problems confronting Germany during his own day. Celtis' efforts to give his countrymen pride in their past and to awaken their consciousness as a nation suggest some of the interests of the Florentine civic humanists, but the analytical perspectives of the Italians are seldom to be found in his writings, which ask more what Germans have done than why they have been able to do it.

Not all Germans were so indifferent to the potential usefulness of humanism. Most famous of those who looked for its practical significance was the Franconian knight Ulrich von Hutten (1488–1523). The class of imperial knights in which Hutten was born was in this period rapidly losing its independence and political power to the territorial princes. The knights looked to the emperor for support and longed for former days when they were more influential. They also thought in pan-German terms because they opposed both the territorial princes and foreign influences, especially the pope.

These attitudes found support in humanist writings, and Hutten early in his career became a follower of the new learning. He wrote poetry that was moral and traditional in form and even tried his hand at manuscript editing, though he never seems to have grasped the real purpose of humanist scholarship. He certainly had no sense of the ambiguities of life. Hutten's overriding concern was his political position, and he was ready to accept help from any quarter. He was at first indifferent to Luther, dismissing the Lutheran movement as another monks' quarrel, but when he saw that it coincided in many ways with his own position, he backed Luther wholeheartedly and castigated the humanists for refusing to join the Lutheran cause. Hutten's humanism thus was temporary and superficial.

Although a later generation of humanists, most notably Luther's long-time friend and colleague Philipp Melanchthon, rallied to the Protestant cause, those German humanists who matured before 1517 were largely unsympathetic to Luther's appeals for support in his attack on the church. As soon as it became clear that the attack was more than simple criticism of clerical immorality, most of them announced their allegiance to the Catholic church and then stayed out of the battle as much as possible. Such a reaction on their part is hardly surprising. The profundity of Luther's ideas was far more likely to be appreciated by the French humanists, because of their greater commitment to moral reform and the role of scholarship in such reform. Not the German Luther but the French Calvin brought humanism truly to bear on the deepest concerns of the Reformation.

Erasmus

In the first part of the sixteenth century one north European humanist stood out from all the rest. Desiderius Erasmus of Rotterdam (1466–1536) shared the deep religious interests of his northern colleagues but at the same time understood the significance of Italian humanism. Erasmus made humanism so much a part of his life that his works, except for their emphasis on religion, seem equivalent to the best products of Italy. For the other great humanists of the North, humanism was only one among several aspects of their outlook on the world, but for Erasmus it was the central fact of his life, the means by which he judged and organized all other paths to knowledge.

Erasmus' success in appropriating humanism's essential attributes is not easy to explain. Neither his early life nor his education was unusual. He was educated in the most noted school at Deventer, but he never spoke highly of the education he received there, and many of his classmates emerged utterly without humanistic interests. In 1488 he joined the monastery at Steyn, where he found a library and an opportunity to study the classics, but no real encouragement. His superiors seemed to feel he was wasting his time, and Erasmus finally found monastic life so stultifying that he spent much of his mature life seeking to be absolved from his vows. His education and experience gave him at most the opportunity to develop his humanism; the impulse to do so came from his own personality, which is revealed to us in his voluminous correspondence. Evidently he was a man who felt an intense need for friendship and human communication, though ironically it appears that Erasmus was not an easy man to get along with. Solicitous of his own physical comfort and refined almost to the point of prissiness, he must have been a difficult house guest. Yet he wrote the most interesting letters in all of Europe, and by 1517 his scholarship and learning had made him famous throughout the Continent. This erudition was always devoted to illuminating and communicating the human condition. Scholastic and abstract disputation never interested Erasmus in the least, and he regarded it as an obstacle to his real pursuits.

Erasmus produced a continual stream of humanist writings in addition to his epistolary work. He wrote a handbook for the education of a Christian gentleman and another for the education of a Christian prince. Both show all of the techniques and values that had characterized Italian treatises on the subject. He also composed a collection of classical sayings with commentaries called the *Adages,* which was used by both scholars and gentlemen as late as the eighteenth century as an easy means of becoming acquainted with the classics. The commentaries stressed the moral lessons to be learned from the classics, while making clear that these lessons depended on a sound grasp of the philology and the exact meaning of the texts.

Erasmus was easily the most well known and generally respected intellectual of his age. Several factors contributed to this popularity and esteem. First, in an age unusually sensitive to the need for reform, Erasmus appeared as a responsible and constructive critic of society. He attacked the superstition and formalism of late medieval religion, offering in their place a simple piety that could appeal to all levels of society. He lampooned both the venality of clergymen and their involvement in ordinary politics. He was repelled in general by war but was particularly incensed at such warlike prelates as Julius II. All these attitudes were phrased clearly, sometimes as gentle satires, sometimes as practical guides to a pious life. During Erasmus' last years Europeans lost much of their taste for his gentle tolerance, but until the religious quarrels between Lutherans and Roman Catholics became so impassioned, Erasmus symbolized an educated and civilized response to the problems of society.

A second source of Erasmus' reputation lay in his editorial work. Humanism by the early sixteenth century had brought men to care about the original texts of the classics, of the early church fathers, and of the Bible itself. Erasmus' prodigious efforts in this field provided nearly authoritative versions of these works. He edited many of the early church fathers and wrote several commentaries on the texts to show his readers how to understand precisely the authors' meanings.

His most important work in this field was the Greek edition of the New Testament, which appeared in 1516. That there was a widespread desire for such an edition is illustrated by the fact that two versions were prepared at the same time in different parts of Europe. While Erasmus worked on his in Basel, the Spanish humanist Cardinal Ximenes was organizing a group of scholars at the University of Alcala to produce the complete Bible in Greek and Hebrew. This Spanish Bible, called the *Complutensian Polyglot,* appeared shortly after Erasmus' New Testament. Not all approved of making the Greek text of the Bible available. Many feared that the traditional Latin version, the Vulgate, would be thrown into question. Erasmus himself was criticized for his efforts and only gradually published those portions of his own Latin translation of the Greek that contradicted the Vulgate.

A third source of Erasmus' reputation is technological rather than intellectual. Erasmus was among the first to take full advantage of the printing press in disseminating his ideas. His texts became authoritative because they could be rapidly spread throughout Europe. Anyone owning one of Erasmus' editions could be sure that his text was as good as Erasmus could make it, unspoiled by copyists' errors. Erasmus was careful in choosing his printers, using only the best — Froben in Basel and Aldus Manutius in Venice. While his editions are not as well proofread as they might have been and often do not rely on the most ancient manuscripts, he always worked closely with his printers to produce as accurate a text as he could. His popularity cannot be understood without realizing the difference between circulating an idea through manuscripts and spreading it through a printed text.

At the core of Erasmus' thought lay a profound appreciation of the ambiguities and ironies of life. He felt that these were not only inevitable but that they gave to life much of its savor and joy. No system could abolish the inconsistencies in nature, and man was the greater because his world could not be carefully organized. Erasmus' unwillingness to take a position devoid of all ambiguity and qualification made him less typical of the sixteenth century than Luther and Calvin, but it also made him more tolerant of other points of view. It is hard to imagine Erasmus wanting to burn anyone who disagreed with him, and in all his disputes with the reformers he never suggested that such a remedy should be applied.

Erasmus expressed the essence of his thought in his greatest work, the *Praise of Folly,* conceived in the form of an oration in which Folly praises herself, but in a way that has long challenged readers to discover its true meaning. The book is an oration in which the personification of Folly praises herself. But is Folly merely being foolish? If so, then the work should be taken in the opposite of its literal sense; what Folly praises we should avoid, and what she condemns we should cling to. But some of the virtues that Folly praises, like Christian love and human companionship, are clearly of such value that we must take seriously Folly's regard for them.

Most of the puzzlement about the meaning of the *Praise of Folly* presupposes that Erasmus held some systematic position on the nature of man and the value of human occupations. That is hardly the case. Indeed, if he had intended to be systematic and unambiguous, he would certainly have chosen another form. The *Praise of Folly,* even more plainly than Machiavelli's *Prince,* is ambiguous to its very core. To systematize it is not to clarify Erasmus' meaning but to destroy it. He presented Folly to us not as an abstraction but as an actual person with a physical presence and human foibles, a person who makes jokes and whose peculiar behavior is not only a subject of humor, but is so similar to Erasmus' own as to constitute almost a self-satire.

By making Folly into an actual person, Erasmus forces us into the very humanistic position of understanding her perspective in order to grasp what she has to say. Folly claims as her own all human activity except reason. Some of these activities are clearly outside of reason's sphere, and here we must agree that Folly is an excellent judge and observer. Thus, when she talks of the pleasures of eating, love-making, friendship, or harmless gossip, she convinces us of the value and humaneness of these pursuits. Folly herself assumes a warm and sympathetic tone. Other activities claimed by Folly are usually pursued within reason's sphere but to the detriment of rational thought. These include superstitious religious practices that interfere with a true understanding of religion, sophistry and pedantic scholarship that obstruct true learning, and warfare that obstructs all humane or rational activities. Here Folly's perspective makes her unfit to judge, because reason is not in her domain, and we are not to regard her intrusion in these fields as beneficial. Erasmus helps us to make this judgment by changing the tone Folly speaks in. A harsh, strident arrogance replaces earlier sympathetic tolerance. Finally, Folly turns to areas of human activity that transcend reason, such as Christian charity and self-sacrifice. Here the nonrational complements reason, and in these sections Folly's tone becomes once again humble and reverent as she contemplates things that from her perspective are clearly above her.

In the *Praise of Folly,* then, Erasmus makes us understand him by forcefully conveying the personal perspective through which he chose to speak. The very limitations of Folly's perspective permit us to see the underlying values but prevent us from reducing them to a simple, systematic position. By combining moral concerns with sensitivity to the variety of human experience and by expressing this combination through the creation of a personal character, Erasmus illustrated both the strengths and the weaknesses of the humanist position. Humanism offered a point of view that was tolerant, humane, and deeply religious; simultaneously it provided a sophisticated perception of human beings in their precise historical settings. On the other hand, it maintained to the end that the essential ambiguity of life precluded the direct, abstract formulations that were the stuff of nominalism and mysticism, the older intellectual traditions of northern Europe. To some sixteenth-century reformers, like Luther, the ambiguity smacked of impiety and robbed the humanist approach of its value. To others, like Calvin, the ambiguities could be resolved without giving up the historical perspective. In the following chapters, we will examine how the three intellectual traditions of humanism, nominalism, and mysticism influenced the great reformers of the sixteenth century.

Bibliography

The classic study of French humanism is Augustin Renaudet's *Préréforme et humanisme à Paris pendant les premières guerres d'Italie, 1494–1517,* 2nd ed. rev. (Paris: Librarie d'Argences, 1953). Franco Simone, *The French Renaissance,* trans. H. G. Hall (London: Macmillan, 1969), has done important work clarifying the relationship between sixteenth-century humanism and early trends in French culture. See also *French Humanism, 1470–1600,* ed. Werner Gundersheimer (New York: Harper and Row, 1970), for an anthology of recent work in the field. Anthony Blunt, *Art* and *Architecture in France, 1500–1700* (London: Penguin Books, 1953), provides a good introduction to French art of the period. Blunt stresses the difficulties of assimilating the Italian models.

Early English humanism has been studied by Roberto Weiss, *Humanism in England During the Fifteenth Century* (Oxford: Blackwell, 1941). For two different perspectives on sixteenth-century English humanism see Fritz Caspari, *Humanism and the Social Order* (Chicago: Chicago University Press, 1954), and Arthur Ferguson, *The Articulate Citizen and the English Renaissance* (Durham, N.C.: Duke University Press, 1965). Caspari stresses the impact of humanism on education, where its effects were socially conservative; Ferguson looks at the ramifications for political thought, where the effects were more subversive.

For Thomas More, Raymond W. Chambers' biography, *Thomas More* (New York: Harcourt Brace Jovanovich, 1935), is still basic. Chambers' view is more favorable to More than the subject warrants. For a recent study of More's activity as a persecutor of heretics see William Clebsch, *England's Earliest Protestants, 1520–1535* (New Haven: Yale University Press, 1964). By far the most sensible treatment of *Utopia* is found in J. H. Hexter's *More's Utopia: The Biography of an Idea* (Princeton: Princeton University Press, 1952).

John Colet's varying relations with Italian humanism have been studied by Sears Jayne, *John Colet and Marsilio Ficino* (Oxford: Oxford University Press, 1963).

A general study of representative German humanists is found in Lewis Spitz, *The Religious Renaissance of the German Humanists* (Cambridge: Harvard University Press, 1963). See also the same author's *Conrad Celtis: The German Arch-Humanist* (Cambridge: Harvard University Press, 1957). Spitz does not consider the German humanists to be antiquarian and presents a different picture from the one found here. See also Hajo Holborn, *Ulrich von Hutten and the German Reformation* (New Haven: Yale University Press, 1937).

The three countries treated in this chapter are of course not the only ones in Europe where humanism had a significant impact; they are treated because the major currents of sixteenth-century thought are found within their boundaries. The most important country from a political perspective during the sixteenth century was doubtless Spain, and humanism was found there also. See Marcel Bataillon, *Erasme et l'Espagne* (Paris: Librairie Droz, 1937), and Otis Green, *Spain in the Western Tradition,* 4 vols. (Madison: University of Wisconsin Press, 1963–1966).

The classic study of Erasmus is Johan Huizinga's *Erasmus and* ⇒ *the Age of Reformation,* trans. F. Hopman (New York: Harper and Row, 1957). See also Margaret Phillips, *Erasmus and the Northern* ⇒ *Renaissance* (London: Hodder and Stoughton, 1949). For an analysis of Erasmus' *Praise of Folly* see Walter Kaiser, *Praisers of Folly: Erasmus, Rabelais, Shakespeare* (Cambridge: Harvard University Press, 1963).

The two most famous texts of the northern humanists, More's *Utopia* and Erasmus' *Praise of Folly,* are readily available in English translation. A selection of the writings of other northern humanists can be found in volume 2 of *Renaissance Philosophy,* entitled *The Transalpine Thinkers,* ed. and trans. H. Shapiro and A. Fallico (New York: Random House, 1969). For another good collection of writings of the northern humanists see Lewis Spitz, *The Northern Renaissance* (Englewood Cliffs, N.J.: Prentice-Hall, 1972).

Part Six
The Sixteenth-Century Reformation

20 Martin Luther

To understand Martin Luther (1483–1546), whose decisive role in the sixteenth-century Reformation is beyond question, we must be mindful of his most deeply felt personal need. Luther required personal and absolute assurance not only of his own worth but of the demands that God made on him, an assurance far beyond anything the intellectual vocabulary of late medieval Europe was equipped to offer. This characteristic can be seen particularly well in Luther's confrontation with Europe's most celebrated humanist, Erasmus.

The Encounter with Erasmus

Humanism was just beginning to make an impression on the German intellectual community when Luther was born, and during his youth it became one of the leading movements of European thought. One of Luther's closest friends throughout his life was Philipp

Melanchthon, a noted humanist scholar. Even the words that Luther wrote on his deathbed seem to display a love for the classics and concern for relating them to Christianity, an attitude so characteristic of the humanists:

> No one who was not a shepherd or a peasant for five years can understand Virgil in his *Bucolica* and *Georgica*. I maintain that no one can understand Cicero in his letters unless he was active in important affairs of state for twenty years. Let no one who has not guided the congregations with the prophets for one hundred years believe that he has tasted Holy Writ thoroughly. . . . Do not try to fathom this divine *Aeneid,* but humbly worship its footprints.

Despite his sympathy for the classics and humanist scholarship, however, Luther never found humanism a satisfactory answer to his problems. A man of great conviction and boundless emotional force, he could neither accept nor understand the humanists' gentle irony and reluctance to commit themselves totally to any specific statement of truth. Profoundly disappointed when few German humanists joined his revolt against the church of Rome, Luther railed against their lack of real religious faith and accused them of lacking the courage to follow their commitments. The relation between Luther's need for certainty and his antipathy to the basic values of humanism is especially well illustrated by his debate with Erasmus over free will.

Initially, Luther looked upon Erasmus as a potential ally and appealed to him for support. But the two men soon fell to quarreling over Luther's basic ideas, particularly the issue of free will, which Luther denied and Erasmus affirmed. The argument broke out in the early 1520s, after Luther's protest against indulgences (1517) had made him famous throughout Europe. In the course of the argument it became clear that Luther was incapable of understanding the reserve and practicality of Erasmus, just as Erasmus failed to understand Luther's fervor and confidence. Erasmus took the position that some issues are so profound that it is neither wise nor worthwhile to speculate on them in public and so confuse the average Christian. "There are certain kinds of truth which, even though they could be known, would nonetheless be unwisely offered for indiscriminate consideration." Erasmus was not trying to suppress ideas. He was expressing his conviction that ultimate questions cannot be known directly with unambiguous clarity. In the preface to his *Diatribe on Free Will,* which Erasmus said was the most important part of the work and which contains the foregoing quotation, he also said,

> So great is my dislike of assertions that I prefer the views of the sceptics wherever the inviolable authority of Scripture and the decision of the church permit — a church to which at all times I willingly submit my own views, whether I attain what she prescribes or not. And as a matter of fact, I prefer this natural inclination to one I can observe in certain people who are so blindly addicted to one opinion that they cannot tolerate whatever differs from it.

Luther found Erasmus' diffidence intolerable and replied to him by saying,

> Not to delight in assertions is not the mark of a Christian heart. Indeed one must delight in assertions to be a Christian at all . . . I mean [by assertion] a constant adhering to and affirming of your position, avowing and defending it, and invincibly persevering in it. . . . Far be it from us Christians to be skeptics and academics.

Luther distrusted a movement that was not completely confident of the truth of its own insights, or that questioned the value of the very sorts of philosophical speculation that could lead to such unshakable truths. While he might assimilate certain aspects of humanism — such as a lively interest in the classics — he did not accept the essential humanist outlook on the world.

The Stages of Luther's Youth

The course of Luther's life testified strongly to his insistence on standards of certainty that the humanists found inappropriate and unnecessary. He was from early youth a man of sensitive conscience and deeply introspective nature. In his later life, he looked back upon his early years as a series of crises bringing these elements of his nature into sharper and sharper relief. The earliest crisis occurred in 1505, when Luther at the age of twenty-two entered the study of law in obedience to the wishes of his father. Returning home from Erfurt where he had recently taken his master of arts degree, he was caught in a sudden and violent thunderstorm. In his terror at the lightning he flung himself to the ground and vowed to Saint Anne that if he survived the storm he would become a monk. A more ordinary and less serious young man might have considered a vow made in terror not to be binding, but Luther kept his word and joined the Augustinian monastery at Erfurt only two weeks later. He took this step of renouncing the world despite the fierce opposition of his father, who proclaimed that the storm and the vow were not God's work but the Devil's.

Years later Luther looked back on this crisis and felt that it had resolved many of the doubts and qualms of conscience that had bothered him during his stay at Erfurt and that had made him increasingly concerned about sin and the salvation of his soul. Whether Luther's memory of his adolescence was accurate or not, the sensitive conscience of the new monk was quickly revealed. His unusual intelligence and energy soon attracted the attention of his superiors, who began entrusting him with important tasks. In 1510 he was sent to Rome to settle an organizational dispute that had arisen between his own cloister and the regional administration of the order. (Luther had chosen a cloister known for the purity and austerity with which it observed the Augustinian rule. The cloister feared that as the whole order became better organized and exerted more control over the individual chapters, the reformed cloisters would become corrupted by association with their more lax neighbors.) In Rome, Luther was shocked by the decadence and ritualism of the Renaissance church. In later life he told of long lines of priests waiting to say mass at certain altars where particularly attractive dispensations were available and of how priests would shout to the celebrant to hurry his mass so that they all could finish before lunch. He told of pilgrimages he made to sacred shrines to redeem his grandfather's soul from purgatory, and how he climbed the twenty-four sacred steps of the Vatican on his knees, saying an Our Father on every step. This last act was considered an especially good way of helping the souls in purgatory. At the top of the steps he suddenly stopped his prayers, as the question came to him, "Is this all true?"

This account of his reaction to the Renaissance church comes, like the story of the thunderstorm, from Luther's later life. Liberal Protestants, who traditionally have regarded the sin of superstition as more grievous than the sin of pride, usually have taken Luther at his word. No one can really be sure that the young Luther saw his problems and doubts so clearly as he did twenty years later, when he reported the incident, but a surer indication of the sensitivity of his conscience comes from the years after he returned from Rome, when he began to have difficulty with the confessional system. Luther's wise and compassionate confessor, Staupitz, listened to him for hours at a time as he dredged his memory for every sin he had committed, apparently feeling such a need to purge himself. Even after one of these grueling sessions, Luther would frequently return a few hours later to confess another sin that he had remembered in the interim. Poor Staupitz labored to convince Luther that his scruples were excessive, finally telling the young monk that he should wait until he had a serious sin like parricide or adultery to confess so that he could recognize what peccadillos he had confessed heretofore.

Staupitz also recommended that Luther study for his doctoral degree so that he could succeed to the chair of biblical studies at the University of Erfurt that Staupitz himself then occupied. Staupitz took this step for two reasons. He hoped that the time and energy spent on study would prevent Luther from engaging in lengthy and unproductive examinations of conscience. More important, he felt that an intensive exposure to the Bible would bring Luther into contact with a more evangelical — that is, a more personal and less legalistic — view of religion and put his scruples into a more sensible perspective. We must keep in mind that the Bible was not part of the normal theological curriculum in the fifteenth century. One of Luther's colleagues, Carlstadt, said that before his conversion to Lutheranism he had never even seen one. Luther accepted Staupitz's charge reluctantly, but with momentous consequences. His studies and lectures on the Bible — especially on the Psalms and the Pauline Epistles — were to lead to a final rejection of the confessional system as a path to salvation.

By 1517, when the controversy over indulgences broke out, Luther had already found the penitential theology on which indulgences were based unsatisfactory and was familiar with the biblical tradition, where this penitential system played little part. He had also shown himself to be forthright and completely honest in expressing himself. It was hardly surprising that he was offended by the manner in which Tetzel sold indulgences, or that he publicly vented his displeasure. It was no more surprising that, when the emperor called him to account at the Diet of Worms in 1521, he refused to accept the authority of the church against the conclusions drawn from his own experience. We cannot be sure whether Luther actually uttered the famous words "Here I stand — I can do no other." But his recorded declaration at the diet was a clearly defiant statement of his right to his own conclusions. Before the assembled princes of the Holy Roman Empire, the magnates of the church, and the emperor himself, Luther refused to recant his opinions or disown his writings. He replied to their demands:

> Since your majesty and your lordships desire a simple reply, I will answer without horns and without teeth. Unless I am convicted by scripture and plain reason — I do not accept the authority of popes and councils, for they have contradicted each other — my conscience is captive to the Word of God. I cannot and I will not recant anything, for to go against conscience is neither right nor safe. God help me. Amen.

Luther's honest and sincere dissatisfaction with the sacrament of penance as a means of coping with his religious problems had given him throughout his youth and into his adulthood frequent periods of intense religious anguish, which could not be assuaged by the usual religious practices of the late medieval church. He had tried pilgrimage, fasting, and self-denial. He had tried to purge his sins through systematic investigation of his conscience. But he remained unsure of his ability to make a perfect act of contrition and acknowledge all the thoughts and deeds for which he might be blamed. He was not even sure of the motives that drove him feverishly to search for rest and assurance. Out of his anguish Luther forged a new religious faith that looked back to the personal religion of Saint Paul and Saint Augustine, but that grew equally out of Luther's own deeply felt personal problems.

Luther attracted a wide following in Europe with amazing speed. Evidently many sensitive Christians were experiencing a religious anguish and despair similar to Luther's own. We ought not to be hasty to pick out the reasons for this, but some contributing factors spring quickly to mind. The century and a half after the Black Death was a particularly trying time for much of northern Europe. The plague had visited the area repeatedly; famines were common; wars engulfed the land — the Hundred Years' War in France, the Wars of the Roses in England, the Hussite Wars in central Europe. During the Hundred Years' War, the English often had to import hay to feed their horses because the French countryside was too devastated to provide fodder. Moreover, the Turkish threat was keenly felt in Germany, and the collapse of the Burgundian state after the death of Charles the Bold in 1477 removed one of the most glittering and stable powers of northern Europe.

Whatever the causes, the results were clear. The great cultural historian Johan Huizinga graphically portrays in *The Waning of the Middle Ages* the popular despair and concern for sin. The rumor spread during the last years of the fifteenth century that no one had entered paradise since the Great Schism of 1378. It takes little imagination to appreciate what effect that rumor must have had on a population deeply preoccupied with salvation. New images appeared in religious art. Although scenes of the Crucifixion or the Pietà were rare in the thirteenth century, in the fifteenth century they were the normal decoration of churches, along with other scenes of the Passion of Christ. Portrayals of the last judgment became more and more excruciating in their detail. Death dominated the imagery of the period. The word "macabre" first appeared in the fourteenth century. Though no representations of the *danse macabre,* or dance of death, can be found before 1400, fifty-two are known from the fifteenth and sixteenth centuries. One treatise on the art of dying went through more than a hundred editions between 1465 and 1500.

All this is not to say that Luther was simply reflecting his times. He was a man of deep and creative originality, but his wide appeal to his contemporaries undoubtedly depended on shared feelings and a perception of similar problems. The need for a more personal religious experience expressed by the intellectuals was equally felt by the less articulate. Their needs were manifest in the new forms of art and religious practice that sprang up with increasing frequency as Europe entered the sixteenth century.

Luther's Thought: The Doctrine of Solifidianism

Not only did Luther strike a responsive chord among his contemporaries, he drew heavily on the intellectual currents of the preceding two centuries. During his own confessional crisis Luther read deeply in the writings of the Rhineland mystics, particularly those of Tauler, and was greatly moved. He was even more strongly influenced by the nominalists. Erfurt was a nominalist university, and much of Luther's theological training was centered around the works of Gabriel Biel. Luther at his maturity was vastly different from either of these traditions, but he gained both perspective and vocabulary from his encounter with them.

Luther's solution to his own personal problems, his contribution to Christian faith, and his significance in Western intellectual history are all expressed in a single doctrine — solifidianism. It is more commonly called "justification by faith." It implies not merely that faith justifies the sinner, but that faith is the only justification — because God's grace is irresistible and prevenient; that is, it comes to the sinner even before he desires it. To say that this doctrine is the basis of Luther's theology fails to do it sufficient honor. It is the essence of his theology. It informs his thought at every level from the most abstruse speculation to the most mundane observation. Dip into Luther's writings at any point and you will find the doctrine openly expounded. Luther frequently admitted that he repeated himself but insisted that the doctrine was so important that it could never be proclaimed too much. In 1531, he lectured on Galatians for the third time, beginning in this manner:

> I have taken in hand, in the name of the Lord, yet once again to expound this Epistle of St. Paul to the Galatians: not because I do desire to teach new things, or such as ye have not heard before, especially since that, by the grace of God, Paul is now thoroughly known unto you: but for that (as I have often forewarned you) this we have to fear as the greatest and nearest danger, lest Satan take from us the pure doctrine of faith, and bring into the Church again the doctrine of works and men's traditions. Wherefore it is very necessary, that this doctrine be kept in continual practice and public exercise both of reading and hearing. And although it be never so well known, never so exactly learned, yet the devil our adversary, who continually rangeth about seeking to devour us, is not dead; likewise our flesh and old man is yet alive; besides this, all kinds of temptations vex and oppress us on every side. Wherefore this doctrine can never be taught, urged and repeated enough. If this doctrine be lost, then is also the whole knowledge of truth, life, and salvation lost and gone. If this doctrine flourish, then all good things flourish: religion, the true service of God, the glory of God, the right knowledge of all things and states of life.

Luther's single-minded devotion to a principle is matched among the great Christian thinkers only by Saint Athanasius in the fourth century, who defended Trinitarianism with equal fervor. The comparison is apt, for the doctrine of justification by faith alone is a touchstone of religion as far-reaching in its implications and as difficult to understand as the doctrine of a triune God.

As a first step toward understanding solifidianism, it must be kept firmly in mind that Luther did not consider faith to be simply assent to a religious creed. Such assent falls into the same category of "works" as pilgrimages, penances, and good deeds. In other words, Luther considered mere affirmation of a dogma, however true it might be, to be no more relevant to our salvation than any superstitious religious observance. Nor did he consider faith to mean love. That, too, is just a "work," even though it is a spiritual act rather than a physical one. Acts of charity and concern are desirable, of course, as is the affirmation of a correct religious doctrine, but they do not bring us closer to true salvation. On the latter issue Luther parted company with his beloved Saint Paul, and did his best to ignore or reinterpret the passage in First Corinthians that says, "Though I have faith so that I could remove mountains, and have not charity, I am nothing."

Luther often coupled faith with trust, and the modern term that most accurately conveys what Luther meant by faith is commitment. We are saved if we are committed to the absolute values of the universe, which are the values of God as he has revealed himself in the Bible and in our own consciences. The commitment should automatically result in acts that reflect and implement these values, but the worth of the acts is determined by the commitment behind them; the acts per se do not create the commitment.

The doctrine of salvation by faith alone is more a series of related notions than a single idea. Three aspects of the doctrine are of particular importance. First, Luther maintained that God so completely transcends the human condition that no human perspectives can truly understand his nature. Second, Luther believed firmly and completely in predestination, the doctrine that we have no control over our salvation because it was decided by God before we were born. Third, and because of the first two tenets, the fundamental religious act of the Christian is a continual process of self-searching to detect signs of an already given grace of faith that brings salvation by its very presence and that results in spontaneous good works.

Luther largely derived his notion of the complete transcendence of God from three main sources: Saint Paul, Saint Augustine, and Gabriel Biel. Luther credited Paul with bringing him out of despair and resolving the spiritual problems of his youth. Sometime between 1517 and the Diet of Worms in 1521, Luther had a deep personal experience of solace at the idea of an overpowering God who saved through his own justice. Years later Luther said that he came to this faith while reading Saint Paul in the privy. This is the famous *Turmerlebnis,* or experience in the tower. Twentieth-century psychoanalysis has used this event to explore both Luther's own psychological makeup and the deeper wellsprings of the support he aroused in the sixteenth century. In any case the Turmerlebnis sho vs us the personal quality of his faith and the intimacy of his encc unter with Paul.

No one so deeply moved by Paul could ignore Augustine, who was himself converted by reading the Epistle to the Romans. Moreover, Luther, as an Augustinian monk, would have been drawn to read him attentively. Augustine speaks more explicitly than Paul of an unfathomable God who is the ground of our personal being, but who utterly transcends the human condition. This is an aspect of Augustine's writings not always stressed in the Middle Ages. Luther found it partly because he came to Augustine seeking to understand Paul more fully.

The influence of Biel and the theology of nominalism on Luther's doctrine of a transcendent God is not so obvious as that of the earlier men, but it should not be ignored. Biel had posited two separate realms, joined to each other only by the unconditioned will of God, and Luther found this division a useful means of understanding the complexities of the human situation. Biel had said that the purpose of the division was to delineate a realm where the Christian could live and adjust himself by his own efforts to the revealed laws of God. Luther adopted a different view and maintained that the Christian exists fully and simultaneously in both realms. In a sense Luther's mature thought is reached as he tries to express effectively his new understanding of Paul and Augustine through the vocabulary and concepts of nominalism.

Luther developed his picture of the two realms slowly. His early writings (1513–1518) talk of a conventional dualism in which the visible world is inferior to the invisible one, the flesh to the spirit, and the creature to the creator. The language is neo-Platonic and reflects intensive reading of the Rhineland mystics, particularly Tauler; thus the two parts of the dualism are also related to each other as copy and original. Sin has destroyed this natural relationship so that men confuse the copy with the original and value the inferior flesh over the superior spirit. The Christian's duty is to correct the confusion by following the example of Christ, who reconciles all dualism in his Passion. "Christ is both God and man, dead and living, mortal and immortal; almost every contradiction is here resolved." And again, "The cross shows that the judgment of God is contrary to the judgment of man. It condemns the things that men choose and chooses what men condemn." In this early formulation Luther conceived of grace as the ability to see the original revealed in the copy, to perceive the invisible behind the visible, and to exalt the spirit over the flesh. In other words, the relation of the two realms was a simple hierarchy.

In the year 1518 or 1519 Luther began to see this dualism in different terms. Rather than progressing from the inferior realm to the superior one, the Christian actually lived simultaneously in both realms. In later life Luther traced this new concept to an insight into what Saint Paul meant by justice. In 1545, writing a preface to his Latin works, he said that this insight was the central strand of his intellectual development and came from his study of a passage in Paul's Epistle to the Romans, which says, "For therein is the righteousness of God revealed from faith to faith: as it is written, the just shall live by faith" (Romans 1:17). Luther interpreted this to signify that the Christian is already totally just in Christ but only partially just in the world, where he must continually progress toward sanctification. To put it in negative terms, the Christian is partially just in the world, but judged before God and without the intercession of Christ he remains totally a sinner.

Luther broke reality apart in this fashion in order to grapple with an important aspect of human experience. He was keenly aware of the tension between the absolute demands of conscience and his incomplete obedience to those demands. His conscience told him that personal salvation and fulfillment were not goals that admitted of degrees. Yet he was equally aware that daily life inevitably involved compromises with principle and God's commands. Luther had to find a way of understanding God's justice that explained why the Christian continued to be sinful but still could attain ultimate and absolute salvation. At first he maintained that the saved Christian was partly just and still partly a sinner, but this solution was unsatisfactory. His reading of the promises and threats of the Bible as well as the experience of his own conscience convinced him that man is capable of being fully just and fully a sinner.

In the concept of two separate but simultaneous realms of existence Luther found the solution he sought. Before God, man is totally just in Christ and totally condemned outside Christ. In the worldly realm of works, the Christian is gradually being healed and sanctified by God's grace; thus he is partly just and partly a sinner. By 1531, when he wrote his last commentary on Galatians, Luther had arrived at a more elaborate conceptual structure for his idea. There were two forms of justice: an active justice, in which we act on our own whether by God's help or not; and a passive justice, in which God acts upon us without any help from us at all. The latter produces salvation; the former produces acts in the world that may be partially good and partially bad but that have no effect whatsoever on our ultimate salvation.

The identification of saving justice with passive justice leads to the second facet of the doctrine of solifidianism: predestination. According to Luther, God has determined the salvation or damnation of every soul before birth; we have no control over this. Luther enunciated this position clearly in his dispute with Erasmus over free will. He acknowledged that human beings have the power to exercise their own wills and make choices, but he argued that the values determining these choices are ultimately beyond our own choosing. This is an ancient and honorable argument in the history of the church and is especially prominent in the writings of Saint Augustine. It is, moreover, hard to deny, not only for a sixteenth-century Christian but for a member of twentieth-century society, where Freud has led us to put such stress on unconscious drives and motives. However much we examine and try consciously to choose our moral standards, there must be a prior set of values that governs the selection of new values and thus lies beyond our control. If this is true, then whether or not our personal values reflect the will of God and are in harmony with the ultimate values of the universe is not within our power to decide. Our basic values can be shaped by any number of secondary causes — environment, heredity, or even physical attributes — but ultimately they come from outside our wills and beyond our power to choose.

The argument that we cannot establish our values without God's help is so strong for a Christian that Erasmus made no attempt to disagree with Luther on the point. Together with most Catholic theologians, he insisted rather that once an inclination to obey God and acquire the proper values is given, we must help it along by gradual sanctification through doing good works. Thereby we will give ourselves the habit of being good and will strengthen the original God-given inclination. By failing to do this, however, we may reject the original gift of grace and refuse our own salvation. Luther denied that we have the power to reject grace. He knew that men can reject the Gospels, that they can resist the most fervent preaching of the faith, but only if God has not given them the grace to believe and accept. Comparing the human will to a horse, he said,

> when God sits upon it, then it desires to go and does go where God wills, . . . when Satan sits upon it, it desires to go and does go where Satan wills, and it has no choice as to which rider it will carry, nor can it seek him, but the riders themselves dispute its possession.

Once the original values have been given, once grace has been imputed, we cannot refuse it by any measure. Grace is not only prevenient (that is, comes before our own efforts), it is irresistible. Thus the crucial point of the doctrine of predestination is not so much that we cannot save ourselves — both Catholics and Protestants agree on this — but that we cannot refuse salvation once it is offered.

Many are tempted to object that determinism robs us of initiative, but Luther's doctrine never called for passivity and submission. On the contrary, it was a call to an active and energetic life. Luther pointed out that however strong the demands of society and the law, we cannot be made to want to follow those demands. Our own values come out of our deepest personal make-up, beyond the control of either ourselves or the power of law. Finally, being bound to the will of God actually makes us free, free from worldly pressures to conform or make ourselves over in society's image. Commenting on Paul's wish that he might live under God, Luther wrote,

> That is to say, that I might be alive in the sight of God. Ye see then that there is no life unless ye be without the law. Yea unless ye be utterly dead to the law, I mean in conscience. Notwithstanding . . . so long as the body liveth, the flesh must be exercised with laws. . . . But the inward man, not subject to the law but delivered and freed from it is a lively, just, and holy person, not of himself or in his own substance, but in Christ, because he believeth in him.

Luther looked on the bondage of the will not only as a call to life but as the touchstone of personal identity. He regarded personal experience of God as the fundamental religious act and defended the individual against all institutions or ways of thinking that might interfere with this experience. He felt that all of God's commands and gifts come through and in the person. Thus Luther does not show man as passive before God in any conventional sense. Furthermore, he speaks often of the individual's ability to exercise his own personal will in accepting God's grace. But he saw that this power to accept was itself dependent on our utter bondage to God's will. Luther accepted and even reveled in this paradox. He did not anticipate Calvin in formulating a systematic doctrine of predestination. Yet he never lost his original insight into our total dependence on the prevenient grace of God. Even his opponents, like Erasmus, rejected the notion that we have completely unconditioned choice. They understood that a random sequence of isolated decisions depending on no persistent values would deprive us of our personal identity. Luther saw that any freedom apart from God's will diluted the force of our personality.

The intensely individual and personal character of Luther's theology emerges even more clearly when we consider the third aspect of his doctrine of justification by faith alone. The doctrine shifted the fundamental religious act of the Christian from a social one to an introspective one. No longer is he charged with gradually purifying himself through spiritual and physical acts that give him the habit of doing good and enjoying it. Since he has no control over his salvation, he cannot be charged with working toward it. Instead he should seek to discover assurances of salvation within him, and use the creative energy of these assurances to perform works in the service of God. These works are acceptable in God's sight not because of their intrinsic worth, but because the doer himself is saved through imputed, Christian justice.

Luther did not claim that this reorientation from moral to epistemological action, from ethics to introspection, would eliminate religious anguish; no major Christian thinker has ever pretended to do that. But he shifted the anguish from the area where it is most damaging and unproductive into an area where Christians should be better equipped to handle it. In Catholic theology the very process of purifying one's soul in preparation for sacramental grace could lead to mortal sin; if we repent of a sin out of fear of hell rather than genuine contrition — in other words, if we commit an act of attrition — the repentance itself becomes a sin. We can easily get into the habit of repenting out of fear until we are incapable of true repentance. In this manner we can reject salvation even while ostensibly seeking to acquire it.

Luther felt this possibility keenly, and it lay behind his anguished soul-searching in the confessional. He sought assurance that he was really contrite, for if he was not, he was giving himself the habit of sinning that would work his own damnation. In his new theology, as with Gabriel Biel, such doubt was eliminated, for a person cannot bring about his own damnation. No amount of repenting out of unworthy motives can change his destiny an iota. We are saved not by works, spiritual or otherwise, but by faith imputed in us by an all-powerful God. Thus there is no danger in self-searching, for the search itself can do us no damage in God's sight.

But the search for assurance of salvation does not guarantee success. Some souls are destined never to be saved, but, more than that, Luther was careful to point out that even the elect have no complete and objective assurance of salvation. The issue is so profound that only the mind of God can know who is saved and who is damned. Luther offered a religion for the strong, for one spends a lifetime searching inwardly for an assurance that can never be absolute. Not everyone can maintain the required level of introspection and self-consciousness and still devote his energies to the secular world. Luther himself was tormented throughout his life with recurring fits of despair in which he worried about his own soul and his religious ideas. His new understanding of justice and faith did not save him from personal anguish, but at least it convinced him that the anguish would not lead to damnation.

Luther's thought represented a fundamental attack on traditional Catholic ethics. Thomistic ethics were eudemonistic, that is, they were designed to bring a person happiness. Thomas sought to create a system that would bring most people's lives into line with objective standards of happiness derived from natural reason and revelation. The nominalists found this ethical system too impersonal and suggested that wavering between fear and hope can be a sign that one is indeed doing one's best on the road to salvation. Luther went much further and maintained that objective standards of happiness, though they may apply to most men, need not be relevant to personal fulfillment and salvation at all. One might be saved without being happy in any socially accepted sense. Luther's critique of Thomistic ethics opened an entire range of human experience to ethical inquiry and radically broadened the ways through which God could manifest himself to man.

Luther's Thought: Other Elements of
the Protestant Tradition

The doctrine of solifidianism is not the only element in the Protestant tradition. Protestants also depart from Catholics in holding that the Bible is the sole source of the truths necessary for salvation and that all true believers are members of the priesthood. Though these two doctrines are a basic part of the Protestant tradition, they were subordinated in Luther's thought to the doctrine of justification by faith alone. This was clearest in the case of the Bible. Luther derived most of the support for his theology from the Pauline Epistles and frequently attacked his Catholic opponents by showing how they failed to take the Bible with proper seriousness. But other parts of the Bible were embarrassing to Luther, just as the Pauline Epistles were to his opponents. For example, the Epistle of James states, "What doth it profit, my brethren, though a man say he hath faith, and have not works? Can faith save him? . . . Even so faith, if it hath not works, is dead, being alone. . . . Ye see then how that by works a man is justified, and not by faith only" (James 2:14, 17, 24).

Luther accepted the challenge from James with characteristic forthrightness. He said the Epistle was so much straw and, while it had some merit, it should never have been incorporated into the canon of the Bible in the first place. This willingness to pick and choose among biblical texts was altogether characteristic. In the preface to his translation of the New Testament into German, Luther declared that the Gospel of Saint John, Saint Paul's Epistles — especially Romans, Galatians, and Ephesians — I John, and I Peter were the noblest books, because they led the Christian to salvation. In other words Luther did not come to the doctrine of salvation by faith alone because it lay before him in the Bible; he came to it out of deep personal travail. He believed the Bible to contain all truths necessary for salvation because he found the crucial doctrine there, but he was convinced of its truth by his own personal experience. For other Protestants the Bible was central, but for Luther it was subordinate to the truth of the basic doctrine he found in it.

Luther's position on the priesthood of all believers was more complicated, for the church had traditionally made two claims for the priesthood. First, the church claimed the power of order, that is, the power conferred by the apostolic succession (the claim of the church that its bishops derive their authority from the apostles) to govern the relation between God and man. From this claim came the sacramental powers: baptism, the mass, penance, extreme unction, marriage, ordination, and consecration. The most striking symbol of the church's power of order is its claim to change the elements of bread and water into the body and blood of Christ at the mass, reenacting thereby the mystery of the Incarnation and Passion. Luther never really disputed the church's claim in this sphere and largely accepted the power of order. But he reduced the number of sacraments to two — baptism and the mass — and rejected the medieval statement of what happens at the mass as too systematic. Thomas had developed a sophisticated terminology for describing the mass. According to him, the elements are transubstantiated, meaning that the "accidents" or appearance of the bread and wine remain but their substance disappears to be replaced by the substance of the body and blood of Christ. Luther sought to avoid such metaphysical terms in describing the mass. They seemed too pagan and unbiblical, and he preferred to maintain the mystery without philosophical explanation. More seriously than to transubstaniation, he objected to Thomas' emphasis on sacrifice in the mass, feeling that the sacrifice of Christ on the cross was perfect and needed no reenactment. These differences apart, Luther's sacramental theology was little different from contemporary Catholic thought.

Luther's acceptance of the sacramental authority of the church did not stem from deep conviction on his part. It evidently was due to a number of causes. The sacrament of the mass is specifically mentioned in the Pauline Epistles, and Luther could not very well deny the sacraments while laying such heavy stress on other aspects of Saint Paul's thought. Also Luther was basically a conservative man. He felt that whenever church practices did not interfere with personal religious life they should be kept. He discarded the sacrament of penance because it was an obstacle, but retained and accepted baptism and the Lord's Supper, as he called the mass, because these were not obstacles. He also allowed church music, clerical vestments, and most of the liturgy for the same reason. He felt that there was no harm in them and that they might in fact underline the truths at the heart of religion.

Luther's attitude toward the sacraments reveals another side of this complex man, a side that would need more stress if this were a social history rather than an intellectual and cultural one. For Luther was not only a thinker; he was a pastor. He saw as a fundamental fact of existence the individual's confrontation with his God. This insight left little room for the sacraments. Yet he realized that men needed a community. Thus he maintained the importance of the church as an expression of this community, not only in theory but in practice, for he devoted much of the last part of his life to the organization of the Lutheran church. Luther, like so many great men, was not preoccupied with maintaining a rigid consistency. He accepted paradox as a part of life.

The church's other claim related to priesthood is the power of jurisdiction. Being descended from the apostles to whom Christ gave authority to loose and to bind, the church claimed jurisdiction over all moral matters and all affairs in which an oath was taken — marriage contracts, treaties, and even certain business agreements. The church's power of jurisdiction also was the basis of its claim to be superior to all secular powers, a court of last resort to which any matter might be appealed. Luther firmly and consistently denied the power of jurisdiction, which put priests in a special class apart from laymen, but his criticism was nothing new in the sixteenth century. Secular rulers had seldom allowed the church jurisdiction over their internal matters, and Dante and Marsilio of Padua had raised important objections to the church's powers of jurisdiction two centuries before Luther.

Although Luther's position was hardly original or extreme, he stated it with new force and vigor. He insisted that because the two realms are separate the visible church on earth cannot claim authority based on its position in heaven as the invisible church. In fact, the priestly calling is no more sacred than any other calling, and the moral strictures of the church have no special authority. The state is the proper guardian of morality and order in this world. As long as its laws do not flagrantly violate Scripture, the state has complete control over the behavior of its subjects. Even when the state commands obedience in opposition to Scripture, Luther felt that the subject should limit himself to passive disobedience, for the state's claim to allegiance is unqualified. Luther carried this principle into practice by opposing a Crusade against the Turks. The church in its spiritual aspect could fight the infidels only through prayer. Wars are not conducted by Christians but by kings, and war against the Turks was no different in Luther's eyes from any other kind of war. In fact he suggested the possibility that the Turks constituted God's punishment for sin; in which case the Crusade would be against the divine will.

Luther's willingness to deny the church all of its traditional power to oversee the moral and political affairs of society springs directly from his sense of religion as a deeply personal experience. Introspection, and the gradual sanctification that is its creative result, needs only peace and stability. The individual needs neither moral guidelines nor the trappings of ceremony. In practice Luther kept church ceremony and advocated strengthening the power of the state in the interests of peace and order. His concern for the latter was most starkly revealed by his reaction to a revolt that broke out among the German peasants in 1525. The revolt was basically economic and political in origin, but some of the leaders sought Luther's support. Luther was at first sympathetic, but as the revolt spread and became more extreme he launched a vitriolic attack on the insurgents, which for bloodthirsty vehemence has few parallels in either sixteenth- or twentieth-century political invective. Acutely aware of the potentially subversive nature of his theology because of its stress on the individual believer, Luther was desperately anxious that the social fabric should not be rent by his attempt at reform.

Luther's great contribution to Western thought lay in his ability to bring his vigorous, uncompromising, and creative mind to bear on problems that had troubled numerous thinkers over the preceding centuries. He stated his view of the human condition with a depth and intensity unknown in medieval Christendom. Most of his ideas can justifiably be traced to Saint Augustine and Saint Paul, but that detracts in no way from Luther's importance. Neither of the two earlier Christians had been so forceful and single-minded in presenting the personal aspects of religious experience and in enlarging the arena of religious concern to include all dimensions of human feeling. Martin Luther expanded the scope of humanity as few others have. He left many shadows, inconsistencies, and problems for his successors to deal with, but his fundamental insight has been impossible to ignore.

Bibliography

The best biography of Luther is still Roland Bainton's classic *Here I Stand* (New York: Mentor Books, 1950). See also Heinrich Boehmer, *Martin Luther: Road to Reformation* (New York: Meridian Books, 1957), and Ernest Gordon Rupp, *Luther's Progress to the Diet of Worms* (New York: Harper and Row, 1964). The obvious psychological aspects of Luther's theology have prompted scholars in the past two decades to look at him through the eyes of modern psychoanalytical theory. The best known of such treatments is Erik H. Erikson's *Young Man Luther* (New York: Norton, 1962), but Norman O. Brown's *Life Against Death* (Middletown, Conn.: Wesleyan University Press, 1966), by emphasizing the *Turmerlebnis,* treats Luther from a more orthodox Freudian standpoint and produces a stimulating though controversial essay.

For a general discussion of Luther's thought see Heinrich Bornkamm, *Luther's World of Thought,* trans. M. Bertram (St. Louis: Concordia, 1958). For more specialized treatments see Carl Wisloff, *The Gift of Communion,* trans. J. Shaw (Minneapolis: Augsburg, 1964), for an analysis of Luther's theology of the mass that stresses its similarity to orthodox Catholicism. For an illuminating though hard-to-read treatment of Luther's intellectual development, see F. Edward Cranz, *An Essay on the Development of Luther's Thought on Justice, Law, and Society* (Cambridge: Harvard University Press, 1959). Finally, James Preus, *From Shadow to Promise* (Cambridge: Harvard University Press, 1969), has examined Luther's methods of studying and interpreting the Bible in context with medieval practices.

John Dillenberger has put together an excellent collection of Luther's writings, *Martin Luther: Selections from His Writings* (Garden City, N.Y.: Doubleday, 1961), which contains many of his most important works and gives a picture of the growth of his ideas. Luther's debate with Erasmus over free will has been translated and edited by E. Winter, *Erasmus-Luther: Discourse on Free Will* (New York: Ungar, 1961).

21 John Calvin

Luther left several crucial areas of thought untouched. Despite his friendship with the humanist Philipp Melanchthon, he never really understood the Renaissance humanism that had become by his death in 1546 one of the dominant intellectual movements of northern Europe. Inevitably this limited his appeal. Another obstacle to the spread of his ideas was the intensely personal nature of his religious concerns. Until late in his life he largely ignored ecclesiastical organization, systematic proselytizing, or any of the other activities that produced a coherent movement. Finally, the demands Luther imposed on the individual's conscience were not suited to all people. Few have the energy, strength, or inclination to devote their lives to the detailed introspection and self-knowledge that Luther prescribed; this is especially true for those who are seeking social and political outlets for their energies. It was in precisely the areas where Luther was weak that John Calvin made his greatest contributions and assured that the Reformation would have a lasting influence on Western society.

Calvin's contributions to the Reformation are often overshadowed by his reputation as a stern puritanical moralist. That reputation is not undeserved. He was diffident and reserved, had a restrained sense of humor, and lacked Luther's warm and sympathetic exuberance. We are told that his friends in college called him "The Accusative Case." But the wildest rumors about Calvin's excesses of zeal are certainly false. (An example of the latter is the statement by the twentieth-century novelist Aldous Huxley that Calvin had a child publicly beheaded for striking its parents.) Nor should Calvin be blamed for the more unpleasant aspects of English and American puritanism. He never compelled the citizens of Geneva to give up all the pleasures of life and spend their days praying. Laws regulating private behavior on religious grounds did exist in Geneva in Calvin's day but dated from medieval codes drawn up by the bishops. The rigid moral codes for which the city became famous were first enacted by Calvin's successors.

Calvin's Life and Career

John Calvin was a Frenchman, born in 1509 in the northern town of Noyon and intended by his family for a career in the church. His father managed the finances of the cathedral chapter at Noyon and possessed the influence necessary to obtain an attractive position for his son. Calvin thus went to Paris in 1523 to study theology. He entered Montague College, which had been reformed by its principal, Standonck, early in the century and became, under Standonck's successor Beda, an even stricter bastion of orthodoxy. (Both Erasmus and Rabelais hated it, and even Calvin never had many tender words for Montague.) While there Calvin was exposed to both nominalism and humanism. He may have studied briefly under the Scottish nominalist John Major, but that movement never made the impression on him that it did on Luther. At the same time he became friendly with William Cop, King Francis' chief physician and a friend of Budé. The friendship with Cop was the beginning of a lasting influence that would make Calvin one of the great humanist scholars of his time.

While Calvin was at Paris, his father lost his position with the chapter at Noyon amid lawsuits and accusations of dishonesty. Since Calvin could no longer expect preferment in the church, he decided to leave his theological studies and embark upon a legal career. The ease with which Calvin seems to have made this decision gives us some indication of the superficiality of his own religious feelings during this period. In stark contrast with Luther, he obviously did not consider a priestly calling to be a matter of grave significance but simply a means to a good career. Law was an equally good career, and in France it was also one of the fields where humanism was most prominent. Calvin studied first under the great French legist Pierre de L'Estoile and then under the even more famous Italian lawyer Alciatus, deepening his acquaintance with the humanist movement.

In 1532 Calvin wrote his first work, a humanist commentary on Seneca's *De Clementia,* clearly revealing the influence of Budé and

Erasmus. Erasmus had commented on this treatise himself only shortly before, and Calvin explicitly claimed to be dealing with things Erasmus had missed. In fact, though Erasmus is mentioned directly only five times in Calvin's commentary, Erasmus' interpretations are used throughout the work as the basis for Calvin's refinements. Budé's influence shows up in the interpretation of Roman law and in the general historical approach for understanding Roman institutions.

Humanism was not a passing phase in Calvin's life; it was the basis of all his mature thought. Several humanist conceptions appear in the commentary on Seneca that were later incorporated into Calvin's theology and his organization of religious life. First and most important was the concern for morality so characteristic of French humanism. Like many other northerners, Calvin greatly respected the stoicism of Seneca, with its self-control and denial of the flesh. He also firmly believed in natural law, which gives even the most depraved the capacity to understand certain basic principles of morality necessary to human society. Thus we have no excuse for contravening basic laws and moral responsibilities.

Second, Calvin appropriated the humanist methodology. His exegetical technique — that is, the capacity to read a text and discover the author's intended meaning — was equal to the best in Europe. He understood how to establish the historical context as the essential first step in the process and then to identify the personality of the author himself. Like any good humanist, Calvin looked upon learning and study as a means of understanding through personal communication. He clearly illustrated this in his approach to Saint Augustine, to whom he felt closest of all the church fathers. The confusion between Augustine's genuine and spurious writings during the sixteenth century (see Chapter 6) made it hard to tell what his actual position had been, but Calvin so accurately perceived the general lines of Augustine's thought that he identified the true works far better than most of his contemporaries. Recent studies of Calvin's use of Augustine show that he seldom quoted from a spurious passage or inaccurately credited an idea to Augustine. The ability to identify Augustine as a historical personage and not just a vehicle for eternal truth is the clearest evidence of Calvin's humanism.

The third humanist attitude running throughout Calvin's work is his commitment to methodological education. Humanists set out to create an educational system that would enlarge human capacities and inculcate social values, and Calvin shared their goal. Calvin's lasting influence has been due in large measure to his belief that the full personality should be developed systematically and intelligently through formal education.

Shortly after he wrote the commentary on Seneca, Calvin underwent a religious conversion. Although with typical reticence he never described the experience in detail, he noted that between 1533 and 1534 his attitude toward religion changed dramatically. Much later, in 1557, he wrote about it in the following terms:

> And at first, whilst I remained thus so obstinately addicted to the superstitions of the papacy that it would have been hard indeed to have pulled me out of so deep a quagmire by sudden conversion, God subdued and made teachable a heart which, for my age, was far too hardened in such matters. Having thus received some foretaste and knowledge of true piety, I was straightway inflamed with such great desire to profit by it that although I did not attempt to give up other studies, I worked only slackly at them. And I was wonderstruck when, before the year was out, all those who had some desire for the true doctrine ranged themselves around me to learn, although I was hardly more than a beginner myself.

Calvin's conversion was sincere, complete, and lasting. He was not a humanist who merely sympathized with the Protestant cause and assumed a veneer of religious concern. He underwent a thorough reorientation that undercut the humanist emphasis on free will and human greatness. He also became absolutely convinced of the rightness of his knowledge, an attitude that directly contradicted the humanist belief in the ambiguities of life. Yet he remained a humanist. The very words he used to express his conversion — "God subdued and made teachable a heart" — are a classic humanist phrase. His earlier humanism continued to influence his thought in important ways that we will consider later in the chapter.

Calvin's conversion differed from Luther's in two important respects. First, the personal needs of the two men were different. Luther from his earliest years was an intense, sincere, and devout man who found conventional religious practices unconsoling and inadequate. His conversion brought him a measure of peace he had not found before. Calvin in his youth displayed only normal religious interests and was apparently indifferent to the failings of the late medieval church. His conversion was the first evidence of an intense religious need; it brought him unrest and disquiet instead of peace.

Moreover, at the time of his conversion Calvin faced a situation far different from that confronting Luther. The latter had been forced to choose, albeit reluctantly, whether to break with the church or not. But in 1534 the church was already split and Calvin's new religious consciousness had only to choose which of the two different types of church was more suitable to his needs and consonant with revealed truth. We must realize this in order to appreciate Calvin's strong belief in the importance of a universal church and his preoccupation with matters of church organization and liturgy.

Calvin converted during a period of royal displeasure against the Protestants, and he had to leave France. He studied theology for a year in Basel and then decided to move to Strassburg, where there was an active Reformation movement. But he happened to detour through the independent city of Geneva, where he met William Farel, who had just expelled the Catholic leaders and begun a religious reform. Recognizing Calvin's talents, Farel urged Calvin to stay in Geneva and help with the work, and he finally won him over in a dramatic scene that Calvin recounted years later:

> After having heard that I had several particular studies for which I wished to keep myself free, when he saw that he was gaining nothing by entreaties, he went so far as an imprecation, that it might please God to curse the rest and quietness I was seeking, if in so great a necessity I withdrew and refused aid and succour. Which word so horrified and shook me that I desisted from the journey I had undertaken: in such a way, however, that, feeling my shame and timidity, I did not want to commit myself to discharge any particular duty.

Calvin's acceptance of responsibilities in Geneva involved considerable personal sacrifice. He was by taste and temperament a scholar and not a church administrator and was unquestionably inclined to pursue a career of scholarship. Throughout his life he devoted great energies to intellectual endeavors. For instance, he learned dogmatic theology in a single year after his conversion, and in that same year wrote his definitive work on the subject. In just four months he learned Greek to the satisfaction of the best legal scholars in France. But Calvin did not believe in pursuing knowledge for its own sake; he had a passionate need to communicate his insights to men and use them to establish social good. Faced with Farel's challenge to put his wisdom into practice, Calvin could not resist. He discovered that his fundamental commitments were actually to preaching and ordering the church rather than to theology and dogmatics; to the cure of souls rather than to abstract speculation.

Many have assumed that Calvin established a theocracy in Geneva. Although he unquestionably dominated the Genevan church, he did not significantly interfere with or change the city's political and economic life. In particular, he cannot be said to have been responsible for Genevan capitalism. Ever since 1387 the city had had laws permitting 5 percent interest on loans, and they were originally enacted to attract trade to the annual fair and compete with the fair at Lyon. Recent research into Geneva's history indicates that most of the administrative and political reforms during the sixteenth century either were enacted while Calvin was away from the city or were part of the continuing policy of the commune. In any case Geneva in the sixteenth century was not a theocracy; it was ruled by secular bodies that resisted any intrusion of the church into the sphere of politics.

Calvin brought three new institutions to Geneva: the consistory, the academy, and the company of pastors. The consistory was a group of church elders charged with overseeing the doctrine and morals of its members. Calvin's concern with behavior and belief was not just a personal quirk. It was shared by the Genevans themselves, and for important reasons. The reformed church in Geneva was newly established, and some sort of control over beliefs was necessary to provide an orderly basis for institutional functions. Moreover, the state itself was recently independent and threatened by foreign enemies, chiefly Catholic France. The records of the consistory occasionally reveal actions that appear rather silly to us in the twentieth century. For example, Genevans were condemned for having their fortunes told by gypsies, for saying that incoming French refugees were raising the cost of living, or for laughing during a sermon. We find a woman of seventy formally forbidden to marry a man of twenty-five. A barber is condemned for tonsuring a priest. Yet most of the offenses that came before the consistory were serious in nature and posed real dangers to the new commune. Furthermore, the consistory's powers over Genevans grew only slowly and with difficulty. Thus, when Calvin first sought to introduce a general confession of faith, he and Farel were both expelled from the city. He was permitted to return in 1541 and immediately became embroiled with the magistracy over the consistory's right to excommunicate recalcitrant citizens; the consistory did not finally acquire that power until fourteen years later. Calvin felt the tensions resulting from this struggle throughout his life.

The difficulties Calvin experienced in establishing the consistory stand in striking contrast to his success with the other two institutional innovations. When he was not quarreling with the magistrates, he devoted much time to forming a system of religious education, for he realized the vital importance of a good education for his pastors. The capstone of his effort was the founding of his academy in 1559. In structure the academy was clearly humanistic. Physical exercise was part of the curriculum as well as mental discipline; moral training was pursued through a study of the ancients as well as through religious works; and humanist exegesis was part of learning formal theology. The academy was remarkably successful in turning out articulate, effective, and reliable pastors. Its success made the school widely influential, and the Jesuits later used the academy as a model for their own schools.

The third of Calvin's institutions was intended to reach beyond Geneva to the rest of Europe. As a Frenchman, Calvin regarded the conversion of his countrymen to be one of his chief missions in life. To this end he established the company of pastors, a group of trained missionaries who systematically infiltrated France, made converts, and organized underground churches. The painstaking attention to detail that characterized all of Calvin's work was especially conspicuous in the way he organized the company of pastors. Not only were the missionaries carefully trained, but their activity on French soil was carefully regulated. Overseers were regularly sent from Geneva to make sure that the doctrine and morals of the new congregations were correct, and the pastors themselves were required to return periodically to be examined at Geneva. An elaborate network of way stations was established on the routes from Geneva into the various regions of France. To this day, there are farmhouses in the Dauphiné that contain hidden staircases and secret rooms where a Calvinist could spend a night unmolested by the king's men. The effectiveness of the company of pastors was dramatic, as will be seen in the next chapter, where the spread of Protestantism is described.

Calvin's life was committed to social and political action. Although he was temperamentally inclined to a life of scholarship, his principles forced him into a wider sphere where he was less comfortable but felt duty bound to go. His theology must be understood in light of his conscious commitment to an active life. He regarded himself first as a pastor entrusted with the care of souls ⚹ and the propagation of God's word to his country; his theological writings were secondary, intended only to aid his pastoral goals.

Calvin's Thought

Calvin's theology was broader, more consistent, and more clearly expressed than Luther's, but it was less original. Not only did Calvin draw heavily on the early church fathers, but he also derived some of his most important ideas from his sixteenth-century contemporaries. His fundamental notions of theology came from Luther, and his concept of the church was taken from the German theologian Martin Bucer. Calvin's own humanist training resulted in his belief that the Bible was the ultimate source of truth, but he had been preceded in this belief by the Swiss reformer Ulrich Zwingli.

Zwingli was one of the first Protestant reformers to come out of the Erasmian tradition. He was born in 1484 and educated for the priesthood at Basel under the humanist Wittenbach. During his studies, he became impressed with Erasmus' work and began to read the early church fathers. In 1518, he was called to the church at Zurich, where he began a series of sermons expounding the Gospel of Saint Matthew according to the literal meaning of the text. That was the beginning of the Reformation in Zurich. In the course of the next six years Zwingli expounded the entire text of the New Testament, commenting on the original Greek. We still have his copy of Erasmus' edition of the New Testament, and from his marginal comments we clearly see the union of religious and scholarly interests so typical of northern humanism.

This scriptural exegesis led Zwingli to criticize one practice after another of the medieval church. First he attacked the lenten fast. Then gradually he began to oppose the use of religious images, the celibacy of the clergy, and eventually the doctrine of the mass. His position was that the mass was simply a memorial service where the bread and wine remained natural elements. That brought him into sharp conflict with Luther. Zwingli did accept the Lutheran doctrines of salvation by faith alone and predestination, but only because they were found in the Scriptures, which he regarded as the sole source of all truth.

Surrounded by his supporters from Zurich, Zwingli died in battle against the troops of the emperor in 1531, shortly before Calvin's conversion. His writings and pastoral work showed the shape of a theology based on humanist study of the Scriptures rather than on personal experience of the existential needs of the soul. His sacramental position was accepted in modified form by Calvin, who maintained that though the elements of body and blood were really present in the mass, their presence was spiritual rather than physical. Calvin succeeded in thoroughly integrating Lutheran theology with scriptural humanism, but the broad outlines of the synthesis were suggested by Zwingli.

Martin Bucer (1491–1551) was a former Dominican monk who had left the church to support Luther, and he was preaching the Gospel at Strassburg when Calvin finally arrived there in 1537 after having been expelled from Geneva. He was one of the few men in either the Catholic or Protestant camp who advocated compromise and conciliation. In his earlier years he had taken extreme positions on the sacraments, favoring Zwingli over Luther, but had become more moderate because he believed that the church should be kept together within a single confession of faith that all could accept. The change in attitude came about largely from his dealings with the radical reformers at Strassburg (see Chapter 24), whose excesses convinced him that firm church discipline and clear confession of faith were essential. Bucer devoted most of his career at Strassburg to working out a theological formula that could satisfy all the reformers and enable them to organize a single church to embody these principles. His efforts culminated in the Wittenberg Concord of 1536, in which Luther agreed to accept a modified Zwinglian interpretation of the Lord's Supper, but Bucer's attempts to form a unified church foundered when the Zwinglians deserted him. Bucer tried all his life to secure his church by irenic or conciliatory methods; Calvin chose more vigorous means and met with greater success, but his intellectual debt to Bucer should not be ignored.

The essence of Calvin's thought is contained in the *Institutes of the Christian Religion*. Few theologians have expressed themselves so completely in a single work. The first edition of the *Institutes* appeared at Basel in 1536 and represented the fruits of a year's study of theology immediately after Calvin's conversion but before his experience at Geneva. It was a relatively small book, little more than five hundred pages in length and designed to be carried in the pocket; it was divided into six chapters. The first four — the law, the creed, the Lord's Prayer, and the sacraments — followed the order of Luther's catechism. Indeed, Calvin labeled the book as a whole a catechism, expressing his desire to educate rather than expound formal and systematic theology. The last two chapters dealt with particular issues of the day and were more polemical in tone.

Successive editions were larger in scope and departed from the form of a catechism to expose more directly the general outlines of Protestant theology. The second edition appeared in 1539, shortly after Calvin's first, brief stay in Geneva. It was three times larger than the first and included two new chapters on the knowledge of God and the knowledge of man. The sections on the trinity, penitence, and justification by faith were also enlarged. The second edition, both in form and theological content, was the model for all subsequent editions. It was more systematic and coherent than the first and included a wider range of quotations from the early church fathers. The first French edition of 1541 (the earliest were in Latin) was intended to be used by the growing Reformed church in France. Subsequent editions, in 1543, 1550, and 1559, appeared first in Latin and then immediately in French.

The last edition of 1559 represented the culmination of Calvin's thought and is the one usually read. Its structure was simplified, even though it contained more chapters than previous editions. It was divided into four books: (1) "the knowledge of God in his titles and qualities as creator and sovereign of the world"; (2) "the knowledge of God the redeemer as he has shown himself in Jesus Christ, which was first known by the fathers under the law and has since been manifested to us in the Gospel"; (3) "the manner of participation in the grace of Jesus Christ, the fruits which come to us therefrom, and the effects which ensue"; and (4) "the external means or aids which God uses to bring us to Jesus Christ his son and to keep us in him." In brief the book deals with God the Father, God the Son, God the Holy Spirit, and the church. Moreover, the format of a catechism had been definitely abandoned in favor of a formal exposition of theology, modeled on the fourfold division of the Apostles' Creed used in the Reformed church.

Commentators have made much of Calvin's consistency during the twenty-five years between the first edition and the last, and according to one, Calvin changed his mind only once. But in fact there were several important changes. In the first edition he said that the only true church was the invisible church, the communion of the elect, and that the visible church on earth was not really so important, because its organization depended on local conditions. But in 1559 he was insisting that the church visible was of vital importance and that the Scriptures and the practices of the early church dictate clear principles of ecclesiastical organization that the visible and universal church must adopt. He also insisted that a church based on scriptural example was the only true church and that all men must join it and receive its sacraments. He similarly changed his position on political matters; though he had said that a bad king was the scourge of an angry God and should be obeyed, in 1559 he enunciated the theory that legally constituted bodies could actively resist the king and that private individuals could passively resist. These changes were essentially movements away from the Lutheran position toward a more active, uniquely Calvinist view. They also prove that Calvin was willing to change his mind in undergoing intellectual growth throughout his life.

Ever since the middle of the nineteenth century, when a German scholar suggested that predestination was the central doctrine in Calvin's theology, there has been a tendency to overemphasize this aspect of his thought. A close examination of the *Institutes* puts the issue in perspective. Calvin devoted more space to predestination in the later editions, but even in 1559 the issue occupied only four chapters and was seldom mentioned outside them. His position on predestination was more systematic though no more extreme than Luther's and in fact it was clearly subordinated to considerations of sanctification and regeneration.

Calvin's basic concept was the majesty of God. He agreed with Luther that God so transcended the human condition that his nature was totally beyond the normal course of human experience. That does not mean, however, that man has no natural knowledge of God whatsoever. Calvin put great stress on our natural sense of God's existence, observing that no society has ever existed without some form of religion; man's own reason suggests a reality beyond itself. This innate sense deprives us of any excuse for not seeking to know God, but it cannot by itself give true knowledge of him. He lies so far beyond and above us that our own nature cannot lead us to him.

Implicit in Calvin's doctrine of the majesty of God is the depravity of man. "Depravity" is the way the doctrine is commonly expressed, and Calvin himself, very early in his *Institutes,* speaks of man's lowly state. But to put the notion in perspective, we must realize that both Calvin and Luther knew what real people were like. They realized that men are capable of conscious self-sacrifice and acts of selfless love. Calvin was trying to stress, however, that ordinary human achievements of self-sacrifice and charity, however good they may seem, are pale reflections of ultimate personal bliss and goodness. Deep within us are realities that so far transcend our accomplishments that they put even our best achievements into shadow. Some people, to be sure, have used the doctrine of human depravity as a means of degrading humanity and counseling despair. But despite its negative terminology, the idea can as easily be a call to joy and hope at the vision of greater worlds beyond daily life. Both Calvin and Luther stressed that man was low and depraved only in contrast with the ultimate personal reality, God himself. Calvin concluded his chapter on human depravity with these words:

> What can man do who is rottenness itself and a worm, when even the very cherubim must veil their faces out of fear? It is this indeed of which the prophet Isaiah speaks, "The sun will blush and the moon be confounded when the Lord of Hosts shall reign," that is, when he shall bring forth his splendor and cause it to draw nearer, the brightest thing will become darkness before it. [*Institutes* 1.1.3]

How then do we know such a God? Calvin considered knowledge of God and of ourselves to be the only true wisdom. We know ourselves when we realize our lowly state in relation to God, and we can acquire this knowledge by looking at our own actions and motives. But to know God we need aid; we must read the Scriptures, where the only true knowledge of God is found. They sharpen our will to know God and give us the possibility of knowing him. Thus, scriptural exegesis stands at the very forefront of Calvin's thought. He placed a far greater emphasis on the Bible than had Luther and asserted that certain knowledge of reality can be derived only from study of the Word. This is a very humanist attitude, for in effect Calvin was saying that truth only exists in the precise communication of personal perspectives. But because the personal perspective expressed in the Scriptures is God's, it is absolute truth. Man cannot reject the Scriptures and rely on another text, for no other text, however convincing, is utterly truthful and completely frees man to worship God rather than an idol. In this manner, Calvin united the humanist notion of the ultimacy of verbal communication with

Luther's demand that we must be completely sure of the basic realities of the universe.

Despite his insistence on the importance of the Scriptures, Calvin never suggested that they should be accepted as superstitiously authoritative merely because the church said so. The Scriptures were true because they would convince anyone who read them with an open mind. "The spirit illumines the word with perfect clarity," and that is what gives the word its power and authority. In this case Calvin meant by the spirit both our own innate standards of what is convincing and the action of God in time that certifies the validity of his word. The spirit adds nothing new to the Scriptures, but it continually certifies them. Calvin abhorred superstition and never claimed that the Bible was literally inspired. Rather, it is a mirror that reflects God; it is not God himself. He frequently ridiculed the fundamentalists of his own day because of their narrow-minded and unimaginative exegetical technique. The whole Bible, he said, Old Testament as well as New, is certainly inspired, but it must be interpreted and certified by the spirit before it can lead us to the true knowledge of God.

Calvin himself set out to demonstrate the Bible's truth by all the humanist methods of source criticism, textual analysis, and historical judgment. He noted, for instance, that the Old Testament makes the Hebrew people and their leaders seem quite human; in addition, the events described in both New and Old Testaments are comprehensible only if we accept the interpretation of them found in the Scriptures themselves. These arguments, if applied to a secular history, would convince us of the accuracy and reliability of the account. Therefore, said Calvin, they ought to convince us with equal force of the truth of the Scriptures. Calvin felt that this sort of argument was very important because it permitted each of us to accept the Scriptures fully and completely by applying his or her own standards of judgment to them. In a sense, Calvin's humanist arguments actually reinforced Luther's individualism. Yet at the same time they provided a role for society, which had to give a person, through education, the techniques to appreciate fully the scriptural message.

Knowledge of God has an important consequence, for through it we come to know creation and understand our place in the universe. We are the goal and culmination of creation. Because the world was created for us, we play a role of unusual responsibility

in it. Man's role is to glorify God, and that is completely independent of our personal salvation. Both the saved and the damned are
commanded to work for God's greater glory. As we shall see, this
position had important implications in the realm of pastoral
theology.

In the second book of the *Institutes* Calvin dealt with our knowledge of Christ and how Christ helps us to escape our fallen state.
Calvin's Christology was quite orthodox, taken mainly from Saint
Augustine. In spite of the gulf between God and man, God partici-
pates fully in the historical process. Thus we have the possibility
of redemption, which is a particular gift of God to every saved soul
based on the original gift of the Incarnation. Calvin explains the
process in the context of the law, distinguishing between Old Testament laws, which are binding only on the people of Israel, and universal laws like the Ten Commandments, which anticipated the
coming of Christ and which he fulfilled. The latter, which are still
binding, have three functions: pedagogical, by showing us what sins
are; political, by hindering the wicked from doing evil out of fear
of punishment; and spiritual, by helping the spirit of the faithful
to mortify the flesh. This last function is especially worth noting
for it developed into the legalism that plagued later Calvinism. In
effect it is saying that man is not made perfect just by being chosen
for salvation. Even though saved he must be nurtured and perfected
by the law, which will diminish his pride and govern his flesh and
prepare him for the eternal bliss that is his predestined gift from
God.

The third section of the *Institutes* further emphasizes the need
to lead a well-regulated and socially useful life on earth, whether
or not we are saved. In this section, which contains the essence of
his social and ethical thinking, Calvin considers the Holy Spirit,
or the manner in which we participate in the grace of Jesus Christ,
and deals with the problem of human action. Here is where he explicitly takes up justification and predestination, and the sequence
is highly significant. The section begins with the statement that we
participate in the indwelling of Christ; the statement is carefully
qualified to exclude any mystical connotation that might diminish
the distance between God and man. Calvin wished to avoid the
anthropomorphism of the Rhineland mystics, who found a bit of
God in every man, which leads to mystical union with the creator.
Next Calvin explained the effects of Christ's indwelling on our val-

ues and attitudes and on the regeneration of a Christian life. Only then did he turn to justification. Finally he mentioned predestination in the overall context of justification, and only as a corollary of the doctrine of solifidianism.

By this sequence of topics Calvin made justification, which concerns our personal relation to God, appear subordinate to sanctification, which concerns our actions in the world, our relations to our fellow man, and our outward obedience to the commands of God. This is not to say that Calvin in fact regarded justification as of secondary importance. Justification touches on the deepest problems of personal fulfillment, and no one can or should maintain that personal salvation is less important to an individual than his contribution to society. The doctrine of the Incarnation teaches that God is a person, and if ultimate reality is personal, then personal problems are ultimate. Calvin knew this, but he was seeking to deal socially and religiously with the fact that justification is completely beyond human control because it was decided, or predestined, before the world began. Luther left man naked before this fact; Calvin sought to offer help by drawing man's attention to the social issue and discourage him from futile worry about his own salvation.

To this end Calvin argued that the fact of election, or being chosen for salvation, tends to have certain effects. In particular, the elect are more likely than the damned to enjoy obeying God and performing good works. Thus, enjoyment of doing good is presumptive evidence of election. On the other hand, the fact that some do not enjoy doing good is not clear evidence that they are damned. No one really enjoys doing good, for even the elect are still subject to pride and must be led to the ways of God through the laws and through social and political pressure. Since we can never completely eliminate pride, it is possible to be chosen for salvation yet never learn to enjoy being good. As Calvin would have said it, a hard heart is perfectly consistent with a state of election.

By these arguments Calvin intended to establish once and for all that man's one, true purpose on earth is to lead a life that glorifies God through obedience to his commandments. Such a life is of course totally inconsistent with introspective brooding, the besetting ill of Lutheran and Roman Catholic theology. Our motives for obeying the commandments are not particularly relevant. It is perfectly acceptable to obey out of fear. If you are among the elect, the mere fact of obedience will tend to condition your will to enjoy the process of sanctification and incidentally assure you of your election. But even that is beside the point, because obedience has no direct bearing on salvation. The real purpose of the law is to establish God's kingdom on earth and work for his glory, and obedience is sufficient. Whether we are inwardly contrite does not affect the value of our acts, for even external obedience to the will of God is a virtue. Strong as these words were, they could not completely eliminate the Lutheran problem. Even Calvin worried from time to time about his own salvation, and some famous Calvinists have gone through life convinced they were not among the elect. But it did change the emphasis of religious life. Calvin gave men social functions to fulfill independent of the search for assurance of salvation. At the same time he showed that it is precisely in fulfilling these functions that we are most likely to receive that assurance.

From the doctrine of sanctification Calvin derived the role of the church. So important did he consider the church on earth that the entire last section of the *Institutes* is centered in it. Calvin accepted Luther's division of the church into a visible and invisible one. But he considered the visible church, which includes both the saved and ♭ the damned, to be crucially important. It is directly concerned with our sanctification and its doctrine and discipline are ordained by God in the Scriptures. The church cannot be governed or ordered by secular powers; it must look to Scripture for its guidance. It is universal, because it includes all human beings, who are without exception called to sanctify themselves by working for the glory of God; but it should be locally governed, because the Scriptures prescribe that sort of organization.

Calvin carefully specified sacraments and regulated ceremonies to support the church. He insisted on infant baptism in spite of the lack of scriptural support because he insisted that membership in the church is not a matter of choice; the fact that it was required by divine command could best be symbolized by admitting people to the church before the age of consent. Contrary to the Zwinglians, Calvin maintained that the Lord's Supper was a major sacrament rather than a simple memorial service. In contrast with Luther, he introduced severe limitations on the use of music and images so that they would not detract from the preaching and the scriptural aspects of the service.

Calvin's church also laid down guidelines for the behavior of its members and established a clear statement of beliefs, embodied in a general confession of faith imposed on all members. The order Calvin introduced was a major ingredient in the success of Calvinism. He offered a definite code of belief and behavior in an age where basic values seemed to be changing rapidly.

Calvin's theology reflected the pastoral concerns that were so conspicuous a part of his life. He developed a conception of God and of man's role in the universe that viewed social and political action as contributing to the glory of God. To be sure, some of Calvin's successors applied his theology in ways that seem hardly humane. Calvin himself, however, clearly was trying to alleviate the severe burdens that Luther had imposed on ordinary Christians. He sought to allow men to use the experience and freedom opened up by Luther without being destroyed by it. Calvinist ideas proved particularly attractive to the second generation of reformers, who had not always been driven to the reform out of personal needs as deep as Luther's, and Calvin's reformed faith spread dramatically throughout Europe.

Bibliography

François Wendel's *Calvin: The Origins and Development of His Thought,* trans. P. Mairet (London: Collins, 1963), offers a splendidly clear, balanced, and sensitive introduction, as well as an excellent bibliography for those who wish to pursue particular problems further. On the issue of Calvin's humanism, which is stressed in this chapter, see Quirinus Breen, *John Calvin: A Study in French Humanism,* 2nd ed. (Hamden, Conn.: Archon Books, 1968). Calvin's impact on Geneva has been most recently discussed by E. William Monter in *Studies in Genevan Government* (Geneva: Librairie Droz, 1964) and in *Calvin's Geneva* (New York: Wiley, 1967). For a recent study of Calvin's ecclesiology see Benjamin Milner, Jr., *Calvin's Doctrine of the Church* (Leiden: Brill, 1970). John T. McNeill has studied Calvin in context with the movement that developed from him; see his *The History and Character of Calvinism* (New York: Oxford University Press, 1962).

Recent studies of Bucer have been mostly in German, but Hastings Eell's *Martin Bucer* (New Haven: Yale University Press, 1931) is still readable and useful. See also Constantin Hopf, *Martin Bucer and the English Reformation* (Oxford: Blackwell, 1946). For Zwingli see

Jean Rilliet, *Zwingli: Third Man of the Reformation,* trans. H. Knight (Philadelphia: Westminster Press, 1964), and Oskar Farner, *Zwingli the Reformer,* trans. D. Sear (New York: Philosophical Library, 1952).

Calvin is more systematic and therefore harder to excerpt without distortion than Luther is. John Dillenberger's recent anthology, *John Calvin: Selections from His Writings* (Garden City, N.Y.: Doubleday, 1971), is less successful than his Luther anthology, although it is still the most comprehensive and useful collection available. Dillenberger presents a more Lutheran Calvin than was actually the case by leaving out many of Calvin's positive comments on the classics. There is no substitute for reading the *Institutes,* which have been translated by F. L. Battles (Philadelphia: Westminster Press, 1960).

22 The Spread of Protestantism

Luther and Calvin were scholars and intellectuals, but their ideas had far-reaching practical effects. They founded new institutional churches and divided Western Christendom into factions. The institutional Reformation associated with Luther and Calvin has been called the magisterial Reformation because it won official acceptance — that is, acceptance from the "magistracies," in important areas of Europe. Other religious leaders, more radical in their views, founded sects that were opposed by all secular rulers and only established political control in scattered local areas for brief periods of time. This radical Reformation, as it was called, was as unacceptable to the magisterial reformers as to the Catholics; it will be treated in a separate chapter.

Two important factors influenced the course of the magisterial Reformation: the political structure of Europe and the vast difference between Luther's and Calvin's concepts of the institutional church. Although the ideas of the great reformers are best viewed in the context of their intellectual tradition, the actual institutional reforms must also take into account the background of regional politics. For example, the Lutheran churches of Germany and Scandinavia were markedly different from the Calvinist churches of France, the Low Countries, and Britain, just as Calvin's thought differed markedly from Luther's. The contrast resulted from a blend of theological and political factors. Luther's religion, because it was fundamentally personal, needed no particular institutional setting. Those who felt sympathy for his ideas could practice their religion within a wide variety of ecclesiastical frameworks, including Roman Catholicism. The growth of national Lutheran churches was not implicit in Luther's writings; it resulted from pressures within Germany and Scandinavia that were not strictly religious.

Calvin, by contrast, tied his ecclesiastical position tightly to his theology. His religion could not be practiced in all ecclesiastical settings; it required a definite form of church organization, liturgical practice, and moral discipline. The split between the Calvinist churches and the Catholic church was thus deliberate and unavoidable. But even here politics had an influence, as we shall see.

The Lutheran Reformation

The Ninety-five Theses were recognized by no one — certainly not by Luther — as an attack on the authority of Rome or as the beginning of a schism. At first Rome hardly noticed them. Pope Leo X, a Renaissance man with a fine political sense, saw the quarrel as a reflection of the rivalry between the Dominicans and Augustinians. The two orders had never been on terms of great cordiality, and for a while Luther's most vociferous opponents were Dominicans. The latter order arranged for Tetzel to acquire a doctorate so that he could publish a reply to Luther, and they also commissioned Sylvester Prieras, a more learned Dominican than Tetzel but still no match for Luther, to counter the attacks. Thus the remark that Pope Leo allegedly made when he heard of the Ninety-five Theses: "Friar Martin is a brilliant fellow. The whole row is due to the envy of the monks." He was not alone in his suspicions. Some who later supported Luther actively, like Ulrich von Hutten, dismissed the issue at first as just another monkish quarrel.

But the theses found active support, and soon the hierarchy became convinced that Luther should be silenced and the abuses that had drawn his fire should be corrected. Tetzel had plainly sold indulgences through extravagant claims, and worse yet, he had lived much too well on his mission. An emissary from Rome, Carl von Miltitz, was sent to stop that scandal. Von Miltitz sternly lectured the unfortunate indulgence seller, berating him for his illegitimate children and for traveling in horse and carriage, and whisked him back to the monastery. Steps were taken to ensure that those who sold indulgences in the future would be more modest in their claims and manners. The curia began to formulate its position on indulgences in more sophisticated language. A papal decretal on November 9, 1518, imposed limitations on the use and effectiveness of indulgences that virtually incorporated the points found in the Ninety-five Theses. If the sale of indulgences and the abuses surrounding it had been the only issues, the quarrel should have been resolved almost as soon as it started.

By the time the church had taken these steps, however, other problems had come to the fore. The attempt to silence Luther had led him to disobey his ecclesiastical superiors directly and turned an acceptable if embarrassing attack on clerical abuses into outright defiance of the church's authority. The first intimation of Luther's determination to defend his position was noted shortly after the theses came to the attention of Rome. Cardinal Cajetan, one of the finest of Italian humanistic churchmen, came to Germany to reason with Luther. Luther talked with him willingly but uncompromisingly, insisting that his understanding of Christianity was orthodox and refusing to acknowledge the cardinal's authority to force him to change.

A lengthy debate at Leipzig in 1519 with the German professor John Eck brought Luther even more in opposition to the authority of the hierarchy. Luther argued that the pope should be obeyed under most circumstances, but that since his authority was of human origin, he could be resisted when his commands contravened the Scriptures. While the debate showed Luther's independence of mind, it made equally clear his desire to avoid heresy and keep a position within the established church. He kept asking Eck to indicate exactly which of his ideas were heretical. When Eck noted that Luther's statements sounded much like those of John Hus, condemned by the Council of Constance, Luther made the tactical error of questioning the wisdom of the council. Though he firmly disavowed any connection with the Bohemian church, any association with Hus was dangerous; the Bohemian church was still very much alive, and Bohemian soldiers had recently ravaged part of Germany. Luther could not expect to attract supporters in that way.

In the year following the Leipzig debate, Luther issued pamphlets calling the German princes to support him and oppose the influence of Rome on the church in Germany; in the same year Pope Leo and the curia decided that stronger measures had to be taken. In 1520 Luther was formally denounced in the bull *Exsurge Domine:* "Rise up O Lord and judge thy cause. A wild boar has invaded thy vineyard." Even at this point, three years after the Ninety-five theses, the hierarchy could find nothing in Luther's already voluminous writings and public utterances that could be singled out as clearly heretical, though they did find forty-one errors described vaguely as "heretical, or scandalous, or false, or offensive to pious ears, or seductive of simple minds, or repugnant to Catholic truth, respectively." The Council of Constance had used the same formulation for John Hus, and in both cases the wording arose from the fact that neither Luther nor Hus was clearly heretical. Virtually everything either man said could be found in the writings of some respectable church father. In both cases the church was less interested in the precise content of the thought than in the possible effects of open defiance.

Luther had become so popular by 1520 that it was hard to get the bull even published; to get it respected was impossible. Luther wrote a diatribe entitled *Against the Execrable Bull of Antichrist* in which he took the pope to task for refusing to say precisely which of his views were heretical and which were not; in it he vowed that he would never recant until proven wrong by Scripture. He put the dramatic final seal on his defiance by publicly burning the bull as well as the canon law and the papal constitutions.

How did this come to pass? Neither Luther nor the church had intended to create the rupture that was rapidly appearing. Luther wanted to make the established church open to new religious insights but professed his willingness to obey the hierarchy on matters not plainly against Scripture. The church only wanted to silence Luther and used methods that had frequently proved fruitful in the past. Only twenty-five years earlier the Dominican monk Savonarola, whose attempts at moral and religious reform in Florence were embarrassing but hardly heretical, had been driven into open defiance of the papacy by a command to be silent. But his defiance had lost him the support of the Florentines and led to his downfall and execution. An established authority will seldom permit another, coordinate authority to be flouted openly for fear of weakening its own control. But Luther's great popularity, his appeal to the national feelings of the Germans against Italian intervention, and the manifest justice of his attacks all combined to make him less vulnerable than Savonarola. And the elector Frederick of Saxony, Luther's temporal ruler, refused to give him over to trial.

Frederick's motives for protecting Luther were certainly more political than religious. He had no interest in theology and claimed to have seen Luther only five times in his whole life. But he was annoyed with the way that the church sold indulgences to his own subjects, for the sale deprived him of needed revenues for the administration of his own state. Furthermore, like all German princes of the period, he was proud of his independence from imperial control. The independence was recent and not wholly secure, and it might be compromised by surrendering one of his own subjects to the imperial tribunal. Frederick's refusal, at first indirect and evasive but eventually forthright and defiant, ensured that the quarrel between Luther and the church would not be settled easily.

Even after Luther burned the papal bull, few thought that the split was irreparable. For the next two decades conciliatory voices in both Catholic and Lutheran camps sought to bring the two movements together into a single faith with a single creed. At the Diet of Augsburg in 1530, Melanchthon prepared a confession of faith designed to satisfy both sides. But the papacy repudiated it and the attempt failed. As late as 1541, Contarini, one of the reforming voices at the papal court, arrived at a statement of justification that appealed to elements on both sides, but again proved unacceptable to the leaders of either. As we look back, the Reformation seems to have been established institutionally and irrevocably by 1525, but contemporaries did not see it so clearly. The church had weathered great schisms and disagreements in the past, some lasting for decades, yet they had always been mended. No one wanted to conclude that this time the split would be permanent.

But the problem went far beyond the defiance of a single monk. Luther's increasing resistance to the pope and Frederick's more and more open support were matched by a widespread reform of religious practices throughout Germany. The first changes appeared almost immediately. By 1520, masses for the dead had become rare in Saxony, and many priests had begun to make important changes in the ritual. Carlstadt, a follower of Luther's, celebrated the mass without traditional vestments and in German rather than Latin. In 1525, Luther married, definitively breaking his monastic vows. The following year he produced a complete text of a Lutheran mass, in which he sought to revise the liturgy to reflect his theological disagreements with Rome, and he especially eliminated any sense that the mass constituted a sacrifice. In 1529, he published a catechism setting forth the doctrinal and liturgical characteristics of the new religion. His interest in bringing the Bible to laymen had led him to translate the New Testament as early as 1522, but he continued to revise and rework the translation of the Bible all his life; it became a model of modern German prose.

By 1521, it was clear that the Lutheran movement would not go away by itself. Luther and his followers enjoyed wide support among all elements of the German population, could rely on the acquiescence if not the active support of a powerful territorial prince, and had formed a distinctive religious life reflecting a Lutheran doctrinal base. They would have to be either accommodated or suppressed by force. The only power in Germany capable of the latter was the Holy Roman emperor, whose opposition to Luther became manifest at the Diet of Worms (1521). Luther refused to recant his works, and on the next day the emperor asked for the support of his electors in attacking Luther and rooting out his teachings:

> I am resolved to stake my lands, my friends, my body, my blood, my life, and my soul. . . . After having heard yesterday the obstinate defense of Luther, I regret that I have so long delayed in proceeding against him and his false teaching. I will have nothing more to do with him. He may return under his safe conduct but without preaching or making any tumult. I will proceed against him as a notorious heretic, and ask you to declare yourselves as you promised me.

Emperor Charles V was determined to suppress the Lutheran movement and persuaded most of the great princes of Germany to join him in signing the condemnation.

Charles seemed to have impressive resources for bringing Luther and his protector Frederick to heel. Not only had he acquired — or, more accurately, purchased — the title of Holy Roman emperor in 1519, but he was hereditary ruler through his father's lineage of Austria and the Netherlands. Moreover, from his mother he had inherited Spain and the kingdom of Sicily. The Spanish New World and the flourishing commerce of Flanders provided him wealth, Germany furnished him troops, and together they should have made him the dominant power in Europe, to say nothing of unquestioned ruler of the Germans. But as events were to ing of the unquestioned ruler of the Germans. But as events were to vast resources. A hostile France, a growing Turkish power, discontent among his diverse possessions, and the resistance of all the German princes — Protestant and Catholic alike — to imperial encroachments on their independence were all factors that worked at one time or another in the thirty-five years after the Diet of Worms to frustrate Charles' design to crush Lutheranism within his empire.

The most serious obstacle was the princes' reluctance to participate in a war against one of their own. Princely independence was
too recently won and too dearly valued. They might fiercely de-
nounce their Lutheran brethren and promise great sums of money
to the emperor's campaign, but few delivered any real support
except when it happened to further their own territorial interests.
As the war dragged on, several princes went over to the Lutherans,
but even from the beginning the emperor had to rely largely on his
own resources.

Charles' personal possessions were not so easily translated into
political and military power as might appear at first glance. Each
of his domains had its own institutions and cultural identity. The
only unity was the person of the emperor himself. The Low Countries were actually sympathetic to the Protestant cause and in addition were loath to see Charles destroy the German princes, for fear
the latter's downfall would result in the loss of their own minimal
independence. In 1539, just as Charles had overcome most of his
other problems, the city of Ghent rebelled against his rule, and to
control the revolt the emperor had to divert troops from the pacification of Germany.

More terrifying, if not in the long run more serious, than the
opposition of the emperor's own subjects was the rise of Turkish
power. Suleiman the Magnificent (1520–1560) extended the Turkish empire into the Balkans, defeated the Hungarians at the battle
of Mohács in 1526, and besieged Vienna itself in 1529. Each time
the Turkish army advanced, Charles had to take forces away from
his campaign against the Protestants to meet the challenge. The
diversion often gave the Protestant leaders respites that were badly
needed. Ultimately the Turkish threat to Europe receded, but not
before Protestantism had become thoroughly established.

The French constituted yet a further problem. Charles' possessions completely surrounded the kingdom of France, and the French
kings could hardly be expected to let pass an opportunity for weakening their dangerous neighbor. Francis I (1515–1547) was Charles'
opponent during most of this period. Rash and warlike (he succeeded in being captured by Charles and taken to Madrid after the
battle of Pavia, in 1525), Francis, supported by the wealth and
population of Europe's largest country, was a constant obstacle to
the emperor's designs. French intervention, too, was often very
timely. By 1547, Charles had crushed the forces of the Protestant

Smalkaldic League, had won over most of the wavering princes in the empire, had imprisoned the elector of Saxony and the landgrave of Hesse, and was on the point of reestablishing Catholicism throughout the empire. At this crucial juncture the new French king, Henry II, breathed new life into the Protestant cause. He intervened militarily, supported by Maurice of Saxony, a former ally of Charles, and the tables were suddenly turned; Charles was forced into ignominious retreat over the Brenner Pass, and his hopes of crushing the Protestants were dashed just when the goal seemed within reach.

In 1555 Charles signed the Peace of Augsburg, giving up all further attempts to impose Catholicism on the Protestant princes. The peace stipulated that the religion of any state in the empire should be chosen by its prince, that people should not be prevented from emigrating to a region practicing their own religion, and that neither side should proselytize the other. Each side had finally realized that it was not strong enough to control all Germany. Charles' own political difficulties were decisive in forcing him into this compromise, but other considerations were also important. By 1555 Lutheranism, in those parts of the empire where it had taken hold, mainly in northern Germany, was an established religion with distinct practices. It had acquired the same sort of support among the people as Roman Catholicism enjoyed in the Catholic parts of the empire, and any attempt to introduce arbitrary change was likely to meet strong resistance. Lutheranism survived as a permanent religion apart from Catholicism not so much by plan or policy as by a complex of political and religious factors. Few wanted the split at the beginning; most accepted it at the end.

The Lutheran Reformation Outside Germany

It is not surprising that Lutheranism won the support of the German princes. Luther was radical only in a religious sense. His one goal was to put the individual into direct and personal confrontation with God, untouched by any institutional intervention. Politically he was conservative. He regarded the state as supreme in its own realm, having power over the secular lives of its subjects and also over the administration of the church. Thus, the Lutheran religion made an excellent prop for princely rule, which, while independent in fact, was theoretically tied to the emperor. Lutheran theology accepted existing powers as the judgment of God and did not question their legitimacy or justification.

Outside Germany Lutheranism enjoyed the favor of the secular monarchs only in Scandinavia, where the kings of Denmark and Sweden found it useful to their political goals. There the Reformation was imposed by the sovereign's direct will and without, at first, many of the signs of popular support that were seen in Germany. Gradually, however, Lutheranism came to be associated with Scandinavian cultural and national feelings. Its popularity lay as much in its ability to symbolize these as in its own merits.

Where Lutheranism did not enjoy the support of the secular authority, it fared poorly. The highly personal nature of the religion tended to discourage sustained attempts at subverting the secular power, and Luther himself strongly and explicitly disapproved of such activity. As a result, the popular support that Luther had attracted all over Europe was easily rooted out except where protected by the state. By 1540, when solid Lutheran roots had been planted in Germany and Scandinavia, Lutheranism had been all but destroyed in the rest of Europe.

Lutheran ideas appeared in England around 1520, and they were swiftly and unhesitatingly repudiated. England had had an earlier encounter with heresy in the person of John Wycliffe (1328–1384), who had attacked the church's powers of jurisdiction and order; he had demanded an abandonment of all clerical property and taught the Gospel in English. Lollardy, the popular movement that grew up after Wycliffe, had conditioned the English upper classes to think of religious protest as equivalent to social revolt, and that made any such ideas highly suspect. Luther's books were publicly burned in 1521, and the bishop of London preached a sermon against them. King Henry VIII wrote a tract against Luther, for which the papacy named him defender of the faith — a move the popes later regretted. Thomas More, in his capacity as chancellor, took a keen interest in persecuting Lutheran heretics, sitting personally as judge in several trials. In spite of all this, Lutheranism acquired a certain following in both intellectual and popular circles and even inspired an English translation of the New Testament that appeared in 1525; but when the leader of the Protestants, John Frith, was burned in 1533, the Lutheran movement in England began to die out. Ironically, Henry's most forceful and effective moves against Lutheran Protestantism coincided with his own break from Rome.

In France, Lutheranism had an even greater initial success than in England. Because of their zeal for moral reform and more meaningful forms of religious expression, French intellectuals found Luther's ideas immediately attractive. Many French humanists read Luther's writings with great sympathy, and soon the movement gained a patron in King Francis' sister, Margaret of Angouleme. Because of her pleading, Francis intervened on several occasions in the 1520s to prevent the Sorbonne (the traditional bastion of conservatism) from suppressing the reform. But late in the decade royal support diminished. Financial difficulties arising from the wars with Charles V forced Francis to appeal to the church for funds; the result was that he was forced to promise to suppress the heretics. At first Francis was halfhearted in this policy, but in 1534 the Protestants made the tactical error of open defiance. In a single night, all over the country, they posted placards denouncing the mass. One was even nailed to the door outside the king's bedroom. Francis regarded this move as a deliberate challenge to his authority and began in earnest to root out Lutheranism in France. In 1540 the movement was officially suppressed by the Edict of Fontainebleau, but it had already been effectively extirpated from the kingdom.

In Spain, by contrast, Lutheranism had little effect. Under the leadership of the great humanist prelate Cardinal Ximenes, the Spanish church had already been cleansed of the abuses so characteristic of the northern churches. Furthermore, an institution was at hand to deal with the problem of Lutheranism immediately. The Inquisition had been founded not to suppress Protestantism but rather to deal with the part of Spain recently won from the Moors, where large numbers of forced converts from Islam or Judaism threatened the orthodoxy of the Christian church. Begun in 1478, the Inquisition was the only truly national institution in Spain, and the kings used it as a valuable tool to reunify the country. As soon as Lutheran ideas and tracts appeared in Spain, the Inquisition turned to deal with the threat. It wiped out the movement so effectively that historians now are not even sure whether Lutheran circles really existed or whether the word *luterano* was just used to describe anyone whose ideas incurred the displeasure of the Inquisition.

By the time of the Peace of Augsburg in 1555, Lutheranism had become a regional religion, confined to Germany and Scandinavia. Although these areas were more significant than Bohemia, the Lutheran church was hardly different from the older Hussite movement, which had also founded a permanent church but was confined to the geographical region that gave it birth and thus was predominantly a national church. Yet Protestantism today is not a regional sect. It is an international and universal religion whose common characteristics transcend local variations. Though Luther may have been the spark that ignited the flame, neither he nor his followers were directly responsible for the movement as we know it. That task was accomplished by the followers of Calvin who carried his Reformed church to France, the Low Countries, Scotland, England, and eventually America.

The Calvinist Reformation

When Calvin was recalled to Geneva in 1541 after four years in exile, he was not immediately in a position to begin the conversion of his native France. His first priority was to consolidate the reform in Geneva itself. Over the next decade, deft use of the consistory and company of pastors enabled Calvin gradually to establish a Genevan church with a solid discipline, a corps of trained ministers, and a distinctive liturgy. In 1555, the same year in which Charles V recognized Lutheran dominion in certain parts of Germany in return for the Lutherans' agreement to forgo missionary activity in the Catholic states, Calvin put down the last anti-French revolt in Geneva, and the company of pastors began to list missionaries formally dispatched to France.

Successful missionary activity depended on keeping Geneva secure. Except for that city, France shared all its borders with Catholic powers and was immune from infiltration through its frontiers. Geneva itself was protected from Catholic interference to the east by the Protestant republic of Bern, but to the west it remained in constant danger of French or Savoyard attack. A determined military effort by France would have seriously threatened and even eliminated the independence of the city, and Calvin was always very careful to conduct missionary activities in secret. Even the magistracy of Geneva was not informed of their extent until long after they had begun, and Calvin continually denied any direct involvement in the political affairs of France.

The infiltration was strikingly successful. The first regular missionaries were sent in 1555; by 1562 these men had converted 3 million Frenchmen, and there were 2,150 Huguenot, or French

Calvinist, churches. By 1559 the French king was sufficiently disturbed to break off his war with the king of Spain in order to devote his energies to suppressing the movement's growth. In 1562, full-scale civil war broke out between Catholic and Protestant parties. This war has the distinction of being the bloodiest in France's history prior to World War I, and it raged until the coronation of Henry IV in 1594. It was marked by legendary massacres (such as the ones on Saint Bartholomew's day in 1572) and dramatic changes of allegiance. The throne itself first attempted conciliation, then outright suppression of the Huguenots, and eventually support of the Protestants. The final settlement, the Edict of Nantes (1598), granted the Reformed church and its followers a measure of political autonomy within the country, including the right to maintain an army and to garrison certain citadels. As long as the edict remained in force, the Huguenots in France constituted a state within a state.

Although France occupied the largest part of Calvin's attention, his greatest success occurred in other parts of Europe. Missionaries dispatched to the Low Countries found a natural sympathy in the Dutch struggle for independence from Spain and soon established a permanent Reformed church in Holland. In Scotland, propaganda printed in Geneva and the effective preaching of John Knox found generous support among those seeking to limit the power of the throne, and by 1560 a Reformed church had been founded and secured in that country.

The case in England was more complex. Strictly speaking, the English church in the sixteenth century was distinctive — not Catholic or Reformed or Lutheran. Henry VIII broke with Rome principally because the church had refused to let him divorce his first wife, who had born him only a daughter. He did not originally intend to depart from Catholic doctrine or practice. Henry reformed ancient abuses, suppressed monasteries, increased taxes on the clergy, and otherwise moved to bring the church under his control, but none of his policies was unusual. Indeed, his control was not significantly greater than that enjoyed by the French kings. On matters of theology he was wholly orthodox and furiously punished every suggestion of Protestant ideas. Late in his life he may have seen the necessity of moving closer to Protestantism, but he made few concrete moves in that direction. Once, in the middle of his reign, he attempted to get support from the Lutheran princes but would not go along with their insistence on the Augsburg confession.

Many of Henry's advisors, including Thomas Cromwell, who had overseen the suppression of the monasteries, were sympathetic to the Reformation. They especially desired to make the Bible widely available in the vernacular. Cromwell patronized Coverdale's translation of the Bible into English and persuaded the king to have it published in 1539. This so-called Great Bible became the basis for the King James version of 1611. But Henry himself was never very sympathetic. In the year the Coverdale Bible was published the king forced the bishops to accept a doctrinal formulation called the Six Articles, which was fully Catholic except for stating that the church was completely subservient to the king.

At Henry's death in 1547, his young son became King Edward VI. Edward had been tutored by Richard Cox, who had great sympathies for the Reformed church. The Catholic party at court had fallen from power shortly before, and one of Henry's last acts was to appoint advisors for Edward who had marked Protestant sympathies. Lord Somerset, the chief advisor, and Edward's tutors constantly corresponded with Geneva. During Edward's short reign the religious service in the Church of England was altered to conform more with Genevan practice. Edward's premature death in 1553 brought the Catholic Mary to the throne, and the Protestant leaders were all executed or exiled. Most of the latter went to Frankfurt, Strassburg, and Switzerland, where they were exposed even more thoroughly to Calvinist influences. But once again politics had its effect. The authorities at Frankfurt, in deference to the emperor, favored the more moderate Englishmen over the Scottish extremist John Knox. As a result, the first exiles who returned to England after 1558 were not so disposed to overthrow the English church as might otherwise have been the case. Elizabeth I succeeded her sister Mary, and the church that emerged during her reign was full of tensions that would not be resolved until the seventeenth century and only then with great difficulty. In discipline and organization it was Catholic, maintaining the episcopal system and some semblance of the apostolic succession; in its national character it resembled the Lutheran churches of Germany and Scandinavia; but in ritual and theology it bore the strong mark of Calvin.

Calvin's remarkable success, which also had echoes in Germany and Hungary, is partly to be explained by the novelty of his operation. The organization and discipline of the Reformed church was unprecedented, as its effectiveness in mobilizing dissident elements within a country into a formidable force amply testifies. The Reformed church was most successful where there were already political factors that undermined the established authority. Calvin himself scrupulously avoided advocating revolution, but he did not object if properly constituted bodies opposed the king. Many of his followers openly supported revolution, conspiracy, and other illicit means of seizing power. Calvin's ideology was sophisticated and appealed broadly to many types of people, and he had a disciplined organization. More than that, he was pragmatic about his means. This combination gave Calvinism a force that Lutheranism did not command. Unlike the Lutheran churches, the Reformed church resulted from deliberate calculation and planning, and despite local variations it became truly universal.

Conclusion

The magisterial Reformation, despite the differences in Geneva, Germany, and England, was held together by important characteristics that clearly distinguished it from Catholicism. They mark a departure from the basic ecclesiastical trends within Catholicism prior to the sixteenth century. The churches of the Reformation sought to institutionalize the need for more personal religious experience in the face of an increasingly organized and efficient society. They departed from traditional Catholicism in two major ways.

First, organization and discipline were always local. Local organization was basic to the Lutheran concept, for Luther gave control over the church to the state. Even Calvin felt that the church should be administered by the leaders of each congregation. These elders were limited in their authority by the demands of Scripture, and Calvin took measures to ensure that the varieties of scriptural interpretation would not get out of hand. Groups of congregations were organized into regional synods, which had the authority to discipline individual congregational pastors. Despite the need for uniformity, Geneva never assumed the powers that the Roman pontiff claimed. The influence of the Genevan company of pastors was strong throughout the sixteenth century in all Reformed churches, but it was purely spiritual. The regional synods were the ultimate authority, and once pastors had left Geneva to work in the field they were essentially independent. Calvin's care in training his pastors and missionaries is understandable. The Reformed church was universal in the sense that Calvin regarded it as the true church, claiming the adherence of all mankind, but it was not centralized.

Second, there was a common commitment among the Protestant churches, in spite of their diversity, to make the liturgy more responsive and meaningful to the needs of the individual congregation. The Catholic mass is primarily a celebration of the Incarnation, the central truth of the faith, through a service in which the created elements of bread and wine are transformed into the uncreated elements of the body and blood of Christ. The implications of the Incarnation and the life of Christ are brought forth in the mass by "propers," sentences and prayers that change with the season. Thus the Catholic service stresses a constant reality and treats different types of human problems through seasonal variations designed to cover the entire range of normal human needs. No particular problem that might arise from daily events is allowed to distort the view of the general human condition. In short, the service reflects the church's desire to stress norms of human conduct and to deal with individuals through the norms.

The Protestant service is basically a preaching service in which broad norms of humanity are subordinated to the needs of the actual congregation. The central truths of the faith are related directly to the Scriptures, and the service is designed to make their meaning clear to particular people faced with particular problems. The pastor is free to choose his text for the day in order to make it timely, and the service is almost exclusively devoted to scriptural reading, preaching, and nonritual prayer. This best describes the service in the Reformed church; among Lutherans and Anglicans the emphasis is similarly shifted to preaching, though they have conserved parts of the Catholic ritual.

Many of the particular differences in religious practice between Catholics and Protestants seem too minor to have caused such strife, but they were often symbolic of major differences in approach. For example, in the Catholic mass, or Eucharist, the point where the words are said to make the bread and wine into the body and blood of Christ is an unusually sacred and important moment. To stress its importance the priest lifts both the wafer of bread, or Host, and the cup containing the wine for the congregation to see and worship. To Protestants such actions underlined the sacrificial character of the mass and the sacramental power of the priesthood, neither of which was a tenet with which they agreed. Consequently that part of the ceremony, called the elevation of the Host, was omitted in many Protestant services. Similarly, in Catholic services the congregation and priest eat the bread in communion, while the priest alone partakes of the wine. The church maintains that Christ is fully present in both, but the practice of allowing the wine only to the priest stresses his special status. Since Protestants do not accord the priesthood a special status, they began to distribute both bread and wine to the congregation.

Both these practices became major points of dispute in the sixteenth century. They are small parts of the ceremony, yet to men of that century they symbolized important areas of disagreement between Catholics and Protestants. The Reformation thus introduced changes into the daily religious life of European Christendom that conveyed through concrete example the meaning of the theological differences between the religious parties.

Bibliography

Both Roland Bainton's *Reformation of the Sixteenth Century* (Boston: Beacon Press, 1952) and G. R. Elton's *Reformation Europe: 1517–1559* (Cleveland: Meridian Books, 1964) contain good narrative accounts of the spread of the Reformation. For a more specialized account of the activities of Calvin's company of pastors see Robert Kingdom, *Geneva and the Coming of the Wars of Religion in France, 1555–1563* (Geneva: Droz, 1956), and *Geneva and the Consolidation of the French Protestant Movements, 1564–1572* (Geneva: Droz, 1967). A good narrative account of the French civil wars can be found in John Neale's *The Age of Catherine de' Medici* (New York: Harper and Row, 1967). The best recent account of the English Reformation is Arthur Dickens' *The English Reformation,* rev. ed. (London: Collins, 1967). William Clebsch has studied Lutheranism in England in *England's Earliest Protestants, 1520–1535* (New Haven: Yale University Press, 1964).

23 The Catholic Church in the Sixteenth Century

Histories of the Catholic church in the sixteenth century generally reveal their biases in their titles. Catholic historians usually refer to the "Catholic Reformation" and emphasize that ecclesiastical reform actually antedated Luther. They see spontaneous reform welling up from the energies of the church itself quite independently of the Protestant Reformation. Protestants, by contrast, usually write histories of the "Counter Reformation" that stress the negative aspects of reaction and zealous suppression of heresy. Fairminded historians of both persuasions recognize that there was a Catholic reform movement not wholly in reaction to Luther, but that the Protestant threat markedly accelerated it. Furthermore, the suppression of heresy was itself nothing new in the history of the church; the weapons deployed against the Protestants in the sixteenth century had an ancient — if not altogether honorable — lineage.

The church has almost always in its history shown a concern for the vitality of the faith. This has generally been manifested in four basic directions: (1) preventing institutions originally designed to meet genuine financial and administrative needs from being turned to the profit of individual churchmen or to aggrandizement of the church's political power; (2) promoting greater personal morality and austerity among the hierarchy, the clergy, and the laity; (3) seeking more spiritual and personal conceptions of Catholic religious life as a counterpoise to inevitable ritual and legalistic tendencies; and (4) steadfastly maintaining the faith in the face of heretical movements. All of these responses were pursued with fresh energy from the end of the fifteenth century onward. We must consider them together as part of a general movement in order to grasp the main lines of Catholic policy during the period in which the Protestant churches became established.

Reform of Abuse

Financial abuses within the church were commonplace, but little could be done beyond correcting the most scandalous cases. The church could not reasonably practice apostolic poverty and still function. Like most complex institutions, it required more money than it could obtain through voluntary and sporadic individual contributions. It had to find sources of regular income, and it hit upon a variety of solutions (see Chapter 15). But by 1500 many of those had been corrupted to the point of obstructing the primary functions of the institutional church. These were the areas that had to be reformed during the sixteenth century. Simony in papal elections was forbidden by a bull of the Fifth Lateran Council (1512–1517). The council was presided over by Julius II and Leo X, Renaissance popes of no conspicuous reforming zeal but of sufficient political sense to recognize a dangerous situation. Indulgences were similarly reformed in order to eliminate the more egregious misuses.

One means of dealing with the situation was to find new sources of income not dependent on the religious functions of the church, and most of the Renaissance popes had actively pursued that strategy. Alexander VI brought areas of the Romagna under his political control and overcame the independence of the Roman noble families, thereby greatly increasing the secular income of the papacy. At his death in 1503, the customs toll of the city of Rome was the chief source of papal revenue. This policy, however, also had disadvantages and drew fire from the same pious souls who had criticized the sale of offices because it inevitably involved the popes in political entanglements and diverted their attention and energies from religious functions. Worse yet, the cost of administering an increasingly centralized and complex church rapidly outstripped the new sources of income. In the end, Alexander himself raised the price of religious offices even further.

The difficulties of reform are clearly illustrated in one of the great reforming documents of the period. In 1534, Paul III was elected as the first reforming pope of the century — except for the short-lived and ineffectual Adrian VI (1522–1523). Soon after his election, Paul appointed a commission of leading churchmen to draw up a program of reform, and in 1537 the group returned the *Consilium de Emendanda Ecclesia (Plan for Reforming the Church)*. The authors were sincere, competent, articulate, and representative of the best elements in the church. They forthrightly attacked the growth of papal power since the Council of Constance and called it the major source of the abuses that were breaking Christendom apart. The document was immediately denounced as heretical by conservative elements in the papal curia, though it raised optimistic hopes among others — notably Protestants — that the church might at last reform itself.

Yet the *Consilium* led to few real results, and when the Protestant leaders studied it more closely, they too were dissatisfied with its superficiality. For example, the *Consilium* pronounced against priests' wearing dirty vestments while celebrating mass — a problem that could be dealt with easily enough but could hardly be expected to work miracles with the church's serious difficulties. One significant abuse pointed out by the council was the issue of absentee bishops. In 1540, Pope Paul ordered eighty absentee bishops then residing in Rome to return to their dioceses. Some protested, but most obeyed — for Rome was not a particularly pleasant place after the sack of 1527. Upon arriving in their sees, some of the bishops actually experienced a genuine change of heart and began to carry out their duties with sensitivity and religious concern. Ten years before the pope's order, Ghiberti (1495–1543), the absentee bishop of Verona, returned to his diocese and began to set an example of upright and godly life and conscientious administration; he had a major influence on the curial reformers who drew up the *Consilium*.

A number of important reforms could be implemented without great financial sacrifice. Resident bishops were actually less expensive than absent ones because diocesan revenues were no longer needed to support the bishop's costly Roman style of living while paying for a resident surrogate in addition. But none of these reforms got at the central problem, that of using the religious functions as a source of money. The *Consilium* recommended that the church stop selling dispensations, indulgences, and other religious services, but the suggestion was ignored by Pope Paul. It has been estimated that dispensations alone brought in twenty thousand ducats annually, and until he found another means of raising money no prudent administrator could be expected to give them up.

Moral and Spiritual Reform

The *Consilium* also drew attention to the second historic area of reform by singling out the Roman hierarchy for conspicuous dereliction in morals, as well as by deploring the general moral tenor of the clergy. Here again the solution was neither simple nor readily available. The church required a wide variety of talents for its administration, and the requirements had been increasing; therefore it was not always possible — nor would it ever be — to make asceticism a necessary prerequisite of service. The worldly popes of the Renaissance were perhaps more willing to forgo this virtue than most of their successors, but even a reforming pope like Paul III lived in obvious comfort and sought to provide for the children he had fathered in his youth. After 1527, the vices of the Italian clergy became less public and the scandals more effectively concealed, but except for a few brief periods in the late sixteenth century, priestly behavior did not bear close inspection. Neither personal immorality nor institutional corruption within the church was remedied in any basic way until the nineteenth century. Let us realize that there are few established churches, either Catholic or Protestant, that have been able convincingly to claim apostolic poverty or moral purity over a significant length of time.

Laymen were also seeking higher moral standards. In Florence the monk Savonarola began a series of sermons in 1490 in which he called to repentance and conversion the residents of that city. His sermons were inspired by visions in which he foresaw doom for Italy. When the invasion of Charles VIII seemed to fulfill Savonarola's prophecies, his reputation increased. He wielded great influence in the government that followed the downfall of the Medici in 1494, organizing the famous bonfires where Florentines burned their vanities. His message struck a deep vein of moral sensibility in Florence — some of the leading neo-Platonists being among his admirers — but, under attack both from Alexander VI and the leaders of the Florentine republic, he fell from popular favor and was executed in 1498. His career shows both the intensity and shallowness of the concern among Italian laymen for significant moral reform.

If not much could be done for the morals of laymen or the secular clergy beyond reducing the public scandal, then the church could perhaps improve the morals of the monastic and mendicant orders.

These had been founded partly for the benefit of those who wished to live an unusually pure and upright life, and it was especially important that they continue fulfilling that function. Most orders, however, particularly the Franciscans, repeatedly fell away from their original purpose to the enjoyment of worldly wealth. In the fifteenth century the begging friars, as the Franciscans were called, became the laughingstock of Europe. Contemporary literature was filled with corrupt, ignorant, and venal friars. If the church wished to make available a personal, spiritual, and austere religious life for those who wished it, then the religious orders would have to be reformed. The pope who set out to promote such a goal was the man whose own personal life was among the most scandalous of his age: Alexander VI (1492–1503). Nevertheless, in 1496 he appointed three abbots to reform all the Benedictine houses in France, giving them the power to excommunicate and depose recalcitrant chapters. In 1501 the cardinal of Amboise was given similar power with regard to the mendicant orders. And in 1494 Alexander had given the king of Spain permission to reform the orders in his own lands, a task entrusted to Cardinal Ximenes, who carried it out with considerable effectiveness.

Leo X (1513–1521) initiated a major step in the reform of the Franciscans by giving control of the whole order to a strict branch called the observants. They had appeared early in the fifteenth century and carefully avoided heretical claims about the necessity of poverty for the whole church, but they insisted that the Franciscans must maintain ascetic discipline in order to serve their function. Because their behavior contrasted favorably with that of the conventual, or regular, Franciscans, the observants were immensely popular with the laity, and the papacy supported them through much of the century. Thus, their victory over the conventuals under Leo was not a new departure but the fruition of a continuing papal policy ever since the Council of Constance.

The New Orders

But the religious orders still remained unpopular and unresponsive to the new demands of the sixteenth century. As a result, during the 1530s there was more enthusiasm to suppress them than to reform them or create additional ones. Proposals were put forward to suppress all conventuals, prohibit new foundations, amalgamate all the orders into four, or abolish their usual exemption from episcopal jurisdiction. The orders were only saved by two basic developments: first, there was a series of attempts to form new orders based on strict observance of the rules of founders of existing orders; and second, an entirely new set of orders was created, the clerks regular, who were to carry their religious discipline out into the world, instead of retreating from it, and engage in a program of work and action.

The first of the new orders in traditional form was that of the Camaldolese Hermits. They had existed since the eleventh century, but their order was completely reformed by the Venetian churchman Giustiniani between 1512 and 1528. Giustiniani was a friend of Contarini and the future Paul III and Paul IV, all curial reformers who later drew up the *Consilium,* and his example was influential in strengthening the notion that existing orders could realistically be purified.

Among the most important of the new orders were the Capuchins. In 1517 several Franciscan friars in the marches of Ancona left their convent to lead lives as hermits and recover the actual poverty of Saint Francis. The most important of them was Matteo da Baccio, who devoted himself not only to contemplation and witness but to active charity. At first he was only desirous of observing the strict rule of Saint Francis in solitude, but he soon attracted a number of followers who insisted on organizing a new order. Clement VII, who had originally given Matteo permission to live apart from the convent, issued the bull founding the order in 1528.

The Capuchins insisted on living in small hermitages made of mud and accumulating no possessions whatsoever. They even avoided regular begging. Moreover, they never interfered with the parish clergy. Unlike even the observant Franciscans, they were reluctant to hear confessions. Instead, they offered their services to the parish clergy in whatever form the latter found useful. The order grew rapidly; by 1535, over seven hundred houses had been founded, covering much of Italy. The Capuchins were characterized from the beginning by rigid discipline and concentration on active charity, and they were remarkably successful in maintaining their standards. In 1619, they became a separate order, independent from the Franciscans.

But more significant than new orders in traditional form were the innovative orders made up of priests who remained active in the world but took special communal vows and lived according to a disciplined rule. The earliest of these groups was formed during the papacy of Alexander VI. In 1494 at Vicenza and in 1497 at Genoa, small brotherhoods were established intended to bridge the gap between the life of the parish priest and that of the monk. The Genoa brotherhood inspired a more famous group at Rome, the Oratory of Divine Love, which was founded by a number of curial prelates and laymen who joined together in the early sixteenth century under the influence of Giustiniani and dedicated themselves to the renewal of the church through prayer and charitable works. The oratory was approved in 1514. Ten years later, members of the oratory, led by Gaetano of Thienne and Carafa, the future Paul IV, organized the Theatine order. This consisted of a body of priests living together and taking vows of poverty, chastity, and obedience, in order to better their apostolic and priestly lives. Though they recited the office together, the emphasis was clearly on work in the world. Dispensations from reciting the office were easy to obtain.

The emphasis on work was an important aspect of the new orders in the sixteenth century. Both the Capuchins and the Theatines avoided pure spirituality or contemplative witness, partly because such contemplation had become associated with Lutheranism, but for other reasons as well. The church wanted to give an opportunity for personal religion but wanted equally to keep such expression within its own framework of relating the spiritual to the mundane. The sixteenth-century church maintained that work within the world should be a means, not a hindrance, to spiritual growth. This attitude was clearest in the most important of all the new orders: the Society of Jesus, known as the Jesuits.

The Jesuits

The rapid growth and undoubted effectiveness of the Jesuits heartened their supporters as much as it appalled their opponents. To many Protestants and even some Catholics the order even today represents the Counter Reformation at its worst: narrow-minded moralism, legalistic casuistry, and intolerant repression of heretics. To others the order is one of the most important instruments for the preservation of the strength of Catholicism in the face of serious threats. Confirmed as a separate order only in 1540, four years later the Society of Jesus had already founded nine establishments; ten years after that, nine whole provinces had been organized — twelve establishments in India, five in Brazil, five in Portugal, nine in Castille, four in Aragon, five elsewhere in Spain, eleven in Italy, and three in Sicily.

Both opponents and supporters of the order have agreed that much of its success is due to the energy and spiritual sensitivity of its founder, Ignatius Loyola (1491–1556); but there is sharp disagreement in interpreting his character. Loyola was born of minor Spanish nobility and, as was normal for his station, entered military service. At the battle of Pamplona in 1521 he was seriously wounded in the leg, which was broken and subsequently became infected, bringing Loyola close to death. As he recovered, he noticed that the leg had been badly set and immediately ordered it broken again and reset. The pain that such an operation must have involved before the day of anesthesia testifies to his strength of will, but scholars disagree as to its meaning. A leading Protestant historian, Heinrich Boehmer, treats the incident as an example of Loyola's inhuman indifference to pain; Boehmer believes it reveals a character that would subject its followers to anything just to achieve a desired end. James Broderick, a Catholic historian, sets the incident in another context. He points out that Loyola had shown previous evidence of vast pride in his military prowess and the keen sense of honor associated with his class; these feelings led him to reset the leg because it endangered his military career and wounded his vanity. In this context Loyola's behavior after Pamplona actually reveals the pride that had to be conquered before he could take up his true religious calling.

A still more important episode in Loyola's personal life took place at the Catalonian town of Manresa. While recovering from his wound, Loyola experienced a religious conversion and decided to take a pilgrimage to the Holy Land. Detained by a plague in Manresa, Loyola began his penance anyway. He practiced extreme forms of religious devotion. He flagellated himself, deprived himself of food and sleep for days at a time, let his hair and beard grow, and begged for his food to induce humility. In a fashion strikingly like Luther, Ignatius began to worry whether he was truly contrite and made detailed and repeated confessions, but also like Luther, he finally gave up this behavior. Instead, he practiced a more reasonable asceticism combined with active service that has set the tone for the Jesuit order ever since. As with Pamplona, however, Protestant and Catholic interpretations of these events diverge.

The Protestant historian Boehmer says that the crucial moment for Ignatius came in the midst of despair when he concluded with the aid of mystical visions that the anguish he felt over his sins was the work of the Devil and should be simply put out of mind. In other words, by a sheer act of will he decided to dismiss unproductive guilt as a product of the Devil and to ignore it. Thus the reputed Jesuit casuistry — the tendency to reason away sins by noting how much more serious other sins might be — can be traced to the fundamental religious perception of the founder.

The Catholic historian Broderick places more emphasis on one event at Manresa in which Ignatius decided to fast until he saw Christ. Ignatius regarded his whole penance as a period of spiritual growth through asceticism and the visions induced by it, and this particular fast was the climax. At the end of the fast, while still trying to satisfy his conscience by mortifying the flesh, he had a vision of meat, but felt that the vision was an insight rather than a temptation. He interpreted the vision to mean that the world and the senses must be accepted and used to build a religious life, not rejected as evil. This interpretation of Manresa is not categorically opposed to the Protestant one, but it stresses Loyola's acceptance of the world as a means to sanctification, whereas the Protestants have stressed his will and calculation.

At Manresa in 1522 Loyola wrote his *Spiritual Exercises,* which determined the character of his order. They are among the most remarkable documents of the century, not so much for their originality as for the manner in which they reflect so many intellectual trends of the period in a program of practical spirituality. Loyola's sensitivity is the more striking for being uninstructed. Later he traveled to study at Alcala, where he found the humanism of Ximenes, and at the college of Montague at Paris, where Calvin, Rabelais, and Erasmus had studied. Many of Loyola's immediate followers were ardent admirers of Erasmus, and he himself found his perceptions enriched and deepened by the further exposure to humanism. Yet the *Exercises* themselves were written long before these travels by a former soldier who, until almost the year he began writing, had hardly ever read a book and was considered unschooled even by the standards of his day. Loyola's perceptions are natural; they spring directly from his own personal needs and experiences — even more so than those of Luther.

The *Exercises* have some known literary sources. During his convalescence at Pamplona, Loyola read Ludolf of Saxony's *Life of Christ* and a hagiography called the *Golden Legend* by Jacopo de Voragine. These books gave him the desire to imitate Christ and the saints, particularly Francis and Dominic, in his own life. At Manresa he read the most popular of the fifteenth-century pietistic treatises, the *Imitation of Christ* by Thomas à Kempis, which gives practical advice for imitating Christ and acquiring the virtues that Eckhart described in starkly mystical terms. There are few ideas in the *Exercises* not found in these sources; what is original is the way Loyola used them in a methodical educational program aimed at developing and controlling introspection and self-knowledge.

The basic purpose of the *Exercises* is to provide the self-knowledge necessary for making a choice, or an election, as Ignatius calls it. They are meant principally to guide the novice in his decision to join the order, but they are also designed to be used in any sort of important decision, and members of the order are expected to do the exercises regularly. They are divided into four major parts, each occupying a week, although Loyola allows for considerable flexibility. The first part consists of an examination of conscience for sin; the second and third, dealing respectively with the Incarnation and the Passion of Christ, involve the search for vocation preparatory to making an election; and the fourth, dealing with the Resurrection, explores the rewards of making the correct election and choosing the true vocation. This last section contains the most mystical elements.

The foundation of the *Exercises* rests on a simple assumption about man and God:

> Man was created to praise, reverence, and serve God, and by this means to save his soul; and the other things on the face of the earth were created for man's sake and in order to aid him in the prosecution of the end for which he was created. Whence it follows that man ought to make use of them just so far as they help him attain his end, and that he ought to withdraw himself from them just so far as they hinder him.

This statement is almost devoid of theological content. Loyola says nothing about systematic theology other than observing that man is created to praise God and that the world is created to help him do it. With the exception of the single clause that man saves his soul by praising God, the statement might almost be the basis of Calvin's *Institutes.*

Similarly, the examination of conscience for sin proceeds not by reference to a systematic hierarchy of sins but by introspection, in which one asks himself what he considers his most grievous sin: "Immediately on rising the man ought to resolve to guard himself carefully against that particular sin or defect which he desires to correct or amend." Loyola provides a general examination to help the individual decide which sin to concentrate on, but this is always subordinated to the particular examination. The fundamental and most frequent question throughout the book is "What do I desire?" The exercises help the individual to guide his desire into channels that work to the glory of God, but personal differences and needs always take precedence over categories and systematic definitions.

The pattern of exercises for the first week illustrates Loyola's method. The exercises direct the exercitant's attention to the first, second, and third sins: the sin of the rebel angels in heaven, the sin of Adam and Eve in the Garden of Eden, and the sin of the individual soul after the fall of man. After a preparatory prayer, the exercitant is asked to visualize the subject of the meditation. Loyola wants him to maintain at all times a connection with the physical world, for this world is created to help him praise God, and he must not reject it. Spiritual things, like the Trinity, which cannot be visualized directly, should still be given a symbolic form that can be pictured by the senses.

After forming an image of the subject of the meditation, the exercitant must ask what he wishes. His desire should reflect a general shame at seeing what great damage sin has done to the world, but it should also arise from personal needs. After these preparations the meditation begins. Ignatius gives several points as guides and draws attention to some peculiar aspects of the three sins that are the subject of the exercise. The meditation concludes with a colloquy in which the exercitant tries to imagine Christ before him. He asks Christ why he made himself a man to die for our sins and then asks himself what he has done to deserve this sacrifice. This colloquy points up a central aspect of Ignatius' approach, for he feels, in common with Erasmus, that men cannot understand general truths when expressed systematically but only when expressed in particular perspectives. By imagining ourselves in personal communication with Christ we are more likely to grasp the nature of sin than if we look at sin in general. This feature of the *Exercises* makes Loyola's affinity to humanism obvious.

By the end of the first week the exercitant should be conscious of the evil of sin, and his desire for things as ends in themselves should have given way to a desire to use them for the greater glory of God. In the second week he examines the desires that remain. The exercises of this week, dealing with the Incarnation, prepare the exercitant for the central act: election. Here Loyola adds a new perspective. The first week dwelt on an interior dialogue in which the exercitant, by associating his senses with his desires, tried to see the harmony between his immediate wishes and his ultimate values. But values are not only personal; they are expressed socially through time. By focusing on the Incarnation, the exercitant is readied to see how his personal values can lead to action in the world. To achieve this end, the exercitant must first contemplate the history of each subject of meditation. For example, when contemplating the Nativity, he should review the journey of Mary and Joseph to Bethlehem before he imagines the scene in the stable where Christ is born. This device also serves to reinforce the connection between personal feelings and the physical world stressed during the first week.

The choice that is to follow the second week's exercises is profoundly personal. Loyola's purpose is not to indoctrinate members into the order but instead to help prospective members ask themselves whether they really want to make such a commitment. Even if the exercitant is seeking to make a choice on some other matters, the personal dimensions of the election remain because the exercises are virtually devoid of specific content. They seek only to give the exercitant a deeper insight into his motives and test the stability of his values. Ignatius himself had clearly accepted the teachings of the church fully and without hesitation, but throughout his life he was deeply sympathetic and patient with those who suffered from periodic doubts about their choice of faith. This attitude was frequently displayed in his intercourse with others and stands at the center of his exercises.

The exercises for the third and fourth weeks ask the exercitant to meditate on the Passion and Resurrection as they test his newly chosen vocation against the whole range of religious feeling. Religious anguish is developed in the third week and religious joy in the fourth, but the same basic method is used as before. The exercises employ throughout military and knightly images, portraying the exercitant as soldier fighting for the Lord.

The *Spiritual Exercises* reflect the two major intellectual trends of sixteenth-century religious life. On the one hand they assume, with Saint Thomas, that all types of experience are interrelated and provide a basis for systematically and objectively ordering man's relation to God. They do not permit the exercitant to sever his connection with the world or reject it as a hindrance to a true religious experience. On the other hand they acknowledge and build on the same personal religious feelings that Eckhart and Luther claimed as the antithesis of system. They begin with introspection and end in contemplation that is clearly mystical. Loyola's achievement was to fuse these two perspectives together, though not in a systematic treatise, which would have been difficult and dangerous, if not impossible. Instead he wrote an educational program, and his fundamental technique was to approach problems in concrete, personal terms. Although Loyola did not put the *Exercises* into their final form until 1541, scholars agree that the essential elements were present from the beginning. They illustrate clearly his remarkable sensitivity to the needs and presuppositions of his contemporaries.

In 1534, when Ignatius and nine companions took vows of poverty, chastity, and obedience to the papacy, they apparently did so so with the vague intention of going to convert the Holy Land. This they speedily recognized as unfeasible, but their missionary zeal was directed to other parts of the world. Even before the order was confirmed, Francis Xavier, one of the nine, left for India, where twelve Jesuit establishments by 1556 testified to his success. The Jesuits' missionary activities also involved them in the fight against heresy, for which they became famous in the century that followed.

The most important contribution of the Jesuits, however, lay in a field Loyola hardly anticipated. From the first he had placed his foundations near universities in order that his men might receive the best training. Though never a scholar himself, he greatly respected the effectiveness of education. The demands of the order soon exceeded the capacity of the universities, and the Jesuits began to train their own priests. By 1550 they had begun to found colleges to educate novices. The humanist education they offered was so much better than that of comparable schools that they were compelled to admit outsiders, too. In 1554 there were twenty-three Jesuit colleges with 2,500 students in Europe; in 1556, twenty-six with 5,700 students. The Jesuits were the first order to act on a large scale as schoolmasters for boys not intended for monastic life, and their efforts provided the model for secular and religious education throughout Catholic Europe.

The Fight Against Heresy

The sixteenth-century church is universally known for its vigorous suppression of heresy. Indeed its laudable attempts at financial and clerical reform are often completely forgotten because the church was simultaneously involved in a policy of intellectual repression that can only be described as an attempt to control the thinking of European Catholics. In retrospect it seems surprising that the Italian church was especially concerned with heresy since it had clearly contained the Protestant threat. Evidently the containment was not so clear to men actually living in the sixteenth century; many continued to fear that Protestantism was a growing tide that could not be turned. It is worthwhile to examine in detail the causes for this concern.

In 1518 a man named Calvi was printing books at Milan, in support of Luther, not so much out of conviction, apparently, but because they sold well. After 1530 large Protestant circles existed at many places in Italy. One circle in Modena, under Cardinal Morone's protection, even included some anti-Trinitarians. Protestant preachers were proselytizing in Milan in 1539. Venice also became an active center for printing Lutheran books, and Lutherans were openly tolerated on the university faculty at Padua until 1550. Many Lutherans could be found in Lucca by 1525 and in Naples by 1528. An active Calvinist church was established in Sicily at Messina, and the duchess of Ferrara, who had become a practicing Calvinist, received Calvin himself in 1536. Italian translations of the *Institutes* appeared in 1545 and 1557.

The seriousness of the situation became fully apparent during the 1540s. In 1541 the vicar general of the Capuchin order, Bernardino Ochino, fled to Geneva and embraced the Protestant cause. This defection from one of the orders newly created to deal with the religious needs pointed up by Protestantism badly frightened the papal authorities and convinced them of the need to take positive measures against the new faith. The Roman Inquisition was established in 1542 under Carafa, the future Paul IV. He tried suspected heretics from all social classes and sought to extend his jurisdiction over all Italy. The persecutions that followed split the ecclesiastical reform movement in two; there were those, like Carafa, who spearheaded the fight against heresy, and those, like Cardinal Morone and Peter Carnesecchi, who were the victims. Morone found himself condemned as outside the acceptable practices of the church, and Carnesecchi, who had been an early member of the Oratory of Divine Love, was executed for unorthodox beliefs in 1567. Eventually the Inquisition turned to regulate thought, drawing up an index of prohibited books, insisting on more austere and religious art, and opposing new scientific ideas. Few would care to defend the persecutions, but the danger that prompted them was not imaginary.

The Council of Trent

As we have seen from the measures discussed so far, the papacy itself was the principal source of ecclesiastical reform and renewal. But from the very beginning of the sixteenth century there was widespread sentiment for calling a general council to correct the abuses that were causing such scandal and to deal with the developing schism with Protestantism. Technically the call for a council depended on papal initiative, for Pius II in the bull *Execrabilis* of 1460 had made it illegal and cause for excommunication to appeal to a council over the head of the pope. Nevertheless, support for a council grew as the split widened, and finally pressure from Emperor Charles V and the threat of Protestantism in Italy overcame Paul III's fear of losing his primacy to a general council. Thus he convoked a council at the north Italian city of Trent in 1545.

The Council of Trent met off and on for almost twenty years, until 1563, and it exercised a remarkable influence on the future development of the church, especially considering the difficulties under which it labored. The first session included only thirty-one prelates, mostly Italians, and was disbanded when the Italian majority tried to move the meeting site to the more comfortable city of Bologna. The second session had to be suspended when advancing Protestant troops threatened to seize the city and the council. The third was better attended, more representative, and conducted in a more orderly fashion, but most of the measures it acted on had been initiated in earlier sessions. Despite these trials, the council established the general lines of theological and ecclesiastical policy that were to dominate the church until the middle of the twentieth century.

Given the preponderance of conservative prelates from Spain and Italy, there was little chance that the council would effect a reconciliation with the Protestants. And in fact by 1545 few believed that such a reconciliation was possible anyway. The council fathers destroyed the last chance for reunion by deciding after long debate to consider the questions of dogma and institutional reform together. Any attempt to make a definitive statement of dogma at this late date would inevitably accentuate the split, and the council made matters worse by deliberately contradicting Lutheran positions. For example, the decree on tradition stated that Scripture and tradition were equally valid sources of truth. The decree on justification, promulgated in 1547, explicitly condemned the Lutheran belief in justification by faith alone. We can hardly blame the council for making no attempt at reconciliation, for it met just after armed conflict between Protestants and Catholics had broken out in Germany — conflict that would continue in one part or another of Europe for decades; perhaps the council should be faulted, however, for failing to aim at a broader statement of Christian belief that might have been the basis for future reunion.

Besides establishing for sixteenth-century Catholics a firm basis for defending their faith against Protestantism, the council achieved two lasting results. First, it confirmed papal primacy beyond any doubt. The popes from Paul III to Pius V, who presided over the church during the period 1545 to 1563, skillfully played the weaknesses of conciliarism to their own advantage and emerged from the last session of the council in absolute control of the church. Their victory is partly explained by the support of a lopsided majority of Italian bishops (of 270 bishops at the last session of the council, 187 were Italians), who, coming mostly from small sees and dependent on papal largesse, lacked the freedom of action enjoyed by the northerners. This implicit bribery, however, was probably less important than the monarchical trend then current in the church and shared with Europe as a whole. Trent simply capped the movement that had begun directly after the Council of

Constance and gave the papacy the prize it had been seeking for over a century.

The council's other result was to establish Thomism as the official theology of the church. The Thomist revival had begun in the last years of the fifteenth century. During the reign of Alexander VI, when so many of the reforming trends of the church began, Thomas de Vio, later Cardinal Cajetan, began his commentaries on Saint Thomas, which initiated a revival of his theology. The advantages of Thomist theology to the sixteenth-century church are obvious. It supported a monarchical conception of government, gave intellectual justification to the ordered and systematic administration of religion, and fully integrated the personal and mystical aspects of religion into the daily demands of life. One pope is reputed to have said of Thomas, "His doctrines are safer."

The adoption of Thomism did not mean that the church retreated into a monolithic and inflexible scholasticism. Numerous schools of interpretation grew up around Thomas' writings, ranging from the literalism of the Dominicans to the comfortable flexibility of the Jesuits. But the adoption of Thomism did mean the disavowal of humanist education and criticism in favor of a scholastic commentary, and that profoundly influenced the attitudes of generations of priests trained in the seminaries set up after Trent in order to create a more educated and effective clergy. More important still, it meant that the church after 1560 had a significantly narrower definition of faith than had been the case during the Renaissance and Reformation. Perspectives once considered legitimate and fruitful were now abandoned or even condemned in favor of the single perspective of Thomism.

Conclusion

The confirmation of papal monarchy, the acceptance of Thomism, and the creation of new orders to provide outlets for personal religious expression were the major achievements of the Roman Catholic church in the sixteenth century. But the reform of abuses that so preoccupied the period was accomplished only in the most superficial way. Great families continued to control benefices into the seventeenth century. The see of Bologna was held by a single family from 1523 to 1563; that of Milan was similarly held from 1511 to 1591; and Parma's was the property of one house from 1509 to

1606. Some of these bishops were exemplary. Carlo Borromeo, one of the finest churchmen of the late sixteenth century, became bishop of Milan through the influence of his family and was made a cardinal at the age of twenty-three by his uncle Pius IV. But more often than not, nepotism exposed the church to men who were manifestly incompetent by reason of age or personal behavior. Pope Pius V, who confirmed the reforming decrees of the last session of Trent, also made cardinals of two eleven-year-old boys — one a member of the Gonzaga family and the other a Medici. The Renaissance at its most scandalous hardly did worse. Financial reforms were equally ineffective. By depriving the popes of political influence in Italy, the Spaniards actually saved the papacy money, but this did not bring an end to the sale of religious offices as a source of papal income. And the Council of Trent even failed to forbid the sale of indulgences. The most that can be said about reform in the sixteenth century is that the church acquired a new puritanical veneer. What had been tolerated with open amusement by the contemporaries of Alexander VI was now bitterly denounced whenever it became public — although it continued to happen in private.

The failures of the church, shocking as they may seem to those accustomed to the ethereal vision of nineteenth-century religion and appalling as they must have been to the real ascetics of the Counter Reformation, should not blind us to its genuine achievements. Faced with the challenge of the Reformation, the church did not react in a negative and unthinking way; it strengthened its institutions, developed a theology that was sophisticated and relevant — though perhaps too narrow — and boldly experimented with new ways to minister to the religious needs of the time.

Practical considerations imposed severe limits on both the church's attempts at reform and its response to Protestantism. Lacking real military force or political power outside the papal states, the church was largely dependent on the territorial monarchs, who exacted their own price in return for help and who pursued their own interests. For instance, Philip II of Spain (1556–1598) was one of Europe's staunchest defenders of orthodoxy. He intervened in France and the Netherlands to suppress Protestant movements and firmly attacked heresy in his own dominions. Yet he resisted any attempt to subordinate the church in Spain to papal control and only promulgated the decrees of Trent after stipulating that his own powers over the Spanish clergy should continue unabated. He even allowed the Spanish Inquisition to imprison the archbishop of Toledo against the long and fervent protests of the pope. Papal attempts to reform the church from its center encountered resistance among the supporters of Catholicism as well as among its opponents.

Bibliography

For examples of standard Catholic histories written before the Second Vatican Council see Pierre Janelle, *The Catholic Reformation* (Milwaukee: Bruce, 1951), or, less blatantly partisan, Henri Daniel-Rops, *The Catholic Reformation,* trans. J. Warrington (Garden City, N.Y.: Image Books, 1964). For a good recent Protestant interpretation see Arthur Dickens, *The Counter Reformation* (New York: Harcourt Brace Jovanovich, 1969). For a more detailed account see Leon Cristiani, *L'Eglise à l'époque du Concile de Trente* (Paris: Bloud et Gay, 1948).

The Protestant historian of the Jesuits referred to here is Heinrich Boehmer, *Ignatius von Loyola,* rev. ed. (Leipzig: Koelher und Amelang, 1945). The Catholic historian is James Broderick, *The Origins of the Jesuits* (London: Longmans, 1940), and *St. Ignatius Loyola: The Pilgrim Years* (London: Burns and Oates, 1956). For recent studies of Loyola stressing the personal spirituality noted here see Hugo Rahner, *The Spirituality of St. Ignatius Loyola* (Westminster, Md.: Newman Press, 1953), and Joseph Guibert, *The Jesuits: Their Spiritual Doctrine and Practice,* trans. W. Young (Chicago: Institute of Jesuit Sources, 1964).

On the Council of Trent see Cristiani's book previously mentioned and Hubert Jedin's *A History of the Council of Trent,* of which two volumes have been translated by D. Graf (London: Nelson, 1957–1961). Some of the debates of that council are found in Hans Hillerbrand, *The Reformation in Its Own Words* (London: SCM Press, 1964).

24 The Radical Reformation

In every age certain forms of thought, modes of expression, and patterns of behavior are considered unacceptable by the vast majority. In the twentieth century, ideas that are clearly outside the mainstream are called radical, but in other ages different terms have been used: Manichaean, Cathar, atheist. In the sixteenth century, people who today would be called radicals were usually referred to as Anabaptists. The established powers, despite their great tolerance for change, persecuted and hounded these radicals in a fashion that is hard to understand, especially if we do not share the intensity of religious conviction that marked that century. Only in a very few places in Europe were the radicals tolerated at all, and on the rare occasions that they attained political power, Protestant and Catholic forces immediately joined together to expel them with armed might.

Radical elements within a historical period, as well as in different periods, have certain common characteristics — great sincerity and enthusiasm, refusal to compromise, and a mode of behavior that disrupts the normal activities of society. These characteristics tempt people to believe that radical movements are monolithic and inter-related, but in fact they are normally more diverse in origin and doctrine than the societies they are criticizing. The tendency to lump all radical groups under a single heading was present during the Reformation just as it is today, and the sixteenth century saw them all as Anabaptists. Henry Bullinger, a Swiss reformer, published in 1560 a classic attack on the Anabaptists, who by that time had spread over much of Europe; his work deeply influenced subsequent interpretations of the movement. Bullinger said that the Anabaptists constituted a single group that sprang from a single source: Lutheranism in Saxony. Recent research, however, has revealed that Bullinger was wrong on both counts. An excellent study by George Williams has made it clear that the radicals sprang from numerous sources and that there were important differences between particular groups. One of the most important of the groups, in fact, grew out of the same Swiss Protestant tradition that Bullinger was attempting to defend.

Each of the three major Reformation movements — Catholic, Lutheran, and Swiss Reformed — gave birth to a separate radicalism. The dominant concern of the Reformation was to provide for personal religious needs that were beyond the scope of medieval institutional Catholicism. The radical movements that grew out of the reformed institutions were, therefore, characterized by a refusal to allow any sort of institution, religious practice, or doctrine to interfere with personal religious life. These diverse movements held certain doctrines in common. Many of them believed in adult, or believer's, baptism rather than the baptism of infants practiced by all the established churches. Many also believed that souls slept after death until the Resurrection. They sought to separate the church from the state. They believed that the church visible was identical with the invisible church and that therefore only the elect should be members. Finally they tended to be pacifists, although there were striking exceptions.

Radical Movements in the Catholic Tradition

The radicals coming out of the tradition of Catholic reform were usually more aristocratic, rationalistic, and individualistic than those emerging from the Protestant movements. The Italian radicals who escaped the growing oppressiveness of the Inquisition after 1540 seldom found the established Protestant churches of the North to their liking. The career of Bernardino Ochino, who defected from the Capuchins in 1541, illustrates many of the problems faced by those who did try to fit in. First Ochino went to Geneva; Calvin welcomed him and arranged for him to assume direction of the Italian parish at Augsburg. Ochino was soon driven from Augsburg by imperial troops and fled to England, where he wrote treatises praising Henry VIII. At the accession of Mary, he had to flee once more and returned to Geneva, but by now the Swiss city was not so welcoming. Calvin had just burned Servetus, a famous anti-Trinitarian, and was becoming as distrustful of doctrinal diversity as the Roman Catholic hierarchy itself. In 1561 Ochino published certain criticisms of Calvin's eucharistic theology, an act not calculated to ease the tension, but fortunately he was residing at the time in Zurich, not Geneva. Nonetheless, his increasingly bitter attacks on Calvin's theology and his denunciation of the burning of Servetus at last led to his banishment from Switzerland. He went first to Nuremberg, then had to flee to Poland, was banished from there, and finally found rest in Moravia, where he died.

Ochino's flight to eastern Europe was not surprising, for it was there that Italian radical reformers had their most lasting influence, in the Transylvanian, Polish, and Moravian churches. The most important thinker among them was Faustus Socinus (1539–1604), a Sienese who gave his name to the movement known as Socinianism. Socinus, in his chief work, *De Jesu Christo Servatore* (1578), enunciated a theme that reappears in the thinking of many different branches of the radical Reformation. Socinus attacked the orthodox concept of salvation, which states that Christ had died for the sins of man, and he purposely blurred all the ways in which Christ is traditionally said to differ from ordinary human beings. With this viewpoint Socinus could tell men that they have the responsibility of working for their own salvation, which they can achieve by following the precepts and imitating the life of Christ as revealed in the Scriptures. Socinus felt that men should do this through voluntary participation in a church specifically organized to this end, with appropriate doctrines and discipline. Such a church, he said, was far preferable to a territorial, state-supported one that included both saints and sinners alike. This belief that good people can confidently be distinguished from the evil and that the good should be gathered together in a single community was a defining characteristic of the radical Reformation; it was also a major reason why the movement was persecuted with such ferocity.

The Italian radicals adopted the rationalistic stance of Catholic Thomism. Socinus' statement of the relation between faith and reason would have been acceptable to most orthodox Catholic thinkers of his day. He said that while revelation contains things above reason, it does not contain anything contrary to reason. The rational sense of Scripture allows one to understand revelation and incorporate its truths into a moral life that can lead to salvation. But the radicals departed from orthodoxy in their evangelical goal of grouping together the good (those who truly understand the Scripture and lead moral lives) into a single church that stands apart from society and whose only function is to provide its members with guidance toward their own salvation.

Radical Movements from Lutheranism

The radical movements that grew out of the Lutheran churches shared with the Italian radicals the belief in full participation in Christ as the way to salvation and an upright earthly life, but the Lutheran radicals departed from the Catholic radicals in being less rationalistic and more concerned with individual religious experience outside of any organized church. As a result the Spiritualists, as the Lutheran radicals have been called, were extremely various in their doctrines and practices and not especially successful in organizing stable churches.

Radical tendencies in Lutheranism appeared very early and can be traced to the period after the Diet of Worms (1521), when Luther went into hiding at Wartburg castle and left charge of the church at Wittenberg to Carlstadt. Despite his early training as an orthodox Thomist, Carlstadt was an enthusiastic convert to Luther's ideas and in Luther's absence began translating them into concrete practice. On Christmas day, 1521, he celebrated the first Protestant communion service, in which no vestments were worn, no reference to sacrifice was made in the words of institution, the Host was not elevated, and communion was distributed to the laity in both kinds. All these measures were designed by Carlstadt to emphasize the importance of the spirit over the letter and were consonant with Luther's eucharistic theology.

As so often happens, the popular reaction to the new service rapidly went beyond Carlstadt's modest changes, and before long the images in the church began to be broken as idols. To keep up with popular attitudes Carlstadt was driven to formulate a eucharistic theology considerably more extreme than Luther's. The Lutheran emphasis on grace and faith diminished the importance of the external sacraments, but Luther had continually maintained that they were necessary aids to preaching and signs of the visible church. Carlstadt began to say that the elements were not even signs or symbols of Christ's body and blood. Instead, the wine is merely a reminder of the covenant of forgiveness of sins and the bread a reminder of the promise of the resurrection of the flesh. Carlstadt soon expanded the spiritual emphasis further by saying that spiritual tribulation itself is a sacrament.

These new ideas were accompanied by increasingly extreme religious practices. In 1524 Carlstadt renounced his priesthood and was refusing to baptize infants. He may even have suspended celebration of the Eucharist. Luther had restored some of the old practices on his return to Wittenberg two years earlier, and by 1524 he and Carlstadt were in open disagreement. The scholastic university professor was no match for Luther, however, either in intellect or persuasive power, and in that same year Carlstadt was banished from Saxony.

Carlstadt was never much of a threat to the stability of the Lutheran church, but others began appearing who did excite the fears of established German society. A circle of radical religious thinkers in Zwickau, led by a weaver named Nicholas Storch, aroused considerable popular support and soon became embroiled in social unrest and revolt. Storch and his followers, called the Prophets, preached radical biblicism and believed in the imminent millennium, which they thought would be preceded by the reign of the Turk as Anti-Christ. They were soon joined by a fiery preacher named Thomas Müntzer (1489–1525). Before becoming pastor of the church at Zwickau, Müntzer had spent some years in reading and contemplation trying to resolve his innermost doubts about the existence of God. Out of this turmoil, he gave the Zwickau Prophets an introspective and spiritual bent that considerably deepened their millenarian doctrine. And the weavers and miners of the Zwickau parish added social radicalism to Müntzer's concerns. He began to preach on the wrongs of society and recommend specific remedies based on the Scripture interpreted literally but with spiritual insight. His social radicalism, as much as his religious ideas, finally led to his banishment to Prague. But soon he returned to Allstedt near Zwickau and began to formulate a theology of the visible elect that included the notion that one must suffer in order to receive the spirit.

Müntzer was not in the least reticent about expressing his ideas. On one occasion he preached before the elector of Saxony, calling him and the congregation to revolution. It is a striking testimony to the remarkable tolerance of those days that the prince patiently sat through the sermon while his own subjects were being urged to revolt. It is highly doubtful that most twentieth-century presidents and prime ministers would show similar restraint. With characteristic temerity Müntzer embraced the cause of the German peasants in the great revolt of 1524–1525. The revolt was reputedly sparked when a group of peasants refused to obey an order of the countess of Lüpfen-Stühlingen to go out and gather snails during haying season. Its true causes were a variety of social and economic ills exacerbated by a severe agricultural depression. There was nothing in the basic aims of the peasants that made this revolt seem different from previous ones. But Müntzer was convinced that it was the work of God and would usher in the millennium. He preached in support of the peasants and identified himself in every way with their cause. When they were finally defeated, he was captured and executed. The revolt terrified the German upper classes, including Luther, and the association of Müntzer and other religious radicals with it wholly discredited the movement. This was ironic, for the peasants had paid little attention to Müntzer and had fought instead for practical goals considerably short of the millennium. The conjunction of the revolt with religious radicalism existed solely in the minds of the radicals. Though they failed to convince the peasants that they were allies, they did convince the aristocracy that they were enemies.

Most Spiritualists were not so eager to identify with violent revolution as were Müntzer and the Zwickau Prophets; they directed their attention instead to individual regeneration. One of the most complete Spiritualist theologies was developed by Caspar Schwenkfeld (1489–1561), a Silesian nobleman and Knight Templar who had converted to Lutheranism as early as 1518. But soon he disagreed with Luther's eucharistic theology and adopted Carlstadt's ideas of an interior Eucharist; he insisted further that the spirit should be free of all institutional restraints. Like most radical theologians Schwenkfeld was passionately concerned with how a Christian could lead a moral life on earth. He was upset that Lutheranism had failed to change the ethical conduct of its followers, and he disputed Luther's position that the saved Christian is at once just and a sinner.

To establish an intellectual basis for his claim that the Christian's life can be improved through regeneration, Schwenkfeld developed a Christology that stressed the bond between the celestial Christ and the regenerate Christian. Although he was the most orthodox of any of the major thinkers of the radical Reformation (he accepted the Nicene formula that Christ is fully man and fully God), Schwenkfeld made a new interpretation of Christ's status as a man. He said that though Christ is flesh, he is not creaturely flesh but celestial flesh. Furthermore, human nature also manifests celestial flesh, and by disciplining our creaturely flesh we can strengthen the bond between ourselves and Christ and bring ourselves to complete regeneration.

Schwenkfeld, like Socinus, emphasized that Christ and man are similar. For orthodox Christians the similarity means that God is able to forgive an undeserving sinner who has persevered in his sinful conduct. But for Schwenkfeld and Socinus it meant something else, namely, that man can achieve through his innate powers the practical result of a visibly moral and upright life that will clearly distinguish him from the unregenerate sinner. In effect Schwenkfeld was applying Luther's spiritual introspection more rigorously in order to derive concrete results, but in so doing he devised a doctrine so extreme as to place himself well outside the mainstream of Christian theology.

Radical Movements from the Swiss Reformed Church

Radical tendencies arose in Zwinglian Protestantism long before Calvin had firmly organized the Reformed church in Switzerland. In the early 1520s groups were formed in Zurich to study the Bible, in accordance with Zwingli's chief interest. By 1524 these groups, which were known as the Swiss Brethren, had become acutely aware of the contradictions between traditional religious practice and biblical practice, especially in the matter of infant baptism, for which no scriptural example can be found. Convinced of the tenuous foundation of the practice, the Brethren petitioned the city magistrates to reform the church in accordance with scriptural examples. The petition was opposed by Zwingli, and a debate ensued between him and the Brethren before the magistrates of Zurich. When the magistrates decided in favor of Zwingli and insisted that the Brethren have their infants baptized, the group decided to resist. To dramatize the necessity of adult baptism, a member of the Brethren, Conrad Grebel, baptized a former priest, George Blaurock, on January 21, 1525. This was too much for the authorities, and they promptly expelled the Brethren from Zurich.

The disruptive force of the new movement soon became clear. The Brethren moved to the nearby village of Zollikon and rapidly gathered converts eager to be rebaptized. An incident there illustrates the extent to which the Brethren were willing to flout social convention and defy authority, so sure were they of their own uprightness. One Sunday, just as the Reformed pastor at Zollikon was stepping up to the pulpit to preach, George Blaurock blocked his path and asked him what he had come to do. The pastor replied, "I will preach the word of God." Blaurock let the man ascend the pulpit, but during the sermon he continually interrupted and heckled until the poor pastor was forced to stop. The congregation then called on Blaurock to preach, but he refused. Instead he seized a rod and beat the pulpit, shouting, "You have made my house a den of thieves." He created such an uproar that the village magistrate finally threatened to jail him.

We can better understand the deliberate provocation of authority and the confidence it implies by examining attitudes and assumptions separating the Brethren from their Zwinglian opponents. These differences crystallized in the decade after 1535 into the Anabaptist movement (and it is here that the term "Anabaptist" is most properly applied), which rapidly became even more radical and left the Swiss Brethren far behind; in the end the latter was one of the most conservative branches of the radical Reformation. The Anabaptist movement spread to the Low Countries and England, as well as to eastern Europe, where, under the leadership of Melchior Hoffman and Menno Simons, it became known as the Mennonite church. In south Germany and Austria, John Denk, John Hut, and Pilgram Marpeck were the Anabaptist leaders. Just as the Swiss Reformed church was the most well organized and institutionally oriented of the reformed churches, so the Anabaptists had the most sophisticated ecclesiology and the most well developed institutional churches among the radicals.

Three basic tenets distinguished Anabaptists from the orthodox Reformation. First, and nearly unique to the Anabaptists, was the belief that baptism is so important that it should be bestowed only on those who understand its meaning and can consent to its responsibilities. This placed an importance on the sacraments surpassing any that Luther and Calvin and even other elements of the radical Reformation could accept. The Spiritualists also rejected infant baptism but principally on the grounds that it gave too much importance to an essentially meaningless sign. The Anabaptists adopted Zwingli's position that the efficacy of the sacrament was dependent on the faith of the participant rather than on the powers of the priest. But they went further and maintained that the sacrament, because it is a sign of adherence to the faith, should be followed by a pure life free from sin. At first they asserted that baptism fills the void left by the destruction of the confessional system. But Zwingli pointed out in rebuttal that the sense of relief experienced in baptism is as temporary as that felt in confession, and the Anabaptists were forced to develop a more sophisticated baptismal theology.

The attempt to do so led at once to divisions within the movement. Some of the difficulties arose over rather superficial problems, such as whether baptism should be administered by immersion or by pouring. Others were more fundamental. The meaning of the biblical texts relative to baptism needs considerable interpretation, and disagreement arose over whether the sacrament of baptism was purely testimonial, redemptive in itself, or a sign of admission to the community that would guide the individual toward redemption. In any case baptism was supposed to bring about a complete reform of the individual's life. The Anabaptists saw themselves as imitating Christ and felt that they should be as pure after their own baptism as Jesus was after the baptism by John.

This sacramentarianism, this great stress on the visible signs of the religion, undercut the central Protestant doctrine of justification by faith alone. The Anabaptists believed that the interior regeneration that brings salvation comes about through the Christian's conscious effort. Regeneration is thoroughly spiritual and is not to be equated with the sort of external penance used in the confessional system, but it was still a work and something that the Christian could actively do. Often it became connected with the external sacrament of baptism. In short, the Anabaptists made the individual Christian again responsible to work for his own salvation — after Luther and Calvin sought to relieve him of that burden. For this reason if for no other, the appeal of the Anabaptist sects was limited to those willing to accept the charge and capable of leading a life of rigorous purity.

The second major tenet of the Anabaptists was that the church visible is identical with the church invisible, a position in accord with that of other radical groups. The church should be organized locally in accordance with scriptural precepts but should include only the saved, who proved that they were truly regenerate by accepting baptism and following the rules of the church thereafter. This claim to distinguish the damned from the elect here on earth and to gather the elect into an exclusive institutional church was the aspect of the radical Reformation that the orthodox found most odious. Such pretensions, they noted, could easily lead to intolerant and inhumane behavior. Although the established religions were hardly in a position to throw stones of this nature, one famous incident lent credence to the accusation. During the years 1534–1535, a group of Anabaptists seized control of the Reformation in the Westphalian city of Münster and expelled the magisterial reformers. The city was promptly besieged by the combined forces of Protestants and Catholics, and the citizens in their extremity gave power over to one John Beukels, who began claiming special revelations, instituted polygamy, and executed all who dared oppose him. The Anabaptists at Münster were finally destroyed amid great carnage, and Beukels was put to death by torture. Though the behavior of the Münster radicals was in flagrant contrast to the sincere pacifism of most of the movement, the incident was long remembered and did much to discredit the Anabaptists.

The third distinctive tenet of the Anabaptists was their Christology. Except for the Swiss Brethren, the movement rejected the orthodox Trinitarian formulation of God in favor of an interpretation that made Christ more human. It is hard for us in the twentieth century to understand why attacks on the Trinitarian formula were so hotly resisted in the sixteenth century. We have to remember that the complex doctrine of the Trinity is one of the chief means by which orthodox Christianity traditionally has resisted oversimplification. A straightforward dualism that divides reality neatly into good and evil is far easier to grasp than the notion of the Trinity, but many would say it is a less accurate picture of reality. Dualisms have always been attractive to radical groups throughout the history of the church.

Dualisms usually assume that it is possible to identify particular acts, events, and people as good, isolate them from the manifestly evil world, and act morally with perfect confidence. Self-confidence is a universal characteristic of radical movements, both during the Reformation and at other times, but the Trinitarian formula fundamentally undermines the possibility of such confidence, because it states that reality consists of three parts — the unchanging values in the universe, the flux of historical time, and the bond between these two, which is a reality in itself not subsumed under them. Thus, although Christ is incarnate in time, no other historical event completely and simply expresses the will of God. Furthermore, the Trinitarian formula maintains that knowledge too is tripartite. It involves, first, objective data; second, a framework of analytical perspectives for organizing the data; and third, the personal perspective of the knower, who is as much a part of the knowledge as the other two factors.

Both of these interpretations of the Trinitarian formula rule out the possibility of completely objective and precisely communicable knowledge. If all understanding contains as a part of its essential nature an element of personal perspective, then no one person's perception of an event is exactly like any other's. And if no two perceptions are exactly alike, how can an event be precisely interpreted as good or evil? Values must remain inextricably mixed in time, to be separated only at the end of history. When they opposed the doctrine of the Trinity, the radical reformers were not merely trying to make Christ more human and a better guide to moral living; they were trying to undercut the orthodox argument that the very nature of reality made it impossible for humans to know with certainty the distinction between good and evil.

The radical reformers' confidence in man's capacity to make exact moral and intellectual judgments lay behind all their doctrines and religious practices and set them clearly apart from the orthodox reformers. That is not to say that Luther and Calvin were unsure of their ideas. Luther fully believed that he had understood some basic attributes of life and that by communicating them he could help men deal with their problems, yet he was less sure of his ability to apply these insights to the acts of his own life. An endearing passage from his *Appeal to the Ruling Classes of the German Nation* illustrates the point:

> I am acting, I confess, as if there were no other in the world than Dr. Luther to play the part of a Christian and give advice to people of culture and education. But I shall not apologize, no matter who demands it. Perhaps I owe God and the world another act of folly. For what it is worth, this pamphlet is an attempt to pay that debt as well as I can, even if I become for once a Court fool. . . . God help us not to seek our own glory but his alone.

Diffidence about the ultimate significance of his own acts was an important part of Luther's grasp of the world. It was related to his sense of the otherness of God and God's complete transcendence of the human condition. Neither Luther's confident attacks on medieval Christendom nor his great assertiveness, which Erasmus complained of, should make us forget his deeply felt personal hesitation. The last sentence of the foregoing passage suggests that Luther was not even sure of his own sincerity in regarding his work as an act of folly: in the end he could only rely on God to decide whether the pamphlet redounded to God's greater glory or not.

The radicals had no such reticence, and that is why the adherents of the magisterial Reformation distrusted them. The radicals saw compromise with principle and refusal to accept the consequences of one's ideas where the orthodox saw a necessary limitation of human capacity. Disagreement on this level was so fundamental that there was little hope of reaching accord on particular issues of theology or church practice. Even if social and economic factors had not exacerbated matters, as in the case of Müntzer and Beukels, it is hard to imagine how the orthodox Reformation churches could ever have incorporated the radical sects that they spawned.

Despite their uncompromising assertion of the truth of their position, the radicals generally felt that the state should not enforce religious conformity. In fact they were among the few open proponents of religious toleration in the sixteenth century. In part this position was a practical one. Almost universally excluded from political power, they saw the state intervene in religious affairs largely to repress their own beliefs. The sincerity of the radicals in championing separation of church and state is beyond dispute, even though at Münster, Beukels used the power of the state to enforce his own religious views. On that occasion he was vigorously opposed by many of the more moderate Anabaptists.

But the radicals' advocacy of religious toleration was more than a practical position. Especially among the Spiritualists, who made religion a matter of individual conscience, a genuine respect for other forms of belief lay behind this opposition to state intervention. Sebastian Frank, for instance, said, "I have my brothers among the Turks, Papists, Jews and all peoples. Not that they are Turks, Jews, Papists and Sectaries or will remain so; in the evening they will be called into the vineyard and given the same wage as we." To understand the full scope of the radical Reformation, we have to keep in mind both this broad-minded individualism and the radicals' direct, uncompromising challenge to the tenets of orthodoxy.

Bibliography

The radical movements during the Reformation have seldom been treated in a balanced way. Secular writers like G. R. Elton tend to be scornful of their religious enthusiasm, while specialized studies have generally been written by adherents to sects that are direct descendants of the sixteenth-century movements and hence overly sympathetic and uncritical. For a comprehensive study of the radical Reformation that is both sympathetic and balanced see George Williams, *The Radical Reformation* (Philadelphia: Westminster Press, 1962). Williams mentions many other good studies in that work. Also of interest is Roland Bainton's account of Michael Servetus, who was burned for heresy by Calvin, *Hunted Heretic* (Boston: Beacon Press, 1953). A recent treatment of the role of mysticism in the radical movements is Steven Ozment's *Mysticism and Dissent* (New Haven: Yale University Press, 1973).

Some of the writings of the radicals have been collected by George Williams in *Spiritual and Anabaptist Writers* (Philadelphia: Westminster Press, 1957).

Conclusion: To Live Appropriately

We have seen the Renaissance and Reformation as parallel though distinct attempts to liberate the human spirit. Both movements unfolded as reactions against the regulation of experience imposed by medieval church, society, and modes of thought; these had validity in their own time, but they had, perhaps through an inevitable process of aging, grown restrictive and repressive. It seemed to men of the Renaissance and Reformation that the traditional categories blotted out the inexhaustible mystery of direct experience. They created a new vocabulary to describe that experience, and by drawing attention to those things that they felt had been neglected, they aimed to open a wider range of experience to humankind. Their goal was nothing less than to increase human freedom and make men more fully alive.

But men need order as well as variety. Formless variety threatens and oppresses. A means of organizing experience is as essential for mental well-being as access to a wide range of experience. Without it experience turns into confusion. We have seen something like this happening at the end of the Italian Renaissance in the extreme particularity of Guicciardini's history of Italy and in the inhuman distortions of mannerist painting. The Reformation, whose concerns were more ultimate and more directly religious, was quicker to sense the need to order its insights. In a sense, Calvin did just that with the insights of Luther. By placing the irrational within clear bounds, he made life easier for the mass of humanity, which finds naked introspection too much to bear. He provided a social form for the new truths about personality and humanity. But the unavoidable danger in the process of ordering is that the new synthesis may itself harden into orthodoxy as repressive and as narrow as the old. Calvinism in seventeenth-century England and America knew nothing of the founder's flexibility, and Jesuits of the same period showed hardly a trace of Loyola's openness.

Toward the end of the sixteenth century, many areas of secular thought showed that they too were searching for a new ordering of experience. Logicians, political theorists, and historians created a new dogma that would incorporate the insights of the Renaissance and Reformation. One of the most systematic statements of the new logic and rhetoric was made by Peter Ramus (1515–1572), a Frenchman who had been influenced directly by Calvinist thought. Although Ramus' criticism of the administration of Geneva under Calvin's successor, Beza made him unwelcome there, he was sufficiently associated with the French Calvinist movement to be killed in the Saint Bartholomew's Day massacre. His system of discourse was based on certain fundamental attitudes that he shared with Calvin, and it became very popular among Calvinists in England and America.

The complex and cumbersome mode of discourse that had evolved in the centuries before Ramus was a fusion of neo-Aristotelian logic and Ciceronian rhetoric that provided a writer or speaker with a detailed, set form for discussing any topic while leaving room for individual variety. Figure 8 shows how a subject was normally approached. The categories are basically arbitrary and cannot be

Figure 8   Traditional System of Discourse

Neo-Aristotelian logic

1. Judgment or disposition (arrangement)
   a. Five predictables (classes of statements)
   b. Ten categories or predicaments (classes of concept)
   c. Definition and division
   d. Method
   e. Propositions
   f. Argument (syllogism, enthymeme, induction, example)
2. Invention (finding subject matter through a list of "places" or topics that overlap with the predicables and categories)

Ciceronian rhetoric

1. Invention (includes places as under logic)
2. Disposition or arrangement (overlaps with judgment or disposition under logic)
3. Style
4. Memory (mnemonic devices)
5. Delivery (elocution)

deduced from simple principles; thus there is a great deal of repetition between the logic and the rhetoric. A twentieth-century student looking at this chart can make little sense of it because mastery of the art required years of intensive training and memorization of established categories and modes of approaching problems. The strength of the method was that it could be applied to almost any topic imaginable, but that was also its weakness. The method was artificial. It was difficult to learn and so complex and arbitrary that it was deeply disturbing to those who had a taste for simplicity or believed that truth that should be grasped on individual terms.

The complexity of traditional logic and rhetoric stemmed from the fact that they were not really a system but an attempt to blend several different treatises of Aristotle and Cicero, along with various commentaries, into a unified synthesis of logical and rhetorical truth. Since the writings were not originally deduced from a unified set of principles, the result had no logical coherence beyond that of the whole civilization that produced it. By the sixteenth century the critical techniques of the Renaissance had made it clear to all that the traditional method of discourse was founded on a mixture of rather disparate elements. The need for a new logic asserted itself.

Ramus proposed a major reform of the system based on the assumption that the fundamental characteristics of clear thought are self-evident to most people, even without extensive training. That being so, logic should not have to waste most of its time proving statements but should be devoted instead to arranging, relating, and

Figure 9   Ramus' System of Discourse

Ramist logic

    1. Invention (finding subject matter)
       a. "Artificial arguments" (new form of categories)
       b. "Nonartificial arguments" (testimony, authority)
    2. Judgment (arrangement)
       a. Axiomatic
       b. Dianoetic (discursive)
          1. Syllogism
          2. Method (includes the three "golden rules of art")

Ramist rhetoric

    1. Style
    2. Delivery (elocution)

presenting them. Similarly, the proper function of rhetoric should not be to arrange ideas — which is the function of logic — but to be concerned primarily with matters of style and delivery. Presented in the form of a chart (Figure 9), Ramist logic and rhetoric may seem as abstruse as the neo-Aristotelian and Ciceronian forms, but in fact it is much easier to use. In order to reduce the problem into categories simple enough to be dealt with, Ramus used the principle of dichotomy, or dividing a category in two and then successively subdividing each of the halves. A very brief introduction to the Ramist method is usually sufficent to allow a twentieth-century student to begin applying it to problems of his own.

The strength of Ramus' method lies in its simplicity. It does not require endless memorization of traditional formulas because it assumes that the basic structure of reality is easily perceived. It has an antiauthoritarian cast because it depends on the individual's own capacity to discriminate the truth. This made it attractive to the followers of Calvin, for Calvin had relied on the individual's ability to understand and accept the revelation found in the Scriptures. At the same time Ramist logic is dogmatic because it assumes that basic truths are constant; they do not vary with individual or historical perspective and can therefore be approached by a single path of investigation. Ramus replaced the rich but confusing variety of the earlier modes of discourse with a clear, simple, and straightforward method that led the individual by his own resources to a single truth prior to any individual insight.

Law was another area that became ordered and simplified during the sixteenth century, producing a new approach to historical inquiry and new political theories. Before the sixteenth century the study of law, like the study of rhetoric, was cumbersome, complex, and highly dependent on rote memorization. The basic code of Roman law, the Pandects of Justinian, had been drawn up in the sixth century to codify and systematize the legal precepts and enactments of all previous governments of Rome. As the texts of the original laws were lost in the centuries after Justinian, the Pandects became the only source of Roman law, and students began to believe that they embodied coherent principles of law deduced from rational postulates. Unfortunately, this was not so. Roman law was positive law — that is, it consisted of particular statutes designed to meet particular problems and therefore had to be revised periodically during the long history of the Roman state.

Thus, the Pandects contained many inconsistencies. A large body of commentary grew up in the course of the Middle Ages attempting to explain the contradictions and help practicing lawyers use the Pandects. By the sixteenth century the commentaries were so involved that ten years of training were required to memorize them.

Training that involved only memorization of commentaries and precepts offended the humanists' ideal of a methodical education, as well as their taste for a simple, conceptual approach to knowledge. As early as the 1450s Valla had attacked the legal profession for the absurdity of its approach and exhorted lawyers to seek out the simple principles underlying the complexity of the Pandects and the commentaries. In the early sixteenth century the French humanist Budé turned his scholarly talents to exposing the medieval mistranslations and grammatical errors that had caused the Pandects to be misinterpreted. But even then Budé was unable to discover coherent legal principles in the Pandects. As his researches proceeded, he came to two conclusions: those who had originally compiled the Pandects had made errors of transcription, and the laws on which the Pandects were based were intrinsically contradictory. He decided, in other words, that Roman law was not based on general principles that could be applied universally. To find these, men would have to broaden their scope and study all laws and all of human history.

Initial reactions to this new task were skeptical. The critical spirit that exposed Roman law now cautioned the humanists against the inevitable biases of historians. Feeling that all records of the past distorted the facts, many scholars doubted that they could even in their own day acquire a sure grasp of world history. How then could one hope to have a basis for new principles of law and statecraft? For a time such doubts were rampant in the intellectual community. By 1560, thinkers in France were seeking an escape from this universal skepticism, or "Pyrrhonism." Melchior Cano pointed out that some form of trust is necessary to carry on the tasks of daily life. If pupils universally doubted everything their teachers told them, down to the very principles of grammar, civilization would collapse. Cano proposed, as a way out of the dilemma, that reliable and generally honest historians should be distinguished from those who had consciously distorted the past. But that approach was only partially satisfying because the judgments were necessarily personal and unsystematic, and they failed to take into account the likelihood that all historians were to some degree dishonest. What was really needed was a critical method for distinguishing reliable from unreliable parts in the works of the same historian.

Jean Bodin's *Method for the Easy Comprehension of History* (1566) proposed just such a method. His goal was to provide criteria for discerning the true facts of the past and a system of historical interpretation for absorbing the information more easily. First of all, Bodin noted that facts reported by impartial eyewitnesses should always be considered valid. Next he set up rules for dealing with biased and partial historians by finding areas where the biases have not made their histories useless. He then considered how to deal with accounts by writers who were not even eyewitnesses to events, showing how we can judge their critical capacities and their understanding of the principles of statecraft.

In the second section of the *Method* Bodin tried to establish the universal principles of law that scholars had been seeking. Partly through exposure to the native cultures of the Americas and partly through a heightened awareness of the diversity of the ancient world, men of the late sixteenth century perceived that human law and custom were far more varied than earlier generations of Europeans had believed. Bodin found an explanation for the diversity in the different climates of the world. Dividing the world into zones from the equator to the north pole, he noted that both physical traits and temperaments changed from zone to zone. Choosing an accepted means of explaining the change, he suggested that the different zones experienced varying astrological influences. This latter explanation makes Bodin's theory seem very peculiar in our eyes, but we have to remember that it was not so in his own time. With its astrological element removed, Bodin's theory is a reasonably comprehensive system for understanding the particulars of history and relating them to one another.

In 1576, ten years after the *Method,* Bodin developed his system into a full-fledged theory of sovereignty in *Six Books on the Commonwealth.* By analyzing every type of government he could find Bodin hoped to discover the bases of political power. In the process he discarded the notions of legitimacy and divine ordination. The question of sovereignty, said Bodin, is empirical. The sovereign is the body or person who exercises authority, and government lies in its unqualified power to command. This was Bodin's most original contribution. At the same time he maintained that sovereign power cannot be totally divorced from its function. The state exists to protect life and property; states that arbitrarily invade these rights are not true states. Bodin's conception of sovereignty as the power to command cast a new light on the law. It was no longer the embodiment of abstract principles and values but rather the will of the sovereign. The essense of power is the right to make laws, and law is nothing more than the sovereign's commands. Thus law, too, is empirical, and to study and understand it one must apply the principles of historical criticism.

Bodin's was not a comprehensive political theory; it was a system for investigation and classification. His ideas on government and law must be extrapolated from his intricate analyses of specific constitutions and his abstruse discussions of how to organize these constitutions. Consequently his political system is not so immediately clear as we have just stated, and scholars have legitimate differences of opinion over Bodin's actual position. Despite this, it is certain that Bodin was deeply involved in the late sixteenth century's search for a new way of ordering experience. His political system, like Ramus' system of logic, was based on observation of experience, but once created it became a means for organizing further experience. By adopting Bodin's method, the student of history or law could free himself from the confused mass of details and penetrate to the underlying structure that bound all details together.

Not every new attempt to order experience resulted in a system independent of that experience. The Anglican theologian Richard Hooker (1554–1600), unlike his French contemporaries, developed a new understanding of the church that recognized the complexities of life and did not oversimplify them. Hooker's reluctance to seek out a new system is partly explained by the problems facing the Church of England during the late sixteenth century. The Protestant exiles returning from the continent after the death of Queen Mary in 1558 had called for the abolition of all practices reminiscent of Roman Catholicism. Yet the country as a whole was relatively conservative and resisted every change introduced into the traditional Roman Catholic liturgy. In addition, Queen Elizabeth opposed the suggestion that bishops and episcopal government should be abolished in favor of the Calvinist system of local government because she feared losing the control over the church she maintained through the appointment of bishops. As a result, the organization and liturgy of the Anglican church that emerged during Elizabeth's reign were based more on political considerations than on strictly religious ones, and it was not easy to justify every church practice on theological grounds. The Calvinists had a clearly articulated theology closely tied to the Scriptures, and they were quick to exploit the weakness of the national church, attacking it as indefensible compromise.

Hooker's response was to write the *Laws of Ecclesiastical Polity,* which remains even today the classic defense of the Anglican church. Essentially, he refused to agree that the Calvinists understood the precise nature of God's will for the church. He carried the issue into the Calvinist camp by showing that the organizational details of their own church at Geneva had resulted from particular problems existing at that moment in the city's history and were not strictly derived from scriptural example. Going further, Hooker observed that even the apostolic church as it is recorded in the Bible reflected historical circumstances, and therefore it is not strictly imitable in another age with different historical circumstances. Hooker claimed that we need not and should not rely on scriptural authority alone. We have other sources of knowledge and other means of discovering God's laws. The most important of these is history, which Hooker used so effectively to undermine the claims of the Calvinists. History reveals certain common patterns of behavior and certain general values that are clearly meant to be followed in all times and places. "The general and perpetual voice of men is as the sentence of God himself. For that which all men have at all times learned, nature herself must needs have taught, and God being the author of nature, her voice is but his instrument" (I. 8. 3). Hooker felt that the beliefs and practices necessary for salvation were basically simple and readily visible and that they could be agreed on by all if men would only try to reconcile their differences.

The search for simple rules behind human history is reminiscent of Bodin, though Hooker did not share Bodin's belief that such rules can be used to criticize the actual institutions history has given us. Underlying Hooker's thought is a profound skepticism about man's ability to understand in detail the fundamental structure of his universe. From the beginning of *The Laws of Ecclesiastical Polity,* he warns of the difficulty of obtaining complete and systematic knowledge, and the warning is repeated through all its books. In the fifth book, arguing that no simple set of religious institutions and beliefs can cure all the ills of mankind, Hooker says,

> General rules, till their limits be known (especially in matter of public and ecclesiastical affairs), are, by reason of the manifold secret exceptions which lie hidden in them, no other to the eye of man's understanding than cloudy mists cast before the eye of common sense. They that walk in darkness know not whither they go. And even as little is their certainty, whose opinions generalities only do guide. With gross and popular capacities nothing doth more prevail than unlimited generalities, because of their plainness at the first sight: nothing less with men of exact judgment, because such rules are not safe to be trusted over far. . . . We must not . . . imagine that all men's cases ought to have one measure. [V. 9. 2]

It was not Hooker's purpose just to point out that no system, however broad, could emancipate man from his experience. Hooker intended to show that personal experience was actually a source of assurance about the validity of basic truths. But to do this he first had to refute man's pretension to unlock every mystery of the universe and to demonstrate that large areas of human conduct are ethically neutral and merely a matter of individual experience or historical creation. More than Bodin or Ramus, Hooker maintained the critical reserve of the Renaissance scholar, even while searching for a more positive basis of understanding.

Hooker bears some resemblance to Guicciardini. The *Laws of Ecclesiastical Polity* and the *History of Italy* are each monumental works in their respective fields; both are fundamentally historical in approach, and both display a minute attention to detail that has made them more often praised than read. Yet Hooker's work is patterned in a way Guicciardini's is not. Hooker believes that there is a rational pattern in the world and that the pattern is so self-evident that it is hardly a subject for argument: "The main principles of reason are in themselves apparent. . . . In every kind of knowledge some such grounds there are, as that being proposed the mind doth presently embrace them as free from all possibility of error, clear and manifest without proof" (I. 7. 5). He also believes in simple norms of human behavior and canons of humanity — which we found as well in the High Renaissance — but tries to give them a positive abstract expression, which the High Renaissance would have thought impossible.

Time has a way of dulling the voice of even the greatest thinkers and writers, and men who spoke with force and cogency to their own age are known only at second hand to another. But two writers of the late sixteenth century escaped the common fate. Michel de Montaigne (1533–1592) in France and William Shakespeare (1564–1616) in England captured the imagination of their own contemporaries and enjoyed great popular success while they lived, and they have continued to speak to the generations that have come after. Both men need to be looked at in the intellectual context of their age. While we certainly do not imagine that the secret of their power will be unlocked in this way, we can gain a clarifying perspective on their contribution. Both Montaigne and Shakespeare produced early works that displayed the Renaissance traits of easy curiosity about the variety of human experience and confidence that the meaning of life lay in this variety. Both abandoned this perspective in mid-career and became more despairing and introspective, with grave doubts about the meaning and coherence of life. And at the end of their lives both men created out of their own personalities a new order for experience, while avoiding the pitfall of distortion and tension that characterized the Italian mannerists.

Montaigne left detailed memoirs, and we can trace his personal development quite accurately. Born near Bordeaux into the minor nobility, he was the only surviving son in his family, and his father devoted great care to his education. The father even hired a German tutor who spoke no French so that the young Montaigne would be forced to learn Latin. Although Montaigne received the basic humanist education that had become popular in northern Europe by mid-century, he was not an enthusiastic pupil and found his formal schooling monotonous and unimaginative. Nor did he acquire much interest in the law, which he was sent to Toulouse to study. From 1557 he was a member of the law court at Bordeaux but seems to have been bored with the proceedings. In 1571, increasingly dissatisfied with his career and depressed by the recent deaths of his father and his close friend Etienne de la Boetie, Montaigne retired from his position and returned to his family's chateau to devote himself to writing and philosophy. The product of his retirement appeared in 1580 as the first edition of the *Essays,* which he reedited several times before his death. Montaigne was never at any time in his life a systematic and thoroughly consistent writer. His thought always operated on many levels of complexity at once and his conclusions were necessarily tentative. The crucial aspect of his contribution was made possible by the form of the essay, which meant literally a "trial" or "test" of judgment; it ranged from anecdotes of momentary interest illustrating some moral lesson to deeply searching introspective analyses. Despite the unsystematic nature of his thought, Montaigne displays three basic stages in his intellectual development. His first writings are clearly humanist in outlook, deeply influenced by the classical movement called stoicism that stressed preparation for death and self-control in the face of pain. Montaigne wrote, "To philosophize is to learn to die," and pessimism lay very close to the surface of his writing throughout this period. "The wretchedness of our condition makes us have less to desire than to fear. . . . To have no ill is to have the happiest state of well-being that man can hope for." Even then Montaigne betrayed a certain skepticism toward his own pessimism and confessed himself unable to explain how some uneducated people, who had not philosophized to learn to die, could meet death with such fortitude.

Around 1576, five years after his retirement, Montaigne experienced his skeptical revolt. He came to have doubts about the stoic humanism he had been following and even about the possibility of real human knowledge. He decisively rejected his earlier philosophy and concluded that his own character did not fit the stoic mold, which was in fact appropriate only for very few. Furthermore, he decided that the classical models, once so inspiring, were not all they seemed; classical heroes were inconsistent in their behavior and frequently unworthy to be imitated. More striking, Montaigne seems to have convinced himself that humans in general are inconsistent and that there is no coherent pattern in human life on which to base a stable ethic and mode of dealing with the world. The essay *On the Inconsistency of Our Action,* written between 1572 and 1574, states, "We are all patchwork, and so shapeless and diverse in composition that each moment plays its own game. And there is as much difference between us and ourselves as between us and others." Skepticism found fullest expression in his *Apology for Raymond Sebond,* which contains the famous question *"Que sais-je"* — What do I know? Yet Montaigne's skepticism, though it revealed the despairing unhappiness and confusion so common among sensitive souls in that century, was never complete. *"Que sais-je?"* was not merely rhetorical; it was a real question. Montaigne distrusted explicit statements of belief, both before and after his skeptical crisis, and even at its height he felt that rationalism and dogmatic systems were more appropriate as targets of attack than was pursuit of understanding in general. He said that his goal was "to crush and trample underfoot human arrogance and pride, to make the rationalists feel the inanity, the vanity and nothingness of man, to wrest from their hands the puny weapons of their reason; to make them bow their heads and bite the ground beneath the authority and reverence of divine majesty." In other words, he did not by his questioning intend to deny the existence of perfect and unchanging truth: instead he would make us mindful of our own limitations.

Montaigne's basic concern was for self-knowledge and happiness. In his third period he set out to find the answers to his questions through direct experience and by studying himself as an individual. Out of this came awareness of common human traits and values. He eschewed the preconceived notions of human destiny that had been characteristic of his early humanistic period and instead freely accepted all human actions and feelings. He concluded that man could learn to be happy by developing his judgment and a sense of his own limitations. The development of judgment is a key concept in Montaigne's later writings, although it has no systematic meaning. Montaigne uses it simply to describe a grouping of experience that allows one to identify certain things as so plain and clear that they constitute assurance of knowledge. In contrast to Hooker, Montaigne does not consider this faculty equivalent to natural reason. It is much more flexible and contingent. Thus, certain "natural" aspects of a human being — like the body, the necessary appetites, the emotions, common sense, and plain good judgment — can bring a person happiness and contentment. "Unnatural" things — like reason untempered by common sense, imagination leading to ambition, presumption, avarice, insatiability and worry — all these lead only to misery: hence the need for self-limitation and moderation.

In his last essays Montaigne talked mostly about himself, his bodily functions, his emotional responses, his ordinary problems. Yet the more he focused on himself the more he seemed to see humanity. As he analyzed the particular, his understanding of the common bonds among men became stronger and he expressed it with more conviction. In short, Montaigne came to believe that truth is thoroughly personal; yet it can be expressed in terms that are basically similar for all well-realized human lives without sacrificing the depth of personal feeling or the intensity of personal expression. His last essay, *On Experience,* concludes, "The most beautiful lives, to my mind, are those that conform to the common human pattern, with order, but without miracle and without eccentricity."

In contrast to Montaigne, Shakespeare chose to express himself in an impersonal literary form, the drama. For this reason little is known about his personal life. None of the characters in his plays, with the possible exception of Prospero in *The Tempest,* seems to have autobiographical significance. Yet Shakespeare's thought evolved along much the same lines as Montaigne's. His early works display a wide-ranging interest in the varieties of human experience and optimistically assume that order and meaning underlie the variety. In *Henry IV, Part One,* young Prince Hal is exposed to an extreme diversity of influences. He learns his father's calculating shrewdness and Hotspur's boldness and valor; he even learns something from his association with Falstaff and the thieves at the Boar's Head Tavern. His greatness is his ability to assimilate all these influences into a consistent personality that recognizes its proper station in life. As Prince Hal says of his ability to take on the manners of the tavern, "To conclude, I am so good a proficient in one quarter of an hour that I can drink with any tinker in his own language during my life."

Shakespeare never lost his intense interest in the variety of life, but around 1600 his plays stop expressing the confidence that society can cope with this variety. This was the period when he wrote sour, unhumorous comedies like *All's Well That Ends Well,* as well as his great tragedies, *Hamlet, Othello, King Lear,* and *Macbeth.* They present a world in which the irrational cannot be contained without devastating convulsions in society. Shakespeare's Renaissance vocabulary is still there; Hamlet praises mankind with words reminiscent of Pico della Mirandola when he says, "What a piece of work is a man, how noble in reason, how infinite in faculties; in form and moving how express and admirable, in action how like an angel, in apprehension how like a god: the beauty of the world, the paragon of animals!" Yet behind the Renaissance vocabulary is a view of a world without order and with no possibility of redemption by earthly means. That same speech concludes, "And yet to me what is this quintessence of dust?"

The world of Shakespeare's great tragedies is somber and forbidding. It explores the depth and greatness of human anguish through dramatic confrontations, just as Luther had confronted Saint Paul. Shakespeare, like Montaigne, found little consolation, only skepticism. Indeed, Shakespeare's attitude during this period is eloquently summarized by Macbeth, who, demented by his own acts, is denied the consolation of growth and repentance:

Tomorrow, and tomorrow, and tomorrow,
Creeps in this petty pace from day to day,
To the last syllable of recorded time;
And all our yesterdays have lighted fools
The way to dusty death. Out, out, brief candle!
Life's but a walking shadow, a poor player,
That struts and frets his hour upon the stage,
And then is heard no more. It is a tale
Told by an idiot, full of sound and fury,
Signifying nothing.

In his last years Shakespeare created a new dramatic form, the romance comedy, which combines the depth of tragic feeling of the middle plays with a new confidence in the ultimate order of the universe and the possibility of redemption and fulfillment. *The Winter's Tale* summarizes in its first few acts the tale of Othello; *The Tempest,* like *Hamlet,* opens with a usurpation. Yet both plots are resolved happily. The late plays recognize and explore the fact that disaster can sometimes be transmuted into a new life and new happiness by seemingly irrational powers. Prospero in *The Tempest* reacts to his deposition and exile not by fruitless and despairing introspection but by creating a new world. He uses his control over good and bad elements on the island of his exile to fashion a life that offers redemption not only to himself but to his enemies; that life springs from his own person but brings solace and relief to humanity in general. Thus Shakespeare, too, arrives at a vision of truth that is highly personal and individualistic but still expresses the human condition in its most exalted state. At the conclusion of *The Tempest,* Prospero breaks his magic wand and surrenders his supernatural powers with these words: "Now my charms are all o'erthrown, / And what strength I have's mine own, / Which is most faint." The gesture may have left him with faint strength, but it was a mighty affirmation of life, bringing to mind Montaigne's advice to the ambitious:

We are great fools. "He has spent his life in idleness," we say; "I have done nothing today." What, have you not lived? That is not only the fundamental but the most illustrious of your occupations. "If I had been placed in a position to manage great affairs, I would have shown what I could do." Have you been able to think out and manage your own life? You have done the greatest task of all. . . . To compose our character is our duty, not to compose books, and to win not battles and provinces, but order and tranquillity in our conduct. Our great and glorious masterpiece is to live appropriately.

"To live appropriately." Could a phrase more aptly capture the spirit of an age? It joins the ethical and social concerns of the Renaissance with the introspective force of the Reformation. The Renaissance taught that man is a social being whose own inner life grows by touching the lives of others. The Reformation taught that he has overwhelming power in his inner life; man is a person before he is a member of society, and he must seek fulfillment first as a person. These two perspectives are not easy to blend into a single system. Yet life depends on each, and by calling us to live appropriately, Montaigne summarizes in full measure the wisdom of both the Renaissance and the Reformation .

Bibliography

For a general discussion of political thought during this period see J. W. Allen, *A History of Political Thought in the Sixteenth Century* (London: Methuen, 1961). Bodin's contributions to the new methodology are discussed by Julian Franklin, *Jean Bodin and the Sixteenth-Century Revolution in the Methodology of Law and History* (New York: Columbia University Press, 1963). Ramus' contribution has been analyzed by Walter Ong, *Ramus: Method and the Decay of Dialogue* (Cambridge: Harvard University Press, 1958), and Perry Miller, *The New England Mind* (Boston: Beacon Press, 1961). Peter Munz has discussed Hooker's significance in *The Place of Hooker in the History of Thought* (London: Routledge, 1952). The best recent studies of Montaigne in English are by Donald Frame, *Montaigne: A Biography* (New York: Harcourt Brace Jovanovich, 1965), and *Montaigne's Essays* (Englewood Cliffs, N.J.: Prentice-Hall, 1969). For a different interpretation of late-sixteenth-century thought than is found in this chapter see Hiram Haydn, *The Counter Renaissance* (New York: Grove Press, 1960). Haydn emphasizes the reaction of these thinkers to earlier values.

Jean Bodin's *Method for an Easy Comprehension of History* has been translated by Beatrice Reynolds (New York: Octagon Press, 1966), and his *Six Books on the Commonwealth* have been abridged and translated by M. Tooley (Oxford: Blackwell, 1953). Hooker's *Of the Laws of Ecclesiastical Polity* is most readily available in the Everyman edition (New York: Dutton, 1964–1965). Montaigne's complete *Essays* have been translated by Donald Frame (Stanford, Calif.: Stanford University Press, 1958).

Index

Abgeschiedenheit, 247
Accoppiatori, 148
Active life, 72
Aemilio, 270
Agricola, Georg, 126
Agricola, Rudolf, 278
Albert of Hohenzollern, 265
Alberti, Leon Battista, 124, 179, 186–188
  Della Famiglia, 94
  De Re Aedificatoria, 187
Albornoz, Cardinal, 17
Alexander VI, pope, 152, 153, 155, 174, 343
  reform of monastic orders, 346, 347–348
Alfonso the Magnanimous, king of Aragon, 101, 103, 146
  and war with Genoa, 149–150
Amerbach, Boniface, 100
Anabaptists, 361, 367–369
Anagni, 16
Anatomy, 139
Annate, 226
Antoninus, bishop of Florence, 108, 114
Apanages, 215–216
Aquinas, St. Thomas, 44, 235–237, 245, 246, 265
Aragon, 220
Architecture, 185–188
Argyropulos, John, 108–109
Ariosto, 157
Aristides, 85–86
Aristotle, 63, 64, 76, 107, 108, 124, 126
  compared with Plato, 234–235
  condemned in 1277, 236
  cosmology, 127–131
Asclepius, see Hermetic writings
Athens, 85

Augsburg
  Diet of, 330
  Peace of, 333, 335
Augustine, 100, 232–234
  and Calvin, 310
  City of God, 68
  Confessions, 67, 69, 234
  and Luther, 297
  and Petrarch, 67–68
  primacy of faith, 233
Averroes, 235
Avignon, 13, 99, 166–167
  and growth of papal government, 224–226
  as humanist center, 60, 268

Baccio, Matteo da, 347
Banking
  and Florence's economy, 25
  in the mid-fourteenth century, 32
Barbaro, Ermolao, 273
Bardi family, 25, 32
Barlaam, 99
Baron, Hans, 78–87
Bartolus of Sassaferat, 101
Beaufort, Henry, 269
Beda, 309
Benefices, 225–226
Beroaldo, 270
Beukels, John, 370
Beza, 376
Bible
  Calvin's approach to, 319–320
  humanist editions of, 102–103, 273, 283, 315
  Luther's approach to, 292, 303–304, 330
Biel, Gabriel, 6, 258–265, 294
  and Luther, 297
Biondo, Flavio, 55

Biringuccio, Vanocchio, 125–126
Black Death, 33–34
Black-White Feud, 60
Blaurock, George, 367
Boccaccio, 55, 71, 74, 81
    conversion of, 40–41
    Corbaccio, 40–41
    Decameron, 39–40
    On the Fates of Illustrious Men,
        41
Bodin, Jean, 379–380
    *Method for the Easy Compre-
        hension of History,* 379–380
    *Six Books of the Common-
        wealth,* 380
Boétie, Etienne de la, 384
Bologna, 22
    Concordat of, 229
    Petrarch studies in, 60
Boniface VIII, 13, 15, 16, 45–46
Boniface IX, 17
Borromeo, Carlo, 359
Botticelli, Sandro
    Adoration of the Magi, 180–181
    and neo-Platonism, 115
    Primavera, 115
Bracciolini, Poggio, 74, 79, 87, 99,
        108, 110, 113, 269
    travels to England, 11
Brahe, Tycho, 134–136
Bramante, Italian architect,
        188–189
Brethren of the Common Life, 244
Briçonnet, bishop of Meaux,
        273–274
Brunelleschi, Filippo, 79,
        186–188, 189
Bruni, Leonardo, 6, 74, 79, 99,
        100, 110, 113
    civic humanism, 80, 84–87, 113
    *Dialogue for Pier Paolo
        Vergerio,* 84–85
    History of Florence, 86–87
    Laudatio Florentiae Urbis,
        85–86

On Studies and Letters, 94
    translation of Aristotle, 76, 269
    translation of Plato, 109
Brutus, 83, 85
Bucer, Martin, 315, 316
Budé, Guillaume, 272, 274, 378
    and Calvin, 309–310
    De Asse, 274
    De Transitu Hellenismi, 274
Bullinger, Henry, 361–362
Burckhardt, interpretation of
    Renaissance politics, 18

Cabala, 116, 118–120, 279
Cajetan, Cardinal, 328, 358
Calvi, 356
Calvin, John, 6, 7, 281, 308–325,
        375, 377
    Academy, 314
    and Augustine, 321
    and Bucer, 315, 316
    company of pastors, 314
    consistory, 313–314
    conversion, 311–312
    De Clementia, 309–310
    ecclesiology, 323–324, 326–327
    and education, 310–311, 314
    and Erasmus, 309–310
    and Geneva, 312–315
    and humanism, 309–311,
        319–320
    *Institutes of the Christian
        Religion,* 316–324
    predestination, 318
    transcendence of God, 318–319
    and Zwingli, 315–316
Camaldolese Hermits, 347
Cambrai
    League of, 154–155
    Treaty of, 155
Camerarius, 226
Cano, Melchior, 379
Capitalism, and Protestantism,
        3–4, 313
Captaincy of the people, 20

Capuchins, 348
Carafa (later Pope Paul IV), 349, 357
Cardinals, College of, 227–228
Careggi, Medici villa at, 112
Carlstadt, Andreas, 292, 330, 364–365
Carnesecchi, Peter, 356
Carrara, Ubertino, 92
Carrara family, 28
Casa Giocosa, 95–96, 100, 270
Castiglione, Baldassare, 157
  The Courtier, 94, 144
Castille, 220
Cateau-Cambrésis, Treaty of, 155
Catherine of Siena, 240–244
Cato, 53
Catullus, 57, 58, 98
Celtis, Conrad, 279–280
Cerchi family, 25, 45
Charles V, Holy Roman Emperor, 331–333
Charles VIII, of France, 153
Charles of Anjou, 16
Charles the Bold, 293
Charles of Valois, 46
Chrysoloras, Manuel, 99, 109
Cicero, 83, 97, 100–101, 108
  letters to Atticus, 64
  Petrarch's letters to, 64–65
Ciompi revolt, 26
Civic humanists, 78–88
  compared to neo-Platonists, 110, 116
Classics
  practical use of, 59, 84–87, 161, 274
  Renaissance attitude to, 57
Clement V, pope, 16
Clement VI, pope, 16, 34, 259
Clement VII, pope, 227
Clerks regular, 347
Colet, John, 275–276
College of Cardinals, 227–228
Columbus, Christopher, 125

Commerce, *see* Trade
Complutensian Polyglot, 283
Compurgation, 211
Conciliarism, 228
Concordat of Bologna, *see* Bologna
Condottiere, 147
Consilium de Emendanda Ecclesia, 345
Constance, Council of, 92, 203–204, 228–229, 269, 328–329
Constantinople, 98, 149
Contarini, Gasparo, 330
Contrapposto, 188
Contrition, 259
  Loyola's doubts about, 349–350
  Luther's doubts about, 293
  problems of, 261
Cop, William, 309
Copernicus, Nicholas, 127, 132–134
  On the Revolutions of the Celestial Spheres, 132
Cortes, 220
Council of Constance, *see* Constance, Council of
Council of Ferrara-Florence, *see* Ferrara-Florence, Council of
Coverdale Bible, 338
Cox, Richard, 338
Critical scholarship, 58
  Petrarch's edition of Livy, 60–61
  and sources, 61, 120–121
  Valla, 100–103
  Veronese humanists, 59
Cromwell, Thomas, 338
Crystalline spheres, 129, 131, 132

Danse macabre, 294
Dante, 5, 43–56, 61, 80–83, 85, 162, 173
  De Monarchia, 44–54
  Divine Comedy, 43, 46, 50, 53
  exile from Florence, 44–46
  Henry VII, 46–48

Denk, John, 370
Descartes, René, 7, 244
Deventer, Erasmus's education at, 281
Dias, Bartholomeu, 125
Dictatores, 77
Diet of Augsburg, *see* Augsburg
Diet of Worms, *see* Worms, Diet of
Dionigi of Borgo San Sepulcro, teacher of Petrarch, 67, 68
Dioscorides, 124
Docta pietas, 114–115
Dominici, Giovanni, 91, 108
Donatello, 79, 188
Donati family, 45
Donation of Constantine, 102
Drugs, Renaissance studies of, 139–140

Early church fathers and the Renaissance, 68
Eck, John, 328
Eckhart, Johannes (Meister), 6, 245–248
    Abgeshiedenheit, 247
    Opus Tripartitum, 245
Education, humanist, 90–98, 314, 354–355
Edward III, of England, 32
Edward VI, of England, 338
Elizabeth I, of England, 381
Erasmus, Desiderius, 102, 103, 244, 281–285, 309
    Adages, 282
    Diatribe on Free Will, 289–290
    and Luther, 288–290
    Praise of Folly, 284–286
Este, Beatrice d', 152
Este, Niccolò d', 96
Euclid, 124
Excommunication, 14–15
Execrabilis, 356
Explorations, 124–125
Exsurge Domine, 328

Fabriano, Gentile da, 179–180, 181
Faith
    Luther's concept of, 295–296
    and reason, 233, 236, 255, 265
Farel, William, 312
Ferdinand of Spain, 154–155, 220
Ferrante of Naples, 146, 151, 152
Ferrara, 96, 104
    University of, 97
    Venetian attack on, 151
Ferrara-Florence, Council of, 99–100, 109
Feudal society, 209–214
Ficino, Marsilio, 110–115
    docta pietas, 114–115
    influence on northern humanists, 272, 275–276, 278
    interest in magic, 115–117
    Libri de Vita, 116
    Theologia Platonica, 112
Fifth Lateran Council, 343
Filelfo, Francesco, 278
Florence, 12, 23–27, 78, 104, 145
    Black Death in, 34–37
    Black-White feud, 45
    civic humanism, 79–87
    factional strife in, 45
    guilds, 24
    historical tradition, 23
    magnates excluded from government, 24–25
    Medici government, 147–149
Florentine Academy, 108
Fontainebleau, Edict of, 335
Fornovo, 154
France
    humanism in, 272–275
    invades Italy, 152–155
    Reformation in, 335, 336–337
Francis I, of France, 155, 332
Frank, Sebastian, 372
Frederick II, Holy Roman emperor, 15

Frederick the Wise, Elector of
Saxony, 219, 329–330
Frith, John, 334
Froben, Johannes, 283
Fronte, Tommaso della, 242

Gabelle, 215
Gaetano of Thienne, 348
Gaguin, Robert, 272
Galen, 139
Galileo, 126–127
Garin, Eugenio, 77–78, 103
Gemüte, 250
Genoa, 27, 31, 149–150
Ghiberti, bishop of Verona, 344
Ghirad'adda, 154
Ghirlandaio, 184
Adoration of the Magi, 180–181
Giotto, 55, 177
Girolami, Remigio di, 38
Giustiniani, 347
Gonzaga, Gianfrancesco, 95
Graphic arts, 120, 173–190,
191–195
Great Schism, 13, 17, 150,
227–228, 294
Grebel, Conrad, 367
Greek
humanist interest in, 98–100
Petrarch and, 62
Gregory XI, pope, 243
Grey, William, 270
Groote, Gerard, 244
Guarino of Verona, 96–98, 99, 270
Guicciardini, Francesco, 145,
196–199, 375, 382–383
History of Italy, 196–199
Gutenberg, Johannes, 125

Henry VII, Holy Roman emperor,
46–48, 54
Henry VIII, of England, 215,
229, 334, 337
Hermetic writings, 116–118

Asclepius, 117, 118, 120
Corpus Hermeticum, 117
Heronymous, George, 270
Hildalgo, 220
Hoffman, Melchior, 368
Holy League
of 1455, 149–150
of 1495, 154
Holy Roman Empire, 12, 48, 54,
79, 218–219
Homer, 62, 71
Honorius III, pope, 15
Hooker, Richard, 381–383
Huguenot church, 336–337
Huizinga, Johan, 249
Waning of the Middle Ages, 294
Humanism, 74–89
active life, 72
attitude toward the ancients,
62–64
and Calvin, 309–311
education, 90–98, 276, 314,
354–355
in England, 269–270, 275–277
in France, 268–270, 272–275
in Germany, 268–270, 277–281
historical consciousness, 64
imitation of the classics, 85–86
letter writing, 65, 67
and Loyola, 350, 352–353
and Luther, 281
philology, 61–62, 77–78
use of dialogue, 70
Humphrey of Gloucester, 269
Hundred Years' War, 33,
214–215, 293
Hus, John, 204, 328–329
Hut, John, 370
Hutten, Ulrich von, 280, 327

Indulgences, 205, 260, 292
Innocent III, pope, 13, 15, 224
Innocent IV, pope, 16
Inquest, 212–213

Inquisition
  Roman, 356
  Spanish, 220–221, 335
Interdict, 14–15, 150–151
Isabella of Spain, 220
Italy
  birthplace of humanism, 74
  urban character, 28

Jeremiah of Montagnone, 58
Jesuits, *see* Society of Jesus
Joanna II, queen of Naples, 146
John XXII, pope, 246
Julius II, pope, 153, 155, 174
Julius Caesar, 83, 85
Justification
  Augustine, 233
  Calvin, 321–323
  Luther, 294–302
  Trent, Council of, 357

Kepler, Johannes, 127, 134,
    136–138
Knox, John, 337, 338
Kristeller, Paul Oscar, 75–77
Kuhn, Thomas, 127

Ladislaus, of Naples, 17, 149
Lascaris, John, 270
Lateran Council, *see* Fifth Lateran
    Council
Latin, Renaissance method of
    teaching, 97
Law
  and early classical studies, 58
  humanist approach to, 379–380
Lawyers, needed in Florentine
    government, 27
League of Cambrai, *see* Cambrai
Lefèvre d'Etaples, Jacques,
    272–274
  Moral Art, 273
  Quintuplex Psalter, 273
Leipzig debate, 328
Leo X, pope, 155, 175

and Luther, 327
reform of monastic orders, 346
Leonardo da Vinci, 55, 120, 144,
    176–177, 194, 199
  Adoration of the Magi, 143,
    176–177, 180, 182–184, 188
  Virgin and St. Anne, 183–184,
    189, 194, 199
Liturgy, 340–341
Livy, 66, 83, 85, 102, 103
  Petrarch's edition of, 60–61
Lodi, Peace of, 149
Lollardy, 334
Lombard, Peter, *Sentences,* 233,
    253
Louis IX, of France, 146
Louis XI, of France, 155
Louis XII, of France, 154–155
Loyola, Ignatius, 349–354
  Spiritual Exercises, 350–354
Lucca, 36
Ludolf of Saxony, 351
Lull, Raymond, 272
Luther, Martin, 3, 6, 103, 288–
    307, 375
  and Augustine, 297
  and Biel, 294, 297
  and humanism, 288–290
  ninety-five theses, 203
  and nominalism, 258, 265, 294
  pastoral concerns, 304–305
  predestination, 299–301
  and St. Paul, 296–297, 298, 387
  and Tauler, 294, 297
  transcendence of God, 296–299

Machiavelli, Niccolò, 6, 48, 143,
    145, 158–171, 196, 199
  appearance and reality, 160,
    165–168
  Discourses on Livy, 159, 160,
    162, 170
  fortune, 168–169, 199
  History of Florence, 169
  humanism, 86, 111, 159, 166

interpretations of, 158
irony, 161–162
Mandragola, 143, 169, 170
political experience, 158–159
Prince, 144, 158–170
Republican sympathies, 159
Magisterial Reformation, 326–
327, 339–341
Calvinist, 336–339
Catholic, 342–360
English, 337–338
Lutheran, 327–336
Magna Carta, 214
Magus, 116, 118, 120, 121
Maillard, 272
Major, John, 309
Manetti, Gianozzo, 108
Mannerism, 192–195
Manresa, 349–350
Mantua, 95, 100
birthplace of Virgil, 66
Manuel II Palaeologus, 99
Manutius, Aldus, 99–100, 124,
283
Margaret of Angoulême, 335
Marpeck, Pilgram, 370
Marsilio of Padua, 266
Martin V, 17, 228
Masaccio, 79, 180
Virgin and St. Anne, 178–179
Mass, Luther's attitude toward,
304–305
Mattingly, Garrett, 161
Maximilian I, Holy Roman
emperor, 154
Medici, Cosimo, 81, 107, 147–148
patronage, 174
and the Platonic Academy,
110, 111, 117
Medici, Lorenzo, 148–149, 150
Medici, Lorenzo di Pierfrancesco,
115
Medici, Piero, 148–149
Medici, Piero di Lorenzo, 152, 153
Medici family, 158–159

as bankers, 32
government of Florence,
147–150
Meister, Eckhart, *see* Eckhart,
Johannes (Meister)
Melanchthon, Philipp, 280–281,
288, 308, 330
Menot, 272
Michelangelo, 55, 120, 174,
184–185, 192
David, 189
Pietà, 189
sculpture, 189
Milan, 12, 18–22, 79–80, 82, 145,
147
Miltitz, Carl von, 327
Ming dynasty, 32
Modern Way, *see* Nominalism
Mohács, 332
Mongols, 32
Montague College, 309, 350
Montaigne, Michel de, 6, 383–386
Essays, 384–386
Monte, Piero del, 269
Montecassino, 59
More, Thomas, 275–277, 334
Utopia, 276–277
Morone, Cardinal, 355–356
Motion, in Renaissance science, 7,
128–129
Motta, in Milanese commune, 19
Münster, 370
Müntzer, Thomas, 361–368
Muret, Jean, 268
Mussato, Albert, 59
Mysticism, 239–252
church's policy toward, 240,
243–244, 246, 248
definition of, 238–240
and St. Paul, 240
speculative, 245–251

Nantes, Edict of, 337
Naples, 27, 101, 104, 145–146
Neo-Platonism, 106–121

influence on northern humanists, 272, 275–276, 278
and science, 135–136
Neumarkt, Johannes von, 268
Newton, Isaac, 120, 127
Niccoli, Niccolò, 80–81, 108
Nicholas V, pope, 174
Nicholas of Clemange, 268
Nicholas of Cusa, 250, 273
Nominalism, 253–267
abstractive knowledge, 255–256
and Calvin, 309
contingency of the universe, 257
intuitive knowledge, 255
and Luther, 258
and modern science, 258
the Modern Way, 258
and penance, 262–265
realms of absolute and ordained
power, 262
and universals, 255–256
Northern Europe, reaction of
Italian humanists to, 11

Ochino, Bernardino, 355, 362–363
Ockham, William of, 6, 253–258
contrast with Aquinas, 253,
254–255
Ockham's razor, 258
Ontology, 235
Oratory of Divine Love, 348
Ordinances of Justice, 23–24
Otranto, 149
Ovid, 71

Padua, 28, 66, 92, 95
early humanism in, 58–59
Painting
influence on religious visions,
241–242
International Style, 179–180,
181–182
Monumental School, 178–179,
180–181
Palladio, Andrea, 188

Palmieri, Matteo, 74
Pamplona, 349
Pandects, 379
Papacy, 13–17
patronage, 174–175
traditional interpretation of, 13
Papal States, 14, 146, 150–151
Machiavelli's interpretation of,
161
Paracelsus, Philip, 139–140
Parallax, 134
Passavanti, Jacopo, 38
Patronage, motives for, 173–174
Paul III, pope, 343–344
Paul, St., 103
and Luther, 296–297
road to Damascus, 240
Pavia, 22
Pazzi family, 153
conspiracy, 150–151
Peace of Augsburg, *see* Augsburg,
Peace of
Peace of Lodi, *see* Lodi, Peace of
Peasants revolt, 306, 366
Pelagianism, 264
Penance, 258–262
nominalist perspective, 262–265
Peruzzi family, 32
Petrarch, Francesco, 6, 54, 55,
60–72, 74, 81, 101, 112
Africa, 61
Ascent of Mt. Ventoux, 66–67,
71
De Viris Illustribus, 61, 71
De Vita Solitaria, 82
edition of Livy, 60–61
founder of humanism, 58,
87–88, 91, 191
Greek studies, 99
northern humanists'
approach to, 269, 278
On his Own Ignorance, 61, 71
Secretum, 68–71
sonnets, 71
Philip II, of Spain, 359

Philip IV, of France, 13
Piccolomini, Aeneas Sylvius, *see*
 Pius II
Pico della Mirandola, 115, 116,
 118–120, 387
 Oration on the Dignity of Man,
 119–120
Pisa, 47
Pius II, 228, 270
Plague, *see* Black Death
Planets, explanation of retrograde
 motion
 Aristotle, 130–131
 Brahe, 135–136
 Copernicus, 132–134
 Kepler, 137–138
 Ptolemy, 131–132
Plato, 52–53, 76, 106, 233
 compared with Aristotle,
 234–235
 dialogues arrive in Italy, 109
Platonic Academy, 100, 107–115
Plenum, 129, 132, 135
Plethon, Gemisthos, 99–100,
 109–110, 112–114
Pliny, 59
Plotinus, 106
Podestà, 20
Pollaiuolo, Antonio del, 188–189
Pontormo, Jacopo da, 193,
 194–195, 196
Pragmatic Sanction of Bourges,
 229
Prague, humanism in, 268
Preaching, response to Black
 Death, 37–39
Predestination
 Calvin, 318, 321–323
 Luther, 299–301
Prieras, Sylvester, 327
Priesthood of all believers,
 304–306
Printing, 96–97, 125–126, 283
Provisors and Praemunire,
 Statutes of, 229

Ptolemy, 131–132, 135
 Almagest, 124
 Geography, 124
Purgatory, 259
Pyrrhonism, 379
Pythagoras, 136

Quintilian, 97, 98, 100–101

Rabelais, François, 309, 274–275
Ramus, Peter, 375–377
Raphael, 144, 174, 184–185, 192
 School of Athens, 185
Raymond of Capua, 243
Reason and revelation, 246
Reconquista, 220
Reformation
 and capitalism, 206
 Catholic interpretations of,
 204, 206
 Protestant interpretations of,
 205
 relationship to Renaissance, 4,
 5–6, 204
Retrograde motion, *see* Planets,
 explanation of retrograde motion
Reuchlin, Johann, 278
Rhetoric, 72
 importance in the Renaissance,
 65
Rhineland mystics, 245–251
 and Luther, 251
Rienzi, Cola da, 17
Rinuccini, Alamanno, 108
Rinuccini, Cino, 81
Roman law, 212–213, 378–379
 in Germany, 219
Romano, Ezzolino da, 59
Romano, Giulio, 195
Rome, 102–103
 sack of, 155
Rosso Fiorentino, 193–194, 196
 Deposition from the Cross, 192,
 194
Rota, 226
Royal domain, 211

Sacramentarianism, 369
Saignet, Guillaume, 269
St. Bartholomew massacre, 337, 376
Salutati, Coluccio, 6, 55, 74, 85, 101, 108
  and civic humanism, 80–84
  De Tyranno, 82–84
  Letter in Defense of Liberal Studies, 91–92
Savonarola, Girolamo, 329, 345
  supported by the neo-Platonists, 114–115
Scala, Can Grande della, 59
Scala, della, family, 173
Scandinavia, Reformation in, 334
Scholasticism, 43
Schwenkfeld, Caspar, 366
Scientia rerum, 92, 93, 98, 103, 104
Scipio Africanus, 61, 68
Sculpture, 188–189
Seneca, 58, 59, 93, 309–310
Sephiroth, 119
Servetus, Michael, 362–363
Sforza, Francesco, 146–147, 149
Sforza, Galeazzo Maria, 147
Sforza, Giangaleazzo, 151–152
Sforza, Ludovico, 151–152, 154
Shakespeare, William, 6, 157, 383, 386–389
Sicily, 27
Sigismund, Holy Roman emperor, 92
Simons, Menno, 368
Sixtus IV, pope, 150–151
Smalkaldic League, 333
Society, Renaissance, 3
Society of Jesus, 348–355
  education, 354–355
  missionary activity, 354
Socinus, Faustus, 365
Solifidianism, 294–302
Somerset, Duke of, 338
Spain, 219–221

  explorations, 125
  invades Italy, 154–155
Spiritualists, 364–367
Spiritus, 118
Standonck, Jean, 309
Staupitz, Johannes, 229
Stigmata, 243
Stoicism, 310, 387
Storch, Nicholas, 365
Strabo, 96, 124
Studia humanitatis, 75
Suleiman the Magnificent, 332
Suso, Henry, 248–249, 272
  Book of Eternal Wisdom, 248
Swiss Brethren, 367–368
Sylvester I, 102
Syphilis, 197–198

Tacitus, 57, 85, 98, 100, 279
Taille, 215
Tasso, 157
Tauler, Johann, 248, 249–250, 272, 297
Tepl, Johann von, 269
Territorial state, 3
Tetzel, John, 205, 292, 327
Theatines, 348
Theophrastus, 124
Thomas à Kempis, 244, 351
Thomas de Vio, *see* Cajetan, Cardinal
Thomism, 358
Tifernate, 270
Toleration, religious, 372
Torre, della, family, 20
Trade
  decline in 1340s, 31–32
  importance of, 33
  in the Renaissance, 3
Transubstantiation, 304
Treaty of Cateau-Cambrésis, *see* Cateau-Cambrésis, Treaty of
Trent, Council of, 356–357
Trinity, doctrine of, 370–371
Troyes, Treaty of, 218

Turks, 98–99
Turmerlebnis, 297

Unigenitus dei filius, 259
Urban VI, pope, 227

Valla, Lorenzo, 100–104, 174, 378
    Donation of Constantine, 102
    Elegantiae, 101–102
    Greek translations, 102–103
    New Testament, edition of, 103
    On Pleasure, 101
Vasari, Giorgio, 55, 177–178, 179
Vaucluse, 66
Venice, 27–28, 79, 104, 124, 146,
        154–155
    Black Death in, 34
    expansion onto the mainland,
        150–151
    Greek studies, 99
    patronage, 175
Vergerio, Pier Paolo, 74, 79, 84,
        95, 270
    *On Noble Manners and Liberal
        Studies,* 92–94
Verona, 64
    early humanism, 59
Verrocchio, Andrea del, 175–176
    sculpture, 188
Vesalius, Andreas, 124, 139
Virgil, 58, 66
Virgin Mary, Cults of, 244

virtu, 163
Visconti, Filippo Maria, 146–147
Visconti, Giangaleazzo, 21, 85,
        149, 154
    attack on Florence, 79–80
Visconti family, 19–21
    patronage, 173
Viterbo, Parliament of, 15
Vitruvius, 167
Vittorino da Feltre, 74, 100, 114,
        270
    Casa Giocosa, 95–96
Voragine, Jacopo de, 351
Vulgate, 103

Walter of Brienne, 36–37
Wars of the Roses, 215, 293
Weber thesis, 206–207
Whethamsted, John, 275
William of Ockham, *see* Ockham,
        William of
Wittenberg Concord, 316
Worms, Diet of, 292, 331, 364
Wycliffe, John, 334

Xavier, Francis, 351
Ximenes, Cardinal, 103, 283, 335,
        346, 350

Zwickau Prophets, 365
Zwingli, 315–316, 367